Computers and Data Processing Today

Computers and Data Processing Today

Steven L. Mandell
Bowling Green State University

West Publishing Company
Saint Paul New York Los Angeles San Francisco

THIS BOOK IS DEDICATED TO ALL OF THE PEOPLE AT WEST PUBLISHING COMPANY.

COPY EDITOR Sonsie Conroy
COLOR AIRBRUSH ARTWORK Dave Pauly Graphics
TECHNICAL ARTWORK Barbara Hack and Li Greiner
COMPOSITION The Clarinda Company

50 West Kellogg Boulevard
P.O. Box 3526
St. Paul, Minnesota 55165

Printed in the United States of America

Library of Congress Cataloging in Publication Data

Mandell, Steven L.
Computers and data processing today.

Includes index.
1. Electronic data processing. 2. Electronic digital computers. I. Title.
QA76.M27474 1983 001.64 82-21753
ISBN 0-314-69663-6

2nd Reprint—1984

A study guide has been developed to assist you in mastering concepts presented in this text. The study guide reinforces concepts by presenting them in condensed, concise form. Additional illustrations and examples are also included. The study guide is available from your local bookstore under the title *Study Guide to Accompany Computers and Data Processing Today*, prepared by Steven L. Mandell.

Photo Credits

Cover and Title Page: Clockwise from upper left: Photo courtesy of DATAPRODUCTS CORP.; courtesy of Bell Laboratories; courtesy of Rockwell International; photo courtesy of Burlington Industries, Inc; courtesy of Paradyne Corporation; courtesy of Motorola, Inc; photo courtesy of DATAPRODUCTS CORP.; courtesy of Paradyne Corporation; *center* courtesy of Intel Corporation.

v courtesy of Paradyne Corporation. **vi** courtesy of Bell Laboratories. **vii** courtesy of Control Data Corporation. **viii** courtesy of Intel Corporation. **ix** photo courtesy of DATAPRODUCTS CORP. **x** courtesy of Paradyne Corporation. **xi** reproduced with permission of AT&T. **xii** photo courtesy of Burlington Industries, Inc. **xiii** courtesy of Quotron Systems, Inc. **xiv** courtesy of Paradyne Corporation. **xv** photo courtesy of DATAPRODUCTS CORP. **3** courtesy of Paradyne Corporation. **5** (top) photo by Norma Morris. **5** (bottom) courtesy of IBM. **6** courtesy of Ohio Citizen's Bank. **7** (top) courtesy of Chrysler Corporation. **7** (bottom) courtesy Texas Instruments, Inc., Digital Systems Group. **8** courtesy Office of the Secretary of Defense. **9** photo courtesy of the Internal Revenue Service. **10** (top) courtesy of Shell Oil Company. **10** (bottom) The National Center for Atmospheric Research. **11** (left) courtesy of Federal Bureau of Investigation. **11** (right) courtesy of Bell Laboratories. **12** courtesy of Bell Laboratories. **13** (top) courtesy Texas Instruments, Inc., Digital Systems Group. **13** (bottom) courtesy of Pfizer, Inc. **14** (top) courtesy of Floating Point Systems, Inc. **14** (bottom) courtesy of the Brookhaven National Laboratory. **15** (top) courtesy of Tektronix, Inc. **15** (bottom) photo by Norma Morris. **17** courtesy of Federal Bureau of Investigation. **26** courtesy of Paradyne Corporation. **29** courtesy of Bell Laboratories. **30** courtesy of IBM. **31** (top) courtesy of IBM **31** (bottom left) courtesy of IBM. **31** (bottom right) Crown copyright. The Science Museum, London. **32** courtesy of IBM. **33** courtesy of IBM. **34** (top) courtesy of IBM. **34** (bottom) courtesy of IBM. **36** courtesy of Sperry Univac. **38** courtesy of Sperry Univac. **39** courtesy of IBM. **41** courtesy of IBM. **42** courtesy of NCR Corp. **43** courtesy of Digital Equipment Corporation. **44** courtesy of Bell Laboratories. **46** courtesy of Paradyne Corporation. **51** courtesy of Paradyne Corporation. **53** courtesy of U.S. Postal Service. **56** courtesy of Paradyne Corporation. **59** courtesy of Control Data Corporation. **61** courtesy of Library of Congress. **69** courtesy of Paradyne Corporation. **73** photo by Norma Morris. **84** courtesy of Paradyne Corporation. **87** courtesy Intel Corporation. **94** (top) courtesy of Bell Laboratories. **94** (bottom) courtesy of the Perkin-Elmer Corporation. **95** (top) courtesy Intel Corporation. **95** (bottom) courtesy Rockwell International. **96** photo courtesy of Hewlett-Packard Company. **97** courtesy of Bell Laboratories. **98** courtesy of Bell Laboratories. **99** all three photos courtesy Intel Corporation. **108** courtesy Paradyne Corporation. **111** photo courtesy of DATAPRODUCTS CORP. **113** photo by Norma

(Continued after Index)

CONTENTS

CHAPTER 1

The Role of Computers in Today's Society 2

CHAPTER 2

Information Processing 28

CHAPTER 3

The Programming Process 58

CHAPTER 4

Computer Hardware

86

CHAPTER 5

Communicating with the Computer: Input/Output Devices 110

CHAPTER 6

Remote Access Communication Systems 136

CHAPTER 7

Storage Devices and Process Design

160

CHAPTER 8

Software

188

CHAPTER 9

System Analysis and Design 224

CHAPTER 10

Computer Systems 254

CHAPTER 11

Computers in our Future 282

PREFACE

In the last few years there has been an explosion in the number of students taking first courses in computers and data processing. This explosion has resulted in the need for a wide variety of books and teaching materials. In the time since the First Edition of *Computers and Data Processing* was published, I've had numerous inquiries into the possible availability of an introductory computer text that would be more concise and briefer than *Computers and Data Processing*, but maintain its clarity and teaching style. Two years of hard work with my publisher have resulted in the book you hold in your hand—*Computers and Data Processing Today*. I believe that this book continues my philosophy of presenting the educational material in a logical, uncluttered manner, while including relevant real-world examples. Additionally, by virtue of its full-color format and extensive use of graphics, I believe this book is one of the most visually appealing introductory computer books yet published.

In structuring the material to be included in this book, I worked closely with my introductory students at Bowling Green State University trying out different teaching approaches. I taught several experimental sections of the introductory computer course, shifting some of the programming material to a very early stage in the course. This afforded the students an opportunity to begin their laboratory experience (BASIC on Apples) after the second week. Tradition has always placed this material after hardware, but I found the students were able to grasp programming concepts prior to knowing the technology. The extremely positive feedback I received from the students concerning this non-traditional approach led to the new organizational structure in this book. This organization was further reinforced by certain first draft reviewers, who in fact, reported that they often teach their courses in this fashion and thus were most receptive to this new ordering of materials. However, even with this new organization the book remains flexible enough for the instructor to reorder the topics in any order he or she chooses. The book, therefore, remains an extremely flexible teaching device.

The basic pedagogical format found in this book is designed to aid in the clear, straightforward presentation of the material, while including motivational real-world examples. Each chapter begins with a brief introductory section that provides a logical link with the previous material. The chapter outline that follows permits the student to develop a frame of reference for the text material. This outline also provides a useful guide when preparing for exams. At the conclusion of the chapter material, there is a point-by-point summary in sentence form followed by approximately ten review questions.

Two additional features in the pedagogical design warrant special attention, and are also related to the title of this book, *Computers and Data Processing Today*. Several Highlight boxes are included in each chapter that present material of current interest. These materials are designed to be motivational and entertaining, while at the same time providing current perspectives that enrich the book's content. The Highlights appear in the margins so as not to break up the flow of the text material. Secondly, because of the tremendous proliferation of microcomputers today, it became apparent that adequate attention had to be devoted to their special requirements. This arose both from my own teaching experience as well as from comments received from instructors all around the country. Rather than just including a separate chapter on microcomputers, the decision was made to integrate this information throughout the book by providing a separate "Focus on Microcomputing" section at the end of each chapter. This section integrates microcomputer concepts and applications into the material discussed in that particular chapter. This should prove to be an extremely valuable addition for students entering a "micro world."

The importance of good flowcharting techniques can never be under-estimated. This was also made clear to me in reviews of a preliminary version. Therefore, in the book, the flowcharting material presented in the text and in the BASIC/Pascal appendices is augmented through the use of a separate appendix entitled "Common Program Logic Flowcharts." Individuals with courses utilizing a language laboratory will find this addition provides significant flexibility in teaching program design. A second appendix, "Career Opportunities," is also included to give students a practical insight into computer-related careers. Finally, at the end of the text is a comprehensive glossary and a separate index.

In order to provide appropriate materials for the widest variety of teaching situations, there are three versions of this book available. First a version with a very complete BASIC language supplement expanded to include microcomputer implementation; second, a version with a Pascal supplement; and finally a language free version.

Finally, as I indicated above, I was very fortunate to have had several outstanding college educators serve as reviewers for this project. It is very difficult to fully express my thanks for their help and aid in shaping this project. Without the professional efforts of the following individuals, this book would not be nearly as effective a teaching vehicle: Don Cartlidge, New Mexico State University; James W. Cox, Lane Community College, Oregon; Richard H. Harms, Santa Ana College, California; Fred L. Head, Cypress College, California; Kathleen Ott, New Mexico Junior College; Curtis G. Rawson, Kirkwood Community College, Iowa; Al Stehling, San Antonio College; Rein Turn, California State University, Northridge; Kenneth W. Veatch, San Antonio College; Louis A. Wolff, Moorpark College, California.

A special debt of appreciation goes to Professor Fred Head of Cypress College and to Professor Kathleen Ott, New Mexico Junior College, who in addition to reviewing the entire manuscript, helped greatly in the completion of the "Focus on Microcomputing" Sections. Their meeting a very tight timetable, their good nature, dedication, and enthusiasm will long be remembered.

SUPPLEMENTARY EDUCATIONAL MATERIAL

The Study Guide to accompany this text includes numerous materials for student reinforcement. Each chapter in the Study Guide includes the following: Key Terms; a Narrative Summary of the chapter; a Structured Learning Section; an extensive set of Questions and Answers (True/False, Matching, Short Answers). The format for the student materials supporting the language supplements is slightly different. For each section in the language supplement there is: Structured Learning, Worksheet, and Programming Problems.

A complete instructor resource package has been designed to reduce administrative efforts. The classroom support includes: Learning Objectives, Detailed Outlines, Answers to Review and Discussion Questions, and Additional Review and Discussion Questions. Extensive materials have been included for language versions of this text. For each section in the language supplement, there are an average of four programming problems; each problem is accompanied by a flowchart and a list of any differences for microcomputers.

A Test Bank of over 1,000 multiple choice questions is also included in the Instructor's Manual. In addition, the WESTEST computerized testing service is available from West Publishing Company with these questions in machine-readable form.

There are over 100 Transparency Masters provided. Most of these visuals are novel, and not mere reproductions of artwork found in the text. Additionally, a narrative script of a tour of a modern computer facility is provided to augment a set of color slides available to adopters from West Publishing Company.

ACKNOWLEDGMENTS

Many individuals and companies have been involved in the development of the material for this book. Numerous corporations and government agencies provided the color pictures found in this book in addition to applications material. Many professionals provided the assistance required for a completion of a text of this magnitude: Rod Harris, Pat Cooke, Robert Szymanski, Rebecca Parks, Patricia Ostrowski on student material; Terrye Gregory and Stephen Gregory with BASIC and Pascal; and Norma Morris, Donna Pulschen, and Candace Streeter in manuscript development. The design of the book is a tribute to the many talents of William Stryker. One final acknowledgment goes to my publisher and valued friend, Clyde Perlee, Jr., for his encouragement and ideas.

Steven L. Mandell

Computers and Data Processing Today

CHAPTER 1

The Role of Computers in Today's Society

INTRODUCTION

Computers are affecting society in ways both great and small. They are being used to make life easier in everyday transactions, such as banking and grocery shopping. They are also being used in complex activities, including weather forecasting and disease diagnosis. It is not difficult to see that our society will become increasingly dependent on the computer as more varied and complex applications are developed.

This chapter focuses on computer applications in business, government, medicine, and education. The issue of privacy and the legal attempts to control the collection and dissemination of sensitive data are reviewed. Finally, computer crime and computer security are discussed. The applications described in this chapter are intended to give a broad overview of the impact computers have had on our society. The reader is encouraged to speculate on the societal impact of future applications.

FACING PAGE
This computer system is specially equipped to handle a wide range of automated design, drafting, and manufacturing operations. Here, the keyboard, a graphics tablet, and an electric pen are all used to design the intricate circuitry of a computer chip.

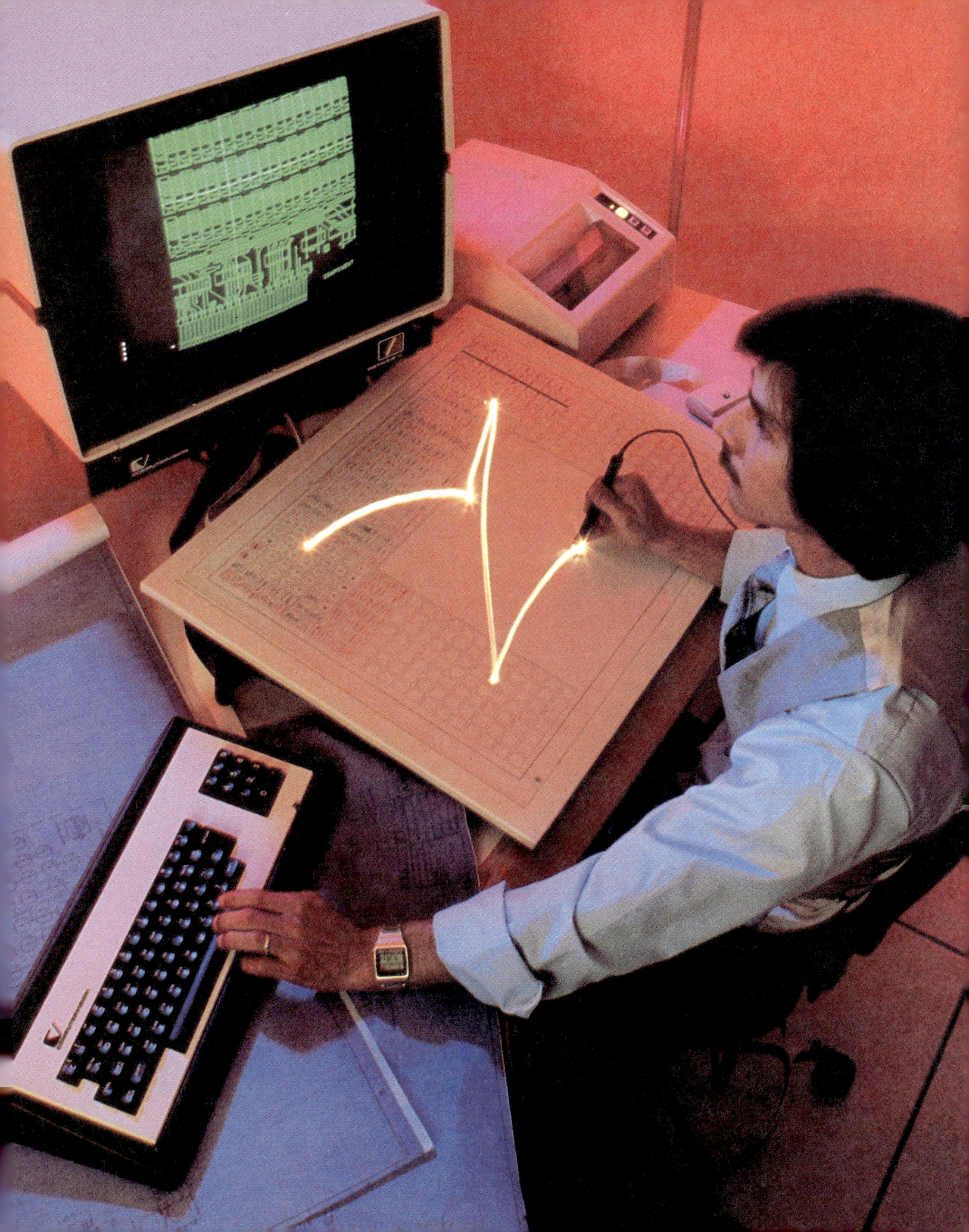

CHAPTER OUTLINE

COMPUTERS IN BUSINESS

Computers have the capability of processing information in a fraction of the time it would take to perform the same types of calculations manually. In any business, large or small, computers can be used to reduce paperwork, thereby reducing the cost of performing routine transactions. Business activities include controlling inventory levels, billing customers for services and products, calculating payroll and tax, paying for inventory and supplies, reporting for decision making by managers, and supporting a host of other business functions. Computer systems can be implemented to perform all of these transactions, thereby increasing the efficiency of an organization's operations.

Hardly a day goes by when we are not confronted by a computer-generated business transaction. Each time we visit the bank, use a credit card, pay a bill, or buy groceries, a computer is behind the scene, recording each transaction. Even a visit to a fast food restaurant involves computer transactions. Whenever business information is to be recorded, more than likely a computer is performing the transaction.

Retailing

Hundreds of people each day pass through the aisles of a grocery store. Counting and recording the number and type of products purchased in a single day would take a person hours of time. However, by use of the **Universal Product Code (UPC)** and **point-of-sale (POS)** terminals (discussed below), a computer can greatly enhance the performance of retail stores.

The UPC is a standardized bar code found on most products in retail outlets. The code is used to identify the product and its manufacturer (see Figure 1–1). The POS terminal is used to record product sales in much the same fashion as a typical cash register. The difference is that a POS terminal has much greater capabilities. Instead of keying in each transaction as would be required on a cash register, the salesperson using a POS terminal merely passes the product's UPC by an optical scanner programmed to read the code (see Figure 1–2). The scanner interprets the code, looks it up on the computer's file, and retrieves the product's name and price. The transaction is then recorded by the computer and a customer receipt printed, listing the item name and price.

Retail computer systems using POS terminals are also used to update inventory levels and calculate sales figures. In addition, these systems allow determination of a customer's credit status. A credit card number can be entered into the system. Within seconds the computer can check the customer's account and determine if the transaction is acceptable. If the transaction is processed, the computer can automatically record the sale in the customer's account.

Banking

The banking industry makes extensive use of computer technology. A bank processes huge amounts of paper in the form of checks, loan records, deposits, savings clubs, investment information, etc. The account balance of every customer must be kept up to date. To facilitate these activities, computers can be found in every banking institution across the country.

One of the newest innovations in banking is the 24-hour banking service. A computer-controlled machine makes it possible to perform banking transactions day or night (see Figure 1–3). The bank customer uses a plastic card and selects the transactions by pushing a series of buttons. These "automatic tellers" are popping up all over the country. Many banks have installed the machines in the outside walls of the bank buildings. The machines can also be found in supermarkets, airports, and on college campuses. Some banks are even constructing shelters to house the machines in parking lots of shopping centers.

Another application of computers in banking is the "bank-by-phone" concept. The Bank of America in San Francisco has a computerized system that allows bank customers to utilize the bank's services by telephone. This system is called BAMTRAC (Bank of America Tracking System). A user can dial in transactions by using a Touch-Tone® telephone. Transactions are performed by entering account numbers and transaction codes through the keyboard of the telephone. The BAMTRAC system even "talks" to the customer. A voice synthesizer is programmed to respond to the customer, giving transaction instructions and information.

Many banks now offer automated services, such as automatic transactions performed each month. For example, a customer can request that his or her

FIGURE 1–1
Universal Product Code

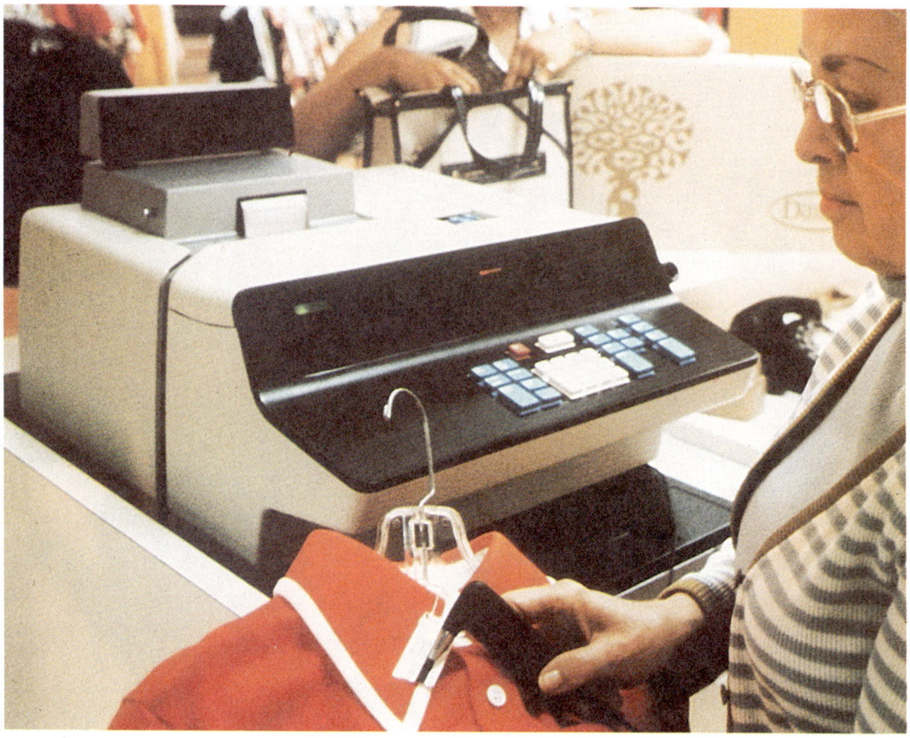

FIGURE 1–2
UPC Wand Reader

HIGHLIGHT
Debit Card Experiment

Debit cards are giving credit cards a run for their money. They're even making the familiar checkbook seem awfully old-fashioned. Indeed, the president of Mastercard International has predicted that within a few years there will be more debit than credit cards in circulation. A preview of what debit card existence will be like for consumers is already on display in Des Moines. Sponsored jointly by NCR, the Iowa Transfer System, and Dahl's Foods, the system allows a shopper to buy groceries at the Dahl's chain by simply passing his or her card through a magnetic-stripe reader built into a point-of-sale terminal at the checkout counter. This process instantly transfers the cost of the purchases from the customer's bank account to the store's account. Setups like this one, experts say, can reduce the check-processing cost for stores to as little as $.35 each instead of the current tab of from $.60 to $1.10 each.

paychecks be deposited directly into an account by the employer. On certain dates of the month, the customer's account can also be accessed to pay utility and credit card bills, as well as to transfer money from checking to savings accounts.

This type of service is made possible by a concept called **electronic funds transfer (EFT)**. This is the automatic recording of account transactions and money transfers. However, no money actually exchanges hands. Predictions for the future indicate that one day we will be living in a cashless and checkless society where all banking and credit transactions will be performed electronically.

Manufacturing

Manufacturing is a large part of this nation's economic activity. The computer revolution has done much to increase the productivity of manufacturing facilities all over the country. Manufacturing involves getting the right product to the right place at the right time in the right quantity. Extensive planning and scheduling is required to do this. Computers are being used to handle the routine scheduling of inventory, machinery, and labor. Computers are also used to simulate future states of the economy and answer "what if" questions about manufacturing demand.

FIGURE 1–3
24-Hour Teller. A customer using OC24 telling machine at Ohio Citizen's Bank.

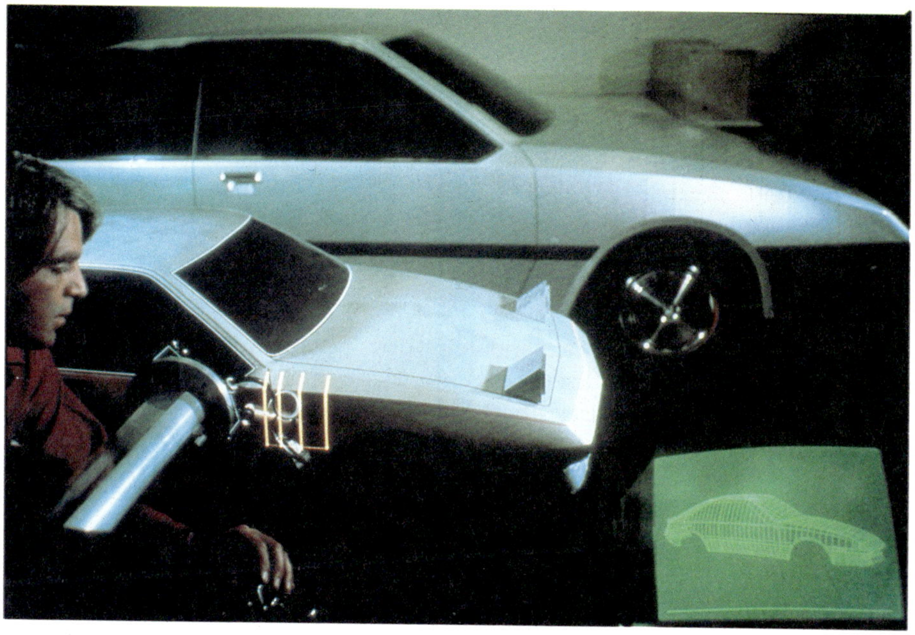

FIGURE 1–4
CAD/CAM. This photograph shows three stages in the design of an automobile at Chrysler Corporation: a computer-generated line drawing on a terminal; a small, ⅜ size model; and the full-size model.

Many programs are available to manufacturing facilities. Inventory control is handled by a complex system called **materials requirement planning (MRP)**. This system allows the manufacturer to enter future demands into a computer and receive a report that lists the scheduling dates and raw materials needed to manufacture the product to meet those demands.

Computer-assisted design and **computer-assisted manufacturing (CAD/CAM)** are two processes that have greatly assisted the manufacturer's job. Engineers and technicians are able to input certain requirements for a product or design and receive a computer-generated picture of the product (see Figure 1–4). In some cases, computerized tasks can take the calculations used to generate that picture and make the finished product.

Small insurance agencies use small business computers to store and access all the information needed in daily operations. Information on the clients, policies, and companies can be easily compiled and summarized for management needs.

Computers and Small Businesses

Until recently, computer capabilities were limited to large businesses and corporations. As the cost of computer equipment continues to decrease, more and more small businesses will be able to utilize computers in their organizations.

Many computer programs for small computers are now available to handle typical business activities. A business owner can purchase programming packages that perform accounts receivable, accounts payable, payroll, tax, and billing operations. The advent of the **microcomputer** has made it possible for entrepreneurs to purchase a complete accounting system. Similar packages are available for lawyers, landlords, shop owners, and a variety of other proprietorship operators.

Computers in the business field serve many other applications. Airlines,

HIGHLIGHT
Computer on Board the Space Shuttle

In order to maintain stable flight in a vehicle the size of the Space Shuttle, reactions to twisting, bending, flexing, or other aerodynamic instabilities must be made in milliseconds. To accomplish this, an all-digital electronic system composed of five on-board IBM AP-101 computers was devised. The five general-purpose digital computers control all systems: guidance, navigation, control, and communications. The five identical computers are interconnected. During launch and landing of the Shuttle, four of these operate together, performing guidance, navigation, and control tasks. The fifth acts as a backup. Inputs are received from the crew and from sensors, while commands are generated by the computers to all engines, jets, thrusters, and brakes. The computers handled 324 billion instructions during the mission's first flight of 54 hours, 20 minutes, and 42 seconds.

travel agencies, and hotels use extensive networks of computer equipment to schedule reservations. Branches of a business may be connected by communication lines across the country. Businesses are installing computers in offices to make clerical duties more efficient. **Electronic mail** systems tie businesses together, providing timely and accurate communication. And the list goes on and on.

COMPUTERS IN GOVERNMENT

The largest user of computers and computer systems in the United States is the federal government. This fact is not surprising when one considers the many government agencies that collect, process, and store information about the population.

Military

Every branch of the Armed Forces is involved in military planning and decision making. Many of the decisions are made by high-level officials with the use of computer-generated information. There exists a network of twenty communication satellites that transmit data to computer centers from all over the world. The North America Air Defense Command near Colorado Springs, Colorado, maintains a huge data base for military control purposes. This data base accepts data from radar and satellite equipment positioned throughout the world. The data can be quickly updated and retrieved at a moment's notice. For example, the computer can calculate the position of rockets and missiles within several seconds after they are launched. The computer can signal and perform the appropriate actions in case of attack.

308th Strategic Missile Wing crew members at the computer center at the Little Rock Air Force Base in Arkansas.

Computers are also used by military planners to simulate wars. Military commanders can practice making decisions based on the lifelike situations that the computer presents. This allows them to gain experience without engaging in real battles; sharpening skills in case a real threat should ever arise.

The concept of war simulation is used at a lower level of military training as well. Video games, similar to those found in game parlors, allow military personnel to practice and sharpen their shooting skills. One novel application is the simulation of tanks. The user is seated in a small compartment, much like the inside of a real tank. The targets are presented on a screen, and the user "fires" the tank by pressing switches and buttons. The computer system then critiques the actions of the user. This process saves millions of dollars, since no real property is destroyed and expensive shells are not fired, yet the result of the training is much the same.

Internal Revenue Service

Every person living in the United States who earns more than a minimal amount of money must report to the federal government for tax purposes. In addition, corporations and businesses file annual tax returns on their businesses. The Internal Revenue Service (IRS) receives millions of tax returns each year. Computers are used by the IRS to monitor these returns and record the information. Without the aid of computers, it would take many years to process just one year's worth of returns.

The IRS also performs audits on selected returns. Computers are used to randomly select tax returns for audits and perform some of the preliminary operations. This reduces the number of manual operations required to perform the audits, increasing the number of audits that can be performed each year.

At the Internal Revenue Service in Washington, D.C., information and data from tax returns are entered on terminals directly into the IRS service center computer system.

At Shell Oil computers are used for environmental research. Here, an engineer records the results of an experiment that tests the effects of water flooding on rock samples.

Planning for the Environment

Many agencies of the government are involved in protecting the future conditions of our environment. The Department of Health and Human Services uses computers to predict and control the effects of industrial waste in our country's rivers and streams. By determining the amounts of oxygen and chemicals in the water, the computers can provide information about the life-sustaining ability of the rivers under study. The system can also analyze the contents of the water to determine the cause of water pollution and suggest corrective courses of action to clean up the river.

Similarly, computers are used by the Environmental Protection Agency to determine the cause and effects of air pollution. The use of computers in environmental planning is becoming more important, especially with the movement toward stronger pollution control laws.

Weather Forecasting

One of the most interesting applications of computers in government is the area of forecasting the weather. Huge computers are used to process complex mathematical equations describing the interaction of a number of variables (air pressure, velocity, humidity, temperature, etc.). The combined use of this data and the mathematical models enables forecasters to predict the weather.

The data is collected from weather stations located throughout the world and processed by supercomputers at centralized locations in time to predict the weather for the next day. Without the use of computers, manual pro-

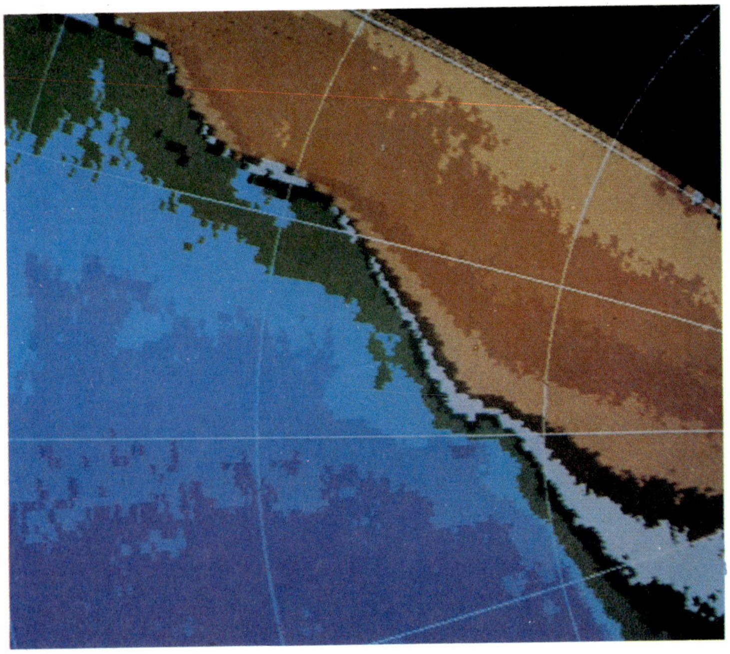

Doppler Radar display. The color contouring shows wind velocity in a severe thunderstorm with a black dot (in the middle left of the picture) depicting the point where a tornado is being produced.

cessing would take so much time that the results would be available *after* the weather conditions had already occurred!

Law Enforcement

Law enforcement agencies such as the FBI and intelligence-gathering agencies like the CIA use computer systems to store information, plan their operations, and track criminals. One government agency, the National Crime Information Center, uses a national network of computer terminals to keep track of police and law enforcement information. A centrally located data bank is available to police stations via terminals connected to state computers. The state computers, in turn, are hooked up to a large computer system located at the National Crime Information Center. This system allows local police to access information about stolen property, criminals, and criminal records from all over the country.

Computers are also found in the court system of the government. Court administrators spend much of their time scheduling courts and selecting juries. Computer systems are used in many courts to help screen qualified citizens for jury duty. The systems also perform the scheduling process, since judges, lawyers, witnesses, and defendents must all be present at a specific time. The system goes so far as to prepare the summonses for defendents and witnesses. Computers are used to record information during the trial. This enables the computer to generate a report about the court activities of a certain case.

The federal government has done much to encourage the advancement of computer technology. Many of the computer capabilities available today are

Computers in law enforcement. *Below left:* This system at the FBI Identification Computer Center is specially designed to read, identify, and store fingerprints. *Below:* This telephone system at the Orange County Sheriff's Office in Florida, uses computer technology to display on screen the caller's number, location, and situation. The Sheriff's office also can route the call to other emergency agencies at the touch of a button.

a result of governmental requests. In the future we can expect to see an increasing number of applications involving computers in government operations. Further advancements in the area of computer electronics will continue to decrease the cost of computer systems, allowing more extensive use of computer technology.

COMPUTERS IN MEDICINE

As the world's population continues to increase in size, demand for health care services will undoutedly be on the increase as well. And considering advances in research that provide an ever-increasing number of cures for ailments and diseases, if properly diagnosed, the problems for the medical profession are obvious. Hospital administrators, doctors, nurses, and researchers must make a wide variety of important decisions and diagnoses based on an ever-increasing number of variables. Without some method of organizing, evaluating, and retrieving the vast amounts of data required by the medical profession, patients could be improperly diagnosed and cures not applied. While computers certainly cannot replace members of the medical profession, they can complement and simplify their duties.

A large amount of data is processed daily in any hospital. A hospital information system is a group of computers and computer equipment that can be used to collect, store, process, and retrieve information. This information is used by hospital personnel to plan and control the operations of the hospital. The tasks performed by a hospital information system can range from routine billing and payroll to training personnel and monitoring patients. The following sections describe some of the many computer applications used by hospitals.

With this hospital's communications management system, doctors and nurses can update computerized records for patients and rooms from any of the hospital's telephones.

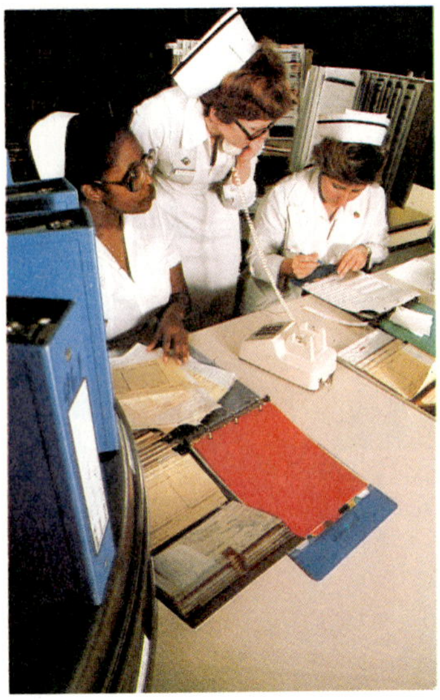

Clerical and Administrative Functions

Computers were first introduced in hospitals as a means of performing record-keeping activities. These activities are necessary to run the hospital in an efficient manner.

Hospital activities resemble those of business in that money must be collected for services rendered, supplies must be ordered, employees must be paid, and decisions must be made by managers. The computer performs many business-oriented functions including patient billing, personnel payroll, accounting, and reporting. Hospital functions also include scheduling beds, equipment, and other facilities, monitoring patients' conditions, and keeping records of patient information. These activities are often performed by computers.

As in any business, supplies and inventory must be obtained. In particular, a hospital necessarily maintains large quantities of many different drugs. Federal regulations require that records be kept on the dispensing of over 300 drugs to comply with drug-control laws. The amount of time required to maintain pharmacy records is substantially decreased by the use of a computer. This allows nurses to spend more time treating patients and less time processing the necessary paperwork.

Maintaining a blood bank also involves a large number of transactions. These transactions include adding and withdrawing volumes of blood, keeping track of and contacting prospective donors with needed blood types, and shipping blood to neighboring hospitals. Demand for blood is unpredictable, and since it can be kept on the shelf for only three weeks, large amounts cannot be stored. Not only can a computer system perform many of the clerical transactions required to maintain a blood bank, but it can also communicate with other hospitals to determine the availability of various types in the surrounding neighborhood.

Computers are also used in planning patient meals. Dietitians can utilize computer-generated menus that include nutritional information. Based on a physician's requirements for a patient, the dietitian can select from a wide variety of meals. The computer can also provide a list of food items low in stock. The result of a computer-assisted menu planning system at Georgia's Central State Hospital has been a wider variety of food for patients as well as a 5 percent decrease in food costs.

Computers are used extensively in the health-care profession. Large amounts of patient information can be stored (such as medical history and test results), and then be retrieved by the physician as needed.

Information Retrieval Functions

When a patient enters a hospital or consults a doctor, it is necessary to have a complete medical history on hand. In the past, this medical history was obtained by a lengthy interview between the patient and the physician or nurse. Many hospitals have recently automated this activity. For example, at the Mayo Clinic in Minnesota, a computer system is used to collect the information. The patient sits in front of a television-like terminal, where questions are displayed on the screen. The patient answers the questions by using a device to point to the correct answer on the screen. Depending on the answer, the computer may ask a series of more detailed questions. For example, the patient is asked if there is any record of heart disease in his or her family. If the answer is no, the computer goes on to the next topic. If the answer is yes, a series of specific questions about the history of heart disease in the patient's family will be asked.

Use of this automated system has greatly reduced the amount of time required of the patient and the doctor. Patients are often more candid with the computer than they would have been with the doctor. The medical history can be printed on paper and sent on to the physician for review. If the information changes, the patient's record can be quickly updated. Additionally, if the patient moves, the data can be transferred to another data bank in another city.

This hip prosthesis (an artificial hip bone) was designed by a computer to maximize resistance to stress.

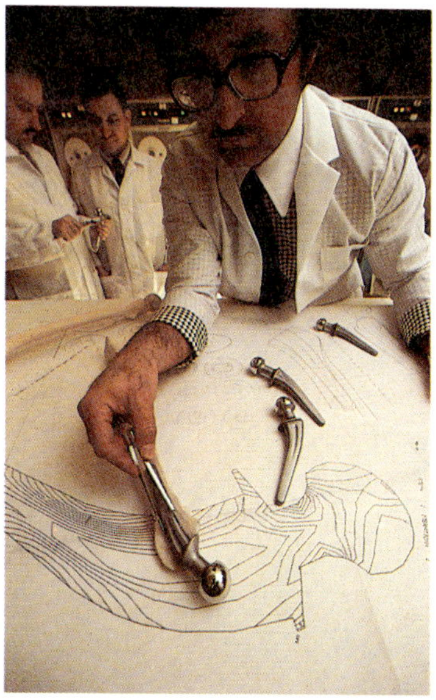

Computer-Assisted Diagnosis

Computers are becoming increasingly popular as a diagnostic tool in hospitals and clinics. One of the latest innovations in medical care is the concept of multiphasic testing. Multiphasic testing occurs when computer equipment is used to perform a series of tests, store the results of the tests, and

report the results to doctors. Physical examinations are performed by trained technicians and paramedics using the computer equipment. Again, this allows the physician to spend more time on diagnosis and treatment.

Multiphasic centers use computer equipment to perform electrocardiograms, x-rays, blood tests, vision and hearing tests, blood pressure tests, and height and weight measurement to name a few. The computer system compares the results of the testing sequence to a set of predetermined standards developed by medical doctors. The physician is then provided with a report of the test results before meeting with the patient. Multiphasic testing can be valuable for preventive health care. Unsuspected diseases can often be detected in this fashion.

As we have seen, the medical field is an area where computers can be used to better the existence of human life. Not only do computers give doctors and nurses more complete information to make better decisions, but they also reduce the time spent on routine activities. The computer's information storage and retrieval capabilities allow hospitals and clinics to process the vast amount of information required to operate efficiently. Computers are also being used in medical research to discover cures and treatments for today's diseases. These innovations have only recently come about, and the possible uses of computers in medicine have just begun to develop.

Above: This medical X-ray scanning device furnishes doctors with a sophisticated diagnostic tool that avoids the perils of exploratory surgery. The color scans produced by this system are used to detect any structural disorders in the patient's brain.
Right: This computer-generated scan of a normal, human brain was created by a system similar to the one pictured above. Scans such as this are used to study not only the structure of the brain, but also its activity and functions. This makes it possible for doctors to diagnose both physical disorders in the brain and certain mental illnesses as well.

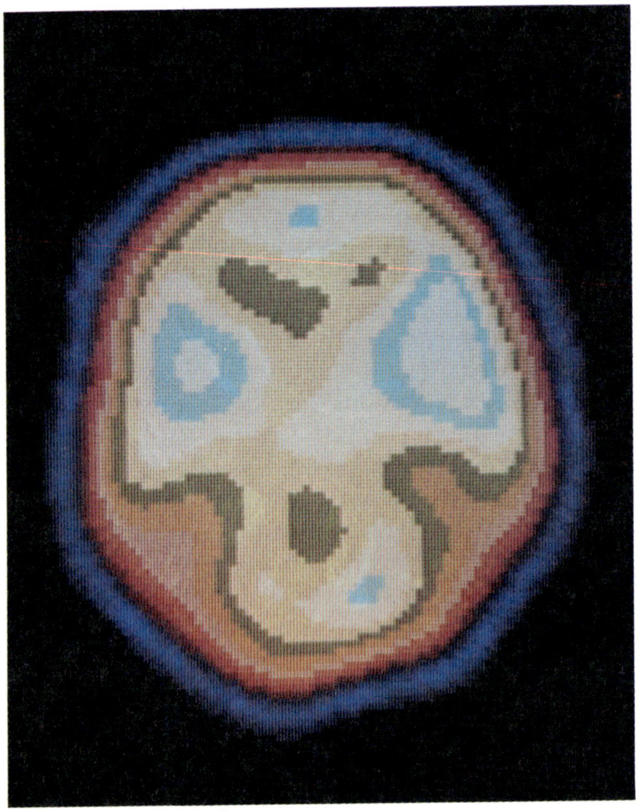

COMPUTERS IN EDUCATION

The potential impact of computers in education is significant. Computers are used for student instruction as well as for administrative data processing. When used for instruction, computers can provide richer, more meaningful experiences in learning, more individualized instruction, and better learning through practice. Computer applications in administrative processes help schools to operate more efficiently.

Computers were first used in the classroom during the 1960s; however, at that time they were utilized as little more than automated flash cards. This type of computer-controlled learning situation is called **computer-assisted instruction (CAI).** Multiple choice questions appear on a screen for students to answer. If the student answers correctly, the computer responds appropriately and asks another question. If the student's initial response is incorrect, the computer tries to steer the student to the correct answer. The computer may supplement the teacher by leading the student through drill work, exercises, remedial or enrichment material, tests, or simply by providing a dialogue with the student.

A classroom with computer-assisted instruction, using Tektronix 4006 graphics terminals.

CAI programs help teach everything from geometry and music theory to sales forecasting and computer programming. At Golden West College in Huntington Beach, California, students are enrolled in sign language courses based on computer-assisted instruction programs. Most of the students have normal hearing, but are interested in communicating with the deaf. A student types in an English word or phrase at the terminal and a drawing showing how to make the appropriate AMESLAN (American Sign Language) sign for the word flashes on the screen within seconds. For basic drill and practice, there's no more patient instructor than a computer!

The summer program at this school offers a computer class for six-year-olds.

HIGHLIGHT
Computerized Auto Sales

Cars can move off the lot faster and with more precise record-keeping details behind them when there is computer assistance. One California used car dealer turned a $30,000 loss into a $5,000 profit via a microcomputer and a software program that provides quick information on such matters as time and amount of sale, cost of space rental per car, depreciation per car, which cars are still on the lot and each of their features, and estimated charges by the Department of Motor Vehicles. Not only does this data help move cars faster, it also acts as a safeguard against errors that can anger customers and elicit reprimands or fines from the Department of Motor Vehicles.

Drill and practice exercises do have their place in education, but the use of computers in the learning environment can be much more effective when applied to other learning situations. Because computers are now simple to operate, and hardware is inexpensive enough for schools to purchase, they are rapidly changing the methodology of education. The student who uses the computer in a math curriculum, for example, learns an effective approach to the solution of any problem. The computer demands that a problem be divided into steps; in writing programs, the student gains a better understanding of problem solving in general.

It is being found that with computers in a classroom, students have a greater desire to learn. The brightest students can be challenged to their limits and slower students can be encouraged to start moving. The handicapped can participate at their own pace. The computer gives a student one-to-one focus and instantaneous feedback. Color graphics enable students to visualize complex engineering and mathematical problems.

For many teachers, computers have opened up a whole new realm of instructional possibilities. Computers can aid with developing curricula, creating and individualizing lessons, and even keeping track of student progress and grades. Computers assist in administrative tasks such as student scheduling, counseling, and grade reporting. Using them to score tests is now a fairly routine application, especially in schools with large classes.

PRIVACY

Data Banks

The widespread use of computers, information systems, and telecommunication systems has created a major concern in recent years—a concern about the invasion of individual privacy. **Privacy** involves an individual's ability to determine what, how, and when information about him or her is communicated to others. Many people are concerned about the use of personal information about them by government and private business; they think that computerized record keeping poses a threat to personal privacy.

Before computerized record keeping became widespread, most business and government decisions concerning such benefits as credit, educational grants, and Medicare were based on personal knowledge of the individuals involved, on limited information obtained from a decentralized system of public records, and from friends and associates of the individuals involved. These individuals' privacy was protected to some extent by the inefficiency of these sources and methods of collecting data. The details of people's lives were maintained in widely separated manually maintained files and in the memories of people who knew them. It was difficult to compile from these sources a detailed dossier on any individual.

With computers, data is easier to collect and store. Enabling information handlers to increase their data-collection activities tends to encourage them to collect more data. Further, computers can transmit data quickly and easily from one location to another. As mentioned above, manual systems pro-

The ease with which computerized information about people can be stored and retrieved has led to an increasing concern that computers may pose a threat to personal privacy. Here a FBI computer assistant files magnetic tapes in the Bureau's huge tape library.

vided an inherent deterrent to privacy invaders because of the difficulty of searching widely scattered records. In contrast, penetrating a single computerized data file gives access to much information, so there is greater incentive to make the attempt. Also, computers make it possible to compile lists of people connected with various types of activities from widely scattered data that probably could not be brought together manually. Previously unknown relationships may be revealed.

Control over personal information has become the accepted definition of privacy. With computers, the individual often has no significant control over what personal information will be collected, whether it will be accurate and complete, or to what uses it will be put. In fact, the individual seldom knows that such collection and dissemination are taking place, even though the results of such activities can effectively determine whether he or she will have access to services, privileges, opportunities, or benefits such as credit, education, medical care, and employment. Figure 1–5 shows examples of different types of data gathered by the federal government.

The main concerns of the privacy issue can be summarized as follows:

- Too much personal information about individuals is being collected and stored in computerized files.
- Organizations are increasingly using these computerized records in making decisions about individuals.

- Much of the personal data collected about individuals may not be relevant to the purposes for which it is to be used.
- The accuracy, completeness, and currency of the data may be unacceptably low.
- The security of stored data is a problem.

Of course, the same computers that are eroding individual privacy are also allowing institutions (private and public) to operate more efficiently. For example, it is obviously beneficial to a business to have enough information about individuals to make decisions that will control the firm's risks when issuing credit. Thus, a solution to the privacy issue must find an appropriate balance between the legitimate needs of organizations for information about people and the rights of individuals to maintain their privacy.

Privacy Law

Since the early 1970s, an increasing number of laws and regulations to protect privacy have been enacted to control the collection, use, dissemination, and transmission of personal data. By far the most numerous have been passed by the federal government, to protect against abuse of the government's own record-keeping agencies. The most sweeping legislation was the *Privacy Act of 1974*. Signed on January 1, 1975, this act was designed to protect the privacy of individuals who have information about themselves maintained by the federal government. This act provided that such individuals must be able to determine what information about themselves is being recorded by governmental agencies and how it will be used. Also, these individuals must be provided with a method of correcting or amending information that they know to be incorrect. In the same vein, information collected for one purpose should not be used for another without the consent of the individual. Finally, any organization creating, maintaining, using, or disseminating personal information must ensure the reliability of the data and must take precautions to prevent its misuse.

Although the act was a giant step in the right direction, it was criticized for its failure to reach beyond the federal government to state and private institutions. Several other laws have been passed by the federal government in an attempt to further control database information misuse. The *Education Privacy Act* is designed to protect individuals' privacy by regulating access to private and public school's computer-stored records of grades and evaluations of behavior. The act provides that no federal funds will be made available to an educational agency that has a policy of denying parents and students the right to inspect and review the student's relevant educational records.

The *Right to Financial Privacy Act of 1978* provides further protection to the individual by limiting governmental access to the customer records of financial institutions; thus protecting to some degree the confidentiality of personal financial data.

The *Freedom of Information Act of 1970* allows individuals to gain access to data about themselves in files collected by federal agencies. It was passed

FIGURE 1–5
Federal Data Banks

because of the potential for the government to conceal its proceedings from the public.

Many state laws regulating government record-keeping practices are patterned after the *Privacy Act of 1974*. Most states have enacted some type of controls on such practices in the public sector. Many of these laws contain provisions that require publication of notices describing the records that each governmental agency maintains; provide for the collection and storage of only data that is relevant, timely, and accurate; and prohibit unauthorized disclosures of data relating to individuals.

The only significant federal attempt to regulate the information practices of private organizations is the *Fair Credit Reporting Act of 1970*, a law intended to deter privacy violations by lending institutions that use computers to store and manipulate data about people's finances. This legislation provides to individuals the right to gain access to credit data about themselves and the opportunity to challenge and correct erroneous data.

States have also begun to regulate the information activities of nongovernmental organizations. Much of the legislation in this area operates to strengthen the protections afforded individuals by the *Fair Credit Reporting Act of 1970*.

Relatively few information privacy violation cases have been litigated. Since one of the problems of information privacy is that data is transferred and disclosed without the knowledge or consent of the subjects, it is not likely that people will even be aware of the use of data about themselves; therefore, they probably will not know that they have a claim to take to court. Further, privacy litigation is something of a contradiction in terms: By taking claims to court, litigants may expose private aspects of their lives to a far greater extent than the initial intrusion did.

COMPUTER CRIME/SECURITY

Two issues of concern to any student of the computer are computer crimes and security considerations. Crimes involving the computer have in most cases used or manipulated data for personal gain and profit. Computer crimes are hard to prevent, let alone detect. Considerable effort is expended by both public and private concerns in attempts to reduce their vulnerability to crimes. Knowledge of the ways in which computer crimes have been committed will aid the system designer in developing methods to deter similar illegal access in new systems.

Computer security focuses on two main problems: how to protect the physical equipment of the computer and how to protect against unauthorized use of the computer facilities by would-be criminals. Good physical protection of the computer does not necessarily assure against criminal use of computer files. The increasing number of telecommunication facilities (discussed in Chapter 6) used by computer installations provides easy access for the criminal desiring illegal access to the computer, even though he or she may be miles away.

Computer Crime

Computer crime is more of a problem than most people realize. Americans are losing billions of dollars to high-technology crooks whose crimes go undetected and unpunished; estimates of losses range from at least $2 billion to more than $40 billion a year. While no one really knows how much is being stolen, the total appears to be growing fast.

The earliest known instance of electronic embezzlement occurred in 1958, just a few years after IBM began marketing its first line of business computers. By the mid–1970s, scores of such crimes were being reported every year; yearly losses were estimated to be as high as $300 million.

Even worse problems appear to be ahead. Home computers and electronic funds transfer systems pose a new threat to the billions of dollars in data banks accessible through telephone lines. Already, crooks have made illegal switches of money over the phone, and more cases can be expected as EFT systems become widespread.

The biggest computer crime case uncovered so far involved the Equity Funding Life Insurance Company of Los Angeles. Officers of the company used a computer to fabricate $1 billion worth of fake life insurance accounts for 64,000 fictitious customers. They sold shares in the phony business to investors and used the computer to create the phony policies and keep track of the vast amount of data associated with them. The $2 billion fraud was discovered when a former Equity Funding employee told a securities analyst, who in turn informed his clients and the authorities. When caught, the officers had at their disposal a program that could have erased all the computer evidence.

This case is only one example of the types of electronic crime being committed: manipulating input to the computer; changing computer programs; and stealing data, computer time, and computer programs. The possibilities for computer crime seem endless. It has recently been suggested that computers are used extensively by organized crime and that a computer-aided murder may already have taken place.

The unique threat of computer crime is that criminals often use computers to conceal not only their own identities but also the existence of the crimes. Law officers worry that solving computer crimes seems to depend on luck. Many such crimes are never discovered because company executives do not know enough about computers to detect them. Others are hushed up to avoid scaring customers and stockholders. It is difficult for a company to admit that computer systems cannot be made "crime-proof."

It is estimated that only about 15 percent of computer thefts are reported to police. Many of these do not result in convictions and jail terms because the complexities of data processing mystify most police officials, prosecutors, judges, and jurors.

To make matters worse, courts are usually lenient in sentencing computer criminals. In one exception to this almost universal rule, a bookkeeper who had stolen $1 million from his employers in six years was charged with sixty-nine counts of grand theft and forgery. He pleaded guilty and was sentenced to ten years, of which he had to serve five and a half. This sentence is one of the longest ever given for a computer crime.

HIGHLIGHT
Computers in Organized Crime

Recent evidence suggests that organized crime, variously known as the Mafia, the Mob, and the Syndicate, is becoming increasingly involved in the use of computers and in computer crime. Most businesses, whether legitimate or illegal, lend themselves to computerization as a way to reduce overall costs. For example, computerizing a gambling racket means larger profits. Officials have already confiscated several betting programs, some of them directly linked to Mafia racketeers.

The Mob is also becoming more active in computer fraud and embezzlement. The growing market in stolen microchips and integrated circuits (as much as $20 million annually) may involve organized crime in New York. Electronic Funds Transfer (EFT) fraud has also been influenced by the Mob; one member was convicted in a $3 million EFT heist from Citibank in New York.

One further aspect of computers the Mob has interest in is the nation's criminal justice computers, such as the FBI's huge data base. Already one case has been reported involving a U.S. Justice Department consultant selling computerized crime dossiers to Mob elements.

Computer Security

Increasing computer crime naturally spawns interest in security measures designed to deter or detect, or at best, to prevent such crime. Computer security involves the technical and administrative safeguards required to protect a computer-based system (hardware, personnel, and data) against the major hazards to which most computer systems are exposed and to control access to information.

Physical computer systems and data in storage are vulnerable to several hazards: fire, natural disasters, environmental problems, and sabotage. Fire is one of the more apparent problems because most computer installations use combustible materials—punched cards, paper, and so on. Further, if a fire gets started, water cannot be used to extinguish it because water can damage magnetic storage media and hardware. Carbon dioxide fire extinguisher systems are hazardous because they would endanger employees, if any were trapped in the computer room. Halon, a nonpoisonous chemical gas, can be used in fire extinguishers instead of carbon dioxide. Halon is more expensive, but the cost of the equipment it protects can usually justify the additional expense.

Many computer centers have been damaged or destroyed by floods, cyclones, hurricanes, and earthquakes. Such natural disasters pose a serious

In order to maintain security, only authorized individuals may approach the locked computer facility.

threat to the computer hardware and wiring. Protection against natural disasters should be considered when the location for the computer center is chosen; for example, the center should not be located in an area prone to flooding.

Usually, computers are installed in buildings that were not originally planned to accommodate them. This practice can give rise to environmental problems. For example, water and steam pipes may run through a computer room; bursting of these pipes could result in extensive damage. Data on magnetic media can be destroyed by magnetic fields created by electric motors in the vicinity of the computer room. Other environmental problems include power failures, brownouts (temporary surges or drops in power), and external radiation.

A standard security precaution—locked doors that can be opened only with specially coded, identification cards.

Sabotage represents the greatest physical risk to computer installations. Saboteurs can do great damage to computer centers with little risk of apprehension. Providing adequate security against acts of sabotage such as destroying tapes, planting bombs, or cutting communication lines is extremely difficult and expensive.

In addition to safeguarding their computer systems from these physical difficulties, companies must protect stored data against illegitimate use by controlling access to it. There is no simple solution to these security problems. Organizations have instituted various security measures; most to restrict access to computerized records, others to provide for reconstruction of destroyed data. Some examples include storing backup copies of data outside the organization's location, giving authorized users special passwords and changing them frequently, allowing access to specific portions of the data base only by those whose jobs require it, restricting access to the data processing department to personnel with special badges and keys, translating or encrypting data into a secret code by using complex coding devices before data is stored and decrypting it after it has been retrieved, and identifying legitimate computer users by fingerprints or voice patterns.

These security measures are not complete, however. They may not prevent internal sabotage, fraud, or embezzlement. How, then, can organizations establish computer security? First, computer users must recognize their role in security. If a high-level priority is assigned to security in the company, employees must be made aware of it and of the security measures that are being taken.

Second, organizations can recognize the need to have a well-trained security force—a department of security guards who specialize in maintaining data security, conducting system audits, and asking the right kinds of questions on a daily and continuing basis.

Third, companies can exercise a great deal of care in the selection and screening of the people who will have access to computers, terminals, and computer-stored data. Companies should choose programmers as carefully as they select attorneys or accountants.

Lastly, companies must discharge employees who violate company rules. Whenever incidents occur, it is imperative that violators be shown that they will not be tolerated and that, however hard the necessary course of action, those responsible for security and protection have the intellectual and ethical integrity to follow through.

SUMMARY POINTS

- Computers are used in virtually every phase of business. In retailing, the Universal Product Code (UPC) and point-of-sale (POS) terminals provide for easy recording of the sale, inventory updating, and even fast credit checks.
- In banking, the computer allows for twenty-four-hour banking services, "bank-by-phone," and other automated services such as direct deposit of paychecks and automatic payment of bills.
- In manufacturing, materials requirement planning (MRP) allows the manufacturer to project when products can be manufactured and the quantity of raw materials required to do so.
- Computer-assisted design and computer-assisted manufacturing (CAD/CAM) are two concepts that have greatly assisted the manufacturer's job. These techniques enable engineers and technicians to input certain requirements for a product design or receive a computer-generated picture of the product.
- In small businesses, the decreasing cost of computer hardware and the increased availability of microcomputers and software provide for complete business accounting systems at a low cost.
- The largest user of computers and computer systems is the U.S. government. For example, the military uses computers to keep track of aircraft along our borders, run operation simulation games, and account for military equipment usage.
- The Internal Revenue Service uses the computer to process the vast amount of data it receives annually from taxpayers.
- The Department of Health and Human Services uses the computer to predict the environmental health of our nation.
- Complex calculations on vast amounts of data are performed by super computers in order to predict the weather.
- A central computer file is used to maintain data regarding criminals for law enforcement agencies. One agency, the National Crime Information Center uses a national network of computers to keep track of police and law enforcement information.
- The computer is used in medicine to organize, evaluate, and retrieve data regarding all aspects of health care. In clerical and administrative functions, the computer is used in much the same fashion as it would be in business—for patient billing, payroll, accounting, and reporting.
- The computer can also be used for information retrieval, where patient histories can be quickly referenced, updated, and compared to other patient histories with similar symptoms.
- Computers can be used in education for drilling, independent study, and for performing clerical tasks for instructors.
- The privacy issue has emerged as more and more computer files are maintained on an individual by federal, state, local, and private institutions. This issue focuses on the degree of control the individual has over personal information.
- Two issues of major concern to the student of the computer include computer crime and security.

- Most of the laws regarding the computer have been passed by the federal government and deal with the privacy issue. State laws usually reflect federal legislation and also deal with privacy. With few exceptions, there has been little attempt to regulate private business practices.
- Computer crime is more prevalent than might be suspected. Due to an unwillingness to publicize crimes, most businesses do not prosecute such criminals. Many crimes that involve computers are concealed by the computers as well, making detection of computer crimes extremely difficult.
- Computer security focuses on two areas: physical security of the equipment and controlled access to the computer and its data. Physical considerations revolve around protection from natural hazards. Efforts to prevent unauthorized access to data attempt to ensure that data is available only for its intended purpose.

REVIEW QUESTIONS

1. Give three examples of how you have seen computers used in business.
2. Show how the advantages of the computer can be put to good use in the diagnosing of medical ailments.
3. Why might the privacy issue be applied to medical records?
4. Do you know of any examples of the use of computers in the military other than those described in the text?
5. What sort of information is maintained about you by the school you are now attending? Do you feel each department or administrative branch needs to maintain the amount of data it does? What problems do you foresee if all this data is pooled together into one file?
6. If you were able to buy a computer to put in your home, what sort of security measures would you take (where would you put it, what would you do with stored files, etc.)? At what point would you not be concerned with security?
7. What advantages do you see in the use of voice synthesizers at retail check-outs?
8. How does EFT benefit employers who "direct deposit" employees' pay?
9. How do you think secretaries feel about using computerized word-processing equipment, and in what ways has the computer changed their tasks?
10. What private information may be too sensitive to allow in government data banks?
11. What traits related to security should an employer seek in a computer-terminal operator?

Personal Computers: As Common as Television Sets

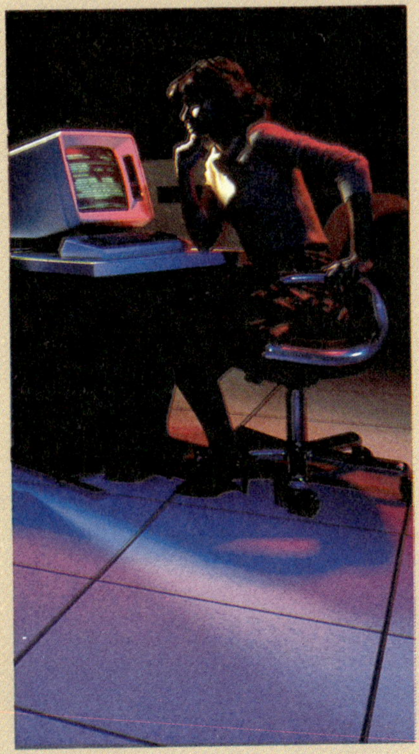

It's all around us. Each of us today is in the middle of an ongoing revolution. Just as the major technological advancements of electricity, air travel, and television changed the very fabric of our day-to-day lives in years past, the proliferation of the microcomputer continues to dramatically alter the way we live today. And, just as these past monumental, technical advancements are now taken for granted, so will the microcomputer and its many applications become an everyday part of our living and working environment. In fact, microcomputers today are becoming as common as television sets. As Hesh Weiner noted, "The computer revolution is the most advertised revolution in world history. Yet one of the funny things about it is that we probably still underestimate its impact."[1]

The uses of microcomputers can be as ordinary as bookkeeping or as diverse as creating music. You can encounter them at the car dealer, the grocery store, the bank or the dental clinic. Or you may even have one in your own home. In 1981 more than 800,000 personal computers were sold in the United States, most to people with little or no prior experience in operating computers. As the market for microcomputers continues to expand, so too does the technology and the number of applications for these computers. What follows are only a few examples of this remarkable microcomputer revolution.

A company in Arlington, Virginia, markets a computer program and electronic components that, when connected to a Heath/Zenith 89 (a small microcomputer that can be built at home), becomes a mechanical servant. One called Fred is controlled with voice commands. Fred turns lights on and off or makes them dimmer or brighter. Fred can turn the television on at a preset time or upon command—or switch the TV off and turn on the stereo at the appropriate time. It also brews coffee, acts as an alarm clock, and controls a security system or thermostat.

Fred is a collection of various electronic parts. The equipment includes a Heath/Zenith 89 computer; an electronic device similar to a signal-controlled garage door opener; a clock; a stereo sound synthesizer; and a sixteen-key pad. The key pad enables the vocabulary of twenty-four instructions to be programmable. The company can add other components to extend the clock and calendar capabilities as well as protect computer programs from accidental erasure.

A family in Burnsville, Minnesota, has an Apple II Plus with programs that control the home environment, act as security (including phoning an alarm to the police), and connect the computer by telephone to an information service. The family also runs a weekly marketing program that measures their growing inventory against needs and use facts. Matching up the information generates their shopping list. The same program manages the family budget.

[1]Hesh Weiner, "Computer Decisions," *Computers and the Future of America*, January 1977.

Another household program for a microcomputer, called Q-PON Helper, organizes discount coupons to reduce the family grocery bill. A printer attached to the microcomputer provides a copy of the information you need to carry with you. First, you type in the program and the shopping coupon facts. Once the program and data are stored, the computer processes the information. The program is written so that particular coupons can be found.

Programs for microcomputers are written either for general application or for a particular task. In a doctor's or dentist's office, a microcomputer can keep an appointment schedule and maintain personal records for each patient. A program called Appointments can be changed by the user; most purchased programs do not have this advantage. The Appointments program stores 23,000 appointments, and printed copy can be made for each doctor's set of appointments.

The search for ancestors (genealogy) is a natural application for computers. Programs that sort alphabetically or chronologically can easily arrange the relationships of 45,000 ancestors. That many could link you back to the seventeenth century. Facts gathered from birth records, church records, or gravestones are fed into the computer for processing. Popular among genealogists are selective statistics such as the frequency of twins or red-headed relatives. Programs that match information do this with ease.

Music is being created on microcomputers, and programs are written to play computer-generated music through your stereo system in high fidelity. One musician with a computer translates easily recognizable songs into computer language and sends them around the country by way of an electronic bulletin board to other owners of Radio Shack's TRS-80.

Sending out information from a microcomputer via the telephone lines is becoming commonplace. A Hollywood script writer who lives in Hawaii uses a word processor and a telephone connector to send scripts to an office in Hollywood where the material is received and recorded on a storage device. Then the scripts are printed on paper by a printer connected to the microcomputer there; the entire process takes thirty-two minutes.

Microcomputers can be used in two ways with other electronic devices. One way is by programming the computer and connecting it to an electronic device. Another way is when the manufacturer builds the device, like a microwave oven, and puts a programmed chip (microprocessor) right inside the device. Another device with functions enhanced by programmed chips is the bicycle odometer, which becomes a bicycle computer or "high-tech odometer."

A consumer electronics firm in East Brunswick, New Jersey, markets computers to use on bicycles. They measure speed, monitor heart rate, and can be programmed to match your position against your preset distance.

To monitor heart rate, either these computers have sensors mounted on the hand-grips or the cyclist wears a belt under his or her clothing around the chest.

Bicycle computers are also timing devices. Cadence is important to a cyclist—that is, how many times the pedal is cranked per minute. The bicycle racer who broke the record for human-powered speed in 1980 used a bicycle computer.

Computers of all sizes are part of our lives, whether we put them in our homes or make a simple transaction at the grocery store. Several universities now require incoming freshmen to own microcomputers and are offering these students plans to buy them through their campus stores. At some universities students are able to access the school's main computer with their micros even after they graduate. The introduction of personal computers into our society is similar to the automobile's introduction when the country was mostly rural. There is little doubt that personal computers will become far more integrated into the daily lives of all people.

DISCUSSION QUESTIONS

1. With so many uses for microcomputers, can you think of any places or applications where microcomputers would be inappropriate or a waste of time?
2. If you were thinking of buying a microcomputer, would you do anything special to prepare for this change?

CHAPTER 2

Information Processing

INTRODUCTION

The computer has become a dominant force in our society. Without the computer, society as we know it would come to a standstill. Business corporations, government agencies, and other organizations depend on computers to process data and make information available for use in decision making. Because of the impact of computers on everyday life, it is essential that people gain a basic understanding of them—their capabilities, limitations, and applications.

This chapter presents a brief history of data processing, beginning with the earliest calculating machines and ending with the state of the art today. The basic strengths and weaknesses of the computer are discussed, along with its use in data processing. Finally, an example of computerized payroll processing is given.

FACING PAGE
Here we see the testing of a "computer on a chip" which contains over 30,000 elements on a chip less than 1⁄10th the size of a postage stamp. Forty probes are used to touch pads on the chip's surface and connect it to a testing system.

CHAPTER OUTLINE

BACKGROUND

The history of the computer is a story of human ingenuity used to develop tools to aid in calculating answers to problems and keeping track of the results. The separate inventions, discoveries, and events that culminated in the creation of the modern-day computer span the ages. Ancient sheepherders tied knots in pieces of string to keep accurate counts of their herd. The abacus, one of the earliest known computational devices, used beads strung on wires to aid addition and subtraction (see Figure 2–1). The mechanical clock, developed in the Middle Ages, continuously calculated the time of day and displayed the results through the positions of two hands on its face.

It was not until the mid–1600s, though, that the first real mechanical calculator was developed. Made by Blaise Pascal, it added and subtracted numbers by using a series of eight rotating gears or wheels. As the first wheel counted out ten digits (one complete revolution), a pin on its edge would rotate the wheel to its left (the ten's place). This second wheel, in turn, would rotate the next, and so on (see Figure 2–2). This same principle is used today in many odometers to keep track of a car's mileage.

Not long after that, in the late 1600s, a man named Gottfried von Leibnitz took Pascal's idea a step further. Leibnitz developed a machine that not only added and subtracted, but did multiplication, division, and square roots (see Figure 2–3). Instructions on how to perform these mathematical functions were programmed mechanically in the way the gears turned one another as they moved, like Pascal's calculator. It was up to the user to enter the numbers and "tell" the calculator which mathematical function was desired (by mechanical interaction).

The weaving industry, of all unlikely places, was the site of the first machine to be controlled not by a human operator, but by a series of previously coded instructions. Previously a loom operator had been required to con-

FIGURE 2–1
The Abacus

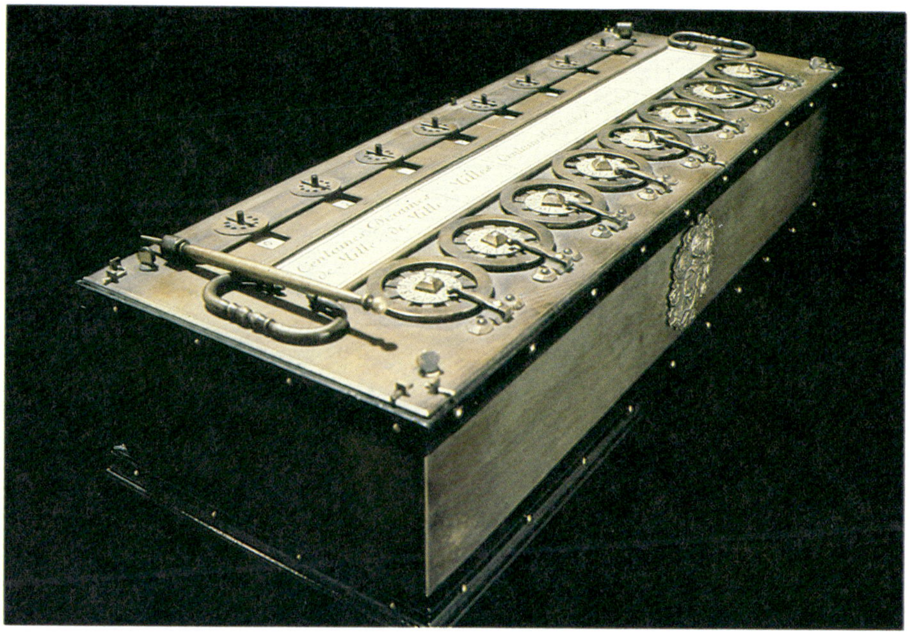

FIGURE 2–2
Pascal's Adding Machine

stantly interact with the machine, adjusting the loom's settings before each operation. Weaving the same pattern a second, third, or fourth time was just as time-consuming as it was the first, even though the series of loom settings were the same. Joseph Jacquard developed a way of recording each loom setting using holes punched in cards. A particular set of holes in a card corresponded to one loom setting. Jacquard next designed a loom that could "read" the punched cards, or "instructions," and translate them into appropriate loom settings. By linking a series of cards together, an entire fabric could be woven without operator adjustments! (See Figure 2–4.) This set of cards, or "instructions," was the forerunner to a similar set of instructions (called a **program**), used to tell the modern-day computer what to do.

One of the tragedies in the history of the computer lies with Charles Babbage, a man ahead of his time. Babbage set out to develop a machine that

FIGURE 2–4
Jacquard's Loom

FIGURE 2–3
Leibnitz's Machine

PROFILE
Ada Lovelace

While Charles Babbage was struggling through the development of his difference engine in the mid–1800s, he was not alone. Working by his side was Lady Ada Augusta Lovelace, daughter of the poet, Lord Byron. Ada Lovelace was considered a mathematical genius and her work with Babbage has earned her the title of the first programmer.

Ada Lovelace began working with Babbage in 1842 after translating a paper from French to English about the difference engine. Her interest heightened as she worked on the project, and the following year, when she was 28 years old, Lovelace had added some of her own ideas to Babbage's. The paper, as it turned out, was tripled in length because of Ada's additions.

Lovelace was married to a man who supported her intellectual growth and was wealthy enough to hire help to take care of their three children. Lovelace continued to put all her energy into Babbage's quest.

One of Lovelace's ideas that earned her the claim as the first programmer was what we now refer to as the concept of a *loop.* She had observed that the same sequence of instructions were often necessary to perform a single calculation. Thus, she discovered that by using only a single set of cards, and a conditional jump facility, the calculation could be performed with a fraction of the effort.

Ada continued to work with Babbage until her tragic death from cancer at the age of 36. Babbage was once again left alone to continue with his labor. Neither Lovelace nor Babbage lived to see the fruits of their efforts. Recently, however, the latest state-of-the-art programming language was named Ada in recognition of the many achievements Ada Lovelace brought to the development of computers.

FIGURE 2–5
Babbage's Difference Engine

could perform calculations without human intervention. The machine was designed to make arithmetic calculations and print the results, avoiding the printing errors so common in his day. His idea relied on the "method of differences," and in the early 1800s he managed to build a small working model (see Figure 2–5). The tragedy was that when he strove to make a larger version of what he called his **difference engine,** parts could not be manufactured to the tolerances required by his machine. The technology simply was not sophisticated enough.

The punched-card concept from the weaving industry was put to good use in the late 1800s by Dr. Herman Hollerith, a statistician. It seems the United States government was encountering problems trying to process data gathered in the census. The last census, taken in 1880, had required some seven-and-a-half years of manual calculations to tabulate. Significant population increases since then would make manual processing of the next census almost unthinkable. Hollerith developed the forerunner of what almost everyone recognizes today as the standard computer card. Each card had twelve rows and eighty columns, and used a coding scheme that is still in use today. This code, called **Hollerith's code**, permitted specially designed machines to sort the census data according to the census' needs (see Figure 2–6). Hollerith's invention reduced the time required to process the census to two-and-a-half years despite a population increase of three million.

Hollerith's successful experience with the government led him to set up the Tablulating Machine Company which manufactured and marketed punch-card equipment for commercial use. His company later merged with others which, over time, became the International Business Machines Corporation (commonly called IBM).

In a different vein, William S. Burroughs was making advances with a mechanical adding machine about the time Hollerith's census machines were working on the 1890 census. The machine was key-driven and operated by a hand crank. It could record, summarize, and calculate, and was sold by the Burroughs Adding Machine Company.

EARLY DEVELOPMENTS TO STATE-OF-THE-ART

From the 1900s on, it becomes more difficult to sort out the various developments preceding the modern-day computer, so fast were they occurring. **Accounting machines** were developed in the late 1920s and early 1930s which supported full-scale record-keeping and accounting functions but did little more than manipulate vast quantities of punched cards (see Figure 2–7). The first real step toward the development of the modern-day computer

FIGURE 2–6
Hollerith's Census Machine

FIGURE 2–7
Accounting Machine

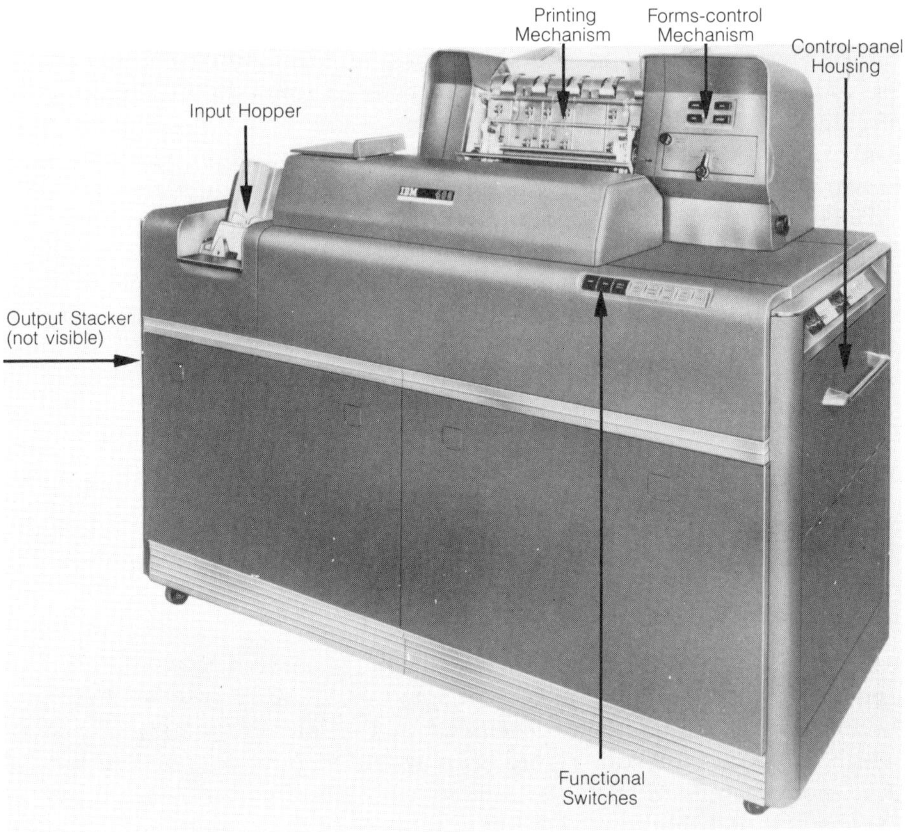

FIGURE 2–8
The Mark I Computer

PROFILE
John Vincent Atanasoff

While working on his Ph.D. in mathematics and physics at Wisconsin, John Atanasoff found himself impeded by the cumbersome task of solving large equations and other complex calculations. After receiving his doctorate in 1930, Atanasoff went to Iowa State as a professor in mathematics and (later) physics. There, again, he was faced with a need for calculating power—this time to help twenty masters and doctoral candidates with their work. None of the various mechanical calculating devices available were adequate; they were too slow and not accurate enough. Atanasoff felt that the solution to his probelm was in the development of a digital computing device based upon electronics. By December 1939, Atanasoff, with the help of his assistant Clifford Berry, had built a prototype computer. The first working model, called the Atanasoff-Berry computer, was completed in 1942. It was a serial, binary, electromechanical machine and employed various new techniques that Atanasoff had invented, including novel uses of logic circuitry and regenerative memory.

Atanasoff's attempts to get either IBM or Remington Rand interested in his invention failed. An attempt to obtain patent rights for himself also failed. Eventually he gave up and the rest of his professional career was spent in various governmental and industrial jobs, including the presidency of two companies he founded, Ordnance Engineering Corporation and Cybernetics, Inc. He received the U.S. Naval Distinguished Service Award in 1945 for his work with the Naval Ordnance Laboratory during World War II.

Although Dr. Atanasoff conceived of and designed the first electronic digital computer, his invention was for many years credited to others. In 1974 a federal judge ruled that Atanasoff was the true inventor of the concepts required for a working electronic digital computer. It is now generally agreed that the design of the Atanasoff-Berry Computer and the use of electronics in the computer provided the foundation for the next advances that took place in the development of the electronic digital computer.

was made with the **Mark I**, the first automatic calculator, designed around 1944 by a team headed by Howard Aiken of Harvard University. (see Figure 2–8). Instead of using mechanical gears like Pascal's or Leibnitz's calculator, it used electromagnetic relays and mechanical counters.

Electronic Processing

It was during this time that researchers were studying the possibility of developing a calculator that used electricity rather than mechanical devices. An electronic calculator had the potential of supporting more complex arithmetical functions since it would not face the limitations of mechanically interacting wheels. It would rely on electricity rather than gears, so it could operate much faster as well. The idea had some problems, however. For instance, numbers are easy to represent on mechanical calculators by the positions of wheels, but how can numbers be represented electronically? An electronic calculator has to rely on electrical currents to control and manipulate numbers, but only two electrical states are recognized easily: "on" and "off" (that is, either the presence or absence of current). A scheme had to be used to represent numbers using only these two states. The binary system, which uses groups of 1s and 0s to represent numbers, appropriately mirrored the "on" and "off" electrical states. Called "the language of the computer," or **machine language**, the binary system was used in these early experiments and is still used in modern computers today. It is the only language that a computer can directly recognize and act upon.

The first true electronic calculator was developed only two years after the Mark I. Called the **ENIAC**, short for the Electronic Numerical Integrator And Calculator (see Figure 2–9), it could perform a multiplication in three-thousandths of a second compared with about three seconds for the Mark I. Instructions to the ENIAC had to be given using a combination of switches, as there was no way for it to store instructions.

It was not until John Von Neumann devised a method of encoding instructions electronically in the same fashion as numbers that it became possible to store instructions within the calculator itself. This was an important development. The calculator could then execute instructions and perform calculations at its own speed, rather than relying on humans to tell it each successive step. The ability to store instructions is one feature separating a computer from a calculator.

FIGURE 2–9
The ENIAC: J. P. Eckert, shown here developed the ENIAC with John Mauchly

Von Neumann's principles spurred the development of the first **stored-program computer.** Two computers were developed around the same time utilizing these principles. The **EDVAC** (Electronic Discrete Variable Automatic Computer) and **EDSAC** (Electronic Delay Storage Automatic Computer) performed arithmetic and logical operations without human intervention, depending solely on stored instructions. These computers marked the beginning of what is called "the computer age." Further refinements after this time focused on speed, size, and cost. These developments are usually divided into four categories: first-generation, second-generation, third-generation, and fourth-generation computers.

HIGHLIGHT
Computer Charting of Airplay

Because almost all radio stations in America select the records they will play by imitating the playlists of a relatively few trend-setting stations, providing these playlists to those who rely on them has become a big business. Until recently, this was done through the charts of such music trade publications as *Billboard*, *Cash Box*, *Record World*, *Radio & Records* and the *Gavin Report*. Now, *Billboard* has introduced a computerized variation to the process. It calls this instant access service "BIN" (Billboard Information Network) and has been selling it to record companies, radio programmers, and record promoters for from $125 a week up. With BIN, a subscriber can instantly discover what records are being played on which stations in which regions of the country and how often, instead of waiting for the magazine to give this information in regular printed form once a week. So are you surprised that radio sounds about the same no matter where you are?

First Generation: 1951–1958

First-generation computers were extremely large and had poor reliability. They used vacuum tubes to control internal operations, which were fairly large and generated considerable heat, much as light bulbs do. Not only was a lot of space required to house the tremendous number of vacuum tubes making up the computer, but special air conditioning had to be installed to get rid of the tube-generated heat. Although first-generation computers were much faster than earlier mechanical or electromechanical devices, they were slow compared to today's computers and their internal storage capacity was limited.

Punched cards were used to enter numbers into the computer. These were cards with holes punched in them according to a coding scheme much like Hollerith's cards. A particular set of holes had special meaning. A machine was used to interpret the punched holes on the cards and translate them into machine language for the computer. The machine language results of this translation were often stored on **magnetic drums**. These were cylinders coated with magnetizable material, rotated at high speeds. Machine language was stored as tiny magnetized spots on the outer surface of the drum, in much the same way that music is stored on audio tapes or cassettes. Read/write heads suspended just above the rotating surface of the drum either wrote on the drum by magnetizing small spots, or read from it by interpreting the already magnetized spots on the drum. Numbers were manipulated by the computer according to the instructions or program given to it. The results of these operations were punched on blank cards, which could then be read by humans.

The first computer to use all of these techniques was the **UNIVAC I** (UNIVersal Automatic Computer), developed by the same people responsible for the ENIAC (see Figure 2–10). Before the UNIVAC I, computers had been one-of-a-kind machines developed specifically for scientific and military purposes. The UNIVAC I was dedicated to business data-processing applications, as its first application by the U.S. Census Bureau shows. For the first time, business firms were exposed to the possibilities of computer data processing. Even then, however, most first-generation computers were still oriented toward scientific applications rather than business data processing. **Scientific applications** require computers that can manipulate numbers according to sophisticated formulas and keep track of the results to many dec-

FIGURE 2–10
The UNIVAC I Computer

imal places. **Business applications** do not usually require such "number crunching," but rather simple calculations like addition and subtraction (for accounting records). The difference is that business applications require inputting large volumes of data on which these simple calculations are performed.

Coding instructions for the computer using the ones and zeroes of computer language was an extremely cumbersome, tedious, and time-consuming task. It was during this period that **symbolic languages** were developed. These languages enabled instructions to be written using symbolic codes (called **mnemonics,** or memory aids) rather than strings of zeroes and ones. One word (or mnemonic) represented a particular machine language instruction (or group of ones and zeroes). Once the series of instructions or words were put together into a **program**, they were translated by the computer into their machine language counterparts (see Figure 2–11).

The computer had to be given instructions on how to translate the mnemonics into recognizable machine language. This set of instructions was a program, too. What this program basically did was to tell the computer to look up each mnemonic it was given in a program and compare it against a list of all possible mnemonics and their machine language equivalents.

FIGURE 2–11
Machine Language versus Symbolic Language

MACHINE CODE TO ADD TWO FIELDS

111110100100000111000000100001010010000000010101100

SYMBOLIC CODE TO ADD TWO FIELDS

AP TOTAL,AMOUNT

When it found a match, it took the machine language code from the table. By doing this for all the mnemonics in a program, it was able to build a program in machine language that it could execute. The first such program for translating mnemonics into machine language was developed by Dr. Grace Hopper in 1952 at the University of Pennsylvania. After this breakthrough, most first-generation computers were programmed in symbolic language. The most popular applications of computers in business at this time were for payroll and billing, since they were easy to program and cost justify.

Second Generation: 1959–1964

In the late 1950s, tiny, solid-state **transistors** replaced vacuum tubes in computers. This greatly reduced heat generated during operation and made possible the development of computers significantly smaller and more reliable than their predecessors. These new computers were faster, had increased storage capacity, and required less power to operate. They were **second-generation computers** (see Figure 2–12).

The magnetic drums of first-generation computers were replaced by **magnetic cores** as the primary internal storage medium. Cores are very small doughnut-shaped rings of magnetic material strung on thin wires. An electrical current passed through the wires on which a core is strung magnetizes the core to represent either an "on" or "off" state. In this way, groups of cores can store instructions and data. The advantage of magnetic cores is that instructions and data can be located and retrieved for processing in a few millionths of a second—faster than with magnetic-drum storage.

This new primary storage of second-generation computers was often supplemented by another form of storage using magnetic tapes. **Magnetic tapes**

FIGURE 2–12
A Second-Generation Computer System—IBM 7070

are very much like recording tapes used for music, only wider. Magnetic tapes provided faster loading of numbers into the computer than with punched cards. The results of computer operation could also be stored faster on tape than punched on cards.

Along with refinements in hardware technology, second-generation computers were also characterized by further refinements in programming lan-

FIGURE 2–13
Comparison of High-Level and Symbolic Languages

SYMBOLIC LANGUAGE Excerpt from payroll program in Assembly Language

```
OVERTIME    AP      OVRTME,FORTY           }
            MP      OVRTME,WKRATE          }
            AP      GROSS,WKRATE           }
            SP      WKHRS,FORTY            } Computer
            MP      WKHRS,ONEHLF           } Overtime
            MP      GROSS,WKHRS            } Pay
            MVN     GROSS+5(1),GROSS+6     }
            ZAP     GROSS(7),GROSS(6)      }
            AP      GROSS,OVRTME           }
TAXRATE     CP      GROSS,=P'25000'        }
            BH      UPPERRTE               } Determine
            ZAP     RATE,LOW               } Tax Rate
            B       TAXES                  }
UPPERRTE    ZAP     RATE,HIGH              }
TAXES       ZAP     TOTAXES,GROSS          }
            MP      TOTAXES,RATE           } Compute
            AP      TOTAXES,=P'50'         } Taxes
            MVN     TOTAXES+5(1),TOTAXES+6 }
            ZAP     TOTAXES(7),TOTAXES(6)  }
            SP      GROSS,TOTAXES          } Calculate Net Pay
            MVC     PRPAY,MASK             } and Edit Print Line
            ED      PRPAY,GROSS            }
            MVC     PRNAME,NAME            } Print Output Line
            XPRNT   LINE,32                }
```

HIGH-LEVEL LANGUAGE Excerpt from payroll program in COBOL Language

```
OVERTIME-ROUTINE.
    MULTIPLY WAGE-PER-HOUR BY 40 GIVING REGULAR-PAY.
    SUBTRACT 40 FROM HOURS-WORKED GIVING OVERTIME-HOURS.
    MULTIPLY WAGE-PER-HOUR BY 1.5 GIVING OVERTIME-RATE.
    MULTIPLY OVERTIME-HOURS BY OVERTIME-RATE GIVING
        OVERTIME-PAY.
    ADD REGULAR-PAY, OVERTIME-PAY GIVING GROSS-PAY.
TAX-COMPUTATION.
    IF GROSS-PAY IS GREATER THAN 250 THEN MULTIPLY GROSS-PAY
        BY 0.20 GIVING TAX ELSE MULTIPLY GROSS-PAY BY 0.14
        GIVING TAX.
    SUBTRACT TAX FROM GROSS-PAY GIVING NET-PAY.
    MOVE EMPLOYEE-NAME TO NAME.
    MOVE NET-PAY TO AMOUNT.
    WRITE PRINT-LINE.
    GO TO WORK-LOOP.
```

guages. Second-generation computers often used high-level languages to instruct the computer how to perform processing tasks. **High-level languages** resembled English a lot more than symbolic languages did, and hence were easier to use. The first high-level language to achieve widespread acceptance was called **FORTRAN** (FORmula TRANslator), developed in the mid–1950s by IBM. The version of the language known as FORTRAN IV was standardized in 1963 and is still used extensively for scientific applications. Because FORTRAN lacked many features desirable for business data processing, another language called **COBOL** (COmmon Business-Oriented Language), was developed in the early 1960s. This language was geared towards processing large amounts of business transactions easily. See Figure 2–13 for a comparison between high-level and symbolic languages.

Third Generation: 1965–1971

Continued technological advances in electronics and solid-state devices brought further reductions in computer size, even greater reliability and speed, and lower costs. **Integrated circuits (ICs)** replaced the transistors of second-generation equipment in machines referred to as **third-generation computers** (see Figure 2–14). Through techniques like etching and printing, hundreds of electronic components could be included on silicon circuit chips less than one-eighth-inch square.

The transition from the second to the third generation occured when IBM introduced the System/360 computers. This family, or series, consisted of six different computers, each offering a different main storage capacity. The se-

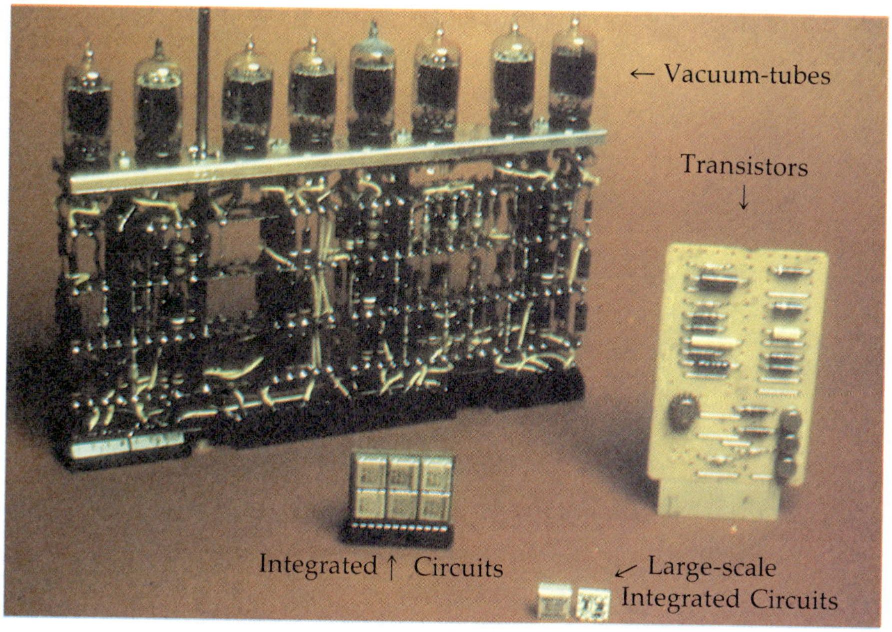

FIGURE 2–14
First-, Second-, and Third-Generation Components

ries was designed to provide all types of processing; its computers were capable of supporting forty different input/output and auxiliary storage devices. Within a short time after the introduction of the System/360, other manufacturers announced their versions of third-generation computers. RCA, Honeywell, Univac, Burroughs, and others began competing with IBM, and before long, over 25,000 third-generation computer systems were installed across the United States (see Figure 2–15).

The advances in solid-state technology that led to third-generation computers also led to the emergence of minicomputers (see Figure 2–16). **Minicomputers** offer many of the same features of full-scale computer systems (such as the IBM System/360), but on a smaller scale. They are physically smaller with less main storage capacity than full-scale machines. They nevertheless provide a powerful computer system and a cost-efficient alternative for small businesses. A small computer manufacturer called Digital Equipment Corporation (DEC) introduced the first commercially accepted minicomputer in 1965 and has since grown into the largest manufacturer of minicomputers in the United States.

Another third-generation innovation involved **remote terminals**—terminals placed at various geographical locations and used to communicate directly (to be **online**) with a central computer. Using such terminals, many users could use the central computer at the same time and receive almost instantaneous results.

FIGURE 2–15
A Third-Generation Computer System—NCR V-8600

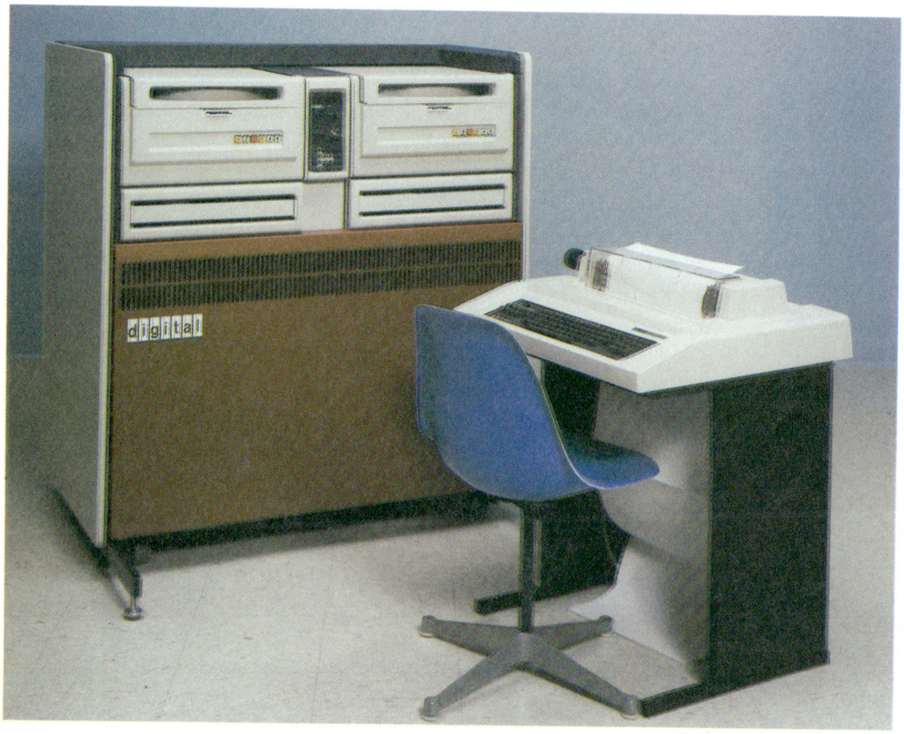

FIGURE 2–16
A DEC Minicomputer That Uses Third-Generation Miniaturization Techniques

Fourth Generation: 1972–?

After the introduction of third-generation computers, further technological developments are not so clearly defined. Some academicians argue that fourth-generation computers are represented by IBM's System/370 computers. In these computers, electronic components were further miniaturized through **large-scale integrated (LSI) circuits.** This process put thousands of transistors on a single silicon chip. These new LSI chips replaced the magnetic core as the primary storage medium and provided faster processing speeds.

Another academic group supports the idea that microtechnology itself is the fourth generation. LSI technology made possible the development of **microprocessors,** which appear in devices people use every day. Many microwave ovens, sewing machines, thermostats, and even late-model automobiles use microprocessors to govern their operations. By using the microprocessor in combination with other LSI chips, scientists have developed an extremely small computer called a **microcomputer.** Microcomputers are now being used in the home for such things as Christmas card lists, educational skill development, tax recording, balancing checkbooks, keeping track of recipes, and amusing people with games. It is argued that these microcomputers, also known as home computers, will play an increasingly important part in everyday society.

Steady progress in complexity and power marks the history of the microprocessor. The chip shown here is Bell Labs' newest and has as much processing power as some minicomputers.

Regardless of which group holds the correct view, there can be no doubt that LSI technology played a large part in the development of fourth-generation computers. As scientists perfect VLSI (Very Large Scale Integration), who knows where the computer will be found next?

Perspective

Today's computer is certainly a complex electronic marvel compared to its modest ENIAC counterpart. Even then it is still quite dumb. It cannot perform any task without prior instructions from a human being. It has no independent intelligence, so, in effect, it has an IQ of zero!

Simplified, the computer is just a beefed-up calculator which can only perform three basic functions: arithmetic operations (addition, subtraction, multiplication, and division), comparisons (test two different values to see if they are equal or if one is less than the other), and storage and retrieval of raw facts. That means the type of instructions that can be given to the computer are quite limited. It is easy to see that computer instructions of this type can just as easily be performed by humans!

What gives the computer the advantage over its human counterparts is *speed, accuracy,* and *memory.* Modern computers are capable of performing millions of calculations in one second. Technological developments to increase this speed are fast reaching the physical limitation of the speed of light, which is about 186,000 miles per second. Obviously, such processing speed far exceeds human ability (see Figure 2–17).

The accuracy of computers is due mostly to the reliability of electronic circuits that make up a computer. This means that the same type of current

TABLE 2–1
Computer Advancements

PERIOD	COMPUTER SYSTEM CHARACTERISTICS
First Generation 1951—1958	Use of vacuum tubes in electronic circuits Magnetic drum as primary internal-storage medium Limited main-storage capacity Slow input/output; punched-card-oriented Low-level symbolic-language programming Heat and maintenance problems Applications: payroll processing and record keeping Examples: IBM 650 UNIVAC I
Second Generation 1959—1964	Use of transistors for internal operations Magnetic core as primary internal-storage medium Increased main-storage capacity Faster input/output; tape orientation High-level programming languages (COBOL, FORTRAN) Great reduction in size and heat generation Increased speed and reliability Batch-oriented applications: billing, payroll processing, updating inventory files Examples: IBM 1401 Honeywell 200 CDC 1604
Third Generation 1965—1971	Use of integrated circuits Magnetic core and solid-state main storage More flexibility with input/output; disk-oriented Smaller size and better performance and reliability Extensive use of high-level programming languages Emergence of minicomputers Remote processing and time-sharing through communication Availability of operating-system programs (software) to control I/O and do many tasks previously handled by human operators Applications: airline reservation system, market forecasting, credit-card billing Examples: IBM System/360 NCR 395 Burroughs B5500
Fourth Generation 1972—?	Use of large-scale integrated circuits Increased storage capacity and speed Modular design and compatibility between equipment (hardware) provided by different manufacturers (customer no longer tied to one vendor) Availability of sophisticated programs for special applications Greater versatility of input/output devices Increased use of minicomputers Introduction of microprocessors and microcomputers Applications: mathematical modeling and simulation, electronic funds transfer, computer-aided instruction, and home computers Examples: IBM 3033 Burroughs B7700 HP 3000 (minicomputer)

FIGURE 2–17
Measuring Units of Computer Speed

UNIT	SYMBOL	FRACTIONS OF A SECOND
Millisecond	ms	one-thousandth (1/1,000)
Microsecond	μs	one-millionth (1/1,000,000)
Nanosecond	ns	one-billionth (1/1,000,000,000)
Picosecond	ps	one-trillionth (1/1,000,000,000,000)

passed through the same electrical circuits will consistently yield the same result. Reliability of this type is proven every day by thousands of people each time they turn a light switch on or off. However, the concept of accuracy applies only to a computer's internal operation. It does not necessarily mean that everything that comes out of a computer is correct. That depends on what information was given to the computer in the first place. If the raw data given to the computer is incorrect, it will be impossible for the computer to manipulate it into meaningful results. Or, if the instructions given to the computer are incorrect, that too, will produce incorrect results. This

This manufacturing facility includes an automatic system for inserting components into circuit boards. The system accurately inserts 7,000 components per hour and "senses" the presence or absence of a component on the circuit board.

concept, called **garbage in—garbage out,** is important to remember when considering potential computer mistakes.

The memory of a computer can be continually expanded so as to be almost limitless. The computer can store vast amounts of facts and retrieve them at incredible speeds. Similar vast quantities of data could be stored in paper files, but they would become extremely bulky and require a good deal of storage space. Not only that, retrieving data from such a file would become increasingly time-consuming as the size of the file increased.

The ability of the computer to store program instructions as well as facts allows it to execute calculations at its own incredible pace. In fact, the ability of the computer to store, retrieve, and process data, all without human intervention, separates it from a simple calculator and gives it its magnificent power and appeal.

So while humans may be able to perform the same functions as the computer, the difference is that the computer can execute millions of instructions in a second, accurately, and store the results in an almost unlimited memory.

DATA PROCESSING

In the past, manual techniques of collecting, manipulating, and distributing data to achieve certain objectives were known as **data processing.** The early electromechanical machines developed to perform these functions provided **automatic data processing (ADP).** Today, the electronic computer is used to perform these same functions in a process called **electronic data processing (EDP).** (The term *data processing* is nevertheless often used as a shorthand reference to EDP.)

The objective of all data processing, whether manual, electromechanical, or electronic, is to convert raw data into information that can be used in decision making. **Data** refers to raw facts that have been collected from various sources but not organized. Data cannot be used to make meaningful decisions. For example, a list of the day's checks and deposit slips may mean very little to a bank manager. But through manipulation of the data in one fashion or another, useful information may be provided—perhaps in the form of a summary report giving the number and dollar value of deposits and withdrawals. **Information,** then, is data that has been organized and processed. Information increases understanding and helps people make intelligent decisions.

To be useful to decision makers, information must be delivered to the right person, at the right time, in the right place. It must be accurate, timely, complete, concise, and relevant. If information fails to meet these requirements, it fails to meet the needs of those who must use it and thus is of little value.

To derive information from data, all data processing follows the same basic flow: **input, processing,** and **output** (see Figure 2–18). **Input** is the process of capturing data and getting it into a form understandable to the computer. **Processing** involves the various steps taken by the computer to

HIGHLIGHT
A Nanosecond

If one person were equivalent to a nanosecond, then it would take the combined populations of the following countries to make up a second:

1. U.S.
2. U.S.S.R.
3. Japan
4. Brazil
5. Nigeria
6. W. Germany
7. Italy
8. U.K.
9. Philippines
10. France
11. Spain
12. Iran
13. Canada
14. Yugoslavia

FIGURE 2–18
Data Flow

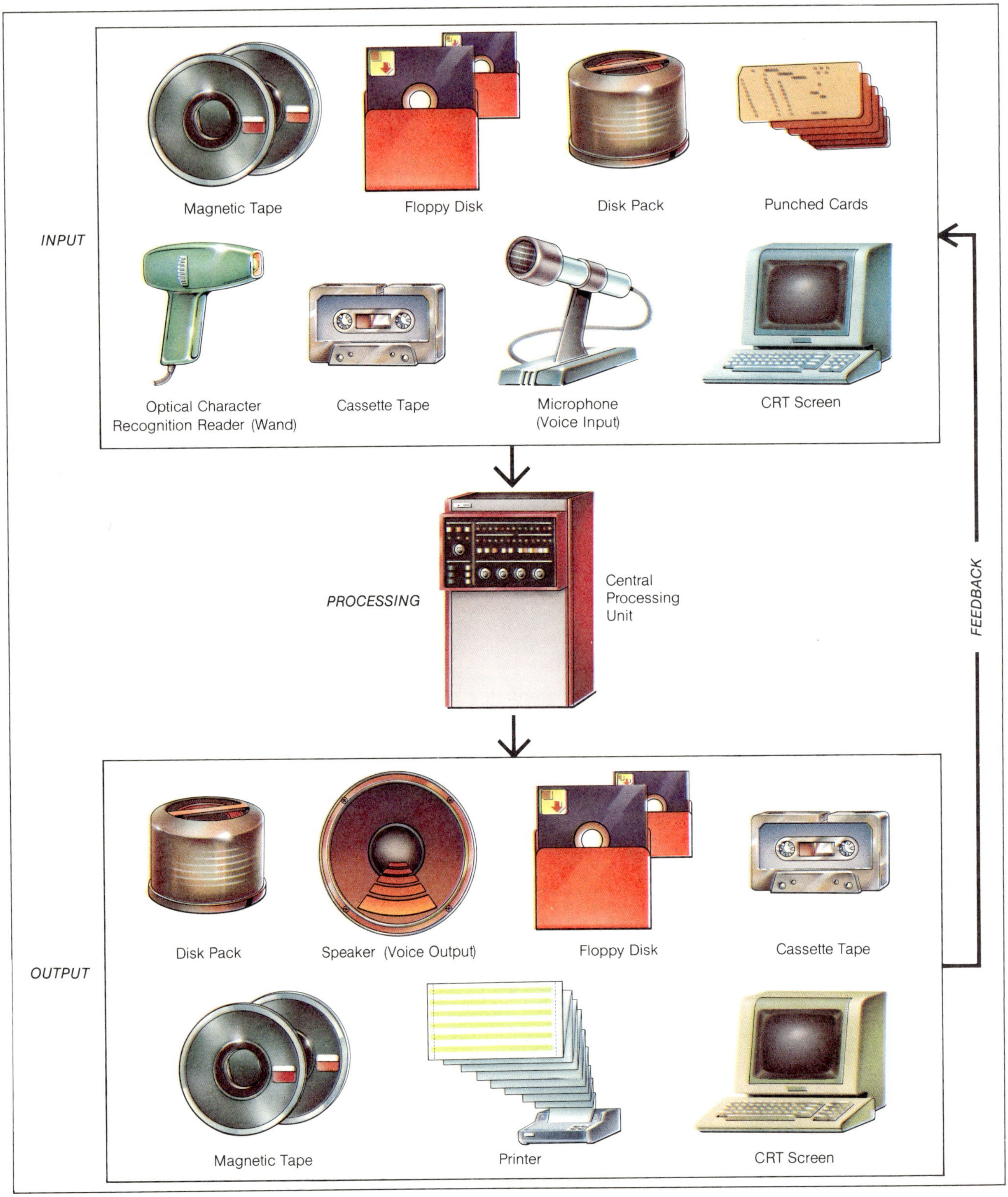

manipulate the data to provide information to management. **Output** is the step where the computed results of processing are made available for use in decision making. **Feedback** is used to evaluate the performance of the processing system.

Input

Three steps are involved in inputting data to the computer: **collection, verification,** and **coding.** Collection pertains to the various processes required to gather data from several sources and assemble it in preparation for processing. During the verification step, the data is checked to determine whether it is accurate and complete, and whether it should be included for processing. The coding step translates the data into machine-readable form so that it can be entered into the data processing system. Data punched onto IBM cards is one example of coding.

Processing

During processing, the computer may perform several tasks on the input data. It may **classify** data by organizing it according to certain characteristics meaningful to the user. For instance, the daily transactions at a bank may be classified as either deposits, withdrawals, or payments. Once classified, the data may be **sorted.** This involves arranging data into a particular sequence to facilitate processing. Sorting the bank's deposits according to account number will speed up processing. Sorting can also be performed on names as well as numbers. **Calculations** may be required to determine a customer's account balance or a student's grade point average. By **summarizing** data, large amounts of data are reduced to a concise, usable form. A top management report summarizing a company's accounting data will help determine its profit performance. Finally, data may be **stored** on a storage medium to facilitate later processing or retrieval. The costs of such storage should not exceed the benefit of having the facts available for later use.

Output

Once processing is complete, the results are available for output. There are three steps involved in the output phase of data flow. In **retrieving** information, the computer pulls information from storage devices for use by the decision maker. By **converting** information, the computer translates information from the form used to store it, to a form understandable by the user (such as a CRT display or a printed report). Finally, **communication** occurs when the right information is in the right place at the right time.

Feedback

Over time, the information provided through processing may lose its effectiveness. It may cease being accurate, timely, complete, concise, or relevant. Feedback is the process of evaluating the output and making adjustments to the input or processing steps in order to ensure that processing results in good information.

"Not only do we not know what's wrong with it, we don't even know what it is."

PROFILE
T. J. Watson

One of the true American success stories is that of Thomas J. Watson, Sr., whose tastes, beliefs, and ideals led to the success of the leader in the computer industry, IBM. This influential man held the position of father figure, leader, and patriarch of IBM for 40 years. Watson was born on February 17, 1874 in Painted Post, New York. His childhood was spent on his family's farm where he trained horses and helped with the farming. Here he was taught the moral values of persistence, respect, loyalty, and optimism, which later helped him to establish an empire of a company.

Watson felt a call toward a teaching career and tried his hand in the classroom—for only one day. He quickly altered his goals and went on to study accounting and business at the Miller School in Elmira, New York. His first job was as a bookkeeper in a meat market, paying $6 a week. Looking for a greater challenge, he joined a travelling salesman named George Cornwell, who hired Watson for $10 a week. Watson travelled all over the country, peddling pianos, sewing machines, and organs, and eventually took over the territory when Cornwell passed away.

Shortly thereafter, Watson moved to Buffalo, New York, and eventually came to work for the National Cash Register Company (NCR). Here he established himself as an enterprising businessman, and went on to work for the Computing-Tabulating-Recording Company (CTR) which was a merger of several smaller companies, including Herman Hollerith's Tabulating Machine Company.

The rest of Watson's life was spent elevating CTR to the company it is today—IBM. In 1924, Watson became the company's chief executive officer. He ran the company in a very family-oriented style, and displayed loyalty, enthusiasm, and commitment to his employees. The company survived the Depression and, in fact, found itself greatly involved in Roosevelt's New Deal Policy.

The rest is history. IBM grew to the position it has today, far surpassing any other company in the information processing industry. Watson died of a heart attack at the age of 82, but not before he saw his son, Thomas Jr., take over as chief executive officer of IBM. In his lifetime, Watson was close friends with three U.S. presidents, numerous international, political, and social figures, and was offered positions as Ambassador to Britian and as Secretary of Commerce. His involvement with IBM saw an increase in assets of 24 times, and an increase in business of 316 times. Truly this man demonstrates the American ideal of integrity and achievement.

DATA ORGANIZATION

To achieve effective data processing, data should be organized in an integrated way so that anticipated needs of users for information can be met. For example, a business firm may want to maintain specific data about its employees, such as home address, social security number, wage per hour, withholding tax, gross income, and the like. Each one of these data items is called a **field.** A collection of these fields that relate to a single unit (in this case, an employee) is a **record.** A grouping of all related records (in this

This microprocessor-based communication system uses the most advanced method of interconnecting display terminals and printers available today.

case, all employee records) is a **file.** The development of more sophisticated software has provided a method of structuring data to satisfy a wider variety of information needs, in a form called a **data base.** This book will consistently use the terms *field, record, file,* and *data base* in this manner (see Figure 2–19).

DATA PROCESSING EXAMPLE

Payroll preparation is suitable for electronic data processing because it involves a well-defined, repetitive procedure and a large number of records. The computer must take the following steps in preparing the paycheck:

INPUT:	Read total hours worked from employee time card.
PROCESSING:	Compute gross pay by multiplying total hours by hourly wage.
	Calculate withholding tax and social security tax.
	Deduct withholding tax and social security tax from gross pay to get net pay.
OUTPUT:	Write paycheck.
	Write payroll report.

FIGURE 2–19
Organization of a Data Base

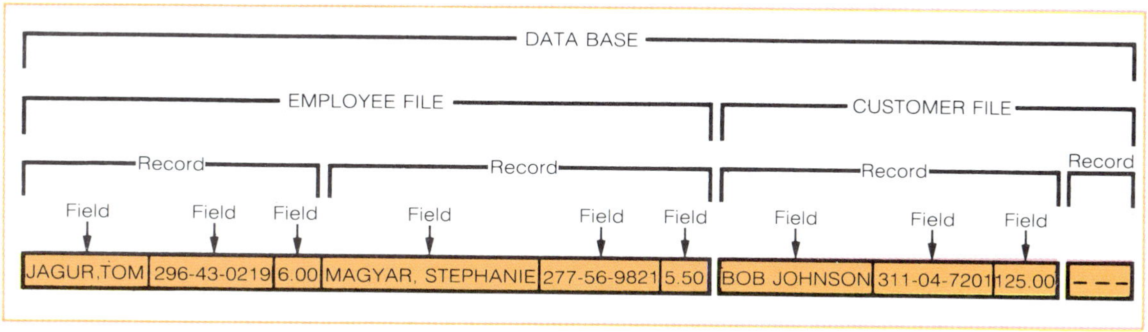

In most payroll applications, the computer must also check for other conditions, such as overtime, maximum or minimum allowable work hours, other deductions, and special wage rates for overtime work.

The payroll report includes summary information such as number of employees paid, total dollar value of payroll for the period, total withholding, and breakdowns of payments for all departments of the company. This summary information helps management make decisions about labor costs, cash-flow planning, and the like (see Figure 2–20).

CONCLUSION

Many people are excited about all the potential uses of computers. Others are concerned about the problems they may create—problems like worker displacement, invasion of privacy, and depersonalization in business operations. The advantages of a new technology are often obvious, but the problems that may arise are much more difficult to assess. This was so with automobiles. It may very well be the case with computers. However, computers are here to stay. We could not maintain our present life styles with-

FIGURE 2–20
Payroll Processing

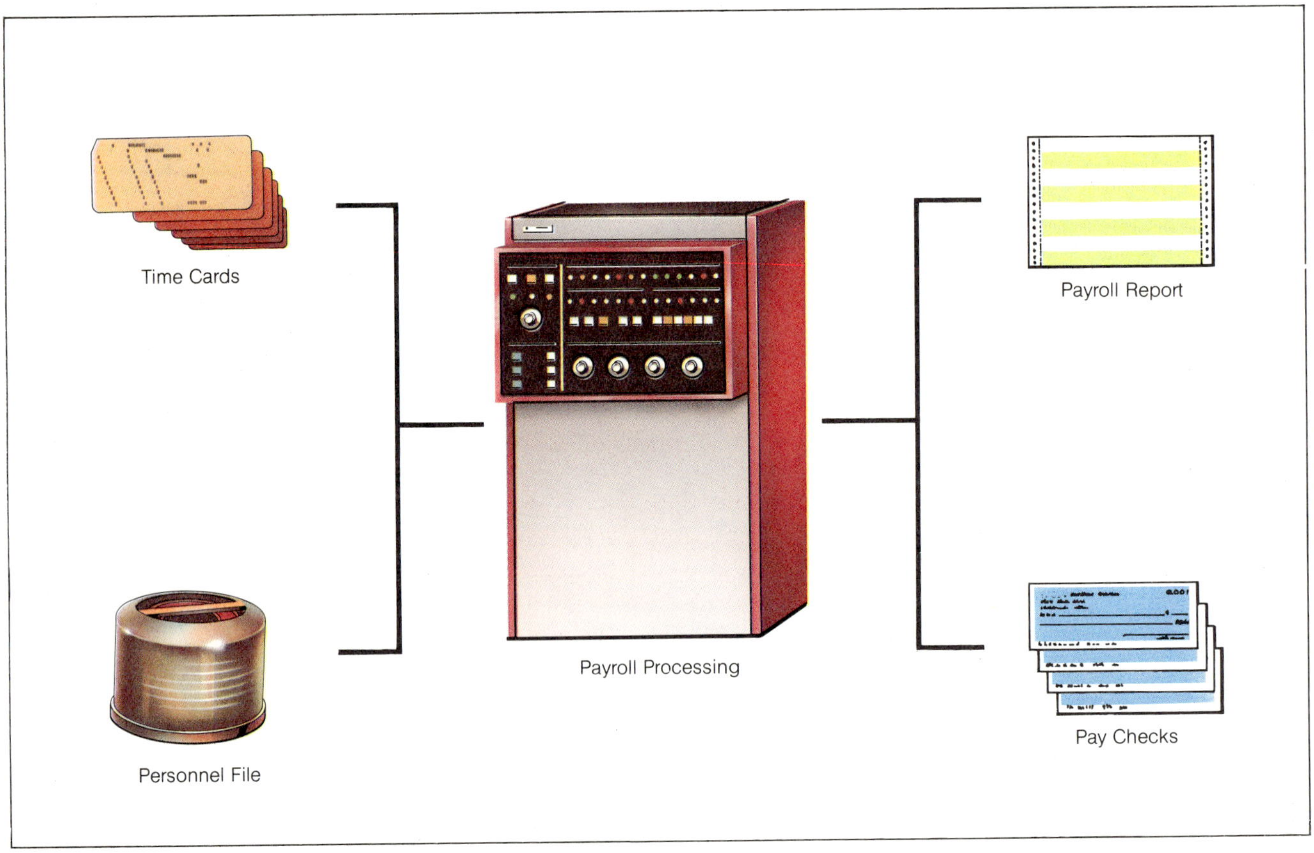

A United States Postal Service operator keying in ZIP codes written on packages as they are processed through one of the twenty-one Bulk Mail Centers throughout the country. After the operator keys in the correct ZIP code, the package moves along the conveyor to the correct bin where it is automatically put in a sack and shipped to its destination.

out them. Indeed, it is essential that we be familiar with their capabilities, limitations, and real and potential social impact. The rest of this text introduces the basic workings of the computer, discusses recent computer innovations, and points to some of the issues facing the generations dealing with computers.

SUMMARY POINTS

- Humans have been preoccupied with calculating the answers to problems and keeping track of the results. Developments preceding the computer that illustrate this trend include the abacus, Pascal's and Leibnitz's calculating machines, and Babbage's "difference engine."
- The weaving industry was the site of the first "programmable" machine, using punched cards to instruct the loom. Hollerith later applied this concept in processing census data, developing machines that could read data punched onto cards. Accounting machines applied the same techniques for processing business data.
- The Mark I was the first automatic calculator, while the ENIAC was the first true electronic computer, even though it had no internal memory.
- Von Neumann proposed storing instructions in the computer using machine language. This breakthrough lead the way for the development of EDVAC and EDSAC, both using internal memory and stored instructions.
- First-generation computers used vacuum tubes to control internal operations. These machines were very large, inaccurate, and generated a lot of heat.

- Second-generation computers relied on transistors for controlling internal operations. Transistors were much smaller, faster, and more reliable than vacuum tubes.
- Third-generation computers used solid-state integrated circuits rather than transistors to obtain reductions in size and cost together with increased reliability and speed.
- Fourth-generation computers rely on large-scale integration and continue to offer improvements in size, speed, and cost.
- A computer possesses no intelligence. It can only perform tasks predetermined by humans. Its functions are quite limited, as it can only perform three basic functions: arithmetic operations, comparisons, and storage and retrieval of data.
- Speed, accuracy, and memory provide the computer with its amazing power and separates it from human or mechanical calculations.
- The collection, manipulation, and dissemination of data is known as data processing. The use of machines to perform these functions is called automatic data processing. When an electronic computer is used, electronic data processing (EDP) is performed.
- Data refers to unorganized, raw facts. Information is data that has been organized and processed so that it can be used to make intelligent decisions. In order for information to be useful, it must be accurate, timely, complete, concise, and relevant.
- The conversion of data to information follows the pattern: input through processing to output. Feedback is used to evaluate the performance of the processing system.
- Data must be organized to be processed effectively. A data item is called a field; a collection of fields relating to a single unit, a record; and a grouping of related records, a file. The structuring of data to support the information needs of a wide variety of users creates a data base.
- The impact of computers on society is growing; we are becoming increasingly dependent on them in our daily lives.

REVIEW QUESTIONS

1. Trace the evolution of computers throughout their early development. What were the significant features of each discovery that led to the development of state-of-the-art computers?
2. Briefly describe how these people have affected the history of information processing: (a) Blaise Pascal, (b) Joseph Jacquard, (c) Herman Hollerith, and (d) John Von Neumann.
3. How do scientific applications differ from business applications?
4. Describe how magnetic cores hold data.
5. For what type of applications is FORTRAN most suited? COBOL? Which is the older?

6. Discuss the features of first-, second-, and third-generation computers. What characteristics distinguish one generation from another?
7. There is some debate as to which technology represents the fourth generation. Explain the differing viewpoints.
8. The transformation of data follows the basic flow of input, processing, and output. Describe the steps involved in each stage.
9. It is stated in the chapter that information may lose its effectiveness over time. Explain how this can happen. What measures can be taken to maintain the relevancy of information?
10. An example of the processing steps involved in payroll preparation is given in this chapter. Perform the same type of analysis for an instructor who wishes to determine grades for a class.

Innovators in the Micro World

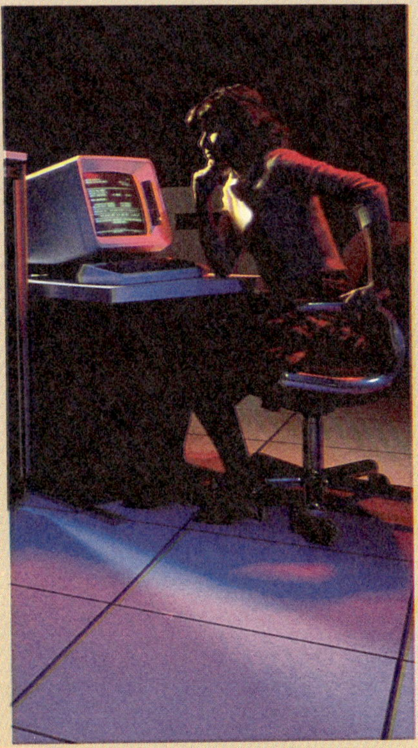

The rapid development of the computer industry has been the result of many ingenious, intriguing individuals. The history of personal computers follows this industry pattern. Let's sample a few of these key figures starting with Jack Tramiel, the founder and vice chairman of Commodore Business Machines.

Tramiel was born in Poland before World War II, a survivor of the concentration camps. After the war, he moved to the United States and drove a taxi for awhile. Eventually, Tramiel started a typewriter repair business that later expanded to include the production and sale of adding machines in Canada. Tramiel predicted then that calculators would someday sell for as little as $10 at the convenient neighborhood drugstore.

Tramiel describes the beginning of his firm's involvement in computers in 1977 as their new computer was introduced at an electronics show. At that time, it was not really known what the computer would be used for. So many people asked about delivery schedules that they were finally told to get in line, send their money in, and when their number came up, delivery would occur. In one month, over $3 million was received, and Tramiel knew that personal computing power was a real need.

The business grew with Tramiel's policy of integrating all business operations involved in the manufacture and sale of computers. When MOS Technology, a semiconductor manufacturer, was acquired, Commodore gained control over the 6502 microprocessor, then in development. Tramiel poured extra money into the project and it paid off. The processor is now found in the Commodore PET, the Apple, and the Atari 400 and 800 computers.

Commodore has since earned a large share of the European market and is gaining popularity in the United States. Tramiel predicts mushrooming personal computer sales as children, trained in computers at school, instigate purchases. He considers today's computer kids as the best salespeople any industry ever had.

Knowing the market's sales potential, Tramiel followed the General Motors philosophy, as he puts it, of having products to meet a broad set of needs at reasonable prices. He aims "to sell to the masses, not the classes." Tramiel now foresees handheld computers becoming as popular as calculators are now by the 1990s.

Another trailblazer in the computer industry is Steven Jobs. Growing up in California's Silicon Valley, Jobs was interested in technology in high school. He attended lectures at Hewlett-Packard and even attracted enough attention from the president, William Hewlett, to get a summer job. Later, Jobs attended college but dropped out after two years and went to work for Atari. His good friend Stephen Wozniak still worked at Hewlett-Packard. In 1976, Wozniak succeeded in building a small, easy-to-use computer, one on which he had been working in his spare time.

Wozniak was pleased with this clever machine, but Jobs had visions of its use in homes and small businesses and talked Wozniak into starting a business. By selling Job's Volkswagon and Wozniak's scientific calculator, the two raised $1300 with which to build the first Apples (named in honor of a pleasant summer working in Oregon's orchards) in Job's parents' garage.

The rest is history. A superb marketing effort has helped Apple blossom in homes and businesses nearly everywhere. With revenues of $335 million in 1981, Apple Computer Company has made Chairman of the Board Jobs a modern-day folk hero and millionaire. Wozniak left the business and returned to college but still remains a major stockholder.

The Apple has weathered a great deal of competition in the past several years. Recently, though, a newcomer to the microcomputer scene, Adam Osborne, has been making predictions that his new firm will grow even faster than Apple. And he may be right!

Osborne, bold and seemingly arrogant, started his firm in 1980 with the profits he yielded by selling twelve computer books published in eight languages. The first Osborne personal computer was shipped in July 1981, and revenues of $10 million were reported at year-end in November. Within sixty days of that first shipment, Osborne's firm had profits—quite a feat! Sales of $250 million have been currently forecast.

Osborne's deal has been hard to beat. He is selling a portable computer that weighs only 24 pounds has a 3½-inch by 2½-inch display screen, has two disk drives, and has five software programs (worth $1500) for $1795. This low price is possible in large part by trading Osborne Computer stock to software suppliers in exchange for much lower licensing fees on the software. So at that price, the Osborne Computer has had no real competition and is appearing in all sorts of places from courtrooms to yachts to the wilds of Kenya.

Charles Tandy, the outgoing, talkative president of Tandy Corporation, pioneered personal computer sales with the TRS-80 by using retail outlets, a marketing technique now being used by such giant companies as IBM and Xerox. With foresight and marketing/management genius, Tandy moved his business from leathercraft and hobby supplies into the rapidly expanding field of electronics. In 1963 he bought a struggling chain of nine retail and mail-order Radio Shack stores and quickly turned them into a rapidly expanding business. His success in the personal computer field came from knowing his market and making his product easily accessible. With the introduction of the TRS-80 in 1977, or the first time a person could walk into a store and purchase a low-priced personal computer. Radio Shack quickly added the TRS-80 Model II for business application, with more memory and twice the speed of the first model.

But men are not the only entrepreneurs finding success with personal computers. Vector Graphics Inc., a six-year-old firm whose sales have risen from $404,000 in 1977 to $25 million in 1981, was founded by two women, Carole Ely and Lore Harp. Vector's success has been achieved by offering to business desk-top computers more powerful than most but less expensive.

When Ely and Harp began, they knew nothing about computers. The business started as a marketing effort to sell a memory board designed by Harp's husband. Six thousand dollars of inventory got the assembly line humming at the Harp home with packing materials stored in a shower and the dining room used for testing. From this humble beginning, the women's company has grown to 400 employees designing, assembling, and selling entire desk-top computers. The founders are now millionaires.

Innovations happen frequently in this industry. These people were ready when opportunity arose. The market, though, is broad, and new people enter the industry daily. That's what keeps the personal computer industry so exciting.

DISCUSSION QUESTIONS

1. What made Tramiel, Jobs, Tandy, Ely, Harp and Osborne so successful?
2. What applications do you see for a portable computer like the Osborne? For the hand-held computer of Tramiel's prediction?

CHAPTER 3

The Programming Process

INTRODUCTION

Most people think computers are cold, calculating machines. In all fairness to computers, they are. Computers have no emotion, independent thought, or voluntary action. The computer is an incredibly fast and accurate machine but with an IQ of zero. Indeed, a computer performs step by step only what it has been told to do. On the one hand, this appears to limit the tasks that computers can perform; on the other hand, it suggests that computers are limited only by people's ability to break down a problem into steps that computers can use to solve it. As economist Leo Cherne suggested, "The computer is incredibly fast, accurate, and stupid. Man is unbelievably slow, inaccurate, and brilliant. The marriage of the two is a force beyond calculation."

This chapter discusses the four steps used to break down a problem into the logical series of steps required for computer solution: defining the problem; designing a solution; writing the program; and compiling, debugging, and testing the program.

FACING PAGE

A programmer looks at a computer printout.

CHAPTER OUTLINE

COMPUTER PROBLEM SOLVING

As any seasoned programmer will tell you, the computer does not "solve" problems the same way we do. Humans solve problems by using reason, intelligence, and intuition. Computers solve problems according to instructions provided by programmers. Any "intelligence" the computer seems to possess is given to it by these programmers. At present, a computer cannot even take general instructions like "calculate each employee's net pay" and turn them into programmatically correct statements it can use to perform the task. Instead, the computer has to be told how to calculate an employee's net pay, step by step.

Each program, then, has to be well thought out. Instructions must be ordered in a logical sequence. The problem must be analyzed to such a level of detail that all logical conditions that may be encountered during processing are anticipated in advance. If an unanticipated condition arises during processing, the program will be executed incorrectly or, in some cases, not at all.

Problem-Solving Process

When programs were first written, there were few rules for programmers to follow because there were few things computers could do. Today, however, with the vast array of programming languages, processing techniques, storage devices, and printing media, a programmer is well advised to use a structured approach to problem solving and program development. Four steps have been found helpful in this process.

- Defining the problem.
- Designing a solution.
- Writing the program.
- Compiling, debugging, and testing the program.

In defining the problem, the analyst/programmer determines the nature and extent of the problem to be solved. In planning a solution, four traditional, basic patterns of program logic are combined in such a way as to provide the required output. In writing the program, the appropriate programming language is selected and program statements are coded in computer-acceptable form. In compiling the program, program statements are translated into a form that can be understood by the computer. Debugging is correcting poorly written program statements and removing logic errors in the program; testing is determining whether the program processes data correctly—that is, whether it works the way it is supposed to work. All of these steps are discussed in more detail below.

DEFINING THE PROBLEM

The first step in defining a problem begins with recognizing a need for information. This need may be expressed as a request from management, users, or a system analyst performing a system study. The analyst/programmer receiving the request must analyze the problem thoroughly in order to understand what is required to solve it. Since such problem-solving skills often differ from the skills required of a programmer, some companies use the system analyst to perform this function. One method used to define the problem analyzes the input, processing, and output required.

Output

Even though output is the last step of computer processing, it can be effectively used as the first step in defining the problem. The solution to a problem must be stated in terms of clear, concise objectives. By defining what output is required of the program, the information requirements of users and management become clear. The analyst/programmer often prepares report mock-ups to show users and asks them to verify the output requirements. In this way, the analyst/programmer can quickly determine whether any omissions or incorrect assumptions about the purpose of the program were made.

Input

Next, the input required to provide this output must be determined. The analyst/programmer reviews current systems to see what data is available and to determine what new data items must be captured in order to provide the required information.

Readers at the Library of Congress in Washington, D.C. have on-line access to cataloging information on books at the Library. Over 3 million terms are contained in the index to the Library of Congress computerized catalog, part of the library's MARC (Machine Readable Cataloging) data base.

HIGHLIGHT
Micromouse

Moonlight Special is the name given to a new micromouse—a small mechanical mouse controlled by four microprocessors. Built for a contest by a team of engineers, the mouse can find its way through a maze. If the mouse hits a wall, it stops, memorizes the location, turns, and continues. After two tries, the mouse has the entire maze memorized and can pass through without touching a wall.

The technology upon which micromouse is based should lend itself to many uses in the future. Artificial intelligence of this kind could be used to free people from monotonous tasks. One application might be a computer-controlled vacuum cleaner; the vacuum could search out the room's walls and clean everywhere in between. Another application might aid farmers—the robots might be able to plow and irrigate fields.

The uses for microprocessors in the future are limited only by imagination and economic feasibility. The cost of microprocessors is already falling, which should open the door for many new applications.

Processing

Finally, given (1) the output specifications developed by the analyst/programmer in close cooperation with the users and management and (2) the required input established by careful evaluation of the current systems, the processing requirements can be determined. Once they are known, the analyst/programmer proceeds to the next step—planning a solution.

DESIGNING A SOLUTION

When the definition of the problem has been completed, the design of the solution begins. This design may take the form of one or more programs. A **program,** as discussed in Chapter 2, is a set of instructions used by the computer to solve a problem. The programmer takes each of the processing segments uncovered in the definition step and works out a tentative program flow; that is, what needs to be done first in the program, what second, and so on. By approaching each segment separately, the programmer can concentrate on developing an efficient and logical flow for that segment.

The programmer does not necessarily need to know the programming language to be used in order to develop a tentative flow. (In fact, knowing the processing requirements first helps the programmer to select the language best suited to those requirements.) To develop a tentative flow, the only thing a programmer needs to know are the four basic logic patterns used by the computer.

Basic Logic Patterns

There is nothing magical about writing a computer program. In fact, the computer can understand and execute only four basic logic patterns: simple sequence, selection, loop, and branch. High-level languages may have more complicated statements, but they all are based on these four patterns. As you read about the patterns, refer to Figure 3–1.

Simple Sequence **Simple sequence** logic involves the computer's executing one statement after another in the order given by the programmer. It is the most simple and often-used pattern; in fact, the computer assumes that all statements entered by the programmer are to be executed in this fashion unless it is told otherwise.

Selection The **selection** pattern requires that the computer make a choice. The choice it makes, however, is not based on personal preference or taste, but on pure logic. Each selection is made on the basis of a comparison that determines whether one item is equal to, less than, or greater than another. In fact, these are the only comparisons the computer can make. Complex selections are made by the use of a sequence of these comparisons.

Loop The computer assumes all statements are to be executed in the order given by the programmer (simple sequence). The **loop** pattern enables the

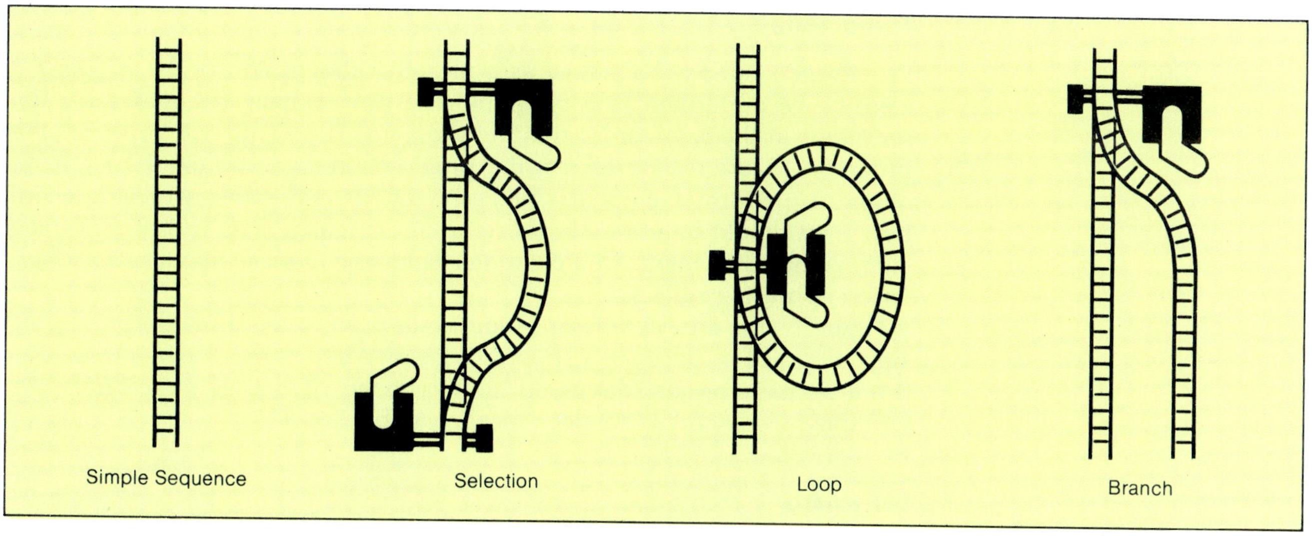

FIGURE 3–1
A Computer's Basic Logic Patterns

programmer to instruct the computer to alter this normal process and loop back to a previous statement in the program. The computer then reexecutes statements according to the simple sequence flow. This is especially useful if the same sequence of statements is to be executed, say, for each employee in a payroll program; the programmer need not duplicate the sequence of statements for each set of employee data.

Branch The last and most controversial pattern is the branch. The **branch** is most efficiently used in combination with selection or looping. This pattern allows the programmer to skip past statements in a program, leaving them unexecuted. Once all employees have been processed, for instance, the computer can branch to the next set of statements in the program.

Branching is controversial for several reasons. If a program uses it too often, the computer must jump frequently from one part of the program to another when executing it. It is extremely difficult, if not impossible, for one programmer to understand another's program when it uses much branching. Such programs are also difficult and time consuming to maintain. For these reasons, the last part of this chapter is devoted to structured programming, which seeks to reduce the use of branching techniques.

It is easy to see why the solution of a program must be well thought out before programming is started. The programmer has to work creatively around the computer's limitations. The problem must be stated in such a way that it can be solved by the use of a series of simple sequence instructions, selections, loops, and in some cases, branches. Even the selections have to be simplified so that they involve only equal to, less than, or greater than comparisons.

When faced with the task of writing a series of programs designed to solve complicated problems, the programmer can easily make omissions and errors in processing logic. Pseudocode and flowcharting techniques can help the programmer to avoid such omissions and errors.

Pseudocode

Pseudocode can be thought of as a narrative description of the processing steps to be performed in a program. The programmer arranges these descriptions in the same order that the program statements will appear in the program. Pseudocoding allows the programmer to focus on the steps required to perform a particular process without necessarily worrying about how they should be phrased in a computer language. (As will be explained later, coding statements in a computer language often requires strict adherence to phrasing rules.)

Figure 3–2 is an example of pseudocode used to describe the processing steps required to calculate a shopper's grocery bill. Notice in the figure how the logic patterns just discussed are expressed. It is easy to see from the example how useful a tool pseudocode can be.

Flowcharts

A **flowchart,** sometimes called a **block diagram** or a **logic diagram,** provides a visual frame of reference for the processing steps in a program. Instead of using the English-like statements of pseudocode, flowcharting uses easily recognizable symbols to represent the type of processing performed in a program. These symbols are arranged in the same logical sequence in which corresponding program statements will appear in the program. Figure 3–3 shows the pseudocode example in flowchart form.

Flowcharts provide excellent documentation of a program. For maintenance, the flowchart can be used to guide the programmer in determining what statements are required to make any necessary changes and where to locate them. Once the flowchart is updated to reflect these changes, it provides good documentation of the revised program. Because of their potential value, flowcharts should be kept complete, up-to-date, and easy to read. To help achieve the latter objective, the American National Standards Institute (ANSI) has adopted a set of flowchart symbols that are commonly accepted and used by programmers.

Figure 3–4 shows some of the ANSI flowchart symbols. The symbol represents the start or stop of a program and so appears at the beginning and end of a program flowchart. The symbol shows a process step such as addition, subtraction, multiplication, or division. Most of the data manip-

FIGURE 3–2
Example of Pseudocode

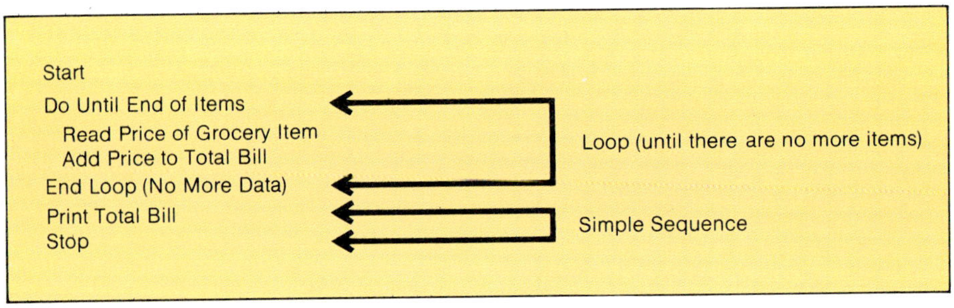

ulation performed in a program is represented by process symbols. A comparison, or decision, is represented by the symbol ◇, which represents a program statement that directs the computer to compare values. The computer may take either of two paths for a decision step. If the result of the comparison is true, one path is executed; if the result is false, the other is taken. Finally, the symbol ▱ indicates that the program requires either input or output of data. Data can be read into the program via punched cards, by the user typing it in at a terminal, or by retrieving it from storage. Output from the program can be directed back to the user, printed on paper, or stored. Figure 3–5 shows how the basic logic patterns are represented using flowchart symbols.

Special Considerations in Solution Design

In solving business problems, computer programmers must be aware of other considerations besides developing the processing steps required for solution: (1) the form of input to the program determines how the program

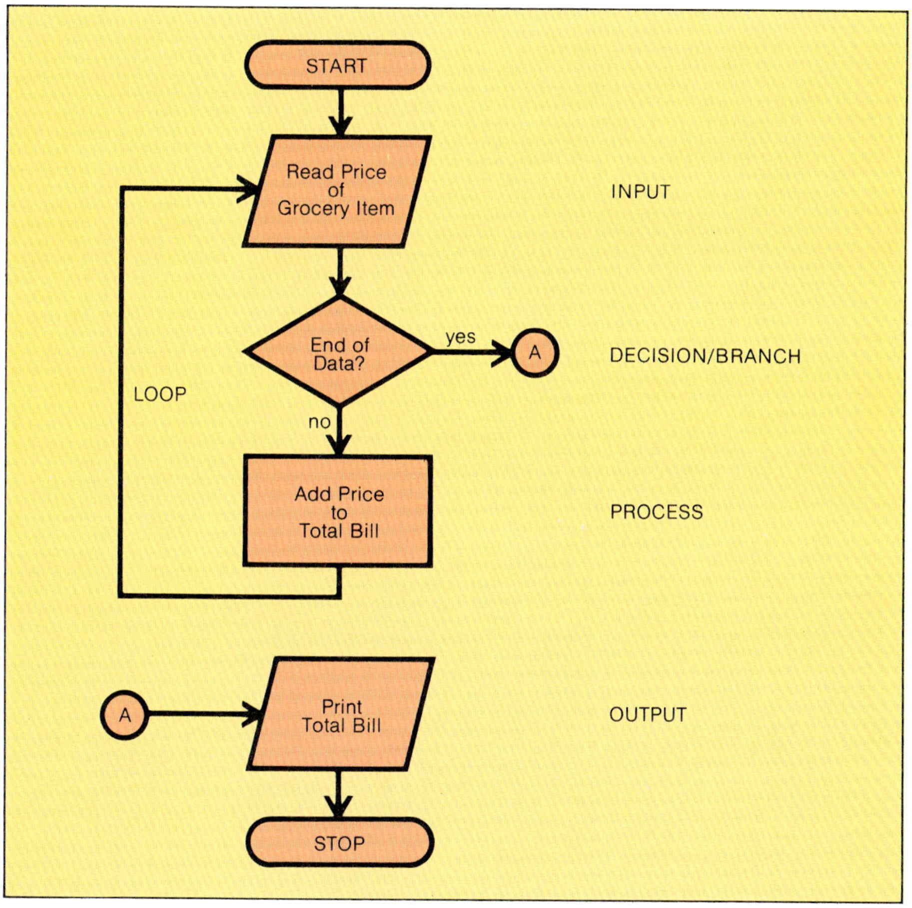

FIGURE 3–3
Example of a Flowchart

FIGURE 3–4
Flowchart Symbols

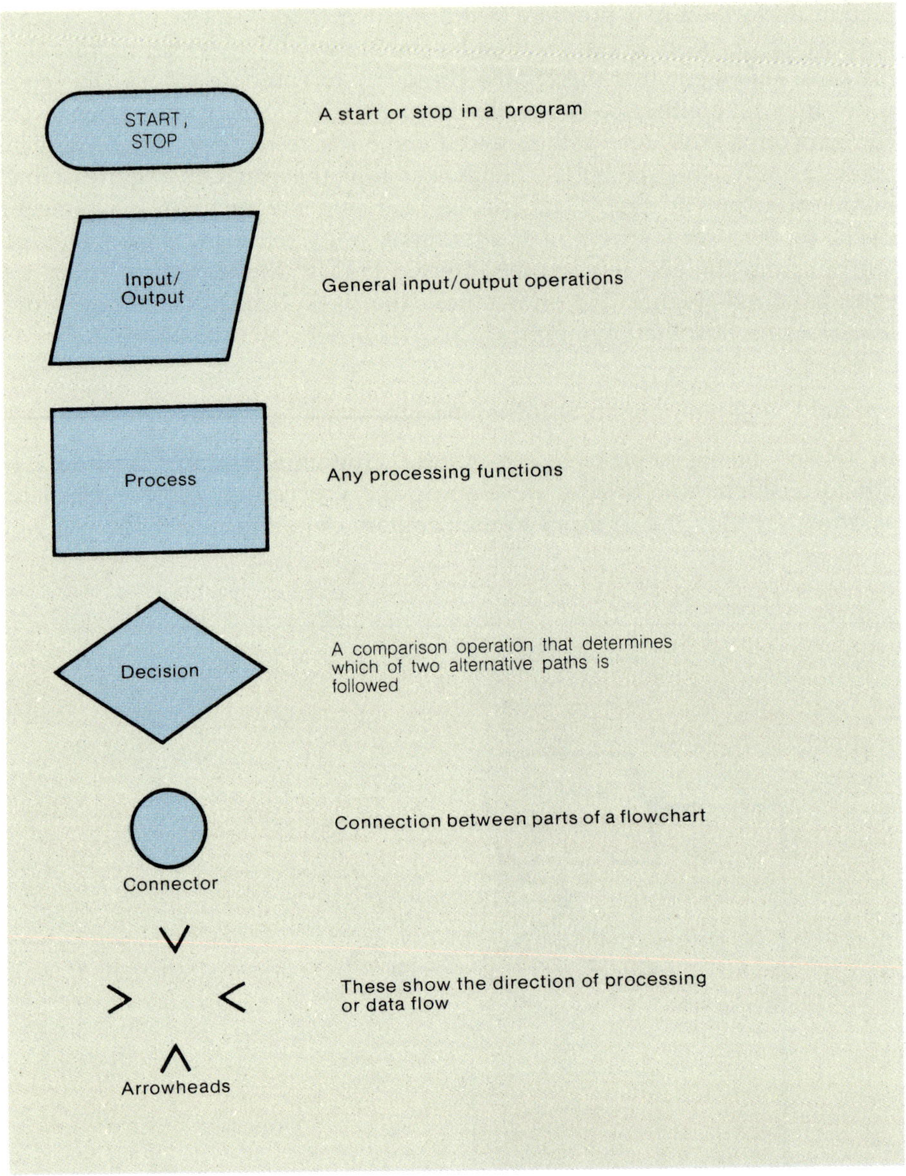

should ask for data; (2) processing steps should verify the accuracy of data and identify potential errors; and (3) the program may be required to produce output that is not in hard-copy form.

Input In today's computer systems, users have a variety of ways to communicate with programs. Given the vast array of input devices discussed in Chapter 5, it is not difficult to see why. The programmer must know in advance which input devices will be used to put data into the program. If the user will input data, the program must be designed to ask for it in a

1. **Simple sequence pattern**
One statement after another, executed in order as stored (A then B)

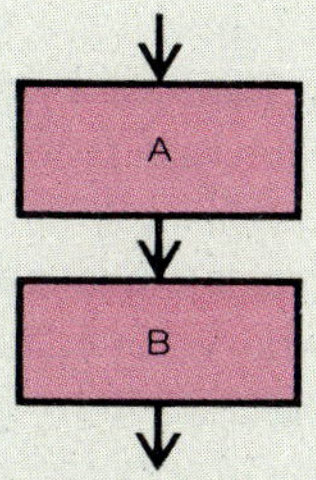

2. **Selection pattern**
Requires a test, and, depending upon the result of the test, one of two paths is taken. For instance, IF A is true THEN do B; ELSE do C.

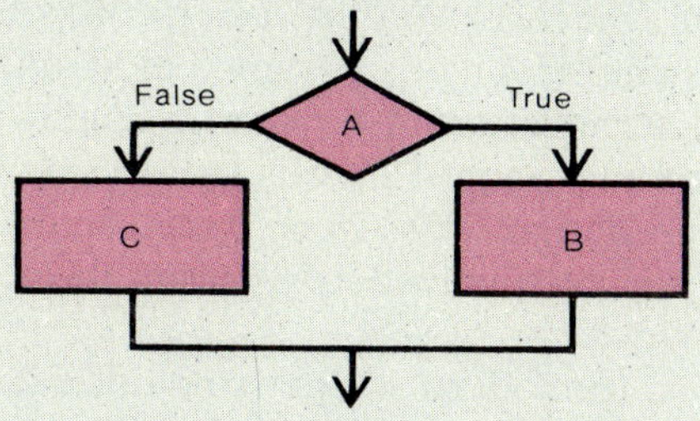

3. **Loop pattern** Execution of E and F continues in a loop fashion as long as D is true. If D is false, the loop is exited. E and F are not executed. The logic is: DO E and F WHILE D is true.

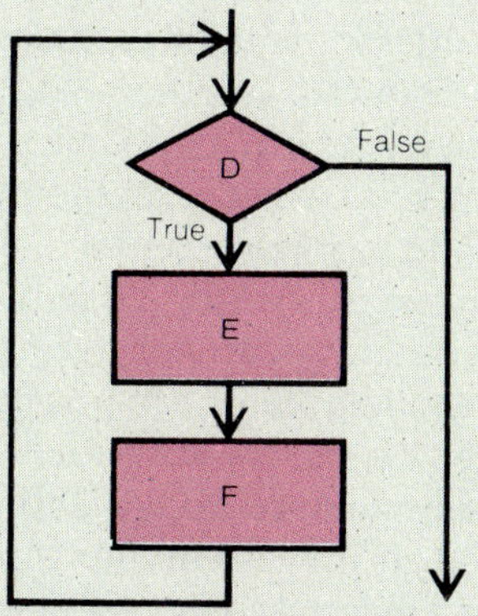

4. **Branch or link pattern**
Control is transferred from the simple sequence flow to another portion of the program. For instance, If G is false, GO TO J. The flow of the program continues with execution of J (rather than H) whenever G is false.

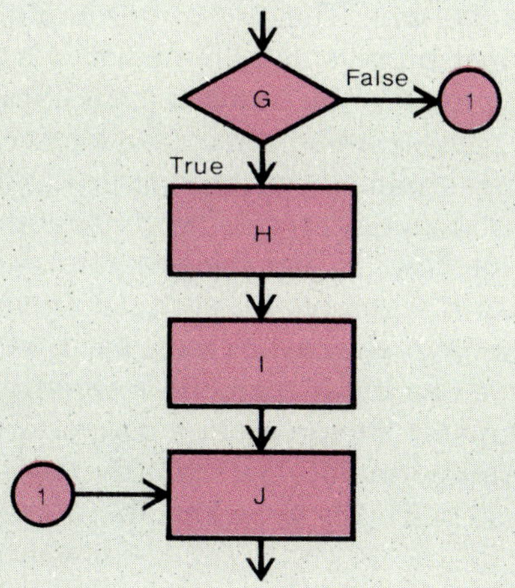

FIGURE 3–5
Four Traditional Program Logic Patterns

way the user will understand. If input will be in the form of tape, the program must be prepared to accept the data in the same way it was stored on the tape. If a data base will provide input, the program may need to actively search and retrieve data from the data base.

Processing Businesses are naturally concerned with the accuracy of data used to provide the information managers use to make decisions. Programmers must do their part to help keep data error-free; merely designing a program with logically correct processing statements providing the required output may not be enough. Most programmers are required to include extensive edit checks on the data before storing it in data files. **Edit checks** are processing statements designed to identify potential errors in the input data. The determination of how many and what kinds of edit checks should be performed on input data is usually made by all personnel involved in the solution design. The users, management, system analyst, and programmer should all be involved in ensuring the accuracy of input data.

Output In modern systems, not all data is entered directly into a program by users nor output fed directly to hard-copy reports. Many systems require the use of interdependent programs in which the output from one program is used as input to another, and so on. The reason for this is that each program may perform a specialized function. If the solution design requires this type of processing, programmers need to ensure that output from one program is in a form acceptable as input to another. Similarly, if the first program in the processing cycle has done extensive edit checks on the input data, later programs do not need to perform the same checks on those data items. (Once data items are put into the computer for processing, they will not change!)

If the information output will be hard-copy reports, the reports should be easy to read. If they seem imposing or confusing to users, the reports likely will be used incorrectly or not at all.

On-Line Systems The trend in computer systems today is to design programs that process data immediately after it is input by the user. The user usually provides the input at a **CRT (cathode-ray tube)** terminal, a terminal with a television-like screen, and receives the output from the program at the same terminal. This type of processing is quite useful in business, but it imposes stringent processing constraints.

One problem is that the program performs a series of input, processing, and output segments for each data item entered by the person at the terminal. This is in contrast to most batch systems, which collect all the data first and have one input segment, a series of processing statements, and an output segment. The program must perform edit checks on each data item as it is entered by the user, even if the item was also entered and checked in an earlier step. To the program, the data item appears new each time it is entered.

Another problem is that as each data item is entered by the user, it may be immediately stored on computer files. Once stored, there are very few

HIGHLIGHT
No More Yelling "Hold the Mayo"

Waiters and waitresses who shout or scribble colorfully cryptic orders to the chef ("Two up, two over, one confused") can now lower their voices and drop their ticket books if they pick the right restaurant to work in. Up-to-date eateries have installed computer terminals in the dining areas into which meal orders can be entered. The orders are then displayed on video or printed out in the kitchen. Besides getting this vital information to the cooks, the systems can also compute and print up each customer's bill, including the proper amount of tax. Managers can refer to the accumulated data to quickly determine which items are the most popular and which waiters and waitresses are turning in the most orders.

Remote programmers using Paradyne's Programming Workstation have the same benefits as those available at the IBM host computer site.

ways of checking the data further. Input checks must be made during the input of data by the user, before it is accepted, processed, and written to the data base.

Finally, the way in which the programmer designs the program to ask the user for data input can have an important effect on how the user feels about the system (and how faithfully he or she checks and feeds in the data). Computer specialists like to refer to programs that ask for input effectively as being "user friendly." The frustration, panic, or boredom that results from improperly designed input segments can destroy the efficiency and effectiveness of a system.

WRITING THE PROGRAM

After the programmer has defined the problem and designed a solution, the program is written in a specific programming language. Programming languages are usually designed for specific types of applications. For example, FORTRAN is a language designed primarily for scientific applications; COBOL is normally used for business applications. A programmer may have no part in the selection of a language for a particular application—there may be a business requirement to use COBOL, for instance, because of its readability.

Desirable Program Qualities

As the program is being coded, the programmer should be aware that generating the correct output is not the only requirement of a good program. There is always more than one way to code a program to provide the correct solution; however, one program can be better than another. The programmer should try to incorporate the following qualities into any program:

- *Programs should be easy to read and to understand.* Data names should be descriptive. Short data names that do not reflect the data represented should be avoided. Statements should be placed in a format that is easy to read and to follow. In other words, the programmer should write the program in such a way that someone else can easily read and understand it.
- *Programs should be reliable.* They should consistently produce the correct output. All formulas and computations, as well as logic tests and transfers of control, must be accurate.
- *Programs should work under all conditions.* Reliability alone is no guarantee of a successful program. Internal logic may be correct, but an incorrect data item (garbage in) could produce incorrect output (garbage out). For example, a program that uses the age of a person may want to test for incorrect ages in the data stream. How would the program react if someone's age were 4,692 or −35?
- *Programs should be maintainable.* They should be easy to update and modify. Programs should be written in independent segments so that a change in one segment does not necessitate a change in others.

COMPILING, DEBUGGING, AND TESTING THE PROGRAM

After the program has been written, it is submitted to the computer. Levels of language and language translation are discussed here to illustrate how a high-level language program is altered to a form the computer can use.

"Dear Dad, my new job as a computer programmer is really great."

Levels of Language

The programmer uses a sequence of instructions to communicate with the computer and to control program execution. As computers have evolved in stages, so have the programming languages they use. Today there are three language levels—machine language, assembly language, and high-level language (see Figure 3–6).

Machine Language **Machine language** is as old as the computer itself. It is the code that designates the proper electrical states in the computer and is expressed as combinations of 0s and 1s. It is the only language the computer can execute directly; therefore, it can be called the language of the computer.

Each type of computer has its own machine language, which is not transferable to another type of computer. Each machine-language instruction must specify not only the operation to be done but also the storage locations

Degree of User Orientation		Degree of Machine Orientation
Low	Machine Language	High
↓	Assembly Language	↓
High	High-level Language	Low

FIGURE 3–6
Language Levels

of data items. Because of these requirements and the nature of the language itself, machine-language programming is extremely complex, tedious, and time consuming. Therefore, other languages have been developed.

Assembly Language **Assembly language** is one step removed from machine language. Programmers using assembly language must be very conscious of the computer and must designate not only the operations to be performed but also storage locations, just as when using machine language. However, assembly language is more easily understood by humans. Instead of the 0 and 1 groupings of machine language, convenient symbols and abbreviations are used. For instance, "STO" may stand for STORE; "TRA" for TRANSFER. Even with these conveniences, programming in assembly language is cumbersome, although not as difficult as machine-language programming.

High-level Programming Languages **High-level languages** provide a great deal of sophistication in programming. Such languages are designed so that most of the programmer's attention can be focused on the problem at hand rather than on details of computer operations. Many high-level languages are English-like and allow the use of common mathematical terms and symbols. The time and effort needed to write a program are reduced and programs are easier to correct and modify.

High-level languages are so called because they are the furthest removed from the hardware; they least resemble the 0 and 1 combinations of machine language. Whereas one assembly-language instruction is generally equivalent to one machine-language instruction, one high-level language statement can accomplish the same result as a half-dozen or more machine-language instructions, principally because the addresses for many of the required storage locations do not have to be specified; they are handled automatically.

Language Translation

Assembly and high-level languages are much more widely used by programmers than machine language. Since these languages cannot be executed directly by computers, they are converted into machine-executable form by a **language-translator program.** The sequence of instructions written by the programmer—the **source program**—is translated by the language-translator program into machine language executable by the computer. The machine language form of the program, known as the **object program,** accomplishes the same operations as a program originally written in machine language.

The translator program for an assembly language is called an **assembler program.** A high-level language translator is called a **compiler program.** Both assemblers and compilers are designed for specific machines and languages. For example, a compiler that translates a source program written in FORTRAN into a machine-language program could not translate COBOL statements (see Figure 3–7).

During the compilation or assembly (the translation process), the object program is generated. The programmer receives an assembly listing or a source-program listing that contains indications of any errors the assembler or compiler detected during translation. The errors are usually violations of the rules associated with the particular programming language and are called **syntax** errors. For example, if a statement that should begin in column 8 begins in column 6, an error message will be generated. Similarly, an error message will be generated if language keywords such as WRITE or COMPUTE are misspelled.

To help the programmer, the compiler can provide a listing of all compiler-detected errors. This error-message listing may give the number of each statement in error and may also describe the nature of the error (see Figure 3–8). Only after all detected errors have been corrected can the object program be submitted to the computer to be executed. Several attempts at successful compilation or assembly may be needed.

The complete process of compilation and execution of a COBOL program is shown in Figure 3–9. In this case, the COBOL source program has been punched on cards, and the data provided as input to the object program has been stored on magnetic tape.

FIGURE 3–7
One COBOL Statement and Corresponding Machine-Language Instructions

(a) COBOL

```
STANDARD-ROUTINE.
  MULTIPLY HOURS-WORKED BY WAGE-PER-HOUR GIVING GROSS PAY.
```

(b) MACHINE LANGUAGE

```
*STANDARD-ROUTINE
           000778
MULTIPLY   000778  F2  71  D  1E8  7  010
           00077E  F2  73  D  1F0  7  012
           000784  FC  42  D  1EB  D  1E5
           00078A  F3  43  6  000  D  1EC
           000790  96  F0  6  004
           000794  58  10  D  21C
           000798  07  F1
```

Debugging is a task at any age.

Debugging the Program

The compiler that translates the program can detect grammatical errors, such as misspellings and incorrect punctuation. However, logical errors are often harder to detect. Such errors may result when the programmer does not fully understand the problem or does not account for problems that may arise during processing.

Errors in programs have acquired the nickname "bugs" over the years. The process of locating, isolating, and eliminating "bugs" is often called **de-**

FIGURE 3–8
Compiler-Detected Errors

Statement Number	Error Code	Error Messages
1972	IKF1080I-W	PERIOD PRECEDED BY SPACE. ASSUME END OF SENTENCE.
1999	IKF1080I-W	PERIOD PRECEDED BY SPACE. ASSUME END OF SENTENCE.
2074	IKF1043I-W	END OF SENTENCE SHOULD PRECEDE 02. ASSUMED PRESENT.
2399	IKF2126I-C	VALUE CLAUSE LITERAL TOO LONG. TRUNCATED TO PICTURE SIZE.
2432	IKF1043I-W	END OF SENTENCE SHOULD PRECEDE 02. ASSUMED PRESENT.
2481	IKF1080I-W	PERIOD PRECEDED BY SPACE. ASSUME END OF SENTENCE.
2484	IKF1080I-W	PERIOD PRECEDED BY SPACE. ASSUME END OF SENTENCE.
2623	IKF1004I-E	INVALID WORD NOTE. SKIPPING TO NEXT RECOGNIZABLE WORD.
2623	IKF1007I-W	MINUS SIGN NOT PRECEDED BY A SPACE. ASSUME SPACE.
2623	IKF1007I-W	**NOT PRECEDED BY A SPACE. ASSUME SPACE.

FIGURE 3–9 COBOL Program Translation and Execution

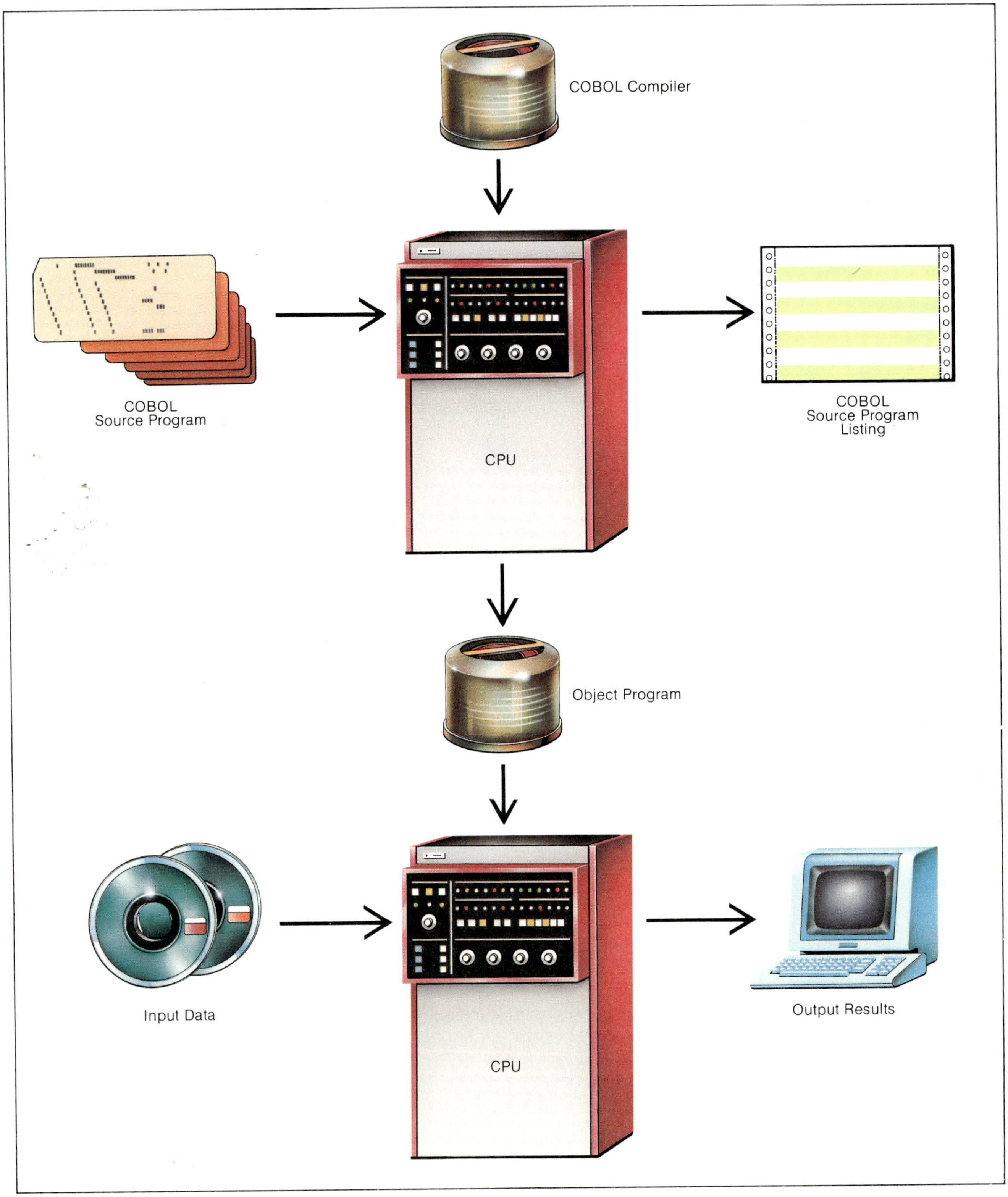

bugging. The amount of time that must be spent in debugging depends on the quality of the program. However, a newly completed program rarely executes successfully the first time it is run. In fact, one-third to one-half of a programmer's time is spent in debugging.

Testing the Program

Testing a program involves executing it using input data that is either a representative sample of actual data or a facsimile of it. Often, sample data that can be manipulated easily by the programmer is used so that the computer-determined output can be compared with programmer-determined correct results. The output should be easy to recognize so that the programmer can see if it is correct.

A complex program is frequently tested in separate units so that errors can be isolated to specific sections, helping to narrow the search for the cause of an error. The programmer must correct all mistakes; running and rerunning a specific unit may be necessary before the cause of an error can be found. The programmer then rewrites the part in error and resubmits it for another test. Care must be taken so that correction of one logical error does not give rise to several others.

Each section of the program must be tested (even sections that will be used infrequently). If instructions for handling exceptions are part of the program, the sample input data should include items that test the program's ability to spot and reject improper data items. The programmer often finds **desk-checking (desk-debugging)** helpful. With this method, the programmer pretends to be the computer and, reading each instruction and simulating how the computer would process a data item, attempts to catch any flaws in the program logic.

After a programmer has worked for a long time to correct the logic of a program, he or she may tend to overlook errors or assume a clarity that in reality does not exist. For this reason, programmers sometimes trade their partially debugged programs among themselves. The programmer stepping through a "fresh" program may uncover mistakes in logic that were unnoticed by the original programmer.

PROGRAMMING CASE STUDY

A teacher has heard about the marvels of computer technology, and would like to try using the computer to help out with one of the more time-consuming tasks of the profession: determining grades. The first step in the problem-solving process is to define the problem. Next, a solution is designed that applies computer processing steps in a logical order to solve the problem. These tentative steps are then used to write a program. Finally, the program is compiled, debugged, and tested.

Defining the Problem

The problem is to calculate students' final grades for a class. The computer is not to be used to evaluate each student's performance and determine the

HIGHLIGHT
The First Computer "Bug"

The first "bug" in a computer program occurred in a very strange way. In the summer of 1945, something went wrong with the Mark II, the large electromechanical device used by the Department of Defense for making calculations. Though the machine was not working properly, no obvious problems could be found. The personnel operating the machine continued their search, and finally discovered the cause of their problems. A large moth had become stuck in one of Mark II's relays, preventing the circuit from being completed and thereby causing an error. The solution to the problem was to remove the bug from the relay, and thus the term "debugging" came into existence.

appropriate grade. The teacher will do that. Rather, once a grade has been assigned for each test given in the class, the computer is to calculate a student's numerical average for all tests, and then assign a letter grade equivalent.

Designing a Solution

The first step in designing a solution is to determine what *output* is required of the program. The teacher would like each student's name, the average test score, and the letter grade equivalent. The *input* to the program will be each student's name and five test scores. The *processing* required of the program will be to add together the five scores, divide by five (the number of tests) to calculate the average, and then assign a letter grade. Letter grades will be assigned on the basis of the following scale:

AVERAGE	FINAL GRADE
90–100	A
80–89	B
70–79	C
60–69	D
0–59	F

The next step in designing a problem solution is to determine a basic instruction flow. Output headings can be printed before the student data is read as input. Since each student has five grades, the student's name and five grades must be input, and the grades added together. When the addition has been completed, the average can be calculated. Once the average has been determined, the appropriate final letter grade can be assigned according to the grade scale. After the final letter grade has been established, the name, average, and final grade can be printed. When the data for one student has been processed, the data for the next student can be read and processed, and so on, until no more statistics are available.

The flow can be placed into steps as follows:

1. Print headings.
2. If all students have not been processed do steps 3 through 8, otherwise go to step 9.
3. Read student's name and five grades.
4. Total the student's numerical grades.
5. Calculate the student's grade average.
6. Determine the final letter grade based on the grade scale.
7. Print name, average, and final letter grade.
8. Go back to step 2.
9. Print message signifying end of the program.
10. Stop.

A flowchart for the solution of this problem is given in Figure 3–10. The relationship between the steps above and the blocks on the flowchart is also pointed out.

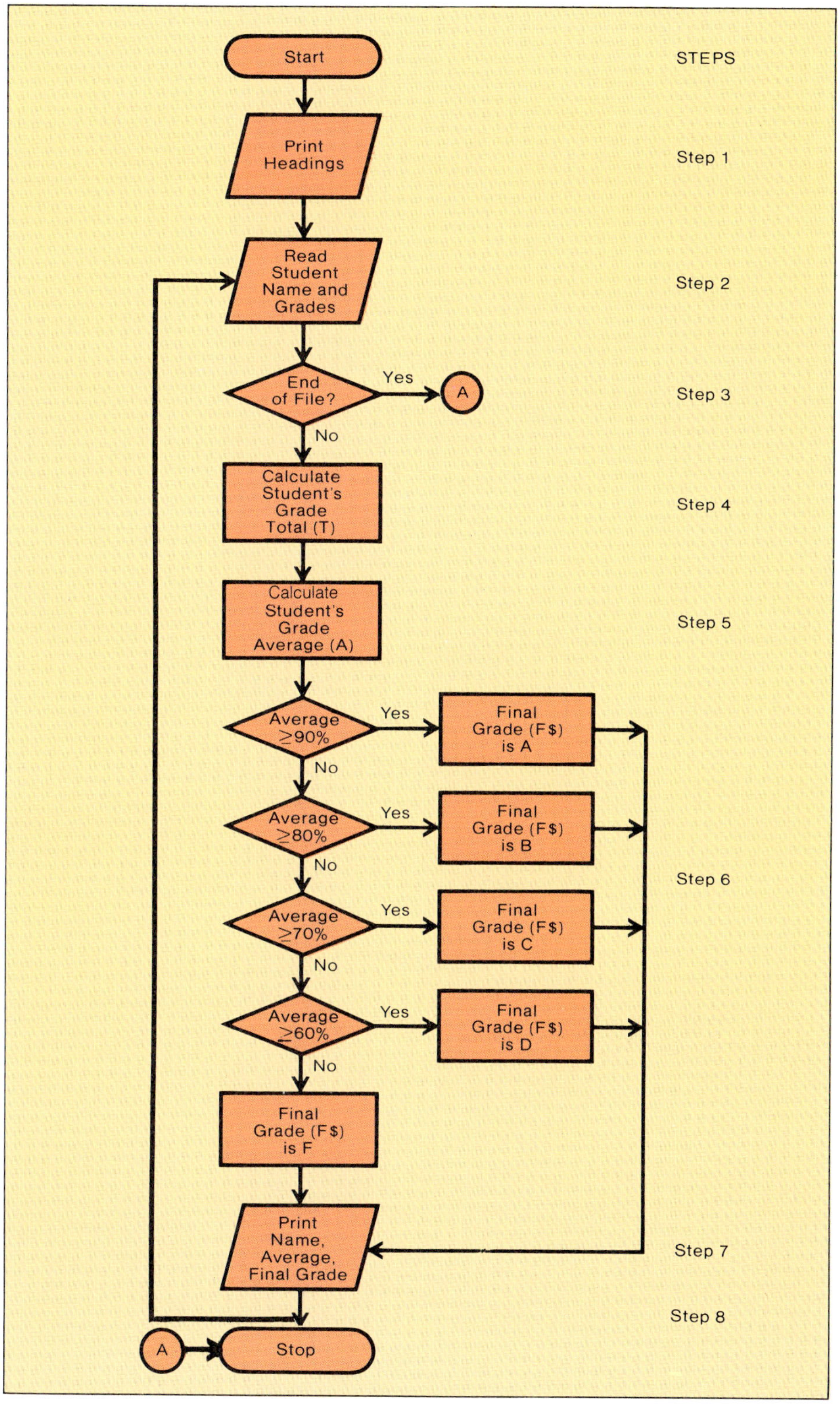

FIGURE 3–10
Flowchart for Case Study

Note: The characters enclosed in ( ) are the variable names used in the BASIC program.

Writing the Program

After the flowchart has been constructed and the logic reviewed, the next task is to express the solution in a programming language—in this case, BASIC (Beginners All-purpose Symbolic Instruction Code, which is discussed more fully in Chapter 8). The completed source program can then be entered into the computer by the programmer. Figure 3–11 shows the source listing for the program.

Compiling, Degugging, and Testing the Program

Once the program has been written, it can be submitted to the computer to be compiled into machine language. A listing of the source program and notification of errors (if any) detected by the computer can be generated.

FIGURE 3–11
BASIC Program with Sample Data for Case Study

```
GRADE     21:54     TUESDAY JULY 27, 1982

100 REM THIS PROGRAM WILL ADD 5 INDIVIDUAL GRADES
110 REM FOR A STUDENT, CALCULATE THE AVERAGE, AND THEN
120 REM DETERMINE THE STUDENT'S FINAL GRADE
130 PRINT 'NAME', 'AVERAGE', 'FINAL GRADE'
140 PRINT
150 READ N$, G1, G2, G3, G4, G5
155 IF N$ = 'END OF DATA' THEN 997
160 LET T = G1+G2+G3+G4+G5
170 LET A = T/5
180 IF A >= 90 THEN 240
190 IF A >= 80 THEN 260
200 IF A >= 70 THEN 280
210 IF A >= 60 THEN 300
220 LET F$ = 'F'
230 GO TO 310
240 LET F$ = 'A'
250 GO TO 310
260 LET F$ = 'B'
270 GO TO 310
280 LET F$ = 'C'
290 GO TO 310
300 LET F$ = 'D'
310 PRINT N$, A, F$
320 GO TO 150
330 DATA 'FRED J. SMITH', 70, 65, 24, 100, 98
340 DATA 'JASON R. JACKSON', 97, 96, 59, 78, 60
350 DATA 'JOHN S. LAWSON', 90, 94, 88, 98, 96
360 DATA 'SUSAN EAKINS', 83, 76, 87, 89, 95
370 DATA 'MARY Q. JOHNSON', 66, 79, 83, 75, 70
380 DATA 'END OF DATA', 0, 0, 0, 0, 0
997 PRINT 'END OF PROGRAM'
998 STOP
999 END
```

Then the program can be executed. Figure 3–12 shows the output produced during the execution of the program.

STRUCTURED PROGRAMMING

Emphasis on the art of programming and on the flexibility that high-level languages provide has sometimes encouraged poor programming techniques. For example, many programs contain numerous branches that continually alter the sequential flow of processing. These programs may work successfully, but their often confusing logic can be understood only by the original programmer. This increases the costs and difficulties associated with program maintenance. Furthermore, without a standardized method of attacking a problem, a programmer may spend far more time than necessary in determining an appropriate solution and developing the program. To counter these tendencies, **structured programming** has been widely publicized.

Structured programming has four objectives:

1. To reduce testing time.
2. To increase programmer productivity.
3. To increase clarity by reducing complexity.
4. To decrease maintenance time and effort.

More simply stated, programs should be easy to read, easy to maintain, and easy to change.

Structured programming encourages well-thought-out program logic and suggests using only three basic control patterns: simple sequence, selection, and loop (see earlier discussion). With these three patterns, programs can be read from top to bottom and are easier to understand. An attempt is made to keep programs as simple and straightforward as possible; structured programming discourages the use of "tricky" logic that is likely to confuse program users (sometimes even the original programmer).

Basic to the concept of structured programming is the use of program modules. Each module is an independent program segment that performs

```
RUN GRADE

GRADE     21:54     TUESDAY JULY 27, 1982

NAME                      AVERAGE        FINAL GRADE

FRED J. SMITH              71.4            C
JASON R. JACKSON           78              C
JOHN S. LAWSON             93.2            A
SUSAN EAKINS               86              B
MARY Q. JOHNSON            74.6            C
END OF PROGRAM
```

FIGURE 3–12
Output for Case Study

only one function. Modules should be small in order to facilitate programming and later debugging. Each module should have only one entry point and one exit point. This allows the flow of control to be followed easily by the programmer. When the modular approach is used, the one-entry/one-exit guideline is easy to incorporate into the program. A program that has only one entrance and one exit is called a **proper program** (see Figure 3–13).

Structured programs are characterized by other special features. Comment statements, or remarks, should be used liberally. Variable names should be definite. Finally, indentation and spacing of program statements should be used.

It must be emphasized that the branch pattern, characterized by the GO TO statement, is not advocated in structured programming. (In fact, structured programming is sometimes called "GO-TO-less" programming or "IF-THEN-ELSE" programming.) A GO TO statement causes an unconditional branch from one part of the program to another. Excessive use of GO TO statements results in the continual changes in the flow of execution. Often the flow is transferred to totally different logical sections of the program. Programs containing many GO TO (branching) statements are difficult to modify because they are obscure and complicated. A programmer may not

FIGURE 3–13
Unstructured versus Structured COBOL Code

```
WORK-LOOP.
    READ CARD-FILE AT END GO TO FINISH.
    IF HOURS-WORKED IS GREATER THAN 40 THEN GO TO
        OVERTIME-ROUTINE.
    MULTIPLY HOURS-WORKED BY WAGE-PER-HOUR GIVING GROSS-PAY.
    GO TO TAX-COMPUTATION.
OVERTIME-ROUTINE.
    MULTIPLY WAGE-PER-HOUR BY 40 GIVING REGULAR-PAY.
    SUBTRACT 40 FROM HOURS-WORKED GIVING OVERTIME-HOURS.
    MULTIPLY WAGE-PER-HOUR BY 1.5 GIVING OVERTIME-RATE.
    MULTIPLY OVERTIME-HOURS BY OVERTIME-RATE GIVING
        OVERTIME-PAY.
    ADD REGULAR-PAY, OVERTIME-PAY, GIVING GROSS-PAY.
TAX-COMPUTATION.
    IF GROSS-PAY IS GREATER THAN 250 THEN MULTIPLY GROSS-PAY
        BY 0.20 GIVING TAX ELSE MULTIPLY GROSS-PAY BY 0.14
        GIVING TAX.
    SUBTRACT TAX FROM GROSS-PAY GIVING NET-PAY.
    MOVE EMPLOYEE-NAME TO NAME.
    MOVE NET-PAY TO AMOUNT.
    WRITE PRINT-LINE.
    GO TO WORK-LOOP.
FINISH.
    CLOSE CARD-FILE, PRINT-FILE.
    STOP RUN.
```

(a) Unstructured Portion of COBOL Program

know how a change in one part of the program will affect processing in other parts. This is not to say that a structured program may not have any GO TO statements, but that they should be used only to implement structured logic. GO TO statements should never cause a branch outside of the program module in which they reside.

Some programming languages are better suited to structured programming than others. Especially well suited are Pascal, PL/I, and ALGOL (a language developed by a coordinated effort of user groups and computer manufacturers and in widespread use in Europe). Languages, such as FORTRAN and BASIC lack some features that many people consider essential for structured programming. For example, it is sometimes difficult to avoid the use of GO TO statements in these languages. However, careful planning, and well-placed GO TO statements can result in well-structured programs, regardless of the language used. (These languages are all discussed in Chapter 8).

The design of a solution to a problem requires a careful definition of the problem. If inadequate analysis has been performed, considerable work will be required to redesign the solution. If the problem has been defined well, the programmer can easily design a solution by following the solution de-

FIGURE 3–13
Continued

```
WORK-LOOP.
    READ CARD-FILE AT END CLOSE CARD-FILE, PRINT-FILE, STOP RUN.
    IF HOURS-WORKED IS GREATER THAN 40
        THEN PERFORM OVERTIME-ROUTINE
        ELSE PERFORM STANDARD-ROUTINE.
    PERFORM TAX-PAY-COMPUTATION.
    PERFORM PRINTING.
    GO TO WORK-LOOP.
STANDARD-ROUTINE.
    MULTIPLY HOURS-WORKED BY WAGE-PER-HOUR GIVING GROSS-PAY.
OVERTIME-ROUTINE.
    MULTIPLY WAGE-PER-HOUR BY 40 GIVING REGULAR-PAY.
    SUBTRACT 40 FROM HOURS-WORKED GIVING OVERTIME-HOURS.
    MULTIPLY WAGE-PER-HOUR BY 1.5 GIVING OVERTIME-RATE.
    MULTIPLY OVERTIME-HOURS BY OVERTIME-RATE GIVING
        OVERTIME-PAY.
    ADD REGULAR-PAY, OVERTIME-PAY GIVING GROSS-PAY.
TAX-PAY-COMPUTATION.
    IF GROSS-PAY IS GREATER THAN 250 THEN MULTIPLY GROSS-PAY
        BY 0.20 GIVING TAX ELSE MULTIPLY GROSS-PAY BY 0.14
        GIVING TAX.
    SUBTRACT TAX FROM GROSS-PAY GIVING NET-PAY.
PRINTING.
    MOVE EMPLOYEE-NAME TO NAME.
    MOVE NET-PAY TO AMOUNT.
    WRITE PRINT-LINE.
```

(b) Structured Portion of COBOL Program

sign steps. By using programming techniques such as structured design, the programming process is enhanced. Programs take less time to develop, are easier to follow, and require less maintenance. Even when maintenance is required, it takes less time and is less costly to perform.

Computers do not provide instant answers to problems. In fact, some problems defy computer solution, either because they are too complex to be reduced to a series of computer statements, or because sufficient data cannot be gathered to make the results of processing meaningful. While the compilation of a program may be "instant," the effort required to prepare the computer to solve problems is not. Tremendous amounts of time are required to define the problem, design a solution, write, test, and debug the program. By using designing tools like pseudocode and flowcharts, programmers not only have a means of visualizing program logic, but have documentation for future reference. By using structured programming, considerable time can be saved both in development and future maintenance.

SUMMARY POINTS

- Computers must be told, step by step, how to solve problems.
- There are four steps to the problem-solving process: defining the problem, designing a solution, writing the program, and compiling, debugging, and testing the program.
- In defining the problem, the analyst or programmer must determine the nature and extent of the problem to be solved. This is often helped by approaching the problem first from the viewpoint of what output is required, what input is available, and then determining what processing will be required.
- In designing a solution, the programmer must develop an approach to the problem using the four basic logic patterns: simple sequence, selection, loop, and branch.
- Development tools are available to help the programmer in the design phase of problem solving—pseudocode and flowcharts. Pseudocode attempts to express in short English phrases the steps the program will take. Flowcharts use standard symbols to visually depict the logical processes within the program.
- In designing a solution, the programmer must make special considerations with regard to input, processing, and output. The method of input, type of edit checks, and form of output will affect how a program should be designed.
- A program is a series of statements the computer can use to solve a problem.
- In writing the program, the programmer should be concerned with the special types of statements that can be used in the language chosen for the program.
- In debugging the program, the programmer attempts to remove syntactical errors in the program. In testing the program, the programmer uses sam-

ple data to execute the program and compares the computer's results to those calculated by hand.

- Structured programming attempts to group sections of the program into segments called modules. Each module is independent and has only one entry and one exit point. Structured programming emphasizes "GO-TO-less" programming.

REVIEW QUESTIONS

1. Consider the problem you face every term scheduling your classes. Can you define the problem well enough that a computer could be used to schedule your classes? Design a solution to your problem. Feel free to use pseudocode or flowcharts to help you in your solution design.
2. Why should a programmer/analyst begin a system by examining the output that is desired?
3. Must you know a programming language in order to design a tentative program flow to solve a problem using the computer?
4. Using only the four basic logic patterns discussed in the chapter, draw a flowchart depicting the steps required by a gas station attendant to fill a car's gasoline tank.
5. When may branching be undesirable and why?
6. What are some benefits of flowcharts?
7. Describe some processing edit-checks that you might use in cashing employee paychecks.
8. Discuss the qualities that can make one program better than another.
9. List and describe the three levels of computer languages.
10. Have you ever had to enter data into a computer system that was not "user friendly?" Describe your experience. In what ways could the programmer have designed the system to make it easier for you?
11. What is a program module and how is it used?

Programs for Your Microcomputer

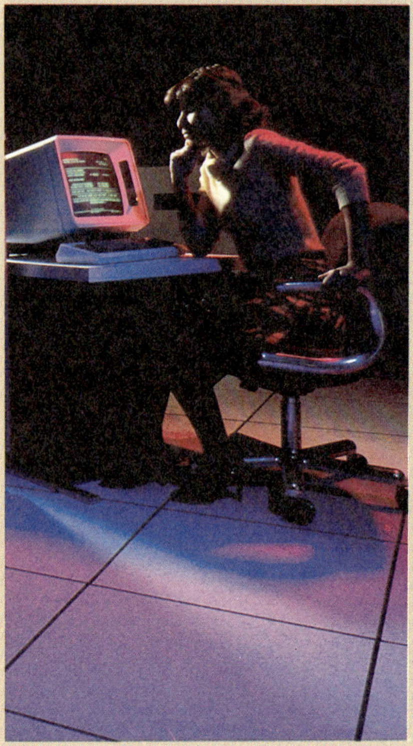

The real power behind any personal computer is the programs that make it run. These programs are called software, to distinguish them from the machines themselves, which are called hardware. One man who recognized the importance of software early in the game is Tony Gold. Gold, along with his collaborator, Larry Alkoff, started Lifeboat, now one of the largest software publishing and distributing firms. Lifeboat is a major success story. Rising out of a small basement apartment in New York, it became a leader in the industry and currently earns an estimated $10 million a year. The company was first conceived as a one-stop source for microcomputer software packages configured for CP/M80 (an operating system that has become an industry standard) and other compatible operating systems. Gold has been credited with being the driving force behind CP/M80. The development and use of a standard operating system like CP/M is important because it enables users, regardless of their brand of computer, to use a wider variety of software products.

According to Gold, there are four basic groups of personal computer users: the professionals—who do some kind of analysis; the transaction-process group, including individuals involved in mailing-list work or accounting; the home computing market; and educators. As of yet, Lifeboat has not entered the latter two markets. But for the business market, Lifeboat is currently selling and supporting well over a hundred software packages and from fifty to seventy-five different computer manufacturers.

The era of business software packages for personal computers began in 1979 with the introduction of Visicorp's VisiCalc, the popular "electronic worksheet" program used in financial applications such as budgeting and planning. The program allows the user to enter or change any data values, alter the format, and answer "what if" questions simply by entering new assumptions via the keyboard. Since the introduction of VisiCalc, many other business software packages have flooded the market. These packages range from general accounting systems to more specific applications such as portfolio management and patient file and billing systems for doctors and dentists.

With the introduction of easy-to-use word processing software, many users are now discovering that their personal computer also offers the ideal way to compose and edit text.

Educational software is a relatively new market that appears to have tremendous growth potential. It offers the advantages of supplying students with immediate feedback; allowing them to do "dry runs" of processing, events, and experiments that otherwise could be too costly, time consuming, or dangerous; and never losing patience with a child.

For home computing, game packages are probably the most popular type of software. Home computers such as the Atari 800 now have a wide variety of games with high-quality graphics. Most personal computers offer a wide variety of these games to suit any taste.

The growth of the numbers and kinds of places that sell software might leave you a little confused about where you should go to buy. There are a number of options available. If you are totally in the dark or would just like to know what's available and where to purchase it, there are clearing houses such as Sofsearch whose sole purpose is to provide you with this information.

Some popular sources for purchasing software are the large publishing and distributing firms such as Lifeboat Associates, New York,; Peachtree Software Inc., Atlanta, Georgia; and Personal Software Inc. of Sunnyvale, California. Other sources are computer specialty stores and mail-order firms.

Before purchasing any software, you should ask to see a demonstration of the program to make sure it meets your needs, is "user-friendly" (featuring English-like commands), and has documentation that is understandable. If at all possible, talk to consumers who have used the program to get their feedback.

It is a good idea to buy only from companies that provide continuing support, for example, newsletters, technical bulletins, enhancements, and solutions to problems.

One store that follows this policy of continuing support is the Software Store in Jericho, New York, which bills itself as the nation's first software supermarket. They stock a wide selection of business, personal, and educational software. Customers can browse through the shelves of software packages, select a program, and then test it on any one of the many models of computers available in the store.

Buying by mail can be very risky. You have no chance to see the software demonstrated, and there is generally a lack of support with mail-order arrangements.

Once you have purchased your computer software and unpacked the disk or cassette, a new thought may sneak into your mind? "My friends would really appreciate having a copy of this program." You had better forget this idea right away because most computer software is protected from unauthorized copying under United States copyright laws, which contain stiff criminal and civil penalties.

After using the recently acquired computer program, its enormous value to you becomes evident. If anything were to happen to this program, you would suffer greatly. The copyright laws recognize the importance of a backup copy and permit you to make one. However, when you try to use the copy utility program supplied by the hardware manufacturer, the operation fails. This happens because the software developer has protected the program from duplication through special coding. What's more the software creator will sell you a second copy only at an exorbitant cost. However, computer programs such as "Locksmith" and "Nibbles Away" and more advanced hardware components such as "Crack-shot" and "Wildcard" have been developed to allow protected software to be copied. All has not been lost: you have outsmarted the software developers and stayed within the copyright law.

For most of the home and business applications that you want the microcomputer to perform, chances are the software is already available or soon will be. We have seen that there are many options available when choosing software and software vendors. Taking the time to select the proper software from an experienced and reliable dealer is your best bet in assuring you of a quality product that will fit your needs.

DISCUSSION QUESTIONS

1. What factors should you consider before purchasing any software?
2. Why is the development of a standard operating system such as CP/M important?

CHAPTER 4

Computer Hardware

INTRODUCTION

One can acquire a general understanding of electronic data processing without making a detailed study of the computer technology involved. However, with a basic understanding of how the computer operates, the student of data processing is better equipped to appreciate the computer's capabilities and limitations and to relate this knowledge to data-processing activities.

This chapter focuses on the parts of a computer; its key components are identified and their functions explained. Differences between analog and digital computers are discussed and stored-program concept is explained. The chapter also examines various forms of primary storage and discusses read-only memory and programmable read-only memory. The chapter concludes with a discussion of how data is represented in ways appropriate for computer processing.

FACING PAGE
The heart of any computer—the microprocessor. Here the size of a computer chip is dramatically shown as it rests on the petal of a daisy.

CHAPTER OUTLINE

DIGITAL AND ANALOG COMPUTERS

Up to now, when this book discussed the term **computer,** it was talking about a specific type—the digital computer. That is because digital computers are by far the most widely used type of computer. There is another type—the analog computer, and it is important to distinguish between these two types.

A **digital computer** operates on the basis of discrete "on" and "off" states represented by its electronic circuitry. As Chapter 2 pointed out, these "on" and "off" states can be represented by 1s and 0s, called **binary digits.** Groups of binary digits can be used to represent numbers, letters, or other distinct symbols. A digital computer receives input and produces output in the form of these 1 and 0 states. The states used for numbers, letters, and special characters can be representd by holes in punched cards or magnetized areas on tapes or disks. They can be translated to easily recognizable printing on paper.

Digital computers achieve varying degrees of precision, depending on their particular construction and machine characteristics. For example, some digital computers can provide results accurate to hundreds or even thousands of decimal places. Such computers are often used in scientific applications. For business applications, results accurate to only a few decimal places are sufficient. Therefore, computer manufacturers build various models of digital computers to meet the varied needs of the ultimate users of these machines.

In contrast to digital computers, **analog computers** do not operate directly on "on" and "off" states represented by binary digits. Instead, they measure continuous physical or electrical magnitudes such as pressure, temperature, current, voltage, length, or shaft rotations. For example, a gasoline pump is an analog device that measures (1) the quantity of gasoline pumped (to the nearest tenth of a gallon) and (2) the price of that gasoline (to the nearest penny). Another example of an analog device is a car speedometer. Here, driveshaft rotations are measured and converted to a number that indicates the speed of the car.

It is important to note that while numerical results can be obtained from analog computers, they are arrived at indirectly. Because digital computers are commonly used in the applications discussed in this book, the remainder of the book focuses on digital computers.

CENTRAL PROCESSING UNIT

It is not necessary to acquire a working knowledge of the internal electronic circuitry of a computer in order to use it. However, a basic understanding of computer technology is essential. The simple diagram in Figure 4–1 shows the principal components of a computer system.

The input to a computer can take many forms: data can be entered on magnetic tape, on punched cards, through the pressing of keys on a terminal keyboard, and so on. (Input devices will be discussed in greater detail in the next chapter.)

The **central processing unit (CPU)** is the heart of the computer system. It is composed of three units: the control unit, the arithmetic/logic unit (ALU), and the primary storage unit. Each unit performs its own unique functions.

The **control unit,** as its name implies, maintains order and controls activity in the CPU. It does not process or store data. Rather, it directs the sequence of operations. The control unit interprets the instructions of a program in storage and produces signals that act as commands to circuits to execute the instructions. Other functions of the control unit include communicating with an input device in order to begin the transfer of instructions and data into storage and, similarly, communicating with an output device to initiate the transfer of results from storage.

The **arithmetic/logic unit (ALU)** performs arithmetic computations and logical operations. An example of a logical operation might be comparing one data item to another to see which is less. Since the bulk of internal processing involves calculations or comparisons, the capabilities of a computer often depend upon the design and capabilities of its ALU. The ALU does not store data but manipulates it.

The **primary storage unit, (internal storage, memory,** or **main storage)** holds instructions, data, and intermediate and final results. At the start of processing, data is transferred from an input device to the primary storage unit, where it is stored until needed for processing. Data being processed and intermediate results of ALU calculations are also stored here. After all computations and manipulations are completed, the final results remain in memory until the control unit causes them to be erased—normally after the results are transferred to an output device.

Among the most widely used of the many types of output devices are printers, which provide results on paper; visual display units, which project

FIGURE 4–1
Computer System Components

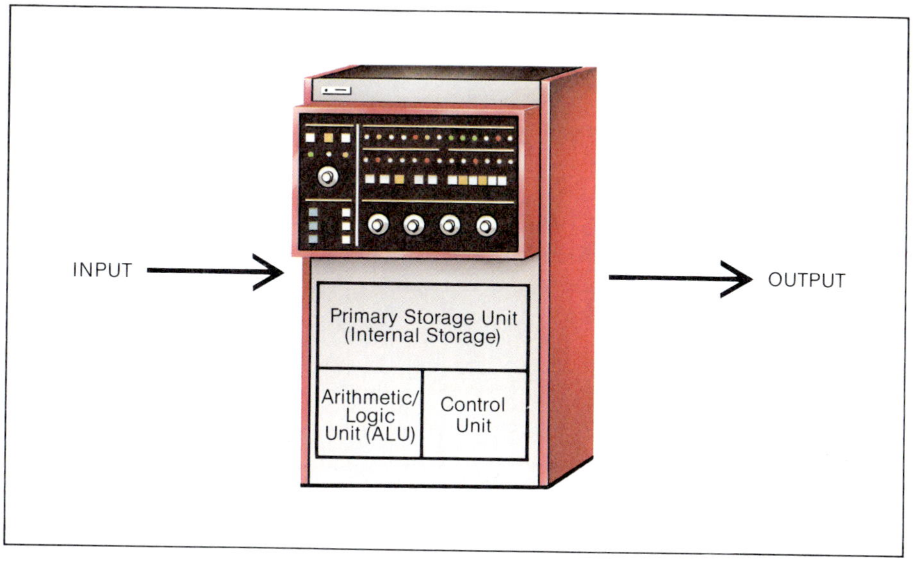

HIGHLIGHT
Analog versus Digital

"Digital" records are causing a revolution in the music business. Even though many of the recordings have prices as high as $19, they have no problem selling.

Traditionally, recordings are made by an analog process. Electronic waves create as close a model as possible of the vibrations caused by the sound waves. This model is recorded on a magnetic master tape, which through repeated use in the record-pressing process, causes the tape to lose its good quality.

In the new digital recordings, each sound wave is sampled thousands of times a second by computer equipment. Each variation of the sound wave is given a numerical equivalent, so when records are pressed, the machine calls back the recorded numbers and reproduces the original sound mathematically. Each copy is free of the distortions created with analog recordings. In listening tests, professional musicians are often unable to distinguish between the recordings and a live performance.

With digital recordings, every copy is as good as the original. Unfortunately, if the recording session turns out poorly, the recording will sound just as bad.

results on television-like screens; and tape and disk drives, which produce machine-readable magnetic information. (These devices will also be discussed in the next chapter.)

INSTRUCTIONS

Understanding how a computer works is essential in writing effective programs and evaluating their performance. A computer **program** is a series of instructions to be executed by the computer. These instructions can be written in any programming language but must be translated into machine language for execution. Each machine language instruction has two basic parts: the operation code and the operand. The **operation code (op code)** tells the control unit what function is to be performed (such as ADD, SUBTRACT, MOVE DATA, or COMPARE). The **operand** indicates the primary storage location of the data to be operated on.

The computer performs instructions sequentially, in the order they are given, unless instructed to do otherwise. This **next-sequential-instruction feature** requires that instructions be placed in consecutive locations in memory. The computer simply goes from one location to the next in executing statements, unless one of these instructions tells it to do otherwise. Since input must be brought into the computer memory to be processed, a separate area must be designated for it. Otherwise, the computer would be unable to differentiate between instructions and data. This is also true for output generated by the program, which is kept isolated from instructions. Figure 4–2 shows this segmentation of memory.

The three units (control, ALU, and storage) interact as follows: Initially, the control unit directs the input device to transfer instructions and data to

FIGURE 4–2
Memory Segmentation

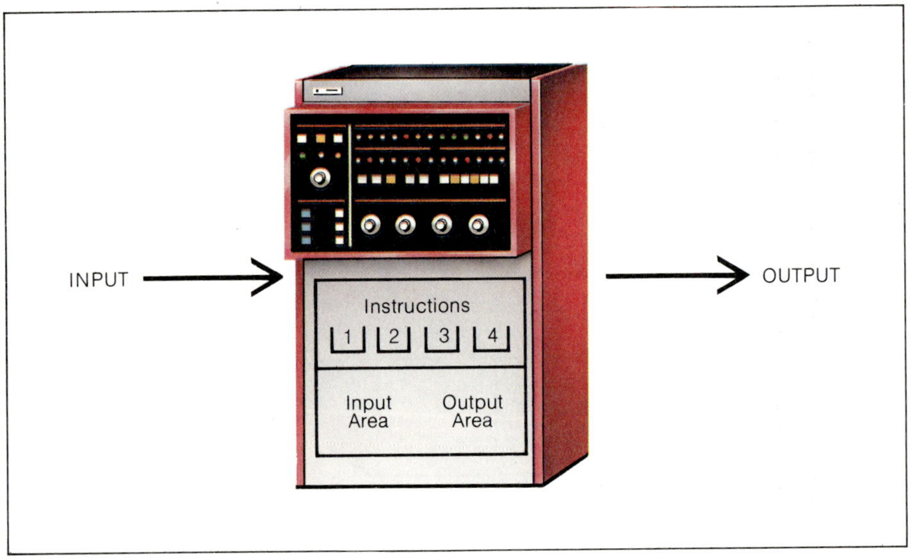

primary storage. Then the control unit takes one instruction from storage, examines it, and sends the appropriate electronic signals to the ALU and to storage to cause the instruction to be carried out. The signals sent to storage may tell it to transfer data to the ALU, where it is mathematically manipulated. The result may then be transferred back to storage.

After an instruction has been executed, the control unit takes the next instruction from the primary storage unit. Data may be transferred from storage to the ALU and back several times before all instructions are executed. When all instructions have been executed, the control unit directs the storage unit to transfer the processed data (information) to the output device.

These steps are shown in Figure 4–3 and are summarized below. Notice that computers, like humans, can only execute one instruction at a time. However, they work at incredibly high speeds (see Figure 4–3).

Step A: Instructions and data from the input device are stored in primary storage under direction of the control unit.

FIGURE 4–3
CPU Operations

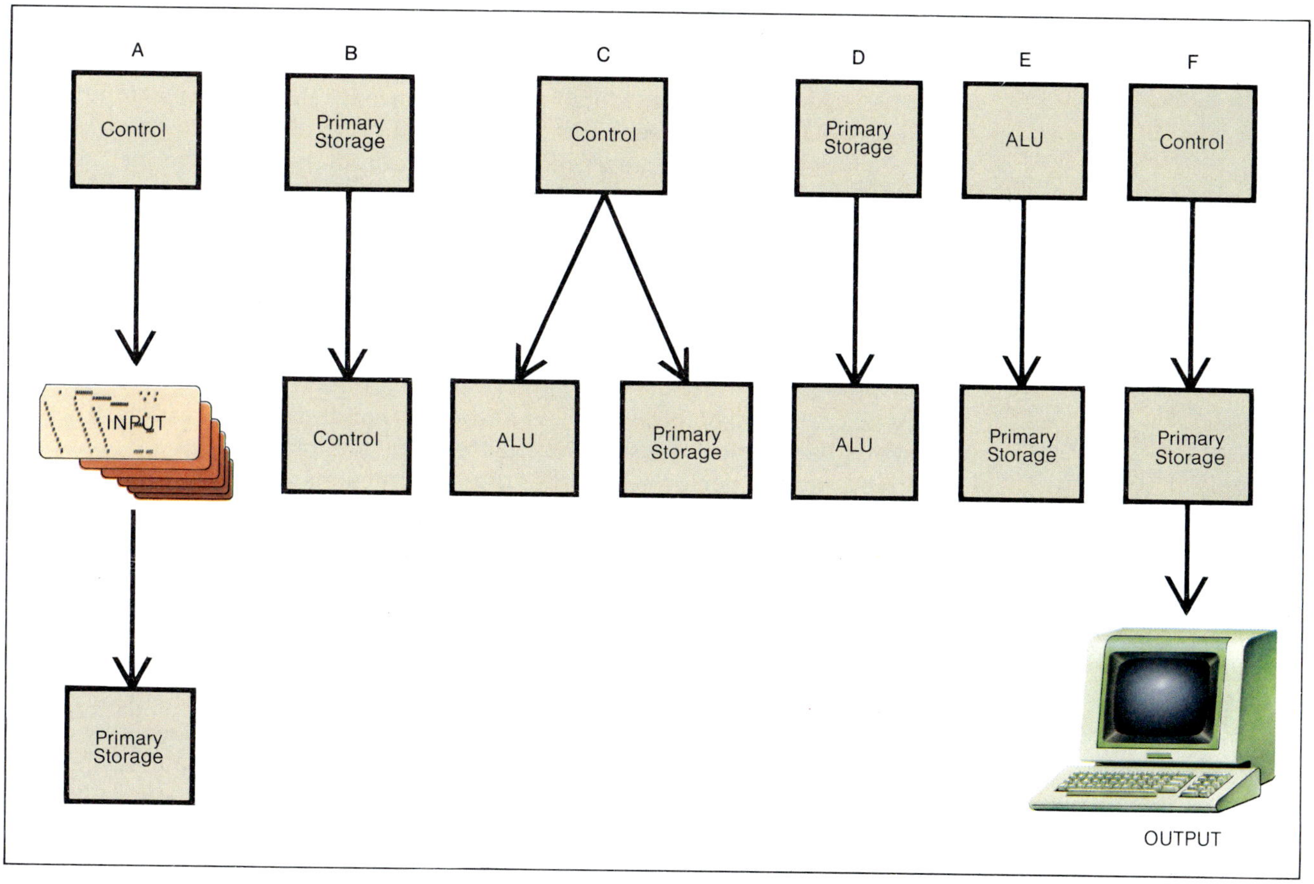

Step B: The control unit examines one instruction and interprets it.

Step C: The control unit sends appropriate electronic signals to the ALU and to primary storage.

Step D: The required data items are transferred to the ALU, where calculations and/or comparisons are performed.

Step E: The result is transferred back to the primary storage unit. Steps B through E are repeated until all instructions have been executed.

Step F: The control unit signals the primary storage unit to transfer the results to the output device.

STORED-PROGRAM CONCEPT

In early computers, instructions had to be either wired on control panels plugged into the computer or read into the computer from punched cards in discrete steps as the job progressed. The punched-card method slowed down processing because the computer had to wait for instructions to be fed in by a human operator. By storing instructions in the computer's memory in electronic form, no human intervention was required during processing. This development, the **stored-program concept,** allowed the computer to proceed at its own speed—almost the speed of light!

Modern computers are stored-program computers. Once the instructions required for a particular application have been determined, they are placed into the computer memory so that the appropriate operations will be performed. The storage unit operates much as a tape recorder does: Once a copy of the instructions and data have been stored, they remain in storage (on the tape) until new instructions and data are stored over them (a new recording is made). Therefore, it is possible to execute the same instructions or process the same data over and over again until a change is desired. This basic characteristic of memory is known as **nondestructive read/destructive write.** Each series of instructions placed into memory is called a **stored program,** and the person who writes these instructions is called a **programmer.**

"Good grief, Farthingsdale, all this and you forget how to turn it on?"

STORAGE

Storage Locations and Addresses

In order to direct processing operations, the control unit of the CPU must be able to locate each instruction and data item in storage. Therefore, each location in storage is assigned an address. A simple way to understand this concept is to picture computer storage as a large collection of mailboxes. Each mailbox is a specific location with its own number or address (see Figure 4–4). Each can hold one item of information. Since each location in stor-

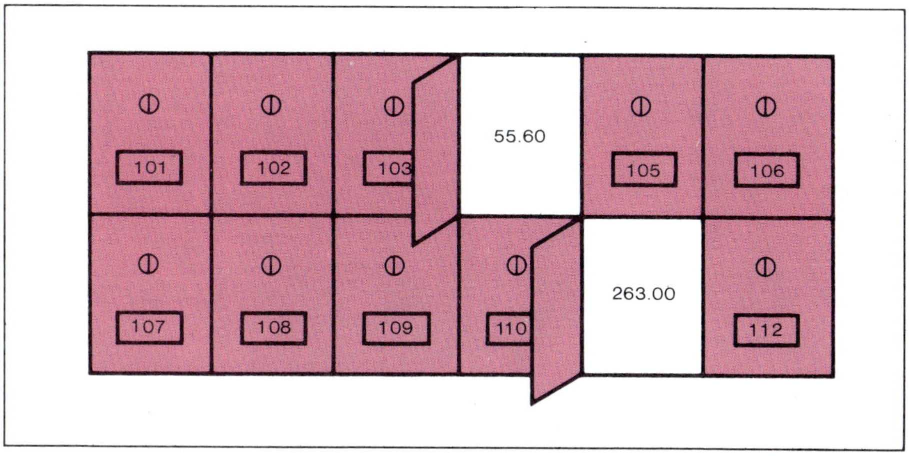

FIGURE 4–4
Each Mailbox Represents a Location in Storage with a Specific Address

age has a unique address, particular items can be located by use of stored-program instructions that give the address.

Suppose the computer is to be directed to subtract TAX from GROSS PAY to determine an employee's salary. Suppose further that TAX is stored at location 104 and has a value of 55.60 and that GROSS PAY is stored at location 111 and has a value of 263.00 (see Figure 4–4). One way to accomplish the desired calculation is to tell the computer to subtract the contents of memory location 104 (TAX) from 111 (GROSS PAY). Although this method works well, keeping track of storage locations in memory by using numbers can be quite tedious.

A better way of keeping track of storage locations is to use symbolic names, or **variables,** such as TAX or GROSS PAY, assigned by the programmer, to represent numerical storage addresses. Using this method, the programmer instructs the computer to subtract TAX from GROSS PAY. The computer interprets this to mean that it should subtract the contents of location 104 from the contents of location 111. It is easier for the programmer to use such names and the computer easily translates them into the specific numeric addresses assigned to storage locations. The term *variable* arises from the fact that while the variable name (the storage address) itself does not change, the data stored at that location may. The values of TAX and GROSS PAY are likely to change with each employee. The addresses of TAX and GROSS PAY will not.

Primary Storage

Primary storage comprises all storage considered part of the CPU. It may, in some cases, be supplemented by **secondary storage** (also called **auxiliary storage**) that is separate from the CPU. Information is transferred between primary and secondary, or auxiliary storage, through electrical lines. The most common secondary storage devices are magnetic tape and magnetic disk units (secondary storage devices are discussed more fully in Chapter 7).

Some primary storage units are composed of magnetic cores. Each core

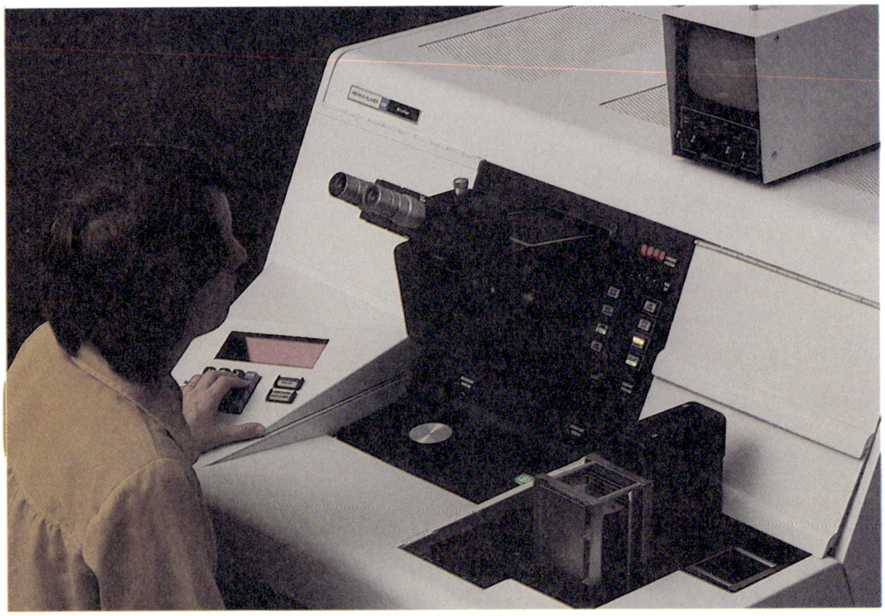

Production of a Chip. *Above:* An engineer first makes a large drawing of the circuitry to be etched on the chip. The drawing will be used to produce a photomask, which will be scaled down to the size of a chip. The circuitry will be etched on a thin "wafer," a piece of silicon about 3 inches in diameter. Each wafer can contain several hundreds of chips. *Right:* The wafer is placed in an oven at a specific temperature to form oxides and other layers of minerals on the surface where the etching will be done. The silicon wafers are then dipped in a photographic-type emulsion and then the photomask of the circuitry is placed over the wafer. Shown here is a worker carefully aligning the mask over the wafer using a high-powered microscope to ensure perfect registration.

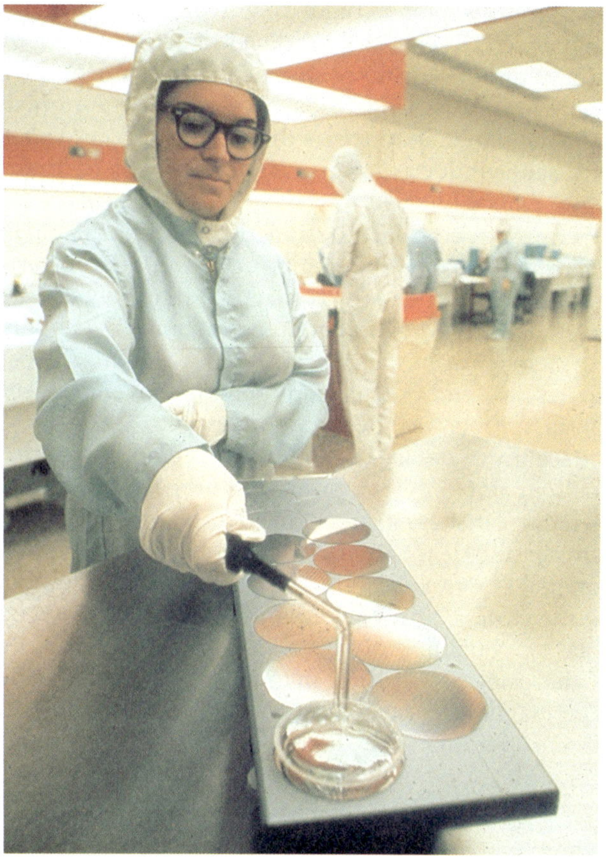

Production of a Chip—Continued. *Left:* Once the mask is in place, the wafer is exposed to ultraviolet light and placed in an acid bath. The parts of the wafer not exposed are washed away in a special wash after the acid bath, leaving the circuitry. Employees who work in wafer fabrication wear protective clothing called "bunny suits." *Bottom:* Seven million tiny transistors are on this silicon-on-saffire wafer designed for military communication equipment. A die cutting machine cuts the wafer into individual chips.

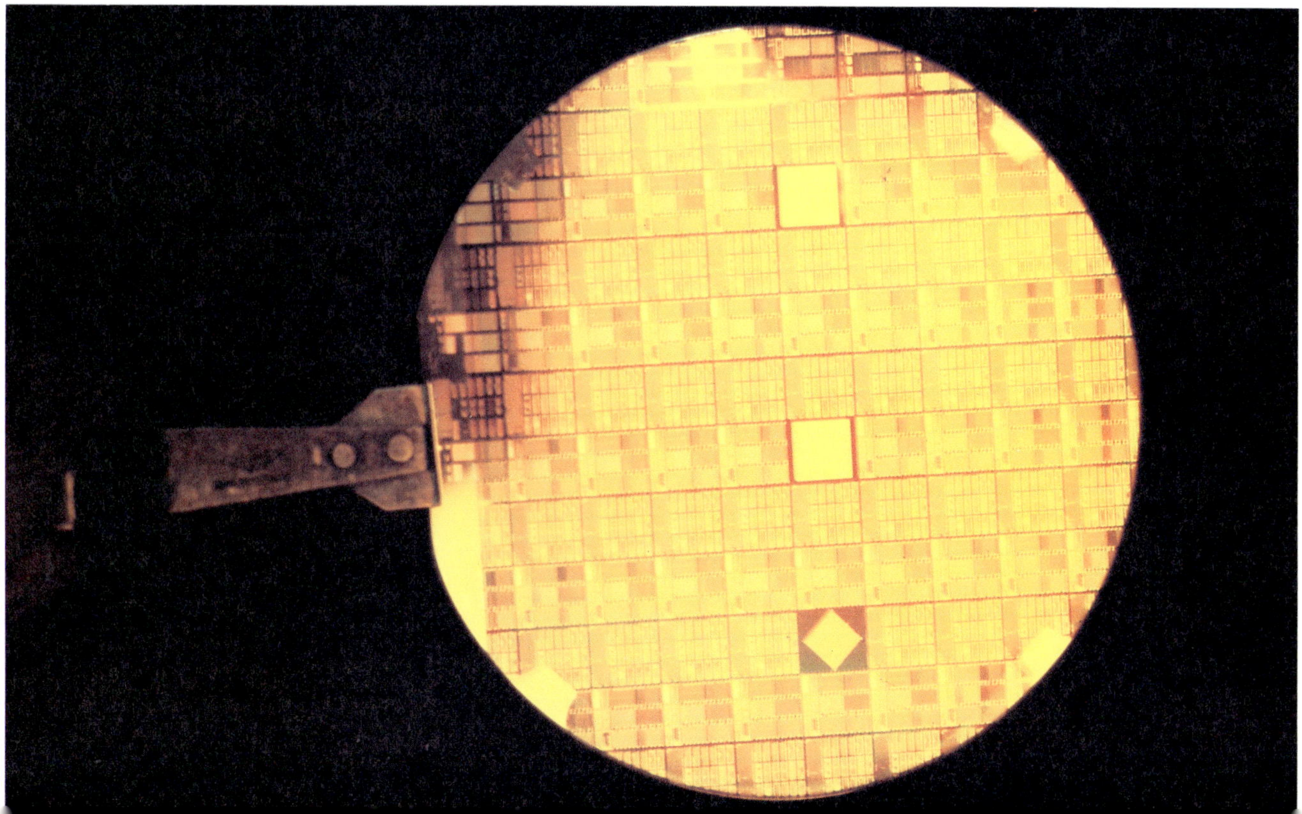

can store one binary digit, or **bit** (short for BInary digiT) by the way it is magnetized. Technological developments have led to the use of semiconductors in other primary storage units. **Semiconductor memory** is composed of circuitry on **silicon chips.** One silicon chip, only slightly bigger than one core, may hold as much as thousands of cores can. The speed of processing with semiconductors is also significantly faster than that with cores (see Figure 4–5).

Semiconductors are designed to store data in locations called **bit cells,** which are capable of being in either an "on" or an "off" state. The bit cells of a semiconductor are arranged so that they can be written to or read from as needed. **RAM (random-access memory)** generally refers to a semiconductor memory unit. Significant improvements in semiconductor technology (size, price, and power requirements) have increased the popularity of semiconductor memory over core memory.

Recently, a device called **bubble memory** was introduced as a replacement medium not only for primary storage but also for auxiliary storage. This memory consists of magnetized spots (or bubbles) resting on a thin film of semiconductor material having polarity opposite that of the semiconductor material on which they rest. Data is stored by shifting the bubbles' positions on the surface of the material (see Figure 4–6). When data is read, the presence of a bubble indicates a 0 bit. The bubbles are similar to magnetic cores in that they retain their magnetism indefinitely. Bubbles are much smaller than magnetic cores, but more data can be stored in a smaller area. A bubble memory module only slightly larger than a quarter can store 20,000 characters of data.

FIGURE 4–5
The incredible shrinking circuitry of today's super computers keeps getting smaller. This tiny memory chip contains the equivalent of 450,000 transistors, and contains the entire "brains" of a computer.

FIGURE 4–6
Bubble Memory Section Magnified 1,500 Times

Some manufacturers have introduced bubble memories in computers; however, a more common use of bubble memories is to provide limited storage capabilities in input/output devices. High cost and difficulty of production have been major factors limiting wide industry and user acceptance of bubbles.

Read-Only Memory (ROM)

Computers are capable of performing complex functions such as taking square roots and evaluating exponents. Such functions can be built into the hardware or software of a computer system. Building them into the hardware provides the advantages of speed and reliability, since the operations are part of the actual computer circuitry. Building them into software allows more flexibility, but carrying out functions built into software is slower and more prone to error.

When functions are built into the hardware of a computer, they are placed in **read-only memory (ROM).** Read-only memory instructions are **hard-wired;** that is, they cannot be changed or deleted by other stored-program instructions. Since ROM is permanent, it cannot be occupied by common stored-program instructions or data. The only method of changing its contents is by altering the physical construction of the circuits.

A direct result of this characteristic is **microprogramming. Microprograms** are sequences of instructions built into read-only memory to carry out functions (such as calculating square roots) that otherwise would have to be directed by stored-program instructions at a much lower speed. Microprograms are usually supplied by computer manufacturers and cannot be altered by users. However, microprogramming allows the basic operations of the computer to be tailored to meet the needs of users. If all instructions that a computer can execute are located in ROM, a complete new set of instructions can be obtained by changing the ROM chip. When selecting a computer, users can get the standard features of the machine plus their choice of the optional features available through microprogramming. Many minicomputers and microcomputers today are directed by instructions stored in ROM (see Figure 4–7).

A version of ROM that can be programmed instead of hardwired is **programmable read-only memory (PROM).** PROM can be programmed by the manufacturer, or it can be shipped "blank" to the end user for programming. Once programmed, its contents are unalterable. Thus, PROM can be programmed only one time. PROM enables the end user to have the advantages of ROM along with flexibility to meet unique needs. A problem with it, though, is that mistakes programmed into the unit cannot be corrected. To overcome this drawback, **erasable programmable read-only memory (EPROM)** has been developed (see Figure 4–8). This memory unit can be erased, but only by being submitted to a special process, such as being bathed in ultraviolet light.

FIGURE 4–7
Microcomputer with various functional parts identified.

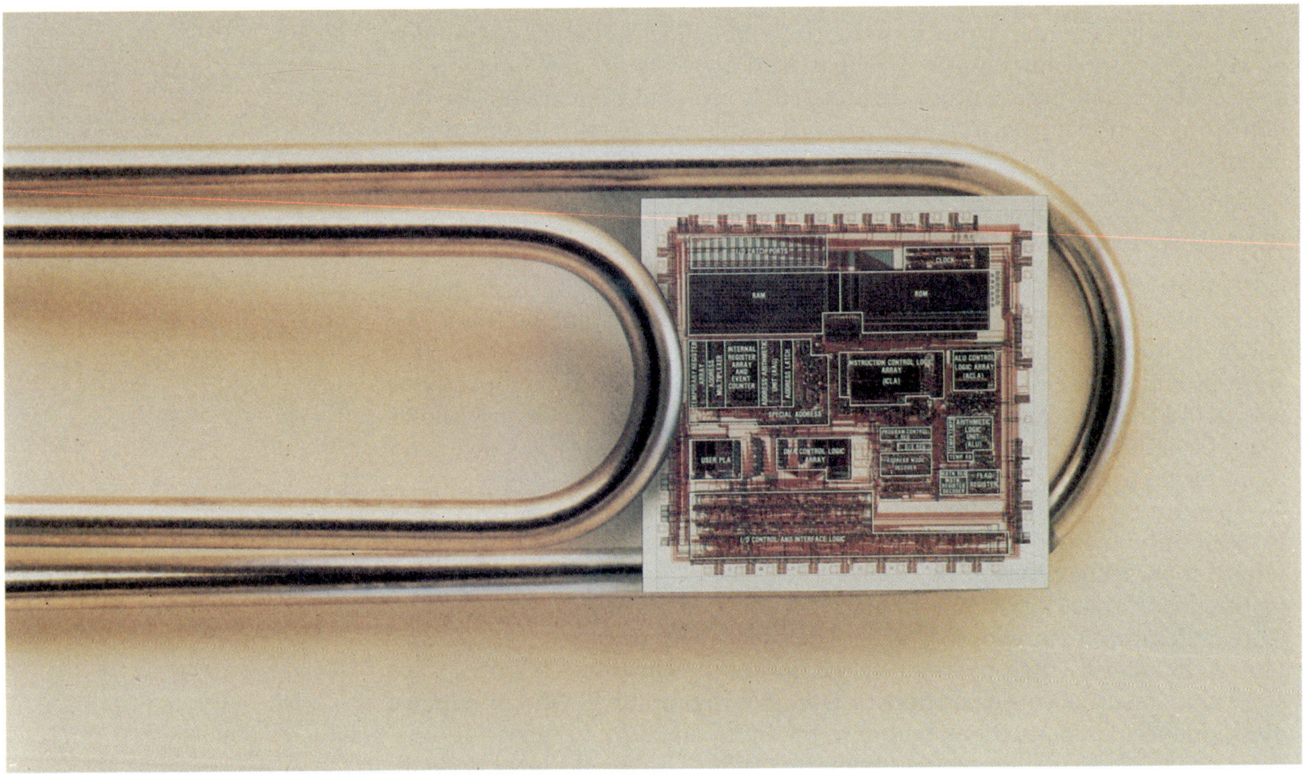

a.

b.

c.

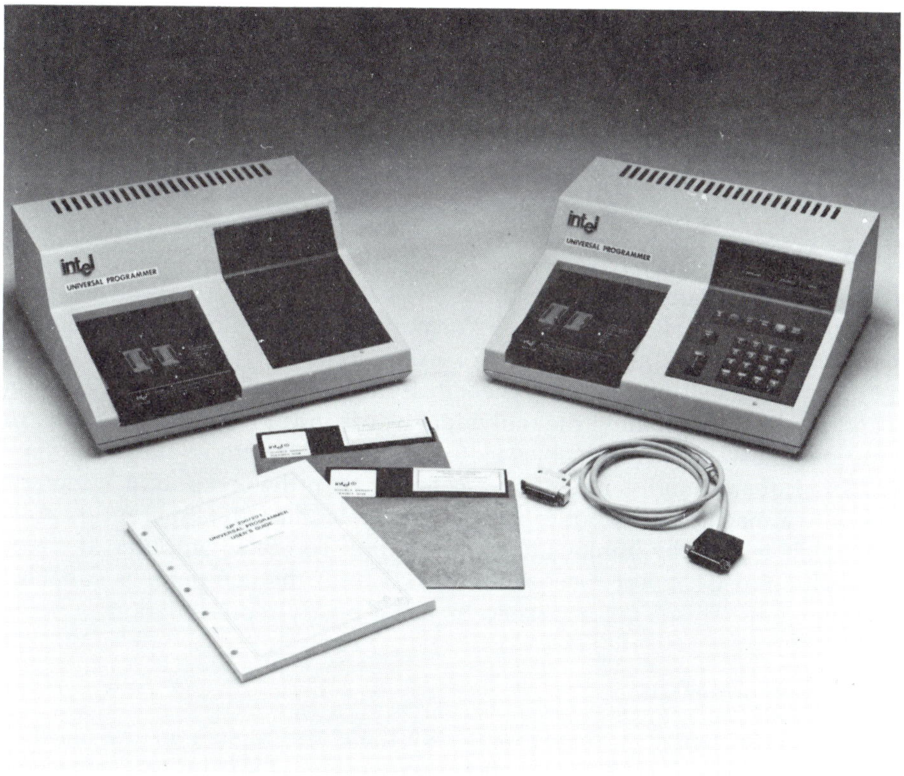

FIGURE 4–8

(a) This chip is Intel 2764—a 5V only, 65,536–bit ultraviolet erasable and electrically programmable read-only memory (EPROM). Its standard access time is 250 ns with speed selection available at 200 ns. Chip-size—153.5 square mil.

(b) The chip is mounted in a plastic carrier with a number of pins that allow it to be plugged into a circuitry board. This one is an Intel 2816 memory, a 16,384–bit electrically erasable programmable read-only memory (E^2PROM). It can be electrically erased and reprogrammed through the use of a 21-volt pulse.

(c) Once the chip is mounted into its carrier, it can be programmed. This PROM (Programmable Read-Only Memory) Programmer made by Intel will program PROM, EPROM, and E^2PROM. The operator plugs in the chip which has been mounted in its carrier and programs by keying in the instructions. By first storing the program on disk, the operator can edit before finally storing the program on the chip.

HIGHLIGHT
Computerized Film Backgrounds

Computerized art—which can simulate what the eye perceives as it moves past a three-dimensional object—may put an end to the building of background sets for movies. By this method, the background is recorded on one piece of film, while the actors are shot on another. The two are then sandwiched and transferred to yet a third piece of film for the final product. The cartoon animator begins with standard two-dimensional photographs of, say, a real building. Once computer-processed, the building photo can be programmed to show how it appears as one walks toward it, past it, around it, etc. While this process is still in a rather primitive stage, it could, if perfected, cut down on location shooting and prop construction costs while adding authenticity of detail since the computer simulations would be based on photos of real objects.

Registers

Registers are devices that facilitate the execution of instructions by acting as temporary holding areas for instructions and data. They are located in the CPU but are not considered part of primary storage. Registers can receive information, hold it, and transfer it very quickly as directed by the control unit of the CPU.

A register functions much as a standard pocket calculator does. The person using the calculator acts as the control unit by transferring numbers from a sheet of paper to the calculator. This paper is analogous to the primary storage unit of the CPU. When the calculation is complete, the calculator displays the result. The person (control unit) then transfers the result displayed on the calculator (register) back to the sheet of paper (primary storage). This process is very similar to the way most modern computers work. Intermediate calculations are performed in registers, and the final results are transferred back to primary storage.

There are various types of registers. Some perform specific functions and are named according to the functions they perform. For example, an **accumulator** is a register that accumulates results of computations (like summations). A **storage register** holds information being sent to or taken from the primary storage unit. During program execution, each instruction is transferred to an **instruction register,** where it is decoded by the control unit. The address of a data item called for by an instruction is kept in an **address register.** Some computers do not have registers with specific uses but instead have **general-purpose registers,** which can be used for both arithmetic and addressing functions.

The numbers and sizes of registers in computers vary. Their purpose however, is the same; they are used as temporary storage areas to facilitate the transfer of data and instructions within the CPU.

DATA REPRESENTATION

Humans communicate information by using symbols that have specific meanings. Symbols such as letters or numbers are combined in meaningful ways to represent information. For example, the twenty-six letters of the English alphabet can be combined to form words, sentences, paragraphs, and so on. By combining the individual words in various ways, we construct various messages. This enables us to communicate with one another.

The human mind is much more complex than the computer. A computer is only a machine; it is not capable of understanding the inherent meanings of symbols used by humans to communicate. To use a computer, therefore, humans must convert their symbols to a form the computer is capable of recognizing. This is accomplished by using binary representation.

Binary Representation

Data is represented in the computer by the electrical state of the machine's circuitry, "on" and "off." This two-state system is known as a **binary system,** and its use to represent data is known as **binary representation.**

The **binary (base 2) number system** operates in a manner similar to the way the familiar **decimal (base 10) number system** works. For example, the decimal number 4,672 can be analyzed as follows:

4 6 7 2

$$2 \times 10^0 = 2$$
$$7 \times 10^1 = 70$$
$$6 \times 10^2 = 600$$
$$4 \times 10^3 = 4000$$
$$4672$$

or

4	6	7	2
10^3	10^2	10^1	10^0

Each position represents a certain power of 10. The progression of powers is from right to left; that is, digits further to the left in a decimal number represent larger powers of 10 than digits to the right of them (see Figure 4–9).

The same principle holds for binary representation. The difference is that in binary representation each position in the number represents a power of 2. For example, consider the decimal number 14. In binary, the value equivalent to 14 is written as follows (see Figure 4–10):

1 1 1 0

$$0 \times 2^0 = 0$$
$$1 \times 2^1 = 2$$
$$1 \times 2^2 = 4$$
$$1 \times 2^3 = 8$$
$$14$$

or

1	1	1	0
2^3	2^2	2^1	2^0

As further example, the value represented by the decimal number 300 is represented in binary form below:

1 0 0 1 0 1 1 0 0

$$0 \times 2^0 = 0$$
$$0 \times 2^1 = 0$$
$$1 \times 2^2 = 4$$
$$1 \times 2^3 = 8$$
$$0 \times 2^4 = 0$$
$$1 \times 2^5 = 32$$
$$0 \times 2^6 = 0$$
$$0 \times 2^7 = 0$$
$$1 \times 2^8 = 256$$
$$300$$

or

1	0	0	1	0	1	1	0	0
2^8	2^7	2^6	2^5	2^4	2^3	2^2	2^1	2^0

10^5	10^4	10^3	10^2	10^1	10^0
100,000	10,000	1,000	100	10	1

FIGURE 4–9
Decimal Place Values

FIGURE 4–10
Binary Place Values

2^6	2^5	2^4	2^3	2^2	2^1	2^0
64	32	16	8	4	2	1

As indicated by the examples above, the binary number system uses 1s and 0s in various combinations to represent various values. Each digit position in a binary number is called a **bit,** as defined previously. A 1 in a bit position indicates the presence of a specific power of 2; a 0 indicates the absence of a specific power. As in the decimal number system, the progression of powers is from right to left.

Hexadecimal Number System

When a program fails to execute correctly, it is sometimes necessary to examine the contents of certain memory locations to discover what went wrong. In such cases, the programmer often finds it useful to have a printout, or **dump,** of the contents of the memory locations (see Figure 4–11). If everything were printed in binary representation, the programmer would be staring at pages upon pages of 1s and 0s. Detection of errors would be difficult, since binary numbers are difficult to read, write, and remember.

To alleviate this problem, the contents of storage locations in computers can be represented by symbols of the **hexadecimal (base 16) number system.** In the hexadecimal number system, sixteen symbols are used to represent the digits 0 through 15 (see Figure 4–12). Note that the letters A through F designate the numbers 10 through 15. The fact that each position in a hexadecimal number represents a power of 16 allows for easy conversion from binary to hexadecimal, since 16 is equal to 2^4. A single hexadecimal digit can be represented in four binary digits.

FIGURE 4–11
Core Dump

```
9000D203 9000C11E 41330004 4650C05A
0010E020 C1220064 E020C186 006407FE
40F0F740 40F0F840 4040F540 40F2F340
40404040 40404040 40F2F340 40F2F340
40F4F640 40F2F540 40F1F240 40F2F440
4040F640 40F6F640 40F8F540 40404040
40F0F840 40F2F540 40F3F140 4040F540
F2F5F640 F7F8F940 F1F2F540 F6F2F440
00000005 00000005 00000006 00000007
0000000F 00000010 00000015 00000017
00000018 00000018 00000019 00000019
00000035 00000035 00000037 00000038
00000055 00000055 00000060 0000007D
0000022B 0000022B 0000022B 0000022B
0000022B 00000315 F0E3C8C5 40E4D5E2
E2D6D9E3 C5C440C1 D9D9C1E8 F1F5F5F5
F5F5F5F5 F5F5F5F5 F5F5F5F5 F5F5F5F5
F5F5F5F5 F5F5F5F5 F5F5F5F5 F5F5F5F5
```

BINARY SYSTEM (PLACE VALUES)				HEXADECIMAL EQUIVALENT	DECIMAL EQUIVALENT
8	4	2	1		
0	0	0	0	0	0
0	0	0	1	1	1
0	0	1	0	2	2
0	0	1	1	3	3
0	1	0	0	4	4
0	1	0	1	5	5
0	1	1	0	6	6
0	1	1	1	7	7
1	0	0	0	8	8
1	0	0	1	9	9
1	0	1	0	A	10
1	0	1	1	B	11
1	1	0	0	C	12
1	1	0	1	D	13
1	1	1	0	E	14
1	1	1	1	F	15

FIGURE 4–12
Binary, Hexadecimal, and Decimal Equivalent Values

Computer Codes

Many computers use coding schemes other than simple binary notation to represent numbers. One of the most basic coding schemes is called **4–bit binary coded decimal (BCD).** Rather than represent a decimal number as a string of 0s and 1s (which gets increasingly complicated for large numbers), BCD represents each decimal digit in a number by using four bits. For instance, the decimal number 23 is represented by two groups of four bits, one group for the 2, the other for the 3. Representations of the number 23 in 4–bit BCD and in binary are compared below:

0 0 1 0   0 0 1 1   4-bit BCD
2   3
0000000000010111   Binary

The representation of a three-digit decimal number in 4–bit BCD consists of three sets of four bits, or twelve binary digits. For example, the decimal number 637 is coded as follows:

0 1 1 0   0 0 1 1   0 1 1 1   4-bit BCD
6   3   7
0000001001111101   Binary

Another approach to data representation is an 8–bit code known as **Extended Binary Coded Decimal Interchange Code (EBCDIC).** The 8–bit EBCDIC can be used to represent uppercase and lowercase letters and additional special characters, such as the cent sign and the quotation mark. The EBCDIC bit combinations for uppercase letters and numbers are given in Figure 4–13. In EBCDIC, the four leftmost bit positions are zone bits and the four rightmost bit positions are numeric bits. The zone bits are used in various combinations with the numeric bits to represent numbers, letters, and special characters.

The **American Standard Code for Information Interchange (ASCII)** is a 7–bit code developed with the cooperation of several computer manufacturers whose objective was to develop a standard code for all computers (see Figure 4–14). Because certain machines are designed to accept 8–bit rather than 7–bit code patterns, an 8–bit verson of ASCII, called ASCII–8 was created. ASCII–8 and EBCDIC are similar, the key difference between them being in the bit patterns used to represent certain characters.

Bits, as described, are very small units of data; it is often useful to combine them into larger units. A fixed number of adjacent bits operated on as a unit is called a **byte.** Since eight bits are sufficient to represent any character, 8–bit groupings are the basic units of memory. In computers that accept 8–bit characters, a byte is a group of eight adjacent bits.

When large amounts of storage are described, the symbol **K** is often used. Generally, one K equals 1,024 (2^{10}) units. Thus, a computer that has 256K bytes of storage can store 256 × 1,024 or 262,144, characters.

FIGURE 4–13
EBCDIC Representation: A–Z, 0–9

Character	EBCDIC Bit Configuration	Character	EBCDIC Bit Configuration
A	1100 0001	S	1110 0010
B	1100 0010	T	1110 0011
C	1100 0011	U	1110 0100
D	1100 0100	V	1110 0101
E	1100 0101	W	1110 0110
F	1100 0110	X	1110 0111
G	1100 0111	Y	1110 1000
H	1100 1000	Z	1110 1001
I	1100 1001	0	1111 0000
J	1101 0001	1	1111 0001
K	1101 0010	2	1111 0010
L	1101 0011	3	1111 0011
M	1101 0100	4	1111 0100
N	1101 0101	5	1111 0101
O	1101 0110	6	1111 0110
P	1101 0111	7	1111 0111
Q	1101 1000	8	1111 1000
R	1101 1001	9	1111 1001

Character	ASCII Bit Configuration	Character	ASCII Bit Configuration
A	1000001	S	1010011
B	1000010	T	1010100
C	1000011	U	1010101
D	1000100	V	1010110
E	1000101	W	1010111
F	1000110	X	1011000
G	1000111	Y	1011001
H	1001000	Z	1011010
I	1001001	0	0110000
J	1001010	1	0110001
K	1001011	2	0110010
L	1001100	3	0110011
M	1001101	4	0110100
N	1001110	5	0110101
O	1001111	6	0110110
P	1010000	7	0110111
Q	1010001	8	0111000
R	1010010	9	0111001

FIGURE 4–14
ASCII Representation: A–Z, 0–9

Code Checking

Computers do not always function perfectly; errors can and do occur. To detect when an error has occurred, most computers have at each storage location an additional bit, called a **parity bit** or **check bit.** Internal circuitry in the computer constantly monitors its operations by checking to ensure that the required number of bits is present in each location. If a parity error is detected, the system may retry the read or write operation occurring when the error was detected. If retries are unsuccessful, the system informs the computer operator that an error has occurred.

The checking circuitry of the computer can detect only certain miscoding of characters. It cannot detect the use of incorrect data.

SUMMARY POINTS

- Computers are usually classified as either digital or analog. Digital computers operate on discrete bits of data (numbers or letters are the most common). Analog computers measure continuous physical or electrical magnitudes such as pressure or temperature. They are less accurate than digital computers.
- The central processing unit (CPU) is the heart of the computer. It is composed of three parts: primary storage unit, the arithmetic-logic unit (ALU), and the control unit. The control unit maintains order and controls the CPU's operation. The ALU is used to perform arithmetic and logical opera-

tions. The primary storage unit holds all data, instructions, and output necessary for processing.

- Instructions are placed in consecutive locations in memory so that they can be accessed and executed consecutively. This process is called the next-sequential-instruction feature.
- The stored-program concept involves storing both data and instructions in the computer's memory. This allows the computer to process at its own speed.
- Nondestructive read/destructive write allows data and instructions to be reread as many times as required for processing until new data or instructions are placed over them.
- The CPU accesses data and instructions in storage using a unique address. Variables, symbolic names for storage addresses, are often used by programmers to facilitate data location.
- Data and instructions can be stored in memory several ways. Magnetic cores store data in the way they are magnetized. Semiconductor storage indicates the value of data by whether or not it passes current. Bubble memory stores data as magnetized spots.
- Read-only memory (ROM) stores data or instructions in a form that cannot be deleted or changed. Microprograms are sequences of instructions built into read-only memory to carry out functions that otherwise would be directed by stored-program instructions at a much slower speed.
- Programmable read-only memory (PROM) is much the same as ROM, except the initial programming of its memory can be done either by the manufacturer or the user. It provides greater flexibility and versatility than ROM.
- Registers are temporary holding areas for data and instructions. They facilitate receiving, holding, and transferring information as directed by the control unit of the CPU.
- Data is represented in the computer on the basis of a two-state, or binary system. A 1 in a given position indicates the presence of a power of 2, a 0 indicates its absence. Special numbering schemes have been developed to group bits in order to facilitate processing and interpreting binary numbers.
- Hexadecimal (base 16) can be used to represent binary data in a concise form. Memory dumps are often printed in hexadecimal for this reason.
- Binary Coded Decimal (BCD) represents numbers using a 4–bit scheme.
- ASCII is a 7–bit code developed with manufacturers' cooperation whose objective was to develop a standard code for all computers.
- Both EBCDIC and ASCII–8 are 8–bit coding schemes.
- Parity bits, or check bits, are used to detect errors in the transmission of data.

REVIEW QUESTIONS

1. Illustrate the difference between analog and digital computers using examples.

2. Discuss the three main components of the CPU. Trace the steps involved in processing a data item. How would the computer process an instruction to multiply ITEM COST by TAX?
3. Explain what the memory characteristic called nondestructive read/destructive write means.
4. What is a variable in programming?
5. Discuss the several types of primary storage. What are the advantages and disadvantages of each?
6. Explain the concept of read-only memory. How does it relate to microprogramming?
7. The stored-program concept was a major discovery. Explain what the stored-program concept is and discuss why it is so important. How were programs processed before this concept was used?
8. Describe the next-sequential-instruction feature. How can this be changed?
9. Convert these binary values to decimal numbers: (a) 10010100, (b) 11111, and (c) 1001101.
10. Convert these decimal numbers into 4–bit BCD code: 14, 383, 9, 1576.
11. What is a K of storage?

Hardware

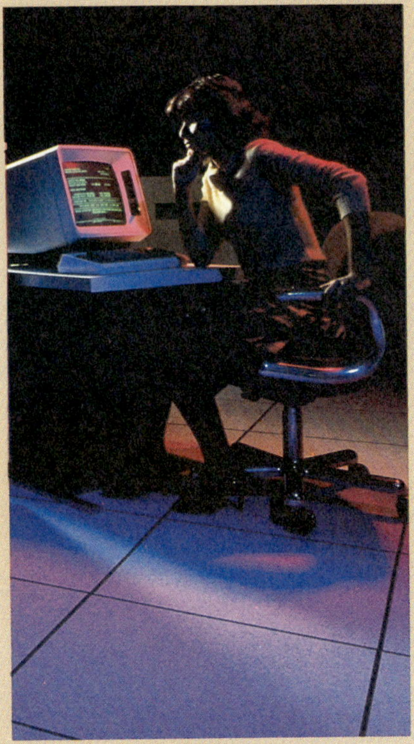

When people discuss the differences between microcomputers and main frames, the most obvious is sheer physical size. A main frame can fill a room, while a typical microcomputer fits nicely on a desk top. There are, however, other differences as well.

At the heart of a microcomputer we find the microprocessor, which is a single, integrated circuit that contains an arithmetic/logic unit as well as control capability for memory and input/output access. It is small enough to fit on a fingertip. Its counterpart, on the other hand, the central processing unit (CPU) of a main frame, is composed of a series of integrated circuits and is much more sophisticated than the microprocessor.

Looking closer at the CPU of a main frame, we find that it has a larger repertoire of more complex instructions and that the central processing unit cycle time, or how fast these instructions can be carried out, is much faster than in microcomputers. This is partly because instructions or data can be retrieved from main memory (memory cycle) much faster in a main frame. A main frame allows for greater word length, which means that more data can be transferred at one time and execution is more efficient. The IBM 370/3033, for example, has a word size of sixty-four bits, while the typical microcomputer has a word size of only eight or sixteen bits. A microcomputer may take several steps just to perform a given operation that a main frame can accomplish in one instruction. The larger word size of the main frame permits a bigger instruction set, access to more memory in a single step, and more rapid large-number arithmetic.

The number and size of *registers* are significant factors in any general-purpose computer. Registers are devices that receive information, hold it, and transfer it very quickly. As mentioned earlier in this chapter, they are designed primarily for temporary storage. Registers are an important key in determining the sophistication of a computer. Their size is based on word size. Because microcomputers have smaller word size and also fewer registers, they are less precise and far slower than main frames. Moreover, there are differences to be found even among microcomputers: Atari, Apple II, VIC 20, and TRS-80 Model III use an eight-bit word size; IBM Personal Computer, Apple III, and TRS-80 Model 16 use a sixteen-bit word size; and the Hewlett-Packard 3000 uses a twenty-four-bit word size.

Another difference between microcomputers and main frames is that microcomputers have only one communication channel connecting the disk units to the computer, which causes the microcomputer to be slower. Main frames introduce *parallelism,* a method where several channels are available for simultaneous data movement, with each channel itself able to transfer more data. Thus main frames allow for multiple users, while microcomputers allow for only one user at a time.

Since primary storage is much larger in main frames, it enables them to manipulate large arrays of data. In applications limited to pure number crunching (the manipulation of large amounts of numbers) associated with large-scale scientific calculations, and in applications involving file management associated with large-scale data bases, the information processors must of necessity be large scale. This is because long word lengths and high execution speeds facilitate long calculations and rapid data searches.

The major advantage of microcomputers is that of cost. Because they are dedicated to one person and/or one task, the operating system is less complex as compared to main frames; this substantially reduces the cost. The prefix "micro" should be interpreted in terms of size and cost rather than capability.

Microcomputers are very powerful in proportion to their size and equal the power of the earlier main frames. To more fully understand the power of the current group of personal computers, let's compare them to a main frame computer of twenty years ago. The IBM 360 Model 30 main frame introduced in the early '60s and today's IBM Personal Computer will serve as our examples. The 360 Model 30 required an air-conditioned room about 18 feet square to house the central processing unit, the control console, a printer, and the desk for a keypunch operator. In addition, the CPU, which was 5 feet high and 6 feet wide, had to be water cooled to prevent overheating. It cost $280,000 in 1960s dollars and could perform 33,000 additions per second at full speed.

In contrast, the CPU of IBM's desktop personal computer is inscribed on a silicon chip smaller than a fingernail. Fully equipped, it costs between $4000 and $5000 and will do 700,000 additions per second. Although microcomputers don't require an air-conditioned room, prolonged use can generate enough heat to require the use of a small fan, which now comes as a standard option with many microcomputers.

For those who would like faster results, there are now chips that can actually speed up the processing capabilities of your microcomputer. Other available microcomputer hardware includes a device that can be added to the existing internal hardware to make your computer work like two computers in one. An example is the SoftCard by Microsoft Computer Products. Designed for the Apple, it allows you to add a Z-80 microprocessor and CP/M operating system that would otherwise not be available for your system.

Other manufacturers are also offering expansion devices. Tecmar Inc., for example, has a complete line of expansion devices for the IBM Personal Computer. Included are devices that increase memory and expand disk capacity by allowing the addition of hard-disk drives. Also, there are practical expansion devices such as a time-of-day calendar, a voice synthesizer, and a device to control lights and appliances.

Although microcomputers are still not as powerful as today's larger computers, the differences will continue to diminish as microcomputers acquire more speed, larger word sizes, larger memory, and more software.

DISCUSSION QUESTIONS

1. Describe some of the differences between main frames and microcomputers.
2. In what type of applications would you use a main frame? A microcomputer?

CHAPTER 5

Communicating with the Computer: Input/Output Devices

INTRODUCTION

A computer system entails much more than just a central processing unit. Data must be provided to the computer in a form it can recognize, and output translated into a form humans understand. Input and output are important activities in any computer-based system because they are the communication links between people and machines. If these people/machine interfaces are weak, the overall performance of the computer system suffers accordingly.

This chapter discusses the various forms input to the computer may take. In addition, newer developments that utilize input devices to communicate directly with the computer (a phenomenon called source-data automation) are discussed. The chapter concludes with a discussion of output devices, including printers and special-purpose output.

FACING PAGE
The daisy print wheel is composed of a set of spokes, each one containing a character. Used on a daisy wheel printer, the wheel rotates until the desired character is then placed where a hammer mechanism presses the character against a ribbon and paper to make the image.

CHAPTER OUTLINE

PUNCHED CARDS

Punched cards were used in data processing long before the digital computer was developed, as we saw in Chapter 2. Today punched cards serve not only as a means of entering data into computers but also as user-oriented documents—time cards, bills, invoices, checks, and the like. The standard punched card has eighty vertical columns and twelve horizontal rows (see Figure 5–1). Data is recorded as a set of holes punched in a particular column to represent a given character. The pattern of holes used to represent characters is known as the **Hollerith code,** after its inventor, Herman Hollerith. Figure 5–2 shows an example of a punched card used to record the sale of an item.

Data is most commonly recorded on punched cards with the use of a **keypunch** (see Figure 5–3). An operator reads a source document and transcribes the data from the document into cards by pressing keys on a keyboard, much as if he or she were using a typewriter. The machine automatically feeds, positions, and stacks the cards, thus allowing the operator to concentrate on the keying operation. Even with these automatic functions, keypunching can be quite costly. One person is needed to operate each machine, and much time is spent keying data.

FIGURE 5–1
Eighty-Column Punched Card and Hollerith Code

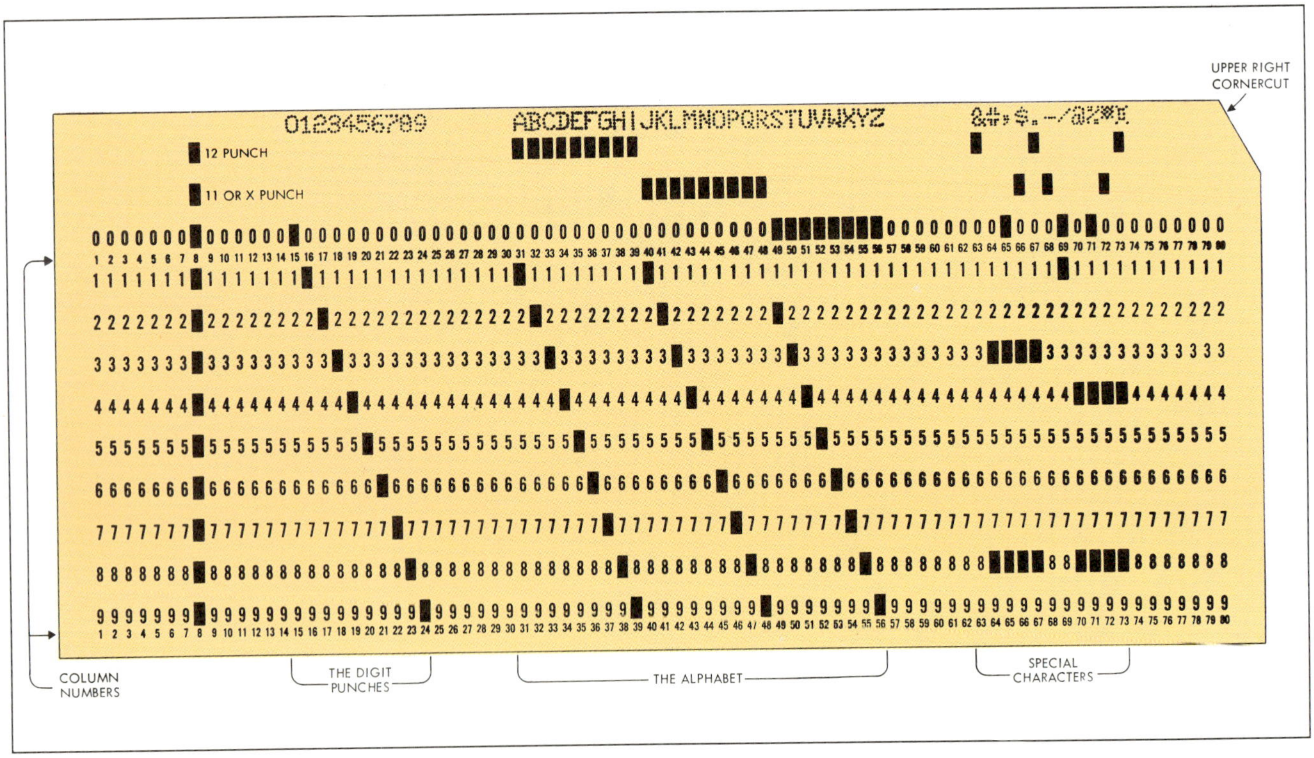

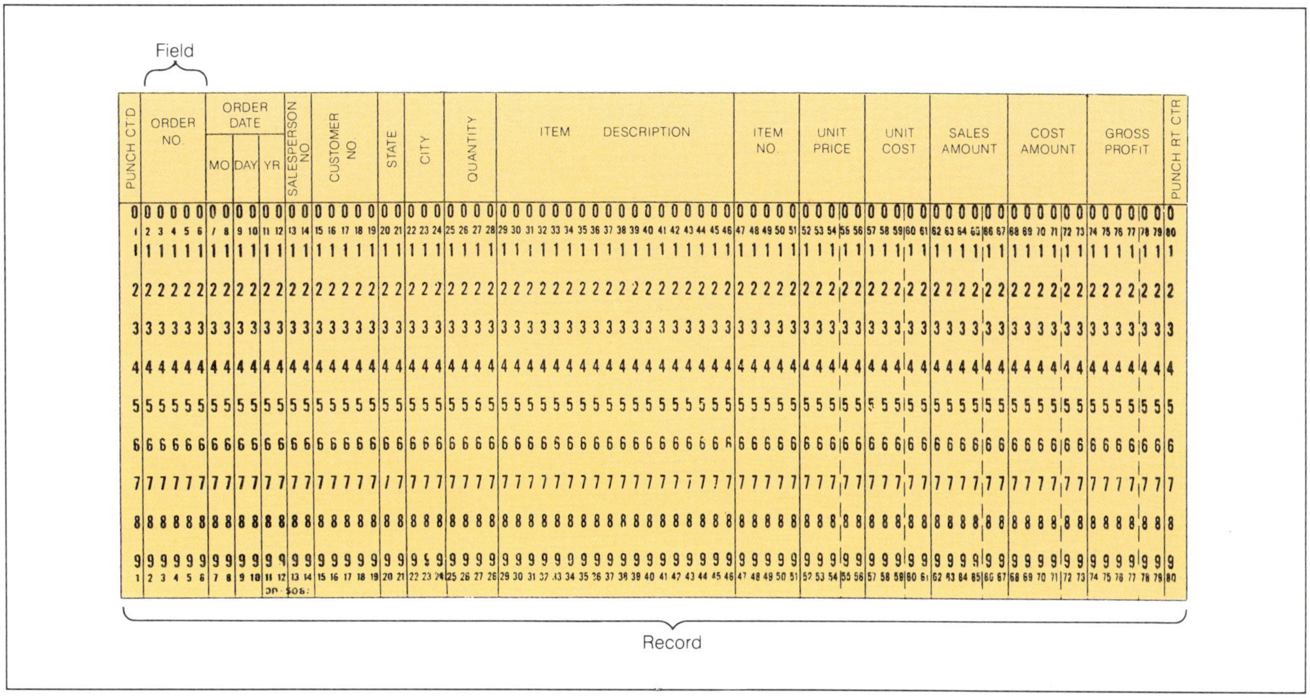

FIGURE 5–2
Punched-Card Record

KEY-TO-MAGNETIC MEDIA

Punched-card systems require much mechanized movement and have many limitations. New methods have been developed to record and enter data using magnetic media such as **magnetic tape** or **magnetic disks** rather than cards. In this process, data is entered in much the same fashion as with the keypunch, but it is stored not as punches on cards but as magnetized spots on the surface of a tape or disk. The data can be stored indefinitely because the spots retain their magnetism. Unlike punched cards, data can be replaced with new data when desired. Tapes and disks can also store much more data in a smaller space; for example, as many as 6,250 characters are commonly stored on one inch of magnetic tape. Data stored on tape or disk can be read into the CPU hundreds of times faster than data on cards. Thus, use of magnetic tape or disk can significantly increase the efficiency of data-processing operations. Most **key-to-tape** systems will eventually be replaced by disks or diskettes as a result of advancing technology.

A typical **key-to-disk** configuration consists of several keying devices, all of which are connected to a minicomputer. Data is recorded onto magnetic disks (see Figure 5–4). Before that, however, it is usually edited by the minicomputer. This editing is directed by the minicomputer's stored-program instructions. If an error is detected, the system interrupts the operator and "stands by" until a correction has been entered. The correct data is then stored on the magnetic disk for input to the computer.

An increasingly popular data-entry system is the **key-to-diskette** system. A flexible (or floppy) diskette is used instead of the conventional (hard) disk.

FIGURE 5–3
Keypunch

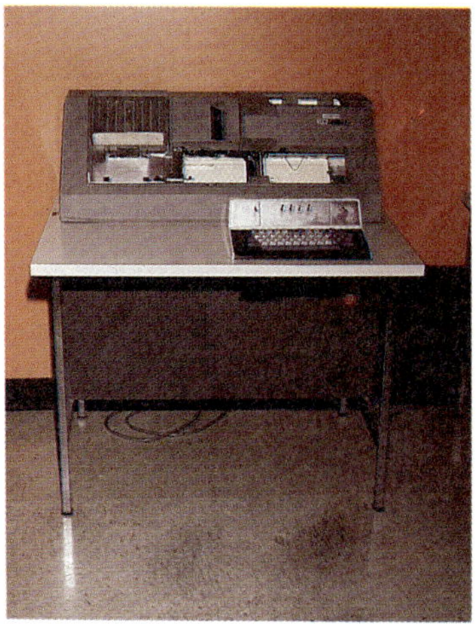

HIGHLIGHT
Ski School Computer

Because its ski school is a major source of income, the Mammoth Mountain Ski Area in California relies on a computer to maximize this important resource. The computer gives the school director a daily and weekly comparison of the school's performance this year with last. It specifies enrollment breakdowns and areas of demand so that instructors can be shifted to where they're needed most, and it computes the payroll for each instructor according to the individual rate and amount of work done. Since the system was installed, personnel spend about 60 percent less time keeping records and gathering information—but they have access to about ten times as much useful information as they had had before.

The data is entered on a keyboard, displayed on a screen for the operator to check, and recorded on the diskette. A key-to-diskette system can operate by itself or with a group of similar devices as described above.

While key-to-tape, -disk, and -diskette systems offer many advantages over punched-card input, they also cost more. Generally, these systems are cost-effective where large amounts of data are prepared for processing on medium-sized or large computers.

SOURCE-DATA AUTOMATION

Data entry has traditionally been the weakest link in the chain of data-processing operations. Although data can be processed electronically at extremely high speeds, significantly more time is required to prepare it and enter it into the computer system.

Consider a computer system that uses punched cards for data input. The data is first written on some type of coding form or source document. Then it is keypunched onto cards by an operator. Next, the keypunched data may be **verified** (checked for accuracy) by duplicating the entire keypunching operation. Incorrect cards must be keypunched and verified a second time. After all data has been recorded correctly on cards, other operations may be required before the cards can be read into the computer. For instance, card files may be copied onto magnetic tape using a special program for later input to the computer, because magnetic-tape files can be read into the computer much faster than card files.

FIGURE 5–4
Key-to-Disk System

This method of entering data into the computer is time-consuming and expensive. Some organizations have turned to the key-to-tape, -disk, or -diskette systems described above to simplify keypunching operations. Another approach to data collection and preparation is also gaining in popularity; it is called **source-data automation.** The purpose of source-data automation is to collect data about an event, in computer-readable form, when and where the event takes place. By eliminating the intermediate steps used in preparing card input, source-data automation improves the speed, accuracy, and efficiency of data-processing operations (see Figure 5–5).

Source-data automation is implemented by use of a variety of methods. Each requires special machines for reading data and converting it into machine language. The most common approaches to source-data automation are discussed below.

Magnetic-Ink Character Recognition

Magnetic ink was introduced in the late 1950s to facilitate check processing by the banking industry. Because magnetic-ink characters can be read by

FIGURE 5–5
Typical Methods of Source-Data Automation

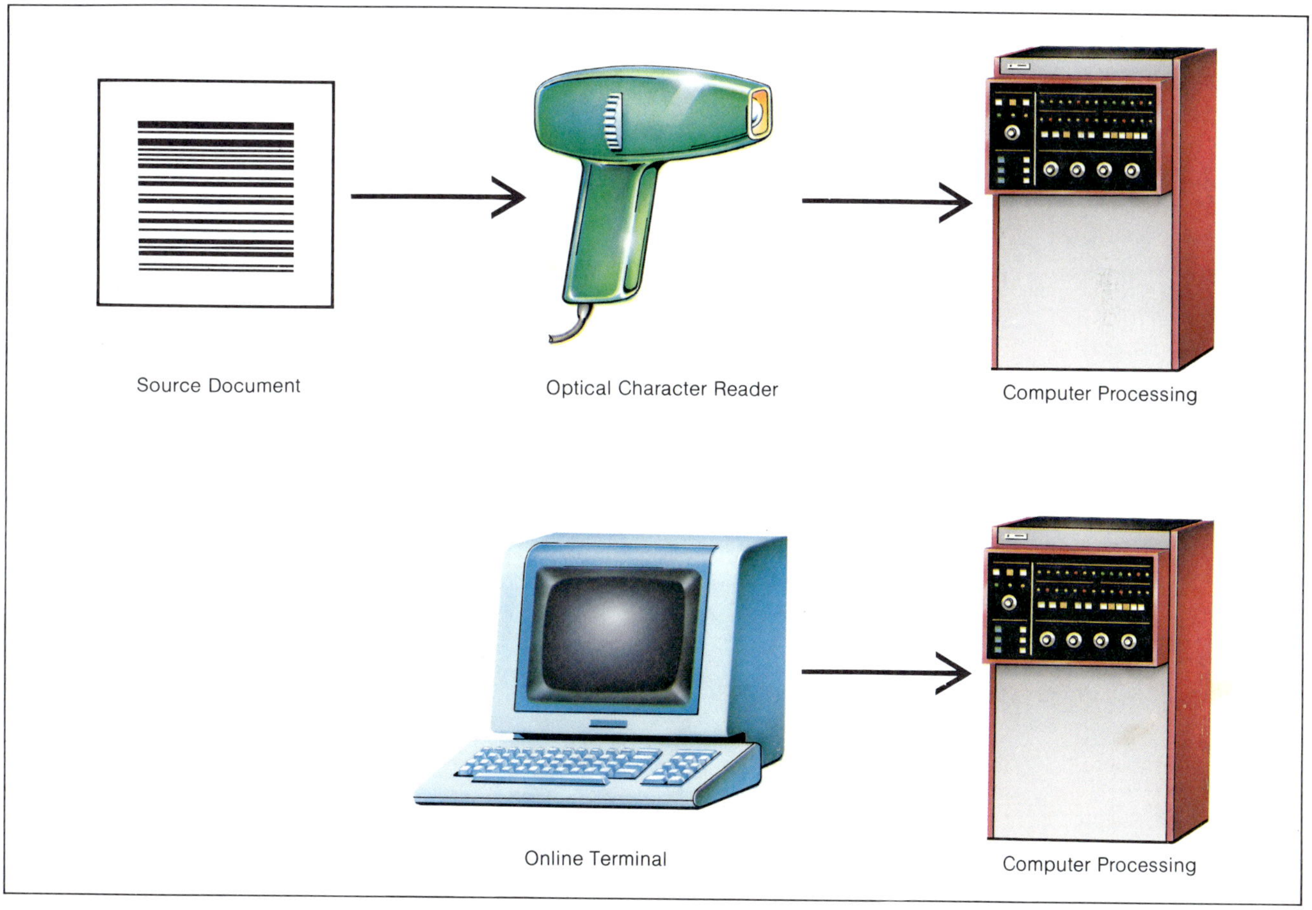

both humans and machines (see Figure 5–6), no special data conversion step is needed. Magnetic-ink characters are formed with magnetized particles of iron oxide. Each character is composed of certain sections of a seventy-section matrix (see Figure 5–7). The characters can be read and interpreted by a **magnetic-ink character reader;** this process is called **magnetic-ink character recognition (MICR).**

All magnetic-ink characters on checks are formed with the standard fourteen-character set (shown in Figure 5–6) as seen in Figure 5–8. (Other character sets may be used in other applications.) As the checks are fed into the MICR device, it reads them and sorts them by bank number at a Federal Reserve Bank and by account number at the issuing bank. In this manner, checks are routed back to each issuing bank and then back to its customers. Between 750 and 1,500 checks per minute can be read and sorted by an MICR system.

HIGHLIGHT
The Songwriter's Helper

A young Canadian musician, David McLey, has invented a computer-based instrument that could be a boon to every songwriter. He calls his invention the McLeyvier and says it will sell for between $22,000 and $55,000, depending on the additions each buyer demands. Featuring a piano-like keyboard and a magnetic disk memory that can store at least six hours of music, the McLeyvier remembers all the sounds the musician plays and all the modifications made in the creative process. It also displays the actual musical score on a video screen as it is being composed. The user need not even know how to read and write music.

Optical Recognition

Optical recognition devices can read marks or symbols coded on paper documents and convert them into electrical pulses. The pulses can then be transmitted directly to the CPU or stored on magnetic tape for input at a later time.

The simplest approach to optical recognition is known as **optical-mark recognition (OMR),** or **mark-sensing.** This approach is often used for machine scoring of multiple-choice examinations (see Figure 5–9), where a person taking the examination makes a mark with a heavy lead pencil in the location corresponding to each desired answer. The marks on an OMR document are sensed by an **optical-mark page reader** as the document passes under a light source. The presence of marks in specific locations is indicated by light reflected at those locations. As the document is read, the optical-mark data is translated into machine language. When the optical-mark page reader is directly connected to the computer, up to 2000 forms of the same type can be read and processed in an hour.

Another type of optical reader, known as a **bar-code reader,** can read special line, or bar, codes—patterns of optical marks. Some bar codes in use today are shown in Figure 5–10. They are suitable for many applications, including **point-of-sale (POS)** systems (discussed later in this chapter), credit card verification, and freight identification to facilitate warehouse operations.

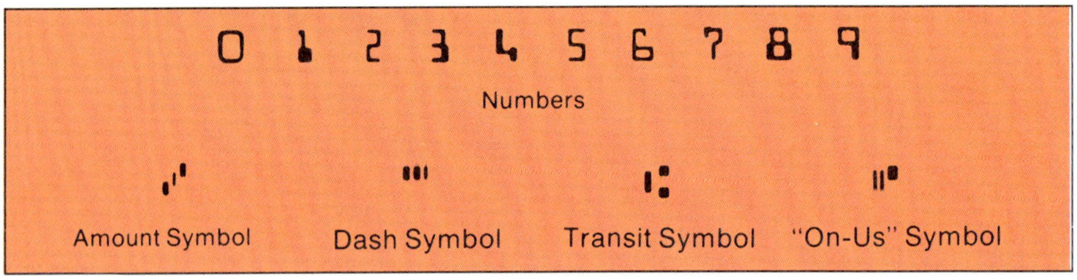

FIGURE 5–6
Magnetic-Ink Character Set

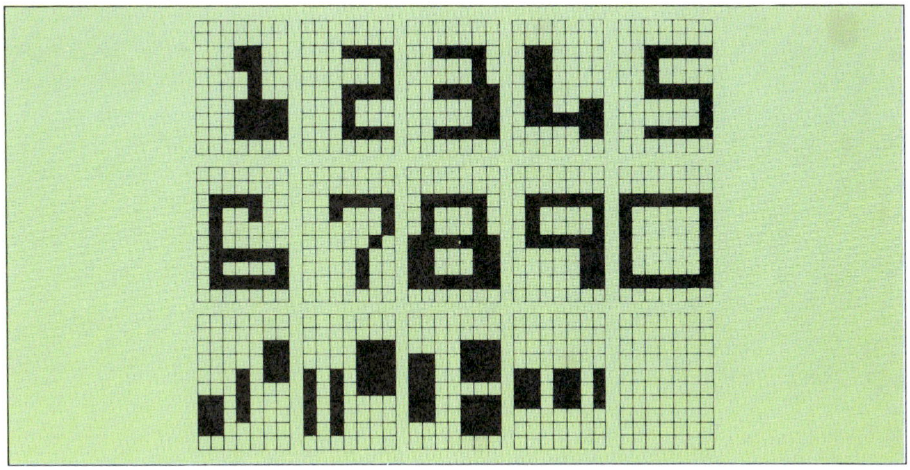

FIGURE 5–7
Matrix Patterns for Magnetic Ink Characters

Data is represented in a bar code by the widths of the bars and the distances between them. Probably the most familiar bar code is the **Universal Product Code (UPC)** found on most grocery items. This code consists of ten pairs of vertical bars that represent both the manufacturer's identity and the identity of the item but not the item's price. The code for each product is a unique combination of these vertical bars.

Optical-character readers can read special types of characters known as **optical characters.** Some **optical-character recognition (OCR)** devices can

FIGURE 5–8
Sample Check with Magnetic-Ink Characters

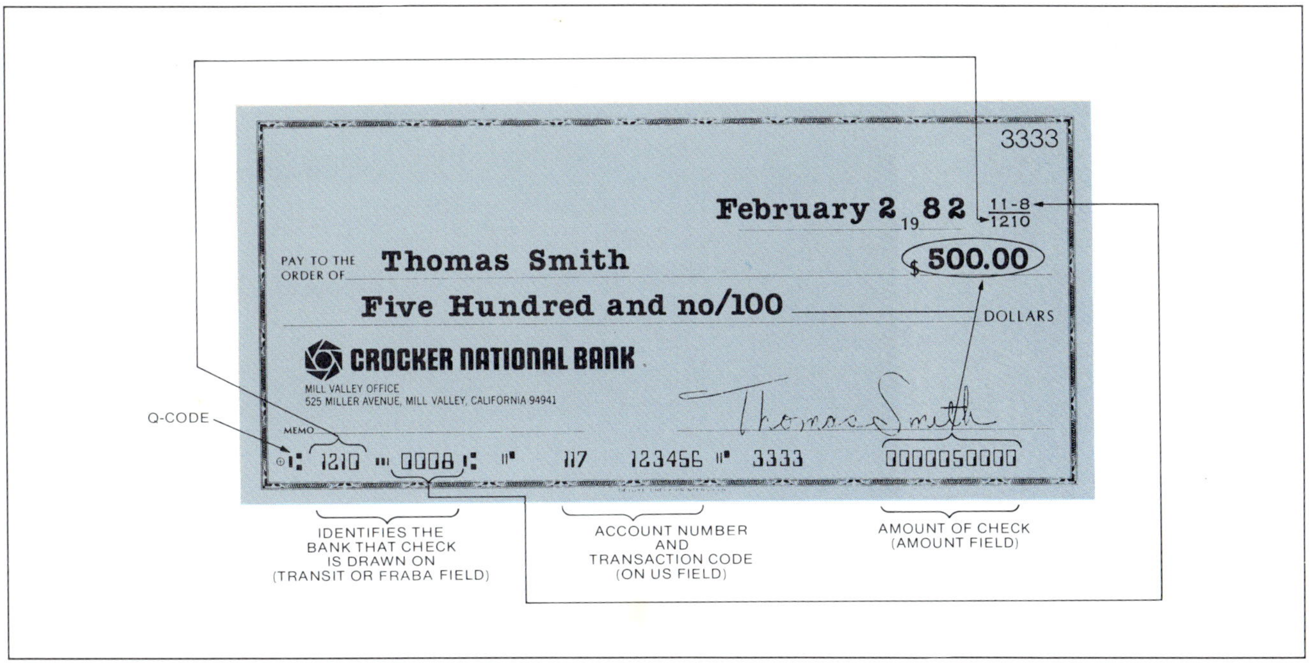

FIGURE 5–9
Optical-Mark Recognition

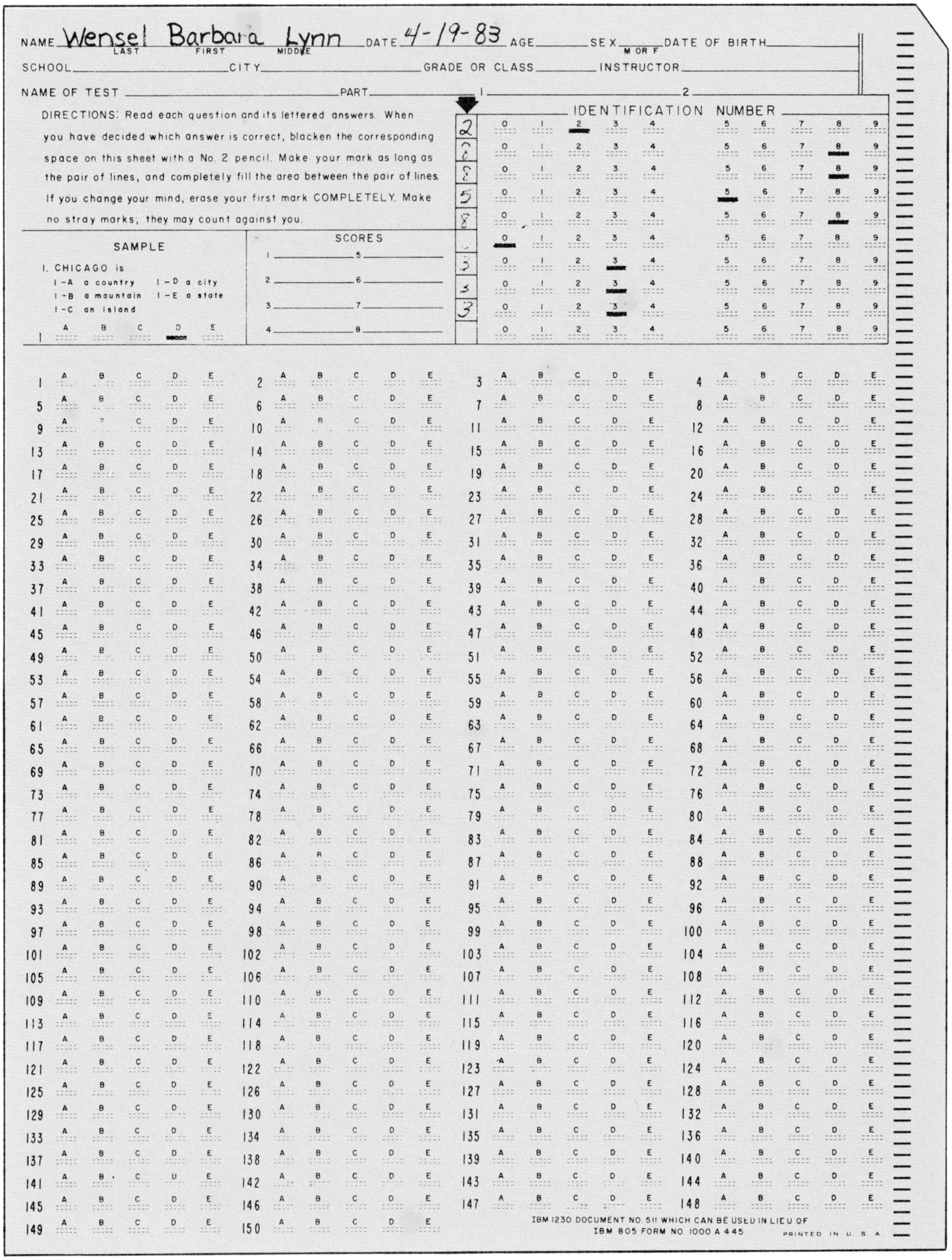
NAME Wensel Barbara Lynn (LAST FIRST MIDDLE) DATE 4-19-83 AGE ____ SEX ____ (M OR F) DATE OF BIRTH ____

SCHOOL ____ CITY ____ GRADE OR CLASS ____ INSTRUCTOR ____

NAME OF TEST ____ PART ____ 1 ____ 2 ____

DIRECTIONS: Read each question and its lettered answers. When you have decided which answer is correct, blacken the corresponding space on this sheet with a No. 2 pencil. Make your mark as long as the pair of lines, and completely fill the area between the pair of lines. If you change your mind, erase your first mark COMPLETELY. Make no stray marks; they may count against you.

IDENTIFICATION NUMBER
2 8 8 5 8 0 3 3 3

SAMPLE
I. CHICAGO is
I-A a country I-D a city
I-B a mountain I-E a state
I-C an island
I A B C D E

SCORES
1 ____ 5 ____
2 ____ 6 ____
3 ____ 7 ____
4 ____ 8 ____

1 A B C D E 2 A B C D E 3 A B C D E 4 A B C D E
5 A B C D E 6 A B C D E 7 A B C D E 8 A B C D E
9 A B C D E 10 A B C D E 11 A B C D E 12 A B C D E
13 A B C D E 14 A B C D E 15 A B C D E 16 A B C D E
17 A B C D E 18 A B C D E 19 A B C D E 20 A B C D E
21 A B C D E 22 A B C D E 23 A B C D E 24 A B C D E
25 A B C D E 26 A B C D E 27 A B C D E 28 A B C D E
29 A B C D E 30 A B C D E 31 A B C D E 32 A B C D E
33 A B C D E 34 A B C D E 35 A B C D E 36 A B C D E
37 A B C D E 38 A B C D E 39 A B C D E 40 A B C D E
41 A B C D E 42 A B C D E 43 A B C D E 44 A B C D E
45 A B C D E 46 A B C D E 47 A B C D E 48 A B C D E
49 A B C D E 50 A B C D E 51 A B C D E 52 A B C D E
53 A B C D E 54 A B C D E 55 A B C D E 56 A B C D E
57 A B C D E 58 A B C D E 59 A B C D E 60 A B C D E
61 A B C D E 62 A B C D E 63 A B C D E 64 A B C D E
65 A B C D E 66 A B C D E 67 A B C D E 68 A B C D E
69 A B C D E 70 A B C D E 71 A B C D E 72 A B C D E
73 A B C D E 74 A B C D E 75 A B C D E 76 A B C D E
77 A B C D E 78 A B C D E 79 A B C D E 80 A B C D E
81 A B C D E 82 A B C D E 83 A B C D E 84 A B C D E
85 A B C D E 86 A B C D E 87 A B C D E 88 A B C D E
89 A B C D E 90 A B C D E 91 A B C D E 92 A B C D E
93 A B C D E 94 A B C D E 95 A B C D E 96 A B C D E
97 A B C D E 98 A B C D E 99 A B C D E 100 A B C D E
101 A B C D E 102 A B C D E 103 A B C D E 104 A B C D E
105 A B C D E 106 A B C D E 107 A B C D E 108 A B C D E
109 A B C D E 110 A B C D E 111 A B C D E 112 A B C D E
113 A B C D E 114 A B C D E 115 A B C D E 116 A B C D E
117 A B C D E 118 A B C D E 119 A B C D E 120 A B C D E
121 A B C D E 122 A B C D E 123 A B C D E 124 A B C D E
125 A B C D E 126 A B C D E 127 A B C D E 128 A B C D E
129 A B C D E 130 A B C D E 131 A B C D E 132 A B C D E
133 A B C D E 134 A B C D E 135 A B C D E 136 A B C D E
137 A B C D E 138 A B C D E 139 A B C D E 140 A B C D E
141 A B C D E 142 A B C D E 143 A B C D E 144 A B C D E
145 A B C D E 146 A B C D E 147 A B C D E 148 A B C D E
149 A B C D E 150 A B C D E

IBM 1230 DOCUMENT NO. 511 WHICH CAN BE USED IN LIEU OF IBM 805 FORM NO. 1000 A 445

PRINTED IN U. S. A.

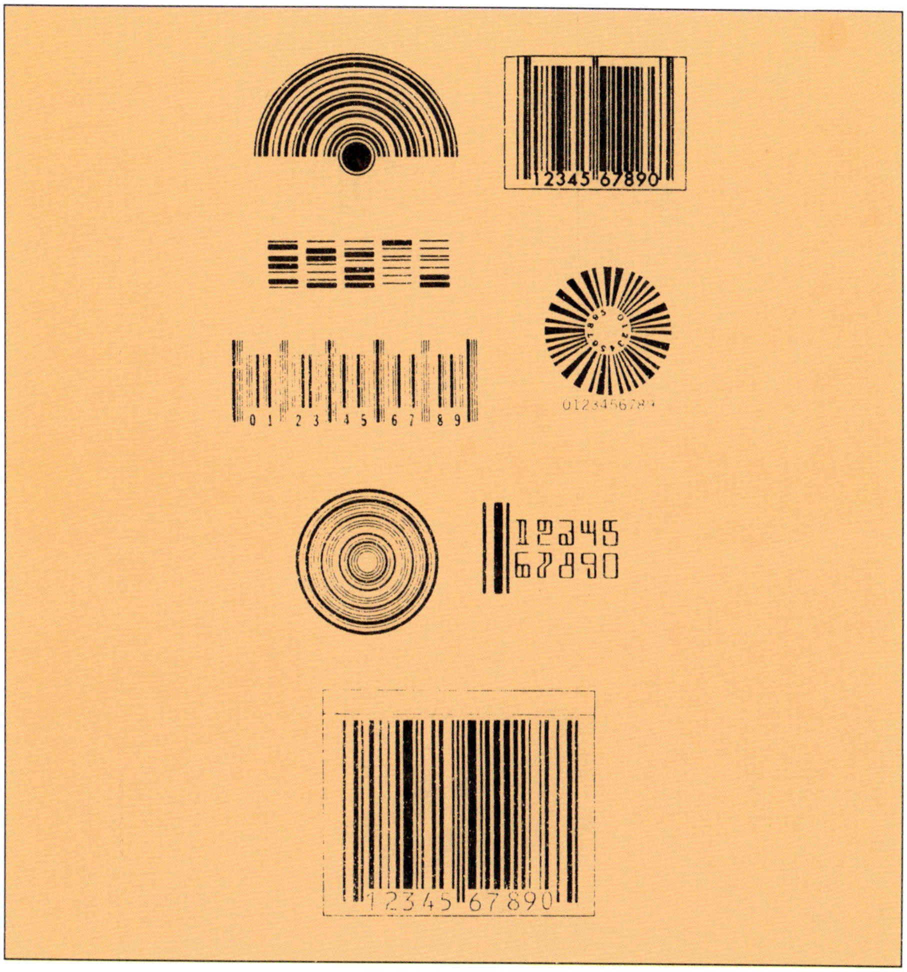

FIGURE 5–10
Types of Bar Codes

read characters of several type fonts, including both uppercase and lowercase letters. The most common font is shown in Figure 5–11.

A major difference between optical-character recognition and optical-mark recognition is that optical-character data is represented by the shapes of characters rather than by the positions of marks. However, both OCR and OMR devices rely on reflected light to translate written data into machine-readable form.

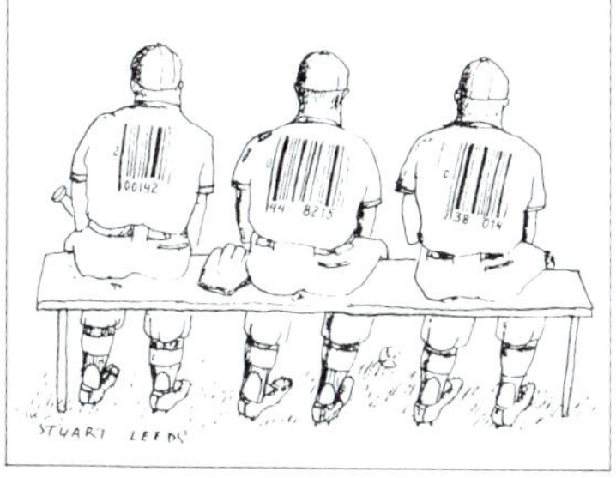

Remote Input

Remote terminals collect data at its source and transmit it to a central computer for processing **(online).** Generally, data is transmitted over telecommunication equipment (in a process described more fully in Chapter 6). The many types of remote terminals available can increase the versatility and expand the applications of the computer. Types of remote terminals to be

FIGURE 5–11
OCR Characters

ABCDEFGHIJKLMN
OPQRSTUVWXYZ,.
$/*-1234567890

discussed here are point-of-sale terminals, touch-tone devices, voice-recognition devices, and intelligent terminals.

Remote terminals that perform the functions of a cash register and also capture sales data are referred to as **point-of-sale (POS) terminals.** Such terminals have a keyboard for data entry, a panel to display the price, a cash drawer, and a printer that provides a cash receipt. A POS terminal typical of those found in many supermarkets is shown in Figure 5–12.

FIGURE 5–12
Point-of-Sale Terminal

Some POS terminals have **wand readers** or a **fixed scanner** that reads the Universal Product Code (discussed earlier) stamped on an item. The sale is registered automatically as the checkout person passes the wand reader over the code; there is no need to enter the price via a keyboard unless the wand malfunctions. Using the UPC symbol, the computer system identifies the product and uses this data to find the item's name and price. Thus, POS terminals enable sales data to be collected at its source. If the terminals are directly connected to a large central computer, useful inventory and sales information can be provided almost instantaneously to the retailer.

Touch-tone devices are remote terminals used together with ordinary telephone lines to transfer data from remote locations to a central computer. The data is entered via a special keyboard on the terminal. Generally, slight modifications must be made to the telephone connection to allow data to be transferred over the line (see Figure 5–13).

Remote terminals that use **audio input** or **voice recognition systems** are suitable for low-volume, highly formal input. Instead of entering data into the computer by punching keys on a terminal, the user may "train" the computer to understand his or her voice. Here, the user must follow only the patterns the computer is programmed to recognize (see Figure 5–14). Computer **audio output** or **voice response units** "speak" by arranging half-second records of voice sounds (phonemes) or pre-recorded words. This approach is being used in the banking industry to report customer account balances and in supermarkets to notify customers of the amount of each purchase. Often the audio response units are coupled with touch-tone terminals for remote data entry. An entire unit may weigh less than ten pounds and some are built into briefcases for easy portability.

FIGURE 5–13
Touch-Tone Device. The Future Phone from Anderson Jacobson is a unique telephone-on-a-chip that combines voice and data communication.

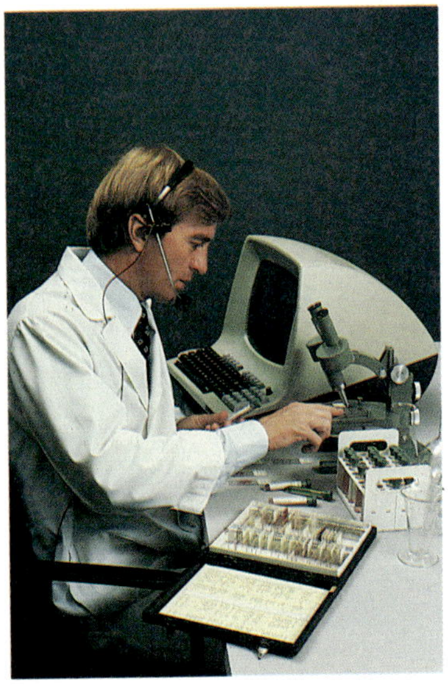

FIGURE 5–14
This lab technician is using an Interstate Electronics voice recognition terminal for voice data entry. Direct data input using the human voice replaces conventional keystroke entry, thereby keeping the user's hands free for other tasks.

Intelligent terminals, still another type of remote device, can be programmed by use of stored instructions. This capability distinguishes them from other terminals discussed earlier in this chapter (sometimes called **dumb terminals**), which cannot be programmed. Intelligent terminals have the same kinds of components as full-sized computers but are limited in their storage capability and in the set of instructions they can perform. They are useful for editing data prior to transmitting it to a central computer; editing and other manipulating functions are directed by programs stored in the terminal's primary storage unit. Most intelligent terminals have a **CRT (cathode-ray tube)** and/or a printer built into them.

PRINTERS

Computer **printers** serve a straightforward basic function—printing processed data in a form humans can read (see Figure 5–15). This permanent readable copy of computer output is often referred to as **hard copy.** To produce it, the printer first receives electronic signals from the central processing unit. In an **impact printer,** these signals activate print elements that are pressed against paper. **Nonimpact printers,** a newer development, use heat, laser technology, or photographic techniques to print output.

Impact Printers

Impact printers come in a variety of shapes and sizes. Some print a character at a time while others print a line at a time. Printer-keyboards, wire-matrix, and daisy-wheel printers are the three principal character-at-a-time devices.

The **printer-keyboard** is similar to an office typewriter (see Figure 5–16).

FIGURE 5–15
Printer

FIGURE 5–16
Printer-Keyboard. This Dataproducts 3-50™ KSR (Keyboard-Send-Receive) terminal provides a throughput of 50 characters per second for letter quality printing.

All instructions, including spacing, carriage returns, and printing of characters, are sent from the CPU to the printers. The keyboard allows an operator to communicate with the system—for example, to enter data or instructions.

Wire-matrix (also called **dot-matrix**) **printers** are based on a design principle similar to that of a football or basketball scoreboard. The matrix is a rectangle composed of pins; usually, it is seven pins high and five pins wide. Certain combinations of pins are activated to represent characters. For example, the number 4 and the letter L are formed by a combination of pins being pressed against paper as shown in Figure 5–17. The dot combinations used to represent various numbers, letters, and special characters are shown in Figure 5–18. Wire-matrix printers can typically print up to 900 characters per minute.

Daisy-wheel printers resemble office typewriters. The daisy wheel itself is a flat disk with petal-like projections (see Figure 5–19). Daisy wheels come in several type fonts that can be interchanged quickly to suit application needs. The daisy-wheel printer offers high-quality type and is often used on

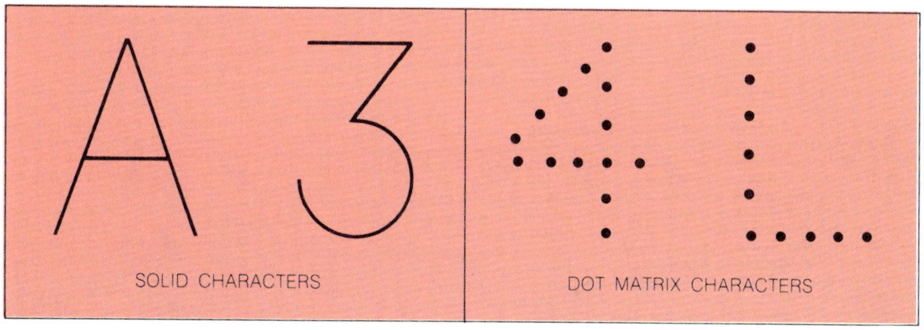

FIGURE 5–17
Wire-Matrix Printer Dot Pattern

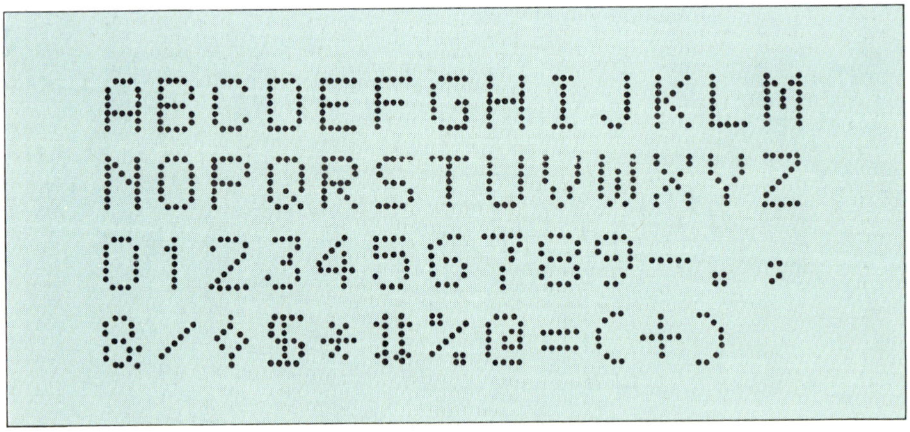

FIGURE 5–18
Wire-Matrix Printer Character Set

word processors to give output a professional appearance. They can produce up to 50 characters per second.

Types of line-at-a-time printers include print-wheel printers, chain printers, and drum printers. A **print-wheel printer** typically contains 120 print wheels, one for each of 120 print positions on a line (see Figure 5–20). Each print wheel contains 48 characters, including alphabetic, numeric, and special characters. Each print wheel rotates until the desired character moves into the corresponding print position on the current print line. When all wheels are in their correct positions, a hammer drives the paper against the

FIGURE 5–19
The daisy wheel is the font carrier used in daisywheel printers. The wheel has a set of spokes, each with a single character embossed at the tip. The hub of the wheel rotates to bring the desired character into position, and is then struck by a hammer mechanism to form an image on paper.

wheels and an entire line of output is printed. Print-wheel printers can produce about 150 lines per minute, which makes them comparatively slow.

A **chain printer** has a character set assembled in a chain that revolves horizontally past all print positions (see Figure 5–21). There is one print hammer for each column on the paper. Characters are printed when hammers press the paper against an inked ribbon, which in turn presses against appropriate characters on the print chain. Type fonts can be changed easily on chain printers, allowing a variety of fonts, such as italic or boldface, to be used. Some chain printers can produce up to 2,000 lines per minute.

A **drum printer** uses a metal cylinder with rows of characters engraved across its surface (see Figure 5–22). Each column on the drum contains a complete character set and corresponds to one print position on the line. As the drum rotates, all characters are rotated past the print position. A hammer presses the paper against an ink ribbon and the drum when the appropriate character is in place. One line is printed for each revolution of the drum, since all characters eventually reach the print position during one revolution. Some drum printers can produce 3,000 lines per minute.

FIGURE 5–20
Print Wheel

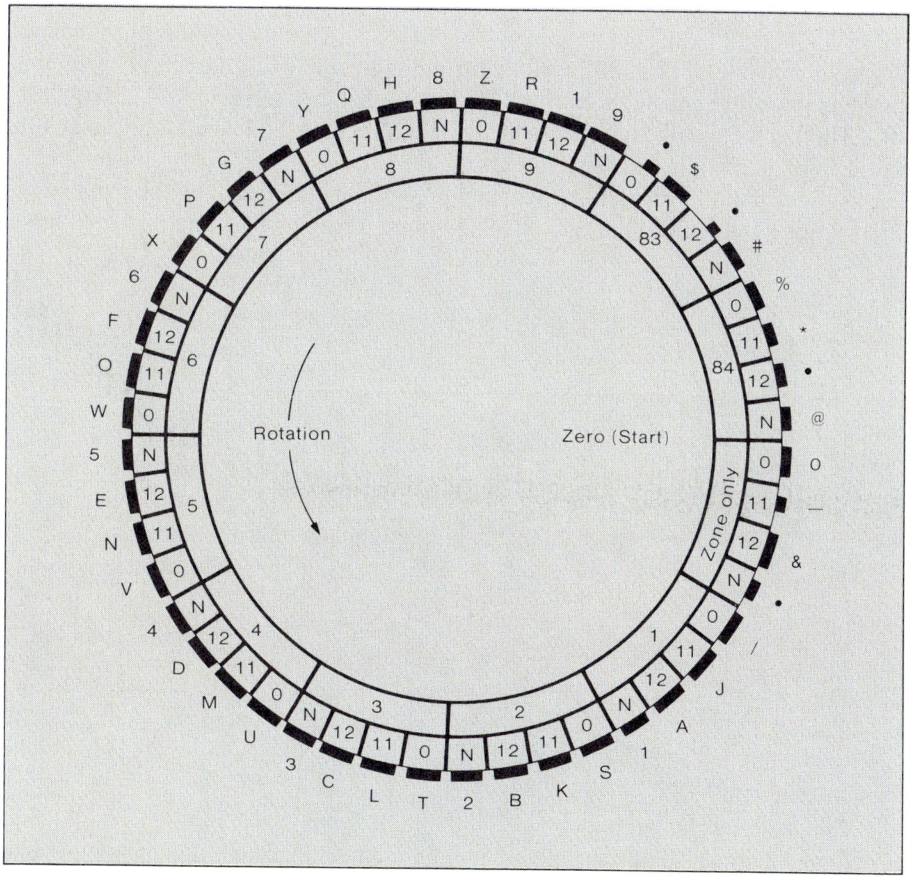

HIGHLIGHT
Computers and Sports

Even the world of sports is being taken over by computers. The Milwaukee Bucks of the National Basketball Association have entered the computer age. The Bucks purchased a microcomputer to computerize team statistics.

Traditionally, keeping game stats meant entering hash marks on a scorecard, followed by many hours of adding columns and typing results. The new system used by the Bucks now virtually eliminates this time-consuming manual process.

The system is a standard, off-the-shelf microcomputer with a special basketball keyboard. The statistics are entered with the touch of a button, and the specially developed statistics programs do the rest of the work. Accurate up-to-date statistics are displayed on video monitors for radio and television broadcasters. Seconds after the game ends, the stats are totaled and printed in box score form. Later the system produces cumulative information along with season highs and lows, in printed form suitable for press releases.

The new system can produce enough statistics to inundate even the most statistically oriented sports fan.

FIGURE 5–21
Chain Printer

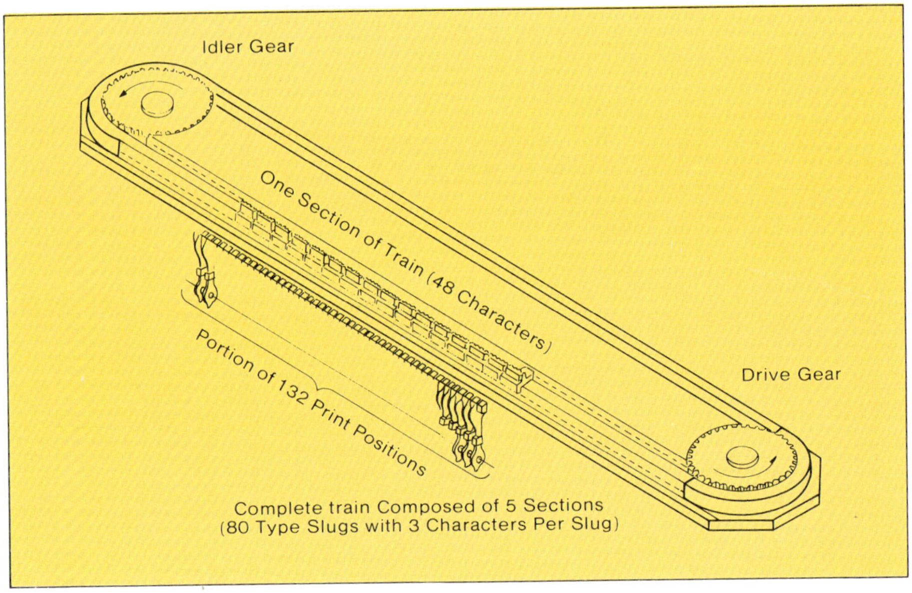

Nonimpact Printers

As mentioned earlier, nonimpact printers do not print characters by means of a mechanical printing element that strikes paper. Instead, a variety of other methods are used. Electrostatic, electrothermal, ink-jet, laser, and xerographic printers will be discussed here.

An **electrostatic printer** forms an image of a character on special paper using a dot matrix of charged wires or pins. The paper is moved through a

This specially designed steel band is used in band printers with speeds ranging from 300 to 1800 lines per minute. Band printers are less commonly used than other types of printers.

FIGURE 5–22
Print Drum

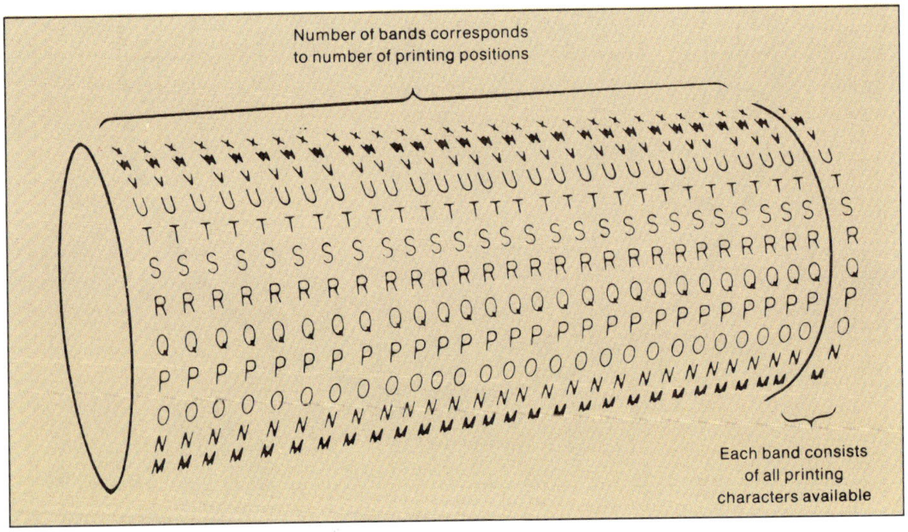

solution containing ink particles that have a charge opposite that of the pattern. The ink particles adhere to each charged pattern on the paper, forming a visible image of each character.

Electrothermal printers generate characters by using heat and heat-sensitive paper. Rods are heated in a matrix; as the ends of the selected rods touch the heat-sensitive paper, an image is created.

Both electrothermal and electrostatic printers are relatively quiet in operation. They are often used in applications where noise may be a problem. Some of these printers are capable of producing 5,000 lines per minute.

In an **ink-jet printer,** a nozzle is used to shoot a stream of charged ink towards the paper. Before reaching it, the ink passes through an electrical field that arranges the charged particles into characters. These printers can print 200 characters per second.

Laser printers combine laser beams and electrophotographic technology to create output images (see Figure 5–23). A beam of light is focused through a rotating disk containing a full font of characters. The character image is projected onto a piece of film or photographic paper, and the print or negative is developed and fixed in a manner similar to that used for ordinary photographs. The output consists of high-quality, letter-perfect images—the process is often used to print books. Laser printers, which can operate up to 21,000 lines per minute, are being considered as a solution to the slower printing speeds of word processors.

Xerographic printers use printing methods much like those used in common xerographic copying machines. For example, Xerox, the pioneer of this

FIGURE 5–23
The 9800 Series laser printers from Datagraphix, Inc. operate at speeds up to 21,000 lines per minute.

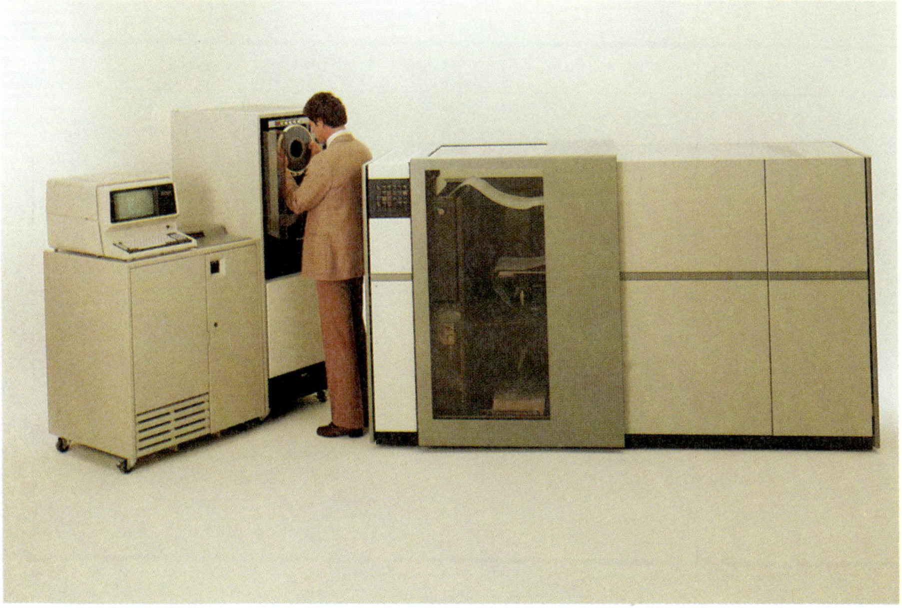

HIGHLIGHT
Psychiatric Programming

Research programmers in Philadelphia have created "Chris," a computerized mental health simulator. Chris will be called into action to train students in the art of psychiatric interviewing; but Chris is the schizophrenic patient, not the well-organized, rational doctor as we might expect. Students must figure out how to deal with Chris when he takes off into chaotic, irrational reveries. Should the computer run into a bug or misinterpret the student's query, the student often cannot distinguish the response from general schizophrenic symptoms.

Another psychiatric research product, "Eliza," recently operated in an interactive mode with Chris. Their conversation was unusually striking, since Eliza is a simulated psychiatrist program designed to train students in a particular diagnostic technique. Using this technique, a psychiatrist takes the patient's statement and responds with a leading question to keep the conversation going. (For example, the patient claims, "My mother hates me," and the interviewer replies, "Why do you think so?") Researchers report that the script of this computer-to-computer session reads out uncannily like some human interactions.

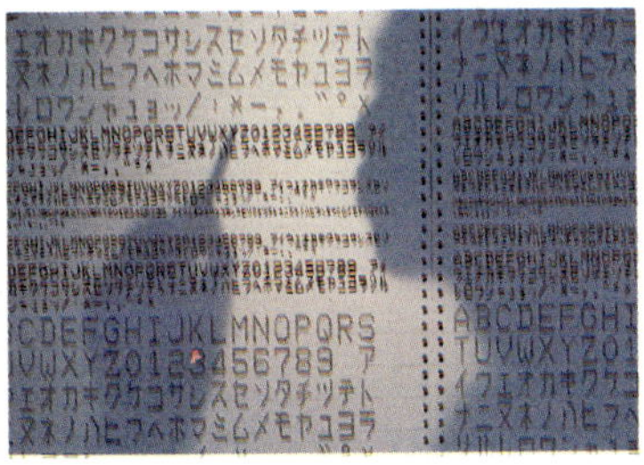

Japanese Katakna characters as well as alphanumeric characters may be printed in a variety of sizes using a special IBM printer developed in Japan.

type of printing, has one model that prints on single 8½-by-11-inch sheets of plain paper. Xerographic printers operate at 4,000 lines per minute.

Table 5–1 shows representative differences in print speeds of impact and nonimpact printers. Since nonimpact printers involve much less physical movement than impact printers, they are generally much faster. They also offer a wider choice of type faces and better speed-to-price ratios than impact printers, and their technology implies a higher reliability because they use fewer movable parts in printing. The disadvantages of using nonimpact printers include their inability to make carbon copies and the special paper some require. However, they can make multiple printings of a page in less time than it takes an impact printer to make one multicarbon page.

New printing systems now being introduced combine many features of the printing process into one machine. For example, collating, routing, hole-punching, blanking out of proprietary information, and perforating may be performed. Some printers produce both text and form designs on plain paper; this reduces or eliminates the need for preprinted forms.

SPECIAL-PURPOSE OUTPUT

In many instances, traditional printers cannot provide certain forms of output. At these times, special output devices are required.

Visual Display Terminals

Visual display terminals in common use display data on **cathode-ray tubes (CRTs)** similar to television screens (see Figure 5–24). A typical screen can hold twenty-four lines, each containing eighty characters (some of the newer terminals have twenty-five lines, one reserved for special messages). These terminals supply what is known as **soft-copy** output; that is, the screen is

TABLE 5–1
Printer Types and Speeds

PRINTER TYPE	PRINTING CAPABILITY
IMPACT PRINTERS	
Character-at-a-Time:	
Daisy Wheel	50 characters per second
Printer-Keyboards	900 characters per minute
Wire-Matrix (Dot-Matrix)	900 characters per minute
Line-at-a-Time:	
Print Wheel	150 lines per minute
Print Chain	2000 lines per minute
Print Drum	3000 lines per minute
NONIMPACT PRINTERS	
Ink Jet	200 characters per second
Xerographic	4000 lines per minute
Electrothermal	5000 lines per minute
Electrostatic	5000 lines per minute
Laser	21,000 lines per minute

FIGURE 5–24
Visual Display Terminal

not a permanent record of what is shown. They are well suited for applications involving inquiry and response where no permanent (printed) records are required, and can be used for capturing data to be transmitted from remote offices to a central computer. Data may be entered on a keyboard on the terminal and displayed on the screen for verification as it is keyed.

Visual display terminals have some advantages over printers. First, they can display output much faster than printers—some CRT terminals can display up to 10,000 characters in a second. Also, they are much quieter in operation that impact printers. It is usually possible to connect a printer or a copier to a CRT terminal; thus, hard-copy output of the screen contents can be provided. These terminals are rapidly gaining recognition as desirable components of information systems.

Another type of CRT, known as a **graphic display device,** is used to display drawings as well as characters on a screen (see Figure 5–25). Graphic display devices are generally used to display graphs and charts, but they can also display complex curves and shapes. With some terminals, data displayed on the screen can be altered by using the **light pen,** a pen-shaped object with a light-sensitive cell at its end (see Figure 5–26). Users can "draw" lines on the screen by specifying the ends of the lines with the light pen and can quickly alter graphs and line drawings by applying the pen at the appropriate locations on the screen. Graphic display devices are being used in highly technical fields, such as in the aerospace industry to aid in the design of new wing structures.

These two displays show the same data: in black and white (above) and in color (below). They demonstrate how color can improve data presentation. The upper display must be studied carefully to understand significant trends; with color, these become obvious.

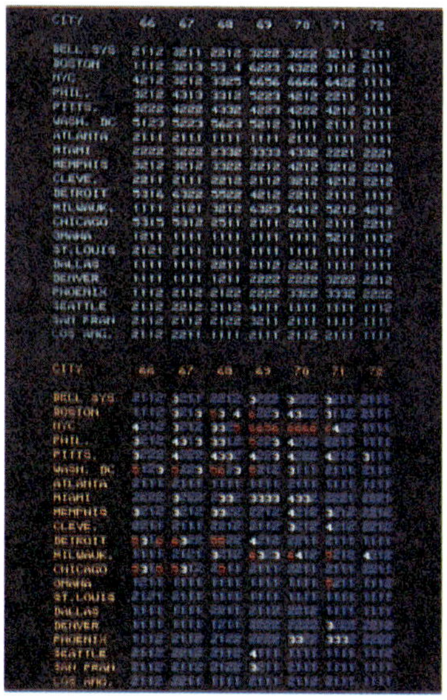

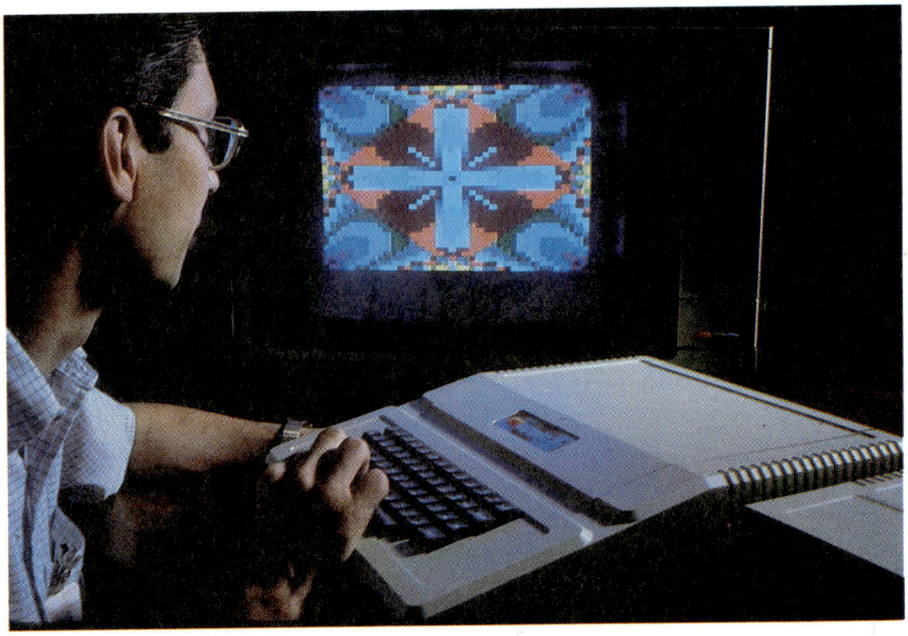

FIGURE 5–25
Graphic Display Device

FIGURE 5–26
Visual Display Device with Light Pen. This operator at Lockheed makes changes in the design of an airplane using an electronic pen and keyboard to alter the drawing.

Plotters

A **plotter** is an output device that converts data from the CPU into graphic form. It can produce lines, curves, and complex shapes. The major difference between a plotter and a graphic display device is that the plotter produces hard-copy output (paper), whereas the graphic display device produces soft-copy output (screen image).

A typical plotter has a pen, movable carriage, drum, and chart-paper holder (see Figure 5–27). Shapes are produced as the pen moves back and forth across the paper along the y-axis while the drum moves the paper up and down along the x-axis. Both the upper movement and the pen movement are bidirectional. The pen is raised and lowered from the paper surface automatically.

The plotter can be used to produce line and bar charts, graphs, organizational charts, engineering drawings, maps, trend lines, supply and demand curves, and so on. The figures are drawn precisely, because the pen can be positioned at up to 45,000 points in each square inch of paper. Some plotters can produce drawings in up to eight colors. The usefulness of the plotter lies in its ability to communicate information in easy-to-understand picture form.

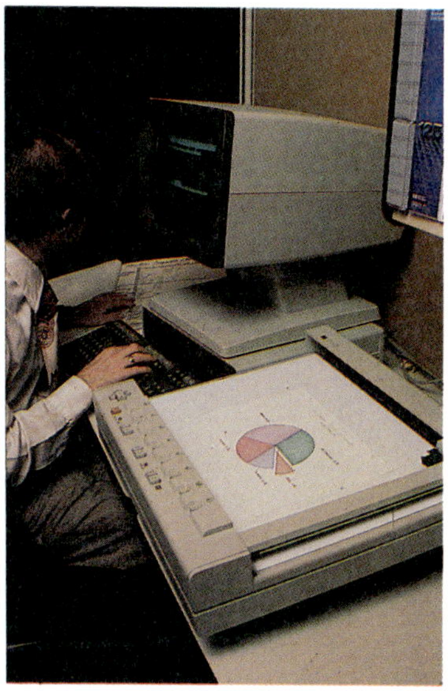

FIGURE 5–27
Business information can be transformed into graphical form for printed presentation on this Hewlett-Packard desktop plotter.

Computer Output Microfilm

In situations where large volumes of information must be printed and stored for future reference, conventional paper output is not appropriate. It uses much storage space, and particular portions of it often are difficult to get to.

This artwork was produced by an engineer using a computer at Bell Labs.

HIGHLIGHT
Biological Computers

The day may be close at hand when tiny computers can be implanted into human tissues to repair and improve intricate physical functions.

Biochemists say the biochip implant could mesh with the human nervous system to banish such ills as blindness and deafness—even endow the brain with capacities it lacked in its unmodified state.

EMV Associates, a small firm in Rockville, Maryland, has already been awarded a grant by the National Science Foundation to test the reaction between an electrode-studded chip and the brain.

Ideally, the implant will become a "living" part of the human system without losing or distorting its original functions.

A possible alternative is **computer output microfilm (COM),** which consists of photographed images produced in miniature by the computer. In some cases, the output is first recorded on magnetic tape. Special photocopying equipment is then used to reproduce the information on microfilm. In an interactive environment, the COM equipment is used to display output on a CRT screen, then the screen is exposed to microfilm. The microfilm copy can be produced as a roll of film or a four-by-six-inch microfiche card. In such a system, the speed of recording can be twenty-five to fifty times faster than traditional printing methods.

The main advantage of COM is that much data can be stored compactly, reducing both space requirements and storage costs. Further, both character and graphic output can be recorded. The use of a transparent forms overlay permits headings to be printed and lines superimposed so that output is highly readable. The cost of producing additional microfilm copies is very low. In the past, high initial investment costs and the inability of the computer to directly retrieve microfilmed data have been disadvantages. However, costs are declining and the number of COM systems in use is increasing.

SUMMARY POINTS

- Punched cards represent data by the position of holes punched in the cards. One card can store up to eighty columns of data.
- Key-to-tape and key-to-disk utilize a magnetic medium to store data. Unlike cards, new data can be stored over old data when it is no longer required.
- Source-data automation refers to capturing data about an event when and where it occurs. Examples include magnetic-ink character readers, optical recognition (optical mark and optical character) and remote input utilizing point-of-sale (POS) terminals, touch-tone devices, and voice-recognition systems. Intelligent terminals can perform data verification and edits before submitting input to the main computer.
- Printers can be either impact or nonimpact. Impact printers can be broken down into line-at-a-time and character-at-a-time printers. Nonimpact printers utilize electrostatic, electrothermal, ink-jet, laser, and xerographic methods.
- Special-purpose output is designed to provide information in a particular way or format. Visual display terminals (also called CRTs) provide soft-copy output of computer information. Plotters provide information summarized and interpreted into graphic form. Computer output microfilm (COM) stores data in reduced size on photographic film.

REVIEW QUESTIONS

1. What are examples of some source documents which may be used as the basis for punching data onto cards or keying data onto a magnetic medium?

2. Compare punched cards to key-to-disk. What are some of the advantages and disadvantages of each? Under what conditions would you recommend the use of punched cards? Key-to-disk?
3. Which part of the data-processing system most frequently contains errors? Why?
4. What is meant by the term *source-data automation?* Describe how it can be beneficial to information systems.
5. Describe two forms of source-data automation.
6. Explain the difference between impact and nonimpact printers. What are advantages and disadvantages of each type?
7. What additional routine tasks may be performed by a modern printing system?
8. Differentiate between hard-copy and soft-copy output.
9. Describe how computer output microfilm (COM) might be helpful to a large banking concern.
10. In what instances would visual display terminals be used? What is the difference between a plotter and a graphic display device? Give some examples of the uses of both types of devices.
11. Distinguish between a light pen and a plotter.

Input/Output

As microcomputers become increasingly popular, many different applications are being developed to make the most of their potential. Along with this has come the need to design new input and output devices and to improve some of the traditional ones.

Data entry has been the weakest link in the data processing operation. Much time and effort has been directed toward improving present and creating new technologies to increase the speed, accuracy, and effectiveness of the input process.

With the onslaught of firms entering the microcomputer business, there has been a variety of input device designs presented as each firm tries to gain a competitive edge for their product.

One area in which a wide variety of differences can be found is in keyboard input. For example, the letters, numbers, and special characters of the Apple keyboard closely resemble that of a conventional typewriter, both in appearance and function. In contrast, IBM has designed a keyboard that divides its keys into three separate sections: one for standard character keys; one for special function keys; and a third for the numeric keys. Both the Apple and the IBM keyboards are of the standard tactile type, where you can feel the keys move under your fingers.

A new twist that is appearing on some of the more inexpensive models such as the Atari 400 is a pressure-sensitive, membrane-covered keyboard. Pressing the appropriate marked point on the membrane cover enters the desired data. Since the more inexpensive microcomputers such as the Atari 400 will often find their way into the hands of younger children, the membrane cover provides excellent protection from spills and other forms of contamination. They may also be appropriate for computer-hostile environments such as factories. This type of keyboard could, however, pose a drawback for those who are accustomed to the traditional keyboard. Since you can't feel the key move (tactile response), you must constantly verify an input by looking up at the screen.

Another variation is multiple capabilities of a particular key. For example, the Commodore VIC 20 uses a typical key that includes upper- and lower-case letters, as well as a choice of two graphic characters. The VIC automatically comes on in "graphics" mode, and by using the SHIFT and the COMMODORE keys you can type upper-case letters and the full graphics set at the same time. There is also a "text" mode, entered by pressing the SHIFT and COMMODORE keys together. This enables you to use the VIC like an ordinary typewriter, with full range of upper- and lower-case letters, plus all the graphics on the left side of the keys. The VIC also offers special editing and programmable keys.

With the advent of video games, joysticks and game paddles have become almost indispensable when purchasing a home computer. These devices input an electrical response that controls the movement of a cursor in such diverse forms on the screen as paddles, missiles, frogs, and pacmen.

As microcomputers continue to grow in popularity, more and more people are trying to discover other ways to use their microcomputers. For those of you with a bit of the artist in your blood, the development of the graphic tablet lets you turn your microcomputer into a canvas. With the appropriate software, the graphic tablet, which utilizes an electronic drawing pen, lets you create your very own masterpiece on your microcomputer's display terminal. Software for the graphic tablet is also available for architects and engineers who use personal computers professionally.

Engineers using computers to aid the design process often find that their initial design can use some modifications. The idea of making changes directly through the CRT screen gave rise to another input device, the light pen. It is a pen-shaped object with a photoelectric cell at its end, used to draw lines or place information on a visual display screen. An engineer can use the light pen to quickly and easily modify a computer-aided design (CAD).

On the leading edge of microcomputer input innovations are spatial digitizers and voice-recognition systems. Micro Control Systems, Inc., has developed a spatial digitizer for Apple and for IBM Personal Computer microcomputers that allows users to record *x*, *y*, and *z* coordinates of any three-dimensional object. The device consists of a clear lucite tablet (Space Tablet) that is mounted on a precision-machined arm. Data are given to the computer by tracing the point of the arm around a three-dimensional object; the three-dimensional nature of the object will be displayed on the screen. The device also allows for two-dimensional use.

One example of a voice-entry system is the Shadow/VET made by Scott Industries. Since the voice-entry system is "trained" to recognize a given vocabulary, the spoken vocabulary reportedly may be anything from English to Ancient Egyptian to the tonal variations given by a severely speech-impaired person.

Voice data entry has many possible applications. Scott Industries already has several installations of its Shadow/VET in place with handicapped persons who would be unable to use a computer except by voice. Other applications of voice-recognition systems include actually telling the computer to turn off the lights or turn on the oven.

Output devices for microcomputers include not only the standard devices such as impact and nonimpact printers and CRTs, but also plotters and graphic display devices. The latter two can display charts, graphs, and complex curves and shapes in a multitude of colors to enhance the analysis of your output.

Because a computer can send information to a printer much faster than the printer can accept it, your computer can be tied up for quite some time as it waits to feed its output to the printer. For those of you who have experienced the frustration of having to wait until the printing of one job is completed before you can use the computer again, there is now a special-purpose device called a spooler that alleviates this problem. Connected to your computer and printer, the spooler buffers (accepts and holds) the output and transmits it to the printer at the printer's specific print rate. It allows you to continue using your computer while your printer does its job.

Devices such as Videx Enhancer II for the Apple allows the keyboard to memorize words or phrases that can then be entered by the use of a single key. A type-ahead buffer allows the keyboard to remember what you typed while the computer is printing or attending some other function. It also allows entry and display of upper- and lower-case letters with fully functional shift keys. With more people using microcomputers for word processing, devices like the Enhancer II will be a welcome addition. In line with this thought is an innovation by Corvus Systems. They have developed a single-unit, dual-orientation screen that can be flipped on its side, allowing a vertical format for word processing and a horizontal format for spread sheets. If your screen doesn't allow for a full 80-column display, devices such as Vista's Vision 80 for Apple computers give your terminal a standard 80-column by 24-line display screen.

Another special-purpose device is the Votrax's Type-N-Talk (TNT), a text-to-speech synthesizer. It can read ASCII text characters from your computer files and pronounce these characters as spoken English words. Devices like this could become a valuable aid in the learning process by providing vocal prompts, exception conditions, and user dialogs with microcomputers.

As development of new and present technologies in the area of input/output devices continues, we are seeing an inprovement in the speed, accuracy, and effectiveness of the data processing operation. As a result, microcomputers can be expected to enter into a wide variety of new and innovative applications.

DISCUSSION QUESTIONS

1. Describe some types of environments in which a membrane-covered keyboard might be appropriate.
2. Why do you think so much emphasis has been placed on the new input/output devices?

CHAPTER 6

Remote Access Communication Systems

FACING PAGE
The power of a central site computer can be available to every remote office, branch, and plant with a powerful distributed data processing computer system specifically designed for remote processing and communication.

INTRODUCTION

Newer, more advanced processing techniques increasingly utilize some form of remote input/output device in direct communication with the computer. POS terminals can communicate sales data directly to the computer as they occur, providing up-to-date sales and inventory figures. MICR applications process checks at incredible speeds, utilizing the computer to keep count of checks and dollar amounts. CRTs can be used for data input as well as information output. Whatever the form, direct communication with the computer can provide fast, up-to-the-minute information by reducing delays in the collection and dissemination of data.

This chapter discusses the concepts and techniques involved in message transmission and introduces the types of equipment that make data communication possible. The concept of computer networks is presented with a discussion of the most popular types. Finally, a brief look is taken at satellite communication systems.

paradyne

CHAPTER OUTLINE

Introduction

Communication Channels
Message Transmission
Grades of Transmission
Modes of Transmission

Multiplexers and Concentrators

Programmable Communications Processors

Networks
Architecture
Distributed Data Processing

Satellite Communication Systems
Current Satellite Usage
Satellite Business Systems

Summary Points

Review Questions

COMMUNICATION CHANNELS

Applications that use remote input/output devices must have some way of communicating with the computer. A **communication channel** is the pathway used to carry data from one location to another. It provides for the exchange of data between remote sites and the computer. Types of communication channels used for data transfer include telegraph lines, telephone lines, coaxial cables, microwave links, communication satellites, and laser beams.

The electronic communication of data from one location to another is referred to as **data communication.** In a data communication system, data are transmitted between terminals and a central computer or even between two or more computers. The combined use of communication facilities such as telephone systems and data-processing equipment is called **teleprocessing,** or **telecommunications.** As the number of information systems utilizing geographically dispersed people and equipment increase, more emphasis will be placed on the development of teleprocessing facilities.

Message Transmission

Data can be transmitted over communication channels in one of two forms: analog or digital. Transmission of data in continuous wave form is referred to as **analog transmission.** This is the type of transmission used on normal telephone lines. An analog transmission can be likened to the waves created in a pan of still water by a stick. By sending "waves" down a wire electronically, one causes messages to be sent and received. In the past, analog transmission was the major means of relaying data over long distances. This was due largely to the type of communication lines provided by American Telephone and Telegraph (AT&T) (see Figure 6–1). **Digital transmission** involves transmitting data as distinct "on" and "off" states; it represents data in the same form the computer does.

FIGURE 6–1
Analog and Digital Transmission

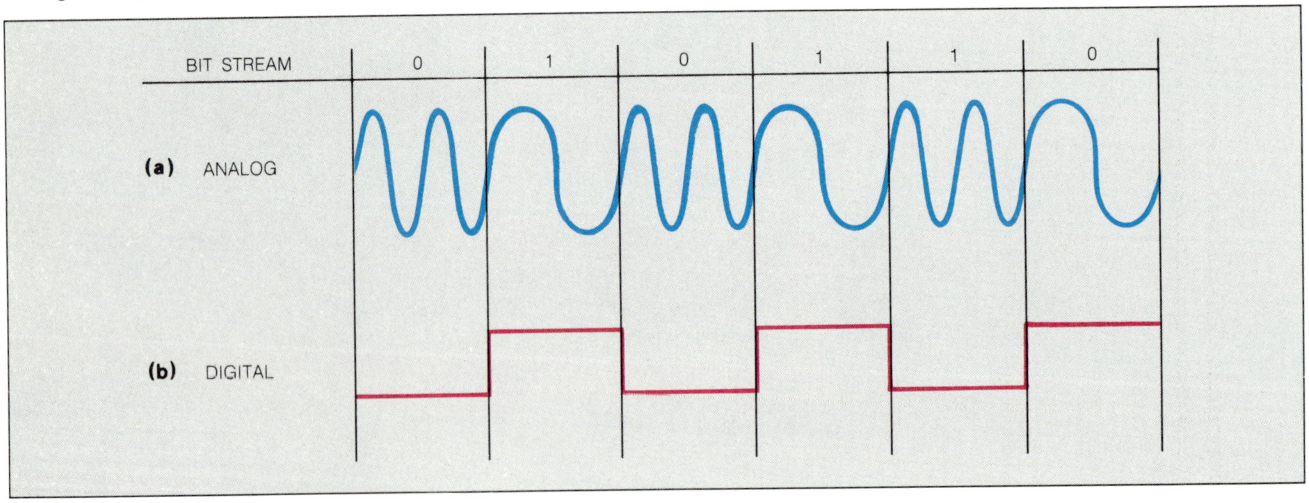

Analog transmission requires that the sender convert the data from the digital (''on''—''off'') form in which it is stored to analog (wave) form before transmitting it. This conversion process is called **modulation.** The opposite conversion—from wave form to digital—is required at the receiving end before the data is entered into the computer. This conversion is called **demodulation.** Both modulation and demodulation are accomplished by devices called **modems,** or **data sets** (See Figure 6–2). The term *modem* is derived from the terms *mo*dulation and *dem*odulation.

Digital transmission requires no conversion of data, since the computer stores data in pulse form. This reduces the time required to send messages. Digital transmission also results in fewer transmission errors than with analog. These two facts mean that users can exchange large amounts of data faster and more reliably using digital, rather than analog, transmission.

Using a special ocean-simulation laboratory at Homdel, New Jersey, Bell Labs is developing a transatlantic lightwave cable (left in photo) that would be more efficient and less expensive than the existing cable system (right in photo).

Grades of Transmission

The **grade,** or **bandwidth,** of a channel determines the rate at which data can be transmitted across the channel. **Narrow bandwidth channels** can transmit data at a rate of 45 to 90 bits per second. Telegraph channels are typical narrow bandwidth channels.

Voice-grade channels have a wider frequency range; they can transmit at rates of from 300 to 9,600 bits per second. Voice-grade channels such as telephone lines are used by the Dataphone and Dataspeed equipment of AT&T's Bell Telephone System, the Wide Area Telephone Service (WATS), and many others.

For applications that require high-speed transmission of large volumes of data, **broad-band channels** are most suitable. Coaxial cables, microwaves, and laser beams belong in this grade. Leased broad-band services are offered by both Western Union and the Bell System; an example of a leased broad-band service is the Telpak system. Such a service is capable of transmitting data at rates of up to 120,000 bits per second.

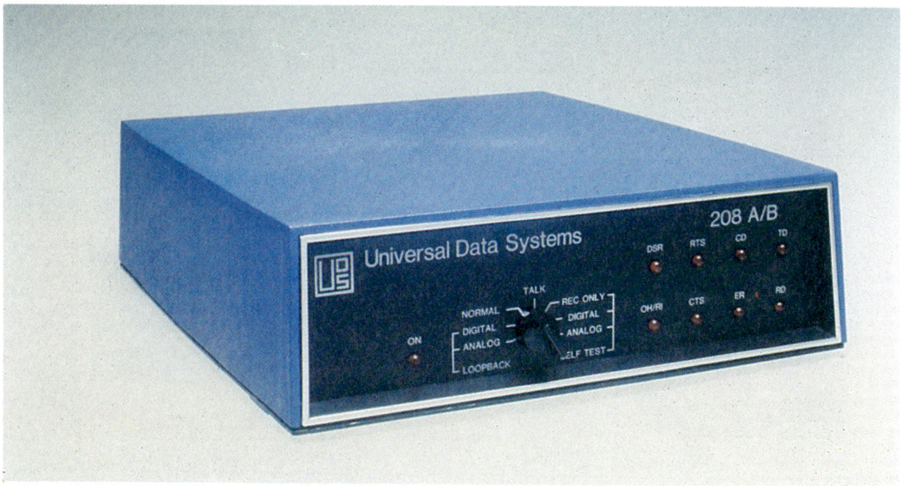

FIGURE 6–2
Modem (Data Set)

HIGHLIGHT
Pager Developments, or "Beefed-Up Beepers"

The overwhelming success of the mobile pager (or beeper) has caused an unexpected traffic jam in the airwaves of many cities. With over 1.5 million pagers already in use, some cities have completely clogged the radio frequencies allowed for paging purposes.

Meta Systems Inc. of California recently introduced a new beeper with built-in memory. This model stores messages up to 940 characters long on a memory chip and then plays them back on command across a display on the pager. Some pagers have a printer, so that a paper copy of the message can be made. While the display or printout is attractive, the best part of the new pager is its speed. It can send fifteen messages, each up to 150 characters long, in the time a current pager can relay one beep and a fifteen-second voice message.

Several other companies are right behind Meta Systems with new memory pagers. So, companies who realize large savings by keeping in touch by beepers will not be haggling with the crowds in the air much longer.

Modes of Transmission

Another method of classifying communication channels is by the mode of transmission they use. Depending on the application and the terminal equipment used, channels operate in one of three basic transmission modes (see Figure 6–3):

- **Simplex.** A simplex channel provides for unidirectional, or one-way, transmission of data. A terminal that transmits via a simplex channel can either send or receive; it cannot do both.
- **Half-duplex.** In the half-duplex mode, communication can occur in both directions but in only one direction at a time. This type of transmission is commonly used in telephone services and telephone networks.
- **Full duplex.** A full-duplex channel can transmit data in both directions simultaneously; thus it is the most versatile mode of transmission.

FIGURE 6–3
Channel Transmission Modes

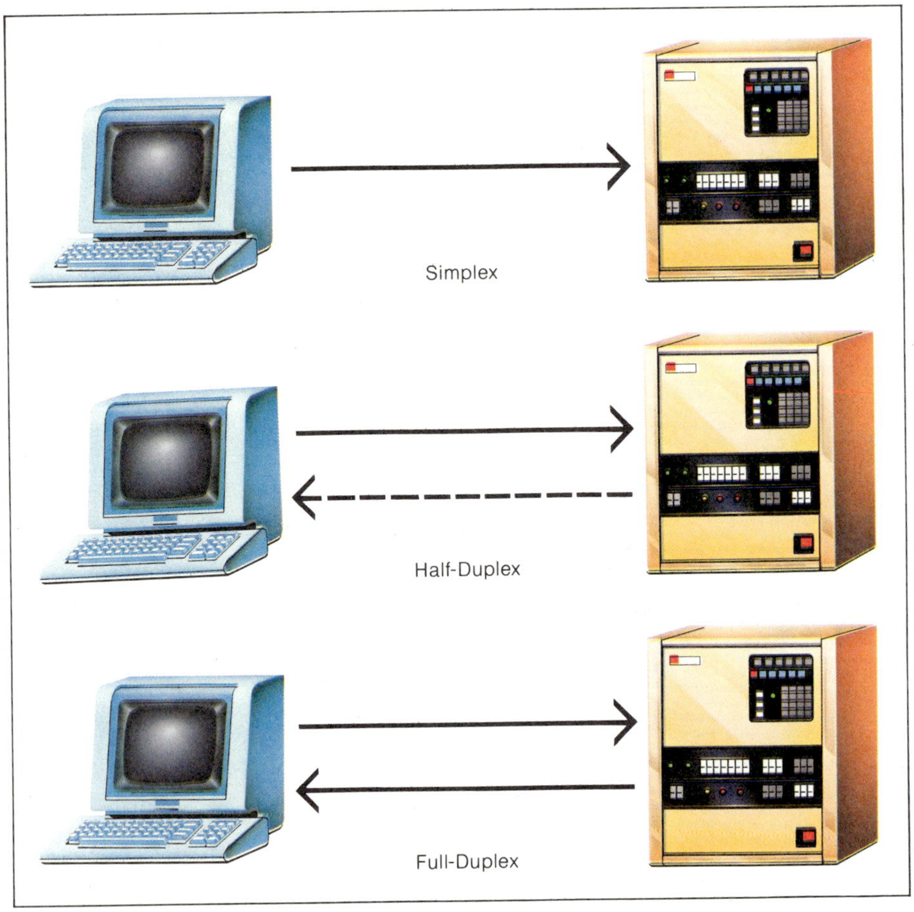

MULTIPLEXERS AND CONCENTRATORS

Multiplexers and **concentrators** increase the number of devices that can use a communication channel. This is necessary because terminals operate at a much slower speed (100 to 150 bits per second) than do communication channels (300 to 9,600 bits per second for voice grade). Thus, a channel is not used to full capacity by a single terminal.

Multiplexing can create a more economical usage of the communication channel. By combining the input from several terminals into a single input stream, data from these terminals can be sent over a single channel. This allows a single communication channel (typically voice grade) to do the job of many other channels otherwise operating at less than full capacity. At the receiving end, a similar unit separates the previously combined input streams for processing.

A concentrator differs from a multiplexer in that it allows data from only one terminal at a time to be transmitted over a communication channel. The concentrator polls the terminals one at a time to see if they have any mes-

Central data centers, such as this one at Informatics General Corporation, can amass huge amounts of information that can be shared by many users through cable or telephone hook-ups.

sages to send. When a communication channel is free, the first terminal ready to send or receive data will get control of the channel and will continue to control it for the length of the transaction. The use of a concentrator relies on the assumption that not all terminals will be ready to send or receive data at a single given time. Figure 6–4 shows examples of communication systems using multiplexers and concentrators.

PROGRAMMABLE COMMUNICATIONS PROCESSORS

A **programmable communications processor** is a device that relieves the CPU of many of the tasks typically required in a communication system. When the volume of data transmission surpasses a certain level, a programmable communications processor can handle these tasks more economically than the CPU. Examples of such tasks include handling messages and priorities, disconnecting after messages have been received, requesting retransmission of incomplete messages, and verifying successfully transmitted messages.

The two most frequent uses of communications processors are message-switching and front-end processing. The principal task of the processor used for **message-switching** is to receive messages and route them to appropriate destinations. A **front-end processor** also performs message-switching as well as more sophisticated operations such as validating transmitted data and pre-processing data before it is transmitted to the central computer.

This Network Management System automatically monitors network conditions, allows the operator to identify any problems, and can even initiate necessary restorative action.

NETWORKS

Architecture

A typical computer system consists of a single main frame linked to a variety of **peripherals** (input/output devices, auxiliary storage devices, and so on). If the peripherals are connected directly to the CPU, the system is said to be a **local system.** However, by utilizing communication channels, terminals may be far removed from the main frame. These terminals, connected to the central computer by a communication channel, result in a system called a **remote system.** When several CPUs are linked together by communication channels, they form a **network** or a **distributed data processing (DDP) system.** Together, these computers allow faster response to inquiries and provide the power needed to perform complex calculations.

As with a single CPU and its terminals, the network's main frames may be hooked together to form either local or remote systems. Several computers can be connected at a central location to enhance computing capabilities. Or, the same computers can be dispersed geographically to the locations of data collection or information retrieval forming a distributed system.

Different types of structures can be used to implement the multiple CPU concept (see Figure 6–5). In a **star configuration,** all transactions must go through a central computer before being routed to the appropriate network computer. The effect is to create a central decision point. This facilitates

FIGURE 6–4 Communication Systems with Multiplexers and Concentrators

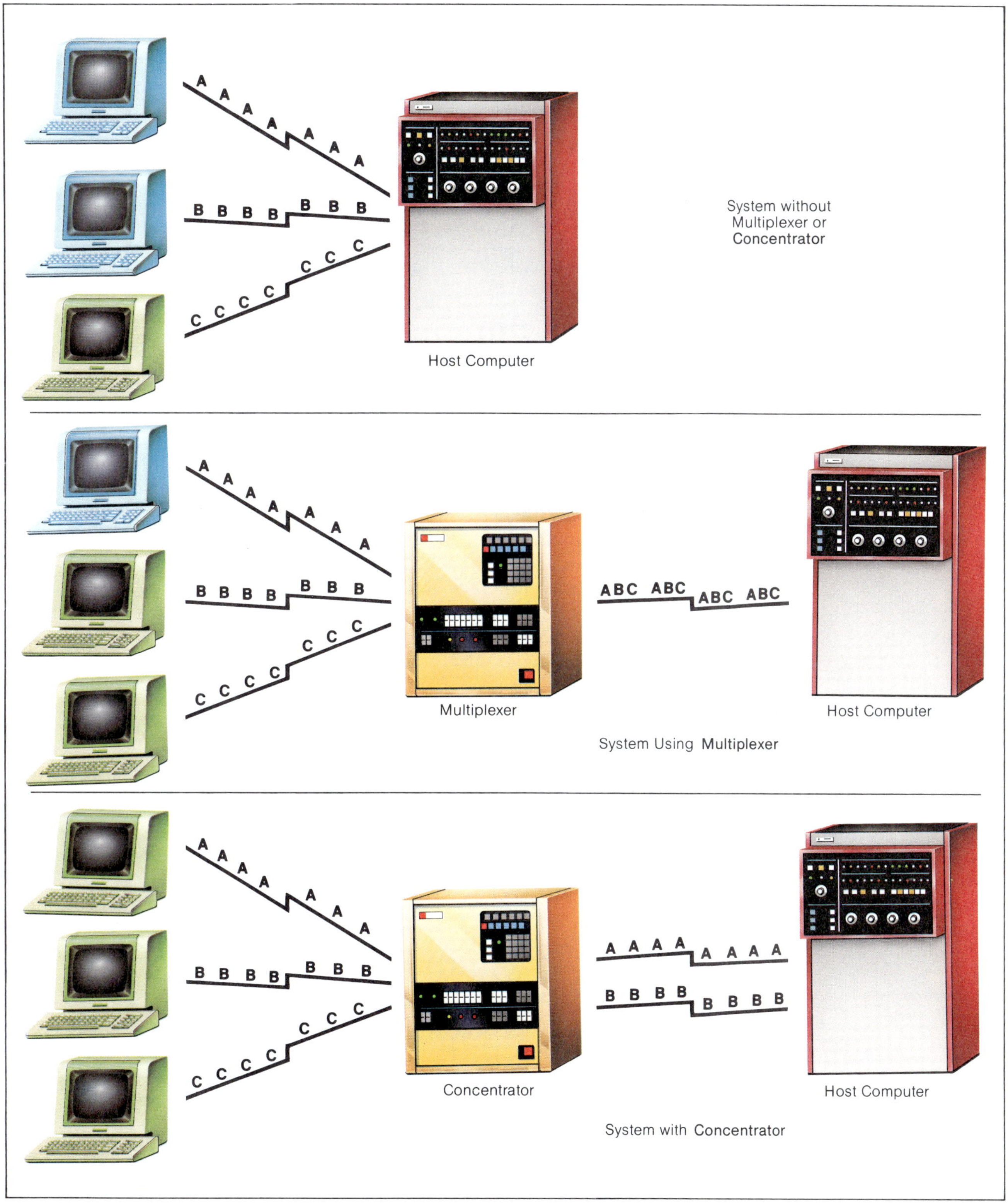

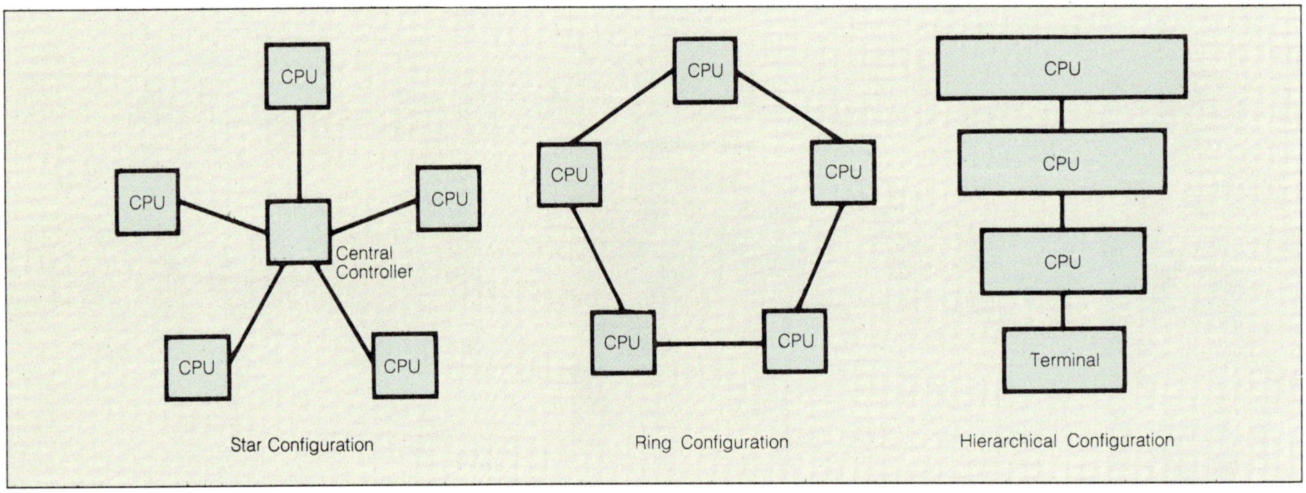

FIGURE 6–5
Multiple CPU Configurations

workload distribution and resource sharing, but it exposes the system to single-point vulnerability. An alternative approach uses a number of computers connected to a single transmission line in a **ring configuration.** This type of system can bypass a malfunctioning unit without disrupting operations throughout the network.

An interesting and more sophisticated approach is the **hierarchical network.** With this approach, an organization's needs are divided into multiple levels that receive different levels of computer support. The lowest is the user level, where only routine transaction computing power is supplied, but this level is connected to the next higher level and its associated information system. At each higher level, the machine size increases while the need for distribution decreases. Thus, such a system consists of a network of small computers tied into a large central computing complex.

Figure 6–6 shows a distributed system consisting of three dispersed minicomputers connected by communication linkages to a large central computer. The three minicomputers are located in three functional departments

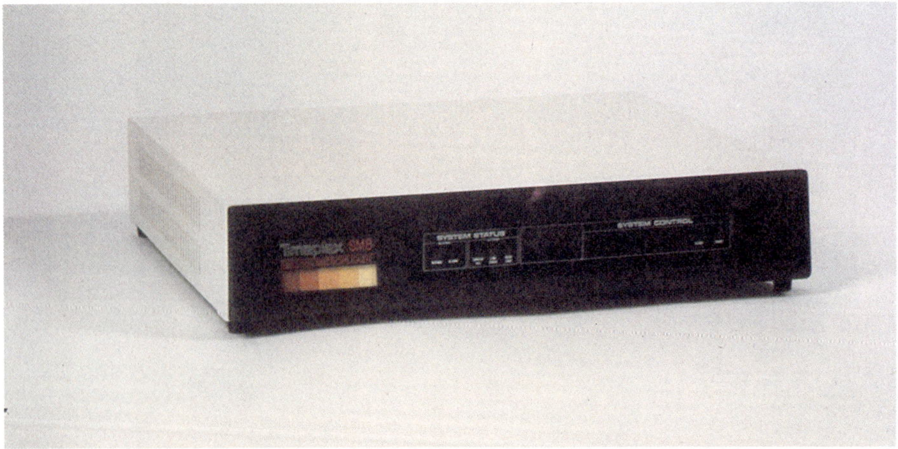

This is an advanced concept in multiplexer design for support of distributed data processing networks. This unit will allow the user to switch between shared-system resources or use in terminal-to-terminal communications.

FIGURE 6–6 Distributed System

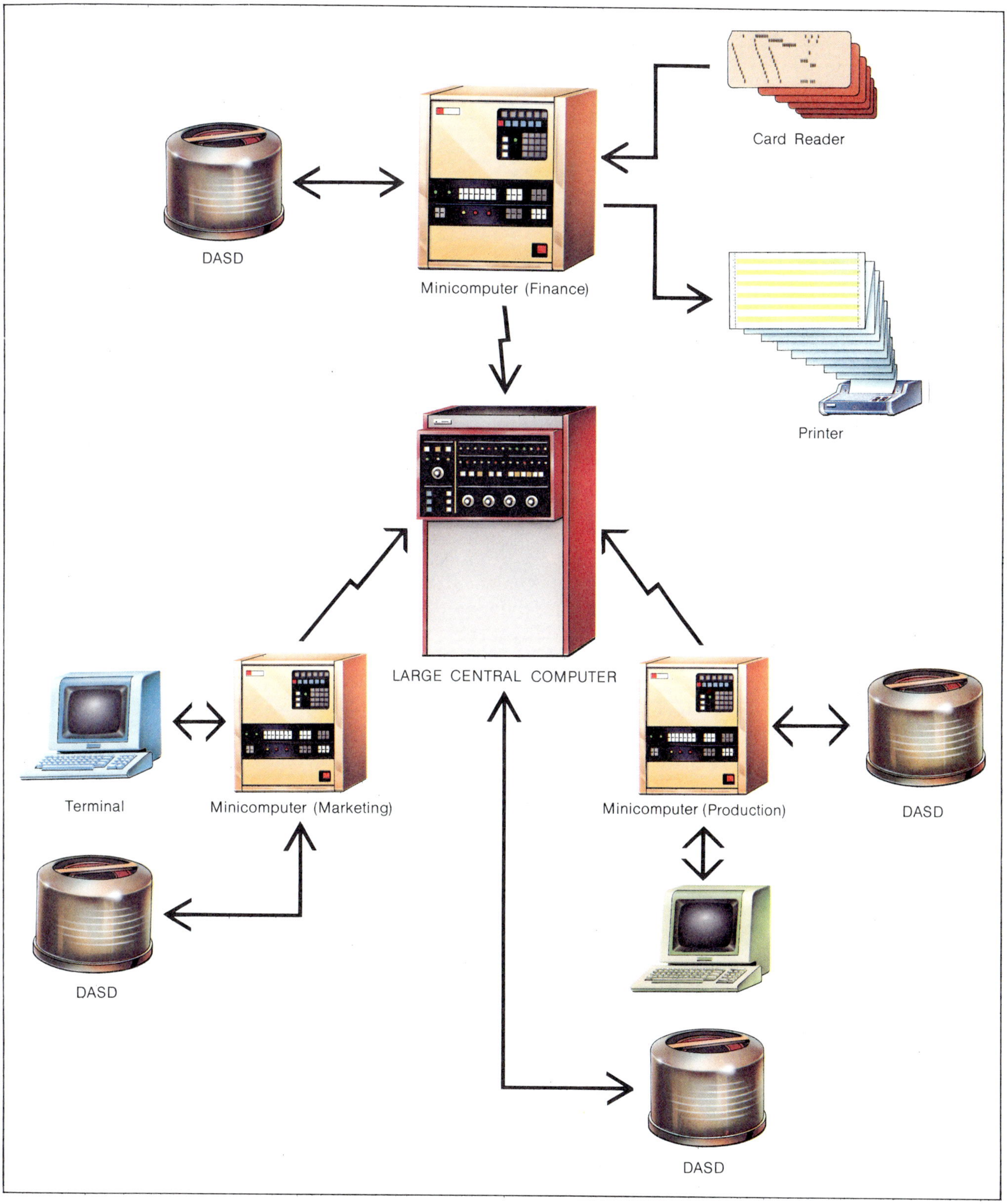

These users are dialing up to connect with their communication network.

of the organization—finance, marketing, and production. Thus, the functional departments can meet their processing requirements locally. Some of the information generated by the minicomputers is communicated to the central computer to be used in corporate-wide planning and control. Such a network provides fast response and great flexibility to local system users. Furthermore, the central facility is available to them for jobs that require computing power beyond the capabilities of the minicomputers.

It is easy to see how the use of networks can greatly enhance a business's data-processing facilities. As more office functions become automated (like word processing) and more applications for minicomputers and microcomputers are developed, computer networks will undoubtedly become one of the more important parts of the data-processing environment.

Distributed Data Processing

Southern Railway Company Southern Railway Company operates a sophisticated network of minicomputers in a distributed approach. This system, located at the Sheffield, Alabama, automatic railroad classification yard, was completed in 1973. The project cost $15 million and took two and a half years to complete. The computer activity is divided into two systems, a management information system (MIS) and a process control (PC) system. Five minicomputers are linked together to form these systems—two on PC, one on MIS, and two on backup (see Figure 6–7).

The system is connected to a large computer installation in Atlanta, Georgia. The information flow begins from Atlanta. About two hours before a train is scheduled to arrive in Sheffield, the Atlanta computer transmits a message to Sheffield. The message consists of the makeup of the train, the

FIGURE 6–7 Southern Railway's Distributed System

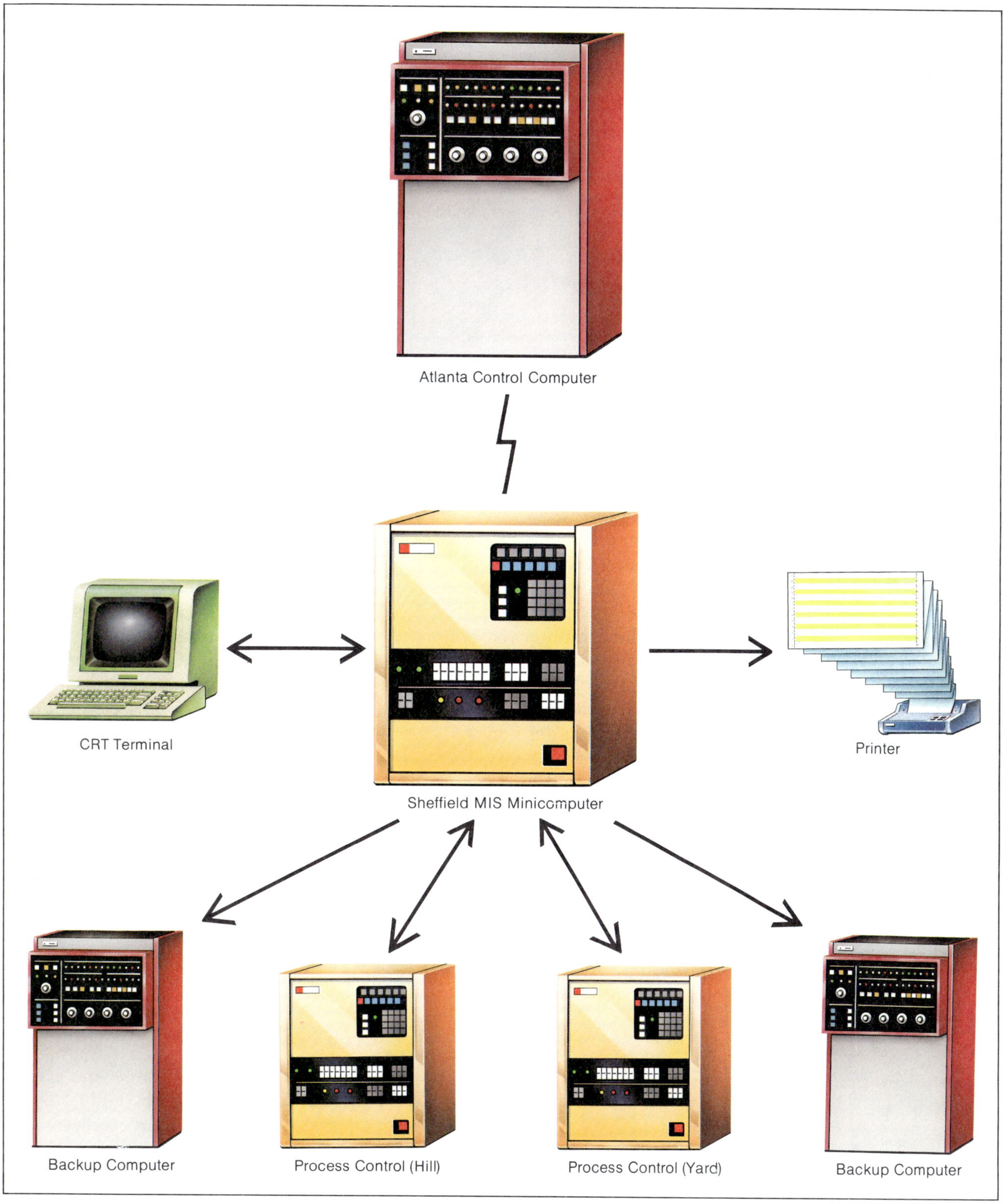

One of the largest computerized message switching complexes in commercial operation, InfoMaster is an integral part of Western Union's communications network. This is the switching center for Mailgram, Telegram, and Cablegram and interconnects Telex subscribers.

car sequence, destination, weight, etc. This data is stored by the MIS minicomputer and printed to assist in planning.

The MIS minicomputer is accessed by the yard supervisor via a CRT. He or she determines which receiving track the cars will go onto and enters this into the computer. From here, the PC minicomputer takes over.

At the end of the receiving track is a small hill. Each inbound car is pushed over the hill and onto one of thirty-two classification tracks. The PC computer determines which classification track is appropriate depending on the car's final destination. The system also controls the speed of the car and car movement. Each car is pushed onto the receiving track at a speed of under four miles per hour. The track switching is also controlled by the minicomputer.

The PC minicomputer is connected to the MIS minicomputer and transmits data about every car, car sequence, destination, and contents, etc. The MIS minicomputer prepares a list of this information and the list is compared to the actual makeup of the train. Thus, a controlled, automated system is achieved. Southern Railway operates its Sheffield station twenty-four hours a day and uses the backup minicomputers in case of breakdown. This application demonstrates how Southern Railway depends on the high reliability of a distributed system.

This financial information system is being used by a broker at a stock exchange.

Bank of America Bank of America maintains 1200 branch banks and 200 Automated Teller Machines (ATMs) throughout California. In addition there are 223 branches, affiliates, subsidiaries, and representative offices in 78 countries abroad. The need to communicate with each of these entities has

resulted in an extensive network of communication channels and computer equipment. The major support for this network comes from two data-processing centers, one located in San Francisco and the other in Los Angeles.

An IBM computer network is used by a southwestern cotton cooperative to provide market information to over 24,000 cotton farmers in Texas and Oklahoma.

An excellent example of a distributed system is Bank of America's Distributed Computing Facility (DCF). The DCF is set up to handle the communication requirements between the branch banks and the IBM host computer located in the data-processing center. Figure 6–8 shows an example of the San Francisco system. The same configuration exists for the Los Angeles system, and the two systems are connected via communication channels.

Terminals at the branch banks are connected by coaxial cable to a control unit, which is also located in the branch bank. This control unit is tied to the DCF minicomputers via telephone circuitry. Connecting the DCF minicomputer to the host computer are six high-speed digital lines that pass customer transaction data from the minicomputers to the host computer. This process allows account balances to be kept up to the minute for all the bank's customers. Customers can inquire about and update information on their accounts.

FIGURE 6–8 Bank of America's Distributed Computing Facility

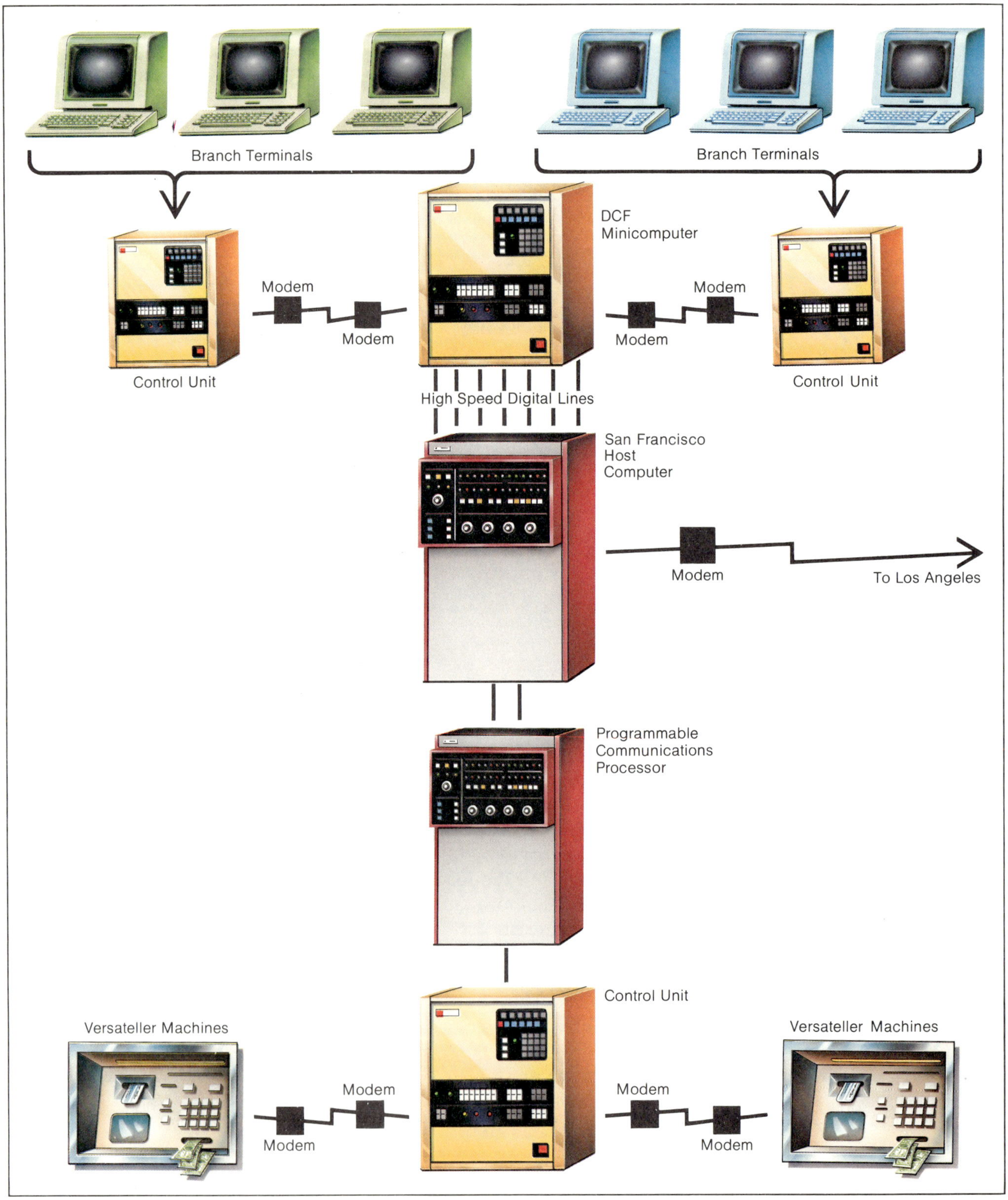

Shipment data is entered into the computer at Santa Fe Railway's data-processing center in Topeka, Kansas. The company is moving toward a distributed computer system in which local, smaller computers will share the overall work with the mainframe units in Topeka.

The DCF system consists of eight independent hardware modules, each handling only a portion of the full customer data base. Thus, if any module goes down, its customer file can be immediately taken over by another module so that teller access is not interrupted.

The DCF is also connected to the Versateller network. Up to eighteen Versateller machines (automated teller machines) are connected to a single control unit via telephone circuitry. Modems at each end of the line make the digital/analog conversion. The control unit is located in the data-processing center and is connected to a programmable communications processor.

These two networks, only a sample of the many communication networks at Bank of America, show how greatly data communication technologies have increased the capabilities and efficiency of data processing in the banking industry.

SATELLITE COMMUNICATION SYSTEMS

The networks discussed so far are earth-based. Today many networks rely on the use of satellite communication channels to extend their ranges to other continents. However, satellite-based networks are very expensive, primarily because they need earth stations (small dish-like antennas) to send and receive messages from the satellites. In the past, satellites have been used mainly for voice and television transmission. However, satellite com-

HIGHLIGHT
Telecommuting: A Modern Alternative

A growing trend all over the world is telecommuting, where employees do their work at home on terminals connected to the company or client's computer via leased phone lines.

U.S. Control Data Corporation is using telecommuting with 60 professional and managerial employees in a voluntary pilot program called "work station." Walgreen, McDonald's, and Mountain States Telephone and Telegraph have installed terminals in the homes of the handicapped in order to enlarge their work forces and to help workers find gainful employment.

Other companies use telecommuting simply because good, qualified workers are increasingly hard to find. For at least one company, offering data base services was the only answer to the problems of no office space and limited company car facilities.

Telecommuting has its drawbacks. Companies are concerned about managing at-home workers. Workers have to contend with the need for self-discipline and with being left out of the office social scene. But, overall the prospects of growing numbers of telecommuters look good.

(a)

(b)

(c)

The Midwest edition of *The Wall Street Journal* is made up into typeset pages at Naperville, Illinois. The pages of the newspaper are then scanned and transmitted by Westar satellite to the earth dish (photo a) at their Bowling Green, Ohio, production plant. There the signals are decoded (photo b) and sent to the laser plate processor (photo c) to make the metal printing plates that are locked directly onto the presses.

munication is looking increasingly attractive for business applications. Satellites can be used by dispersed companies to save time and money in the transfer of voice and data. Communication can be extended across the country or across the world (see Figure 6–9).

In the development of satellites over the past two decades, several problems have emerged that do not exist with terrestrial networks. While satellite communication is a cost-effective method for large companies, it is a very capital- and equipment-intensive industry and satellites must compete with AT&T's existing land-based network. It is generally agreed that satellites are not a substitute for ground networks. Measures must be taken to guard against such things as time delays (also called **propagation** delays), **downtime** (the time the system is not working because of equipment problems), security problems, natural disasters, and even war. And since satellites are often connected to land-based networks, precautions must be taken to avoid possible incompatibility.

Current Satellite Usage

Part of the attractiveness of satellite systems is the capability of transmitting data using a wide bandwidth. This means that more data can be transmitted at a faster rate than with narrow bandwidth (such as telegraph lines) or voice grade bandwidth (telephone lines). In addition, the ability to transmit data from a multitude of locations adds to the effectiveness of satellite usage.

Satellite systems consist of earth stations, or "dishes," that send and receive signals to an orbiting satellite. Located on the satellite itself are a number of **transponders,** small amplifiers that receive the signals from the earth station and reflect them to the appropriate receiving location. A single satellite usually consists of 24 transponders. Each transponder can carry 1 television channel or 1200 voice channels, or it can be used to transmit a stream of data.

To set up a satellite system, the satellite must first be built and launched, requiring a substantial capital investment of between $8 and $40 million for

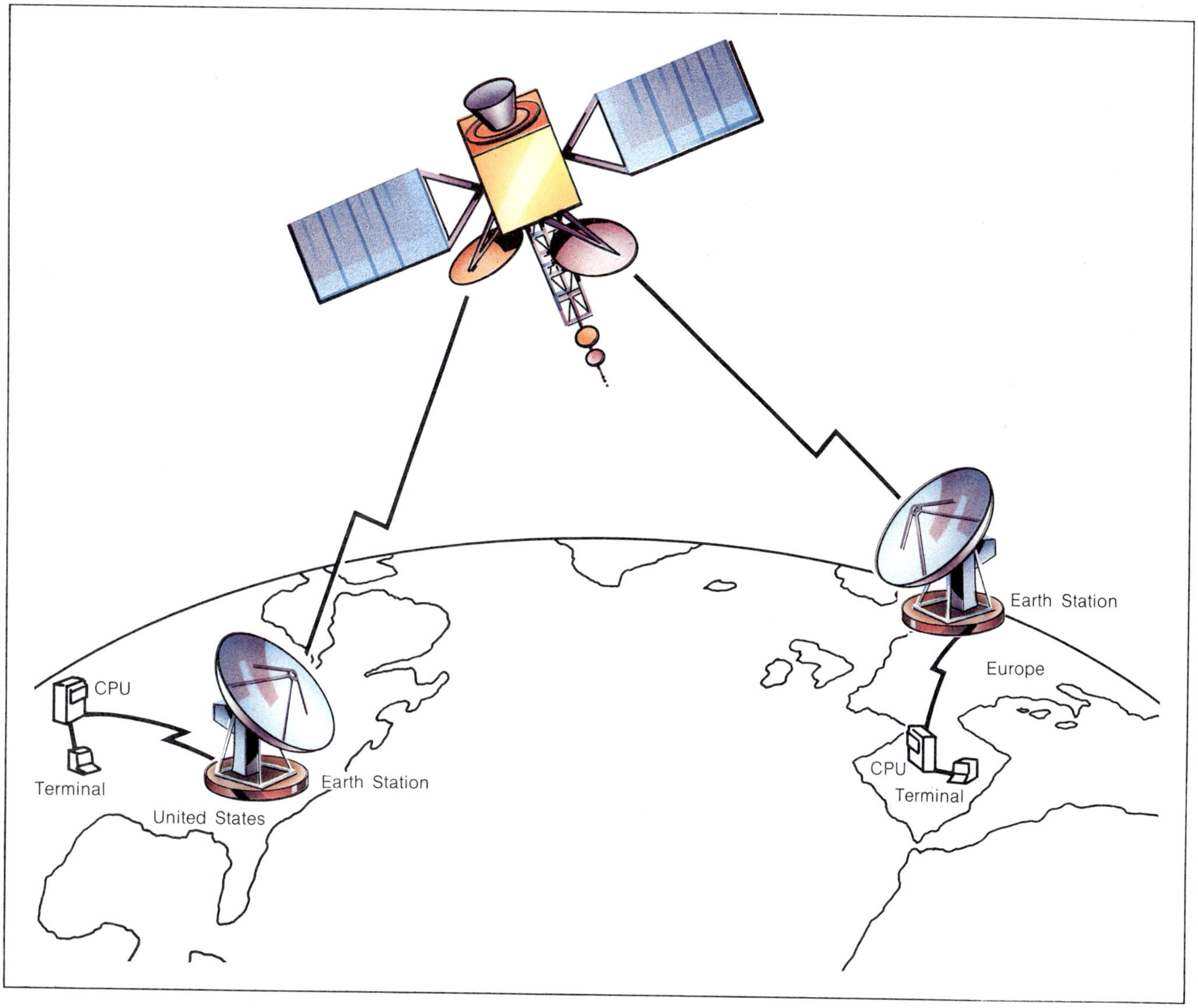

FIGURE 6–9
Satellite Communications

the company. Once the satellite is in orbit, other companies may lease service from the owner of the satellite. Those companies then must either lease or buy an earth station. For example, AT&T presently leases a satellite from Comsat for telephone traffic. The cost of leasing to AT&T, who owns its own earth stations, is $1.3 million per month.

Western Union, another leader in the communication industry, was the first company to establish a commercial system whereby companies lease satellite services. Western Union satellites, referred to as the Westar system, are being used in a multitude of services; Westar not only provides services to the broadcast industry, but also is being used for transmitting text and photographs for regional printing of *The Wall Street Journal, U.S. News and*

HIGHLIGHT
Medallions Help System Subscribers

A new program is offering extra protection and fast aid for emergency situations. The computer-based system is particularly useful to elderly people living alone.

A typical emergency situation involved an elderly lady in Massachusetts who fell and broke her hip. Finding herself unable to move, she sent a signal to the "lifeguard" network by pressing a button on the watch-sized medallion around her neck. Twenty minutes later she was on her way to the hospital in an ambulance, her relatives had been notified, and her doctors alerted.

All this occurred smoothly because her medallion was able to contact the computer service by using an FM signal and telephone lines. Once the signal alerted the computer, her file was secured from the data base. An operator confirmed the emergency by phone. (If no one answers after four rings, an emergency is assumed and the operator begins placing the necessary emergency calls.)

The medallion system is capable of detecting smoke and heat, and the medallion itself can be equipped with a screech alarm. The extra security available to subscribers of the system must be very reassuring.

World Report, Time, People, and *Sports Illustrated.* In addition, Western Union has entered the new and expanding area of video conferencing. For example, Texas Instruments, Inc. leased time from a Westar satellite to broadcast its annual stockholder's meeting. The meetings, held in Dallas, were shown in twenty-two regional offices.

Satellite Business Systems

Satellite Business Systems (SBS) differs from AT&T, Western Union, and other satellite companies in that it caters specifically to the business world. One of SBS's major advantages is its exclusive use of digital transmission to transmit streams of data as well as voice and video. This is particularly advantageous since business computer equipment operates on digital pulses rather than analog, or wave, transmission. This means that digital data can be transmitted via satellites without transforming the data into analog form. SBS also offers technologically advanced satellites that can be used with smaller, less expensive dishes, even in congested cities.

SBS, a joint venture of IBM, Aetna Life & Casualty, and Comsat General Corporation, is located in McLean, Virginia. After a $600 million investment and six years time, SBS's plan was to market its high-speed data communication network to the nation's 100 largest companies. This Communications Network Service (CNS) was designed to handle customers with large amounts of communication needs. The CNS included communication in the form of telephone conversation, video teleconferencing, data transmission,

This equipment, used at Atlantic Richfield, receives geophysical data by satellite.

and document distribution. As of early 1982, SBS had fallen behind projections, with only 25 corporations showing interest. This is because the demand for voice communication is still four times greater than the demand for data transmission in the business world. Some companies using the CNS system are IBM, Boeing Computer Services Company, and Insurance Systems of America Communications, Inc. (Isacomm). IBM has six earth stations in place and uses CNS to enhance their voice communications. Isacomm has six ground stations as well, and Boeing Computer Services uses three earth stations.

Because of the slower-than-expected growth in the demand for CNS, SBS has changed its strategy. Now concentrating on the voice-only market, SBS is competing with well-established companies such as AT&T and MCI Communications Corporation. Because the competition in this market is severe, SBS is making an appeal to smaller companies by offering shared earth stations. This gives companies who cannot afford to lease an earth station by themselves the opportunity to use the SBS network. The Data Exchange Service (DXS) is primarily for small- and medium-size customers with high-volume telephone requirements. The rates for service are said to be priced below AT&T's Wide Area Telephone Services (WATS).

SBS is further providing services to businesses by extending its network into the international market, enabling companies to communicate with overseas offices. The network has already been extended into Canada and arrangements with British firms are waiting the approval of the Federal Communications Commission (FCC).

Remote access systems can greatly enhance the effectiveness of an information system. Considerable time and effort must be expended, however,

Shown here is the control room for NBC television in Burbank, California.

> **HIGHLIGHT**
> ***Computer Maps***
>
> The U.S. Air Force has authorized the Hughes Corporation to produce a system that will display on a TV screen in an airplane detailed maps of the territory it is flying over. These maps will be electronically generated by a computer and will show realistic pictures of the terrain, including features such as roads. If the system lives up to the hopes of its designers, it will enable an airplane to fly low to the ground safely, regardless of light and weather conditions. The system will store up to 250,000 square miles and use more than 1,500 bits of data for each square mile.

to determine the correct match between the input/output device, communication channels, and CPU. Companies are now using communication specialists to analyze their communication needs, evaluate the available hardware, and recommend an effective input/output configuration. For it is only when telecommunication facilities are used effectively that their potential benefits will be fully realized.

SUMMARY POINTS

- Data communication is the electronic transmission of data from one location to another. Communication channels are used to carry data between remote sites and the computer. Types of communication channels include telegraph and telephone lines, coaxial cables, microwave links, and communication channels. The combined use of telephone equipment and data-processing equipment is referred to as teleprocessing.
- Analog transmission is the transmission of data in wave form, while digital transmission transmits data in pulse form. Modems, or data sets, are used to transfer data from digital to wave form (modulation) and back to digital form (demodulation). This conversion is required to send data through telephone channels.
- Communication channels are classified according to grade, or bandwidth; that is, the rate at which data can be transmitted across the channel. The three types of channels in increasing order of volume are: narrow bandwidth, voice-grade, and broad-band channels.
- Channels are also classified by the mode of transmission used. The simplex mode provides one-way transmission, half-duplex allows communication in two directions but in only one direction at a time, and full-duplex channels allow transmission in two directions simultaneously.
- A multiplexer combines the input from several terminals into a stream to be sent over a single channel. Concentrators allow data transmission across a communication channel from one terminal at a time, but will switch from one terminal to another. Both of these increase the number of devices that can use a communication channel.
- To relieve the CPU of the many tasks required in a communication system, a programmable communication processor is used. This device performs message-switching (receiving and routing messages), and, in some cases, front-end processing (preprocessing data).
- Peripherals connected directly to the CPU make up a local system. When communication channels are added to link peripherals to the CPU across a long distance, the system is said to be remote. A network is a configuration of several CPUs and multiple peripherals. This is also called a distributed data-processing system. Types of networks include the star configuration, ring configuration, and hierarchical configuration.
- As businesses expand operations geographically, a greater demand for satellite communication systems results. With advanced technology, satellite communication is becoming a practical and efficient method of communication.

- Satellites are subject to many natural phenomena, including storms, hail, rain, and fog. Precautions must be taken against war and sabotage. Transmission problems may occur because of propagation, or time, delays.
- Satellites provide multipoint locations for data transmission. In addition, the wide bandwidth allows more data to be transmitted at a faster rate. Transponders are small amplifiers located on the orbiting satellite; these devices receive signals from ground stations and reflect the signals to the appropriate location.
- Satellites are used for voice transmission, data transmission, and video transmission. Business applications include videoteleconferencing and electronic transmission of magazine and newspaper text. Business firms lease the use of satellites from a satellite company, and either lease or buy earth stations (dishes) to receive and send data.
- Satellite Business Systems (SBS) is dedicated to providing satellite services for the business environment. Companies of all sizes can link into the SBS networks. SBS is also expanding its network internationally, thereby increasing the efficiency of international data communication.

REVIEW QUESTIONS

1. Distinguish between the terms *local system* and *remote system.* Give examples of a business that would use these systems. How does each apply to single and multiple computer systems?
2. What are modems? What purpose do they serve in data communication systems?
3. Why is digital transmission of data generally preferred over analog transmission?
4. How do multiplexers aid processing?
5. Describe the star configuration, ring configuration, and hierarchical network methods used to tie together several CPUs.
6. Why is the concept of distributed computers extremely important for operations that require complete reliability? Relate this to both the Bank of America application and the Southern Railway application.
7. What is the difference between terrestrial-based communication systems and satellite communications systems? Give examples of companies that would have a need for satellite systems. In what cases would a company prefer a satellite system over a land-based system?
8. What are the major drawbacks of using a satellite system? List some of the business applications for satellite usage.
9. What characteristic of a channel determines the rate of data transmission? Describe the three levels of this characteristic.
10. How does Satellite Business Systems differ from other satellite companies? What is SBS's new marketing strategy and why?

Communication Networks

A. C. Markkula, Jr., President of Apple Computers, predicts that by the year 2000 a personal computer will be as necessary as an automobile is now. His projection is based on the anticipated use of microcomputers as telecommunicators between the individual and huge data banks. Nearly everyone will have as much information available as could be provided by the best of libraries—and it will be easier to access. Location of the individual will no longer be a hindrance to good information, nor will the cost associated with transmission.

Cropping up all over the country are many networks established by and for individuals with shared interests. These electronic mail systems allow individuals to exchange a wide range of information from favorite recipes to the latest in home computer games.

Computer networks are not restricted to the ingenuity of the individual. There are several commercial network services available to subscribers. Two of the largest are *The Source* and *Dow Jones*. A third, *CompuServe, Inc.*, owned by H & R Block, provides an example of the development and growth of this industry. This firm offers a huge data bank full of interesting information. As you can see from the partial listing that follows, the variety of topics offered is indeed wide.

- Home record keeping
- SAT test information
- Silver prices
- Stocks and bonds
- Stamp collecting
- New York Times
- Trivia quizzes
- Travel
- Horse racing
- Science and medical news
- Theater listings
- College financial aid
- Los Angeles Times
- Washington Post
- Tax advice

With CompuServe, news, weather, and sports arrive via wire services; home information with supplementing articles from the current *Better Homes & Gardens* can be accessed. Stocks and financial information, personal finance services, games, and even electronic editions of some major newspapers such as the *New York Times* and *Washington Post* are all popular listings. Subscribers can hook into Aunt Nettie's column of advice on life, love, and trivia. Letters are received throughout the week, and Aunt Nettie replies each Friday. The CB simulator can be used to talk to another good buddy. A line printer art gallery is also available. For a price ranging from about $5 to $20, artwork by the computer will depict Neil Armstrong on the moon, Star Trek's Mr. Spock, Mona Lisa, kittens, or mountains. New graphics are added frequently.

Currently, CompuServe reaches its customers via ComLink networks in about 300 cities. The cost to use

CompuServe is $5 per hour over these lines leased from AT&T. (In areas where ComLinks have not been established, customers pay an additional $2 per hour to connect through MicroNet, a CompuServe-owned computer, time-sharing service.)

CompuServe has had to experiment with and improve upon network structures as the field of home information servicing expanded. Initially, the network was structured in a "star configuration": one long-line circuit connected each remote communications processor with the Columbus, Ohio, computing centers. While functional and cost-effective, such a design had only one communication path for each message; reliability was a worry.

Then, as the network grew, a new structure was developed as a "ring," or "wagon wheel," configuration. Remote links run to more than one processor so that if the direct path breaks down, the message can be routed around the ring and then into Columbus. While more costly, this structure has provided the necessary reliability.

When building the networks, CompuServe aims to balance reliability with cost, flexibility, and performance. Thus, some communications paths are dedicated entirely to particular commercial customers whose needs require very quick response times. So many government information requirements are serviced by CompuServe that a new transmission path will link Washington, D.C., directly to Columbus computer centers. This link will be the first wideband circuit in the network.

CompuServe is also involved with Warner Amex Cable Communications Inc. and Atari in a project using interactive (two-way) cable. An interactive cable TV system, called QUBE, has been used in Columbus, Ohio, since 1977 and allows viewers to "talk back" to their television screens by pushing response buttons on a small console. The system has been particularly useful in gathering consumer information.

Now CompuServe has become available over the QUBE interactive cable by hooking Atari 800 personal computers to television sets. The first cooperative QUBE/CompuServe link was installed in Columbus City Hall to explore how the technology might benefit municipal operations. Although the firms involved are still looking at all the possibilities, some cable applications anticipated are home shopping and banking.

The FBI and other agencies are preparing to fight a new-age crime—electronic thefts. While electronic thievery has been around for many years, the widespread use of personal computers and easy access via phone lines to data banks have aroused a new rash of stealing. Many of these "long-distance hauls" are being made by young people using microcomputers. The FBI has already sent nearly 500 agents to school for courses in electronic crime detection. In addition, auditors of computerized firms are training in the techniques of programmed controls to prevent or detect such abuses. And a bill has been introduced in Congress to make computer tampering a federal crime. In fact, a whole new industry is growing to help protect computer-stored information. Products on the market include software to restrict computer access to data banks, hardware to scramble output being transmitted to other computers, security advice, and detective services. So far, however, no foolproof scheme has managed to eliminate the worry of unauthorized access to business computer files by home computer users. This area will be one of innovation as technology continues to improve long-distance access routes.

Despite some present problems with security, it appears microcomputers are here to stay. Computer network services are greatly increasing their services and amount of information available to the personal computer user. If this is any indication of consumer interest, we can expect to see the personal computer soon become an integral part of our everyday lives.

DISCUSSION QUESTIONS

1. Describe why the "ring" configuration would be more reliable than the "star" configuration network.
2. What topics other than those shown in the sample listing for CompuServe would be of use to the personal computer owner for home or business?

CHAPTER 7

Storage Devices and Process Design

INTRODUCTION

Business organizations maintain a considerable amount of data regarding production, employees, customers, inventory levels, and other data required to perform their business function. Each application will have specific job requirements regarding the timing, costs, and volume of data processed that will largely influence the design of the computer-based files.

This chapter examines the two most popular types of data storage media, magnetic tape and disk. In addition, the three most common types of file arrangements utilizing tapes and disks (sequential, direct-access, and indexed-sequential) are discussed. Finally, considerations regarding the use of mass storage in file design are covered.

FACING PAGE
Rows and rows of disk drives at AT&T's computer center at Knightsbridge, New Jersey.

CHAPTER OUTLINE

CLASSIFICATION

A computer system generally includes two types of storage: **primary storage** and **auxiliary,** or **secondary, storage.** Primary storage, discussed in Chapter 4, is actually part of the CPU and is used to store both instructions and data. In many instances, the amount of data required by a program or set of programs exceeds the capacity of primary storage. In such cases, the data is stored in auxiliary, or secondary, storage. Secondary storage is not part of the CPU. The most common types of secondary storage are magnetic tapes and magnetic disks. Media such as punched cards, mass storage, and magnetic drums are also used. These auxiliary storage media cost much less than primary storage and thus make storage of large volumes of data economically feasible.

The secondary storage media are connected to the CPU, and once data has been placed in them it can be retrieved as needed for processing. However, the retrieval of items from secondary storage is slower than from primary storage. After processing has been completed, the data or results can be written back onto the auxiliary medium (see Figure 7–1).

Access to data in auxiliary storage can be either direct or sequential. The method depends on the storage medium used. Storage media such as magnetic tape and cassette tape provide **sequential-access storage.** The computer must start at the beginning of a tape and read what is stored there until it comes to the desired data. In contrast, storage media such as a magnetic disk or magnetic drum do not have to be read sequentially; the computer can get access to the desired data immediately—hence the name **direct-access storage.** Direct-access media, then, provide faster retrieval than do sequential-access media.

SEQUENTIAL-ACCESS MEDIA

Magnetic Tape

A **magnetic tape** is a continuous plastic strip wound on a reel, quite similar to the tape used in reel-to-reel stereo recorders. The magnetic tape's plastic base is treated with a magnetizable coating. Typically, the tape is one-half inch in width. It is wound in lengths of 2,400 feet on ten-and-a-half-inch diameter reels. Magnetic tapes are also packaged in cartridges for use with small computers.

Data is stored on magnetic tape by magnetizing small spots of the iron oxide coating on the tape. Although these spots can be read by the computer, they are invisible to the human eye. Large volumes of information can be stored on a single tape; densities of 1,600 characters per inch are common, and some tapes are capable of storing up to 6,250 characters per inch. A typical tape reel of 2,400 feet can store as much as 400,000 punched cards (see Figure 7–2).

A magnetic tape is mounted on a **tape drive** when the information it contains is needed by a program. The tape drive has a **read/write head** (actually an electromagnet) that creates or reads the bits as the tape moves past it (see Figure 7–3). When it is reading, the read/write head detects the magnetized

FIGURE 7–1 Secondary Storage for a Computer System

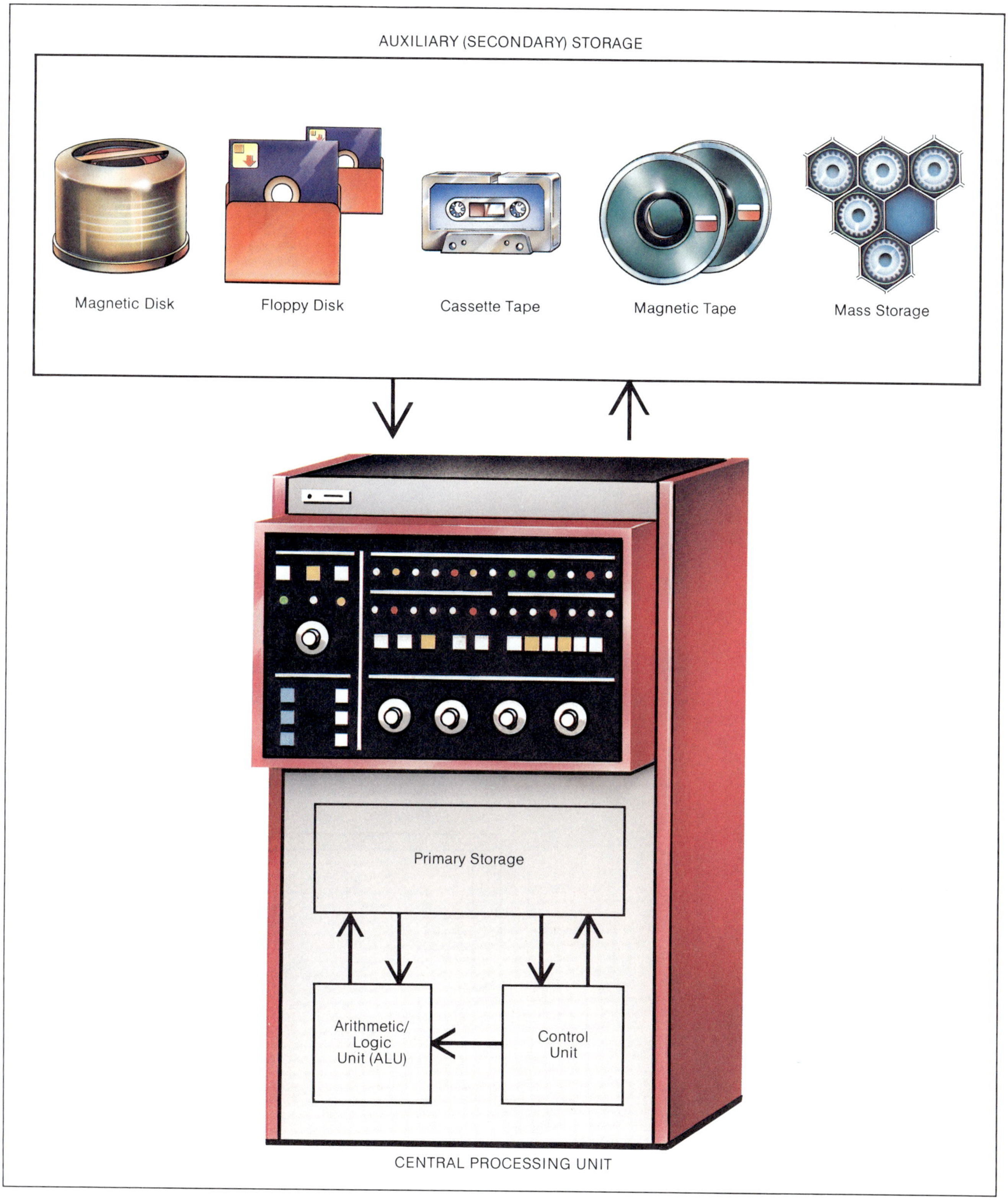

FIGURE 7–2
Magnetic-Tape Drive

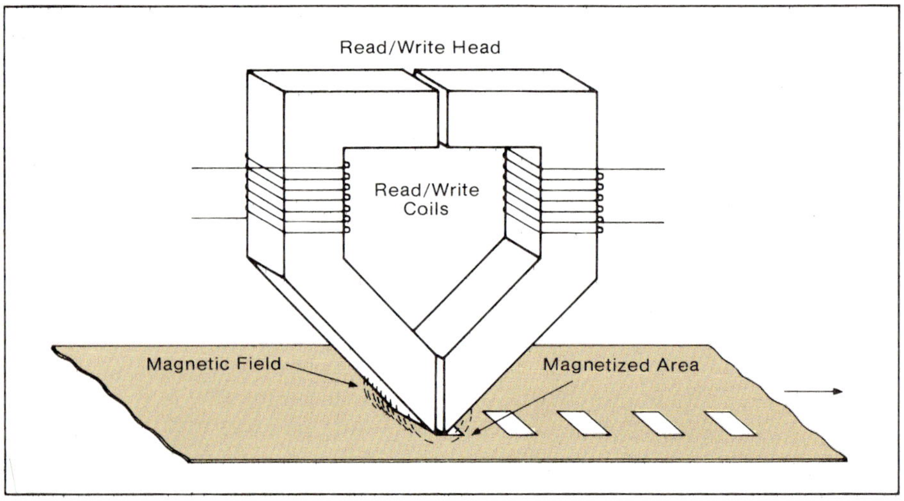

FIGURE 7–3
Recording on Magnetic Tape

areas and converts them into electrical pulses to send to the CPU. When writing, the head magnetizes the appropriate spots on the tape, erasing any previously stored data. Thus, writing is destructive and reading is nondestructive.

Individual records on magnetic tape are separated by **interrecord gaps (IRGs),** as shown in Figure 7–4. These gaps do not contain data but perform another function. A tape is rarely read in its entirety, all at once. Rather, it is stopped after the end of a record is reached. The tape must then be accelerated to the correct speed to allow the next record to be read correctly; otherwise the result would be similar to what happens when a phonograph record is played at the wrong speed. The IRG allows the tape to regain the proper speed before the next record is read. The length of the interrecord gap depends on the speed of the tape drive; if the tape drive is very fast, longer gaps are needed, while slower speeds require shorter gaps.

If records are very short and divided by equally long IRGs, the tape may be more than 50 percent blank, causing the tape drive to be constantly stopping and accelerating. To avoid this possibility, records may be grouped, or blocked. These **blocked records,** or **blocks,** are separated by **interblock gaps (IBGs),** as in Figure 7–5. Now instead of reading a short record and stopping, reading a short record and stopping, and so on, the read/write head reads a block of short records at once and then stops, reads another block and stops, and so on. This method reduces the overall input/output time. An entire block of records can be transferred to primary storage for processing. Blocking also reduces the wasted space on the tape, permitting more records to be stored on a given length of tape.

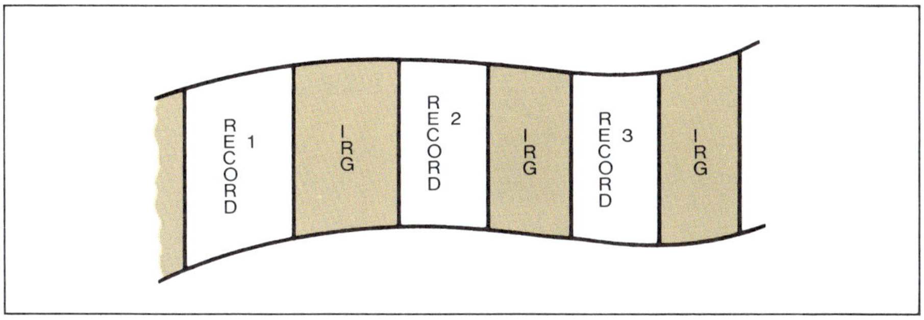

FIGURE 7–4
Magnetic-Tape Records

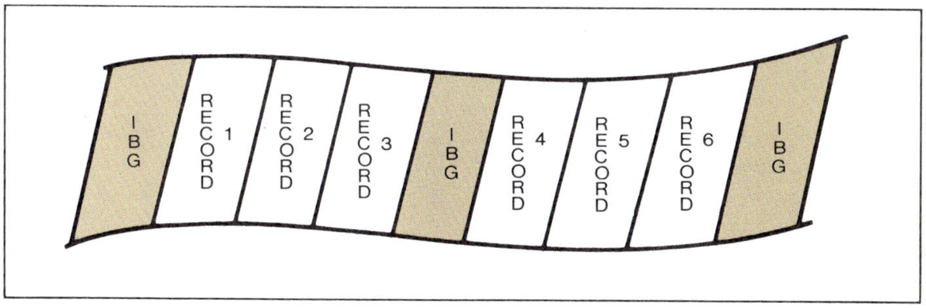

FIGURE 7–5
Blocked Records

HIGHLIGHT
Computer Sales Pitches

If you've been succumbing to telephone sales pitches lately, maybe you're being sweet-talked by a computer. Well, it's not exactly the computer talking—it's a computer telling a real person how to talk away your sales resistance. The system that does this, Salesnet, is a product of the venerable Dun & Bradstreet Corp. Salesnet provides telephone salespeople with computer terminals on which can be called up prospects' names, phone numbers, and customized sales scripts. As the prospect responds to the sales pitch, his or her responses are fed into the computer. It then flashes back a counterresponse for the salesperson to use. It's not clear what the proper counterresponse is to a loud click at the other end of the line.

Cassette Tape

Small computer systems may not need a large amount of auxiliary storage. For these systems **tape cassettes** have been developed. Tape cassettes look like those used in audio recording, and some can even be used with a typical cassette player/recorder. The major difference between the two types of tape cassettes is the tape: tape cassettes used for storing data use higher-quality, high-density digital recording tape (see Figure 7–6).

Because of the low cost and convenience of tape cassettes, their use for input, output, and storage has increased greatly in minicomputer and microcomputer systems. Tape cassettes are an ideal storage system for home computers. They can be used with a standard cassette player purchased for roughly $50 to $60. Tape cassettes are easy to store and also provide security, since they can be removed from the system and carried with the user.

SEQUENTIAL DESIGN

If we need to find a particular record and the set of records in a file is very small, then it may not be difficult to search the file from the beginning to find the record. For files containing large numbers of records, however, this method is impractical. A special ordering technique is needed so that records can be retrieved more easily. For this reason, employee records, for example, may be arranged according to social security number. Figure 7–7 shows an example of what an employee file might look like. Similarly, rec-

FIGURE 7–6
The data tape cassette is the same size as audio cassettes; it is, however, built to more exacting standards with much better quality materials.

ords in an inventory file may be arranged according to item number. The identifier used to locate a particular record in the file is called a **key.** Since a key is used to locate a particular record, it must be unique—that is, no two records in a sequential file can have the same key value. The group of records ordered according to their key values form a **sequential file.**

Updating involves two sets of files: the basic file containing all existing records is called the **master file,** and the file containing changes to be made to the master file is called a **transaction file.** The master file is organized according to the identifier chosen as a key. Since records on the master file must be read sequentially, processing is greatly enhanced if the transaction records are sorted according to the same key. That is, the transaction file should also be sequentially organized.

In updating, both the master file and the transaction file serve as input to the computer system. The computer compares the key of the first master record with the key of the first record on the transaction file. If the keys do not match, the next record on the master file is read. When a match between the transaction record and a master record occurs, the master record is updated. If a master record has no matching transaction record, it is left unchanged. If a transaction record has no matching master record, an error or warning message may be generated.

The updated master record can be longer or shorter than it was before the updating occurred. In some cases, a transaction may require the insertion, in sequence, of a new master record. In other cases, a transaction may delete an entire master record. Since records are stored one after the other on a sequential file, these types of transactions cannot be handled using the old master file alone. To allow such processing, a new master file is created whenever changes are made to the old master file. Every master record not explicity deleted must be written into the new master file, whether or not it is changed. A new master record can easily be inserted in the file by writing

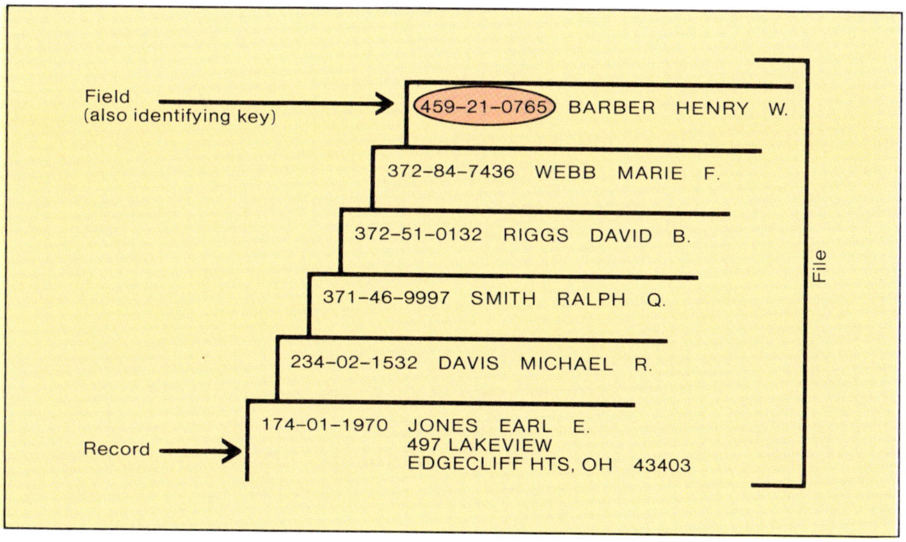

FIGURE 7–7
Employee Data—ABC Company

"The following changes of address are effective as of December 24."

it into the new master immediately after the old one it follows and before the next old master is copied from the old file. The process of creating an entirely new master file each time transactions are processed is called **sequential processing.** When sequential processing is utilized, there is no way to directly locate the matching master record for a transaction. Every time a given master record is to be updated, the entire master file must be read and a new master file created. To eliminate a great deal of unnecessary processing, transactions are collected for a given time period and then processed against the master file in one run. This approach is called **batch processing** (see Figure 7–8).

The amount of time required to update a record in the sequential processing mode includes the time needed to process the transaction, read and rewrite the master file until the proper record is reached, update the master record, and complete rewriting the master file. To reduce the time needed, the transactions are sorted to reflect the order of the master file. For security, the old master file and the transaction records are retained for a period of time; then, if the new master is accidentally destroyed, it can be reconstructed from the old master and the transaction files. In many instances,

FIGURE 7–8 Batch Sequential Processing

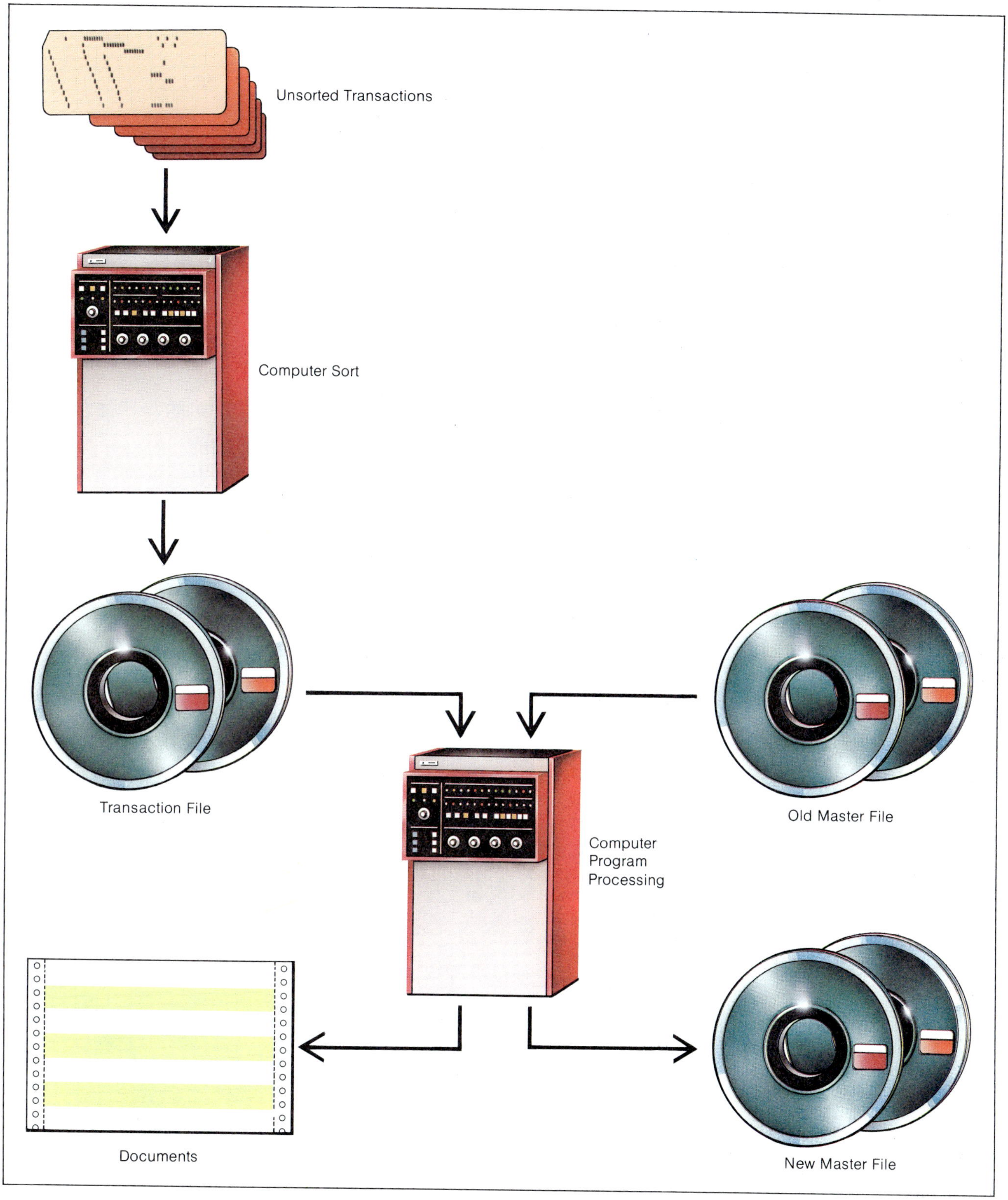

two generations of old masters are kept, giving rise to the terms "father" and "grandfather" backup copies.

Example of Sequential Processing

The billing operation is well suited to sequential processing. Customers' bills must be prepared, but only at scheduled intervals. Standard procedures apply, and large numbers of records must be processed.

Processing customer records results in the preparation of bills for customers and updates of the amounts they owe. Magnetic tape is an appropriate medium for this application because the customer records can be arranged in customer number order and processed in sequence accordingly.

The procedure for preparing the billing statements involves the following steps:

Step a: The transaction cards indicating which items have been shipped to customers are keypunched and verified. One card is used for each item shipped (see Figure 7–9a).

Step b: The data on the cards is transferred to magnetic tape. The card-to-tape program also edits the input data. Editing checks include tests to make sure the contents of fields are within reasonable limits, numeric fields have numeric data, alphanumeric fields have al-

Here FBI computer operators are staging magnetic tapes for processing.

phanumeric data, and so forth. The card-to-tape run provides a report of invalid transactions so that they can be corrected (see Figure 7–9b).

Step c: The transaction records are sorted according to customer number, because the customer master file is arranged in customer number order (see Figure 7–9c).

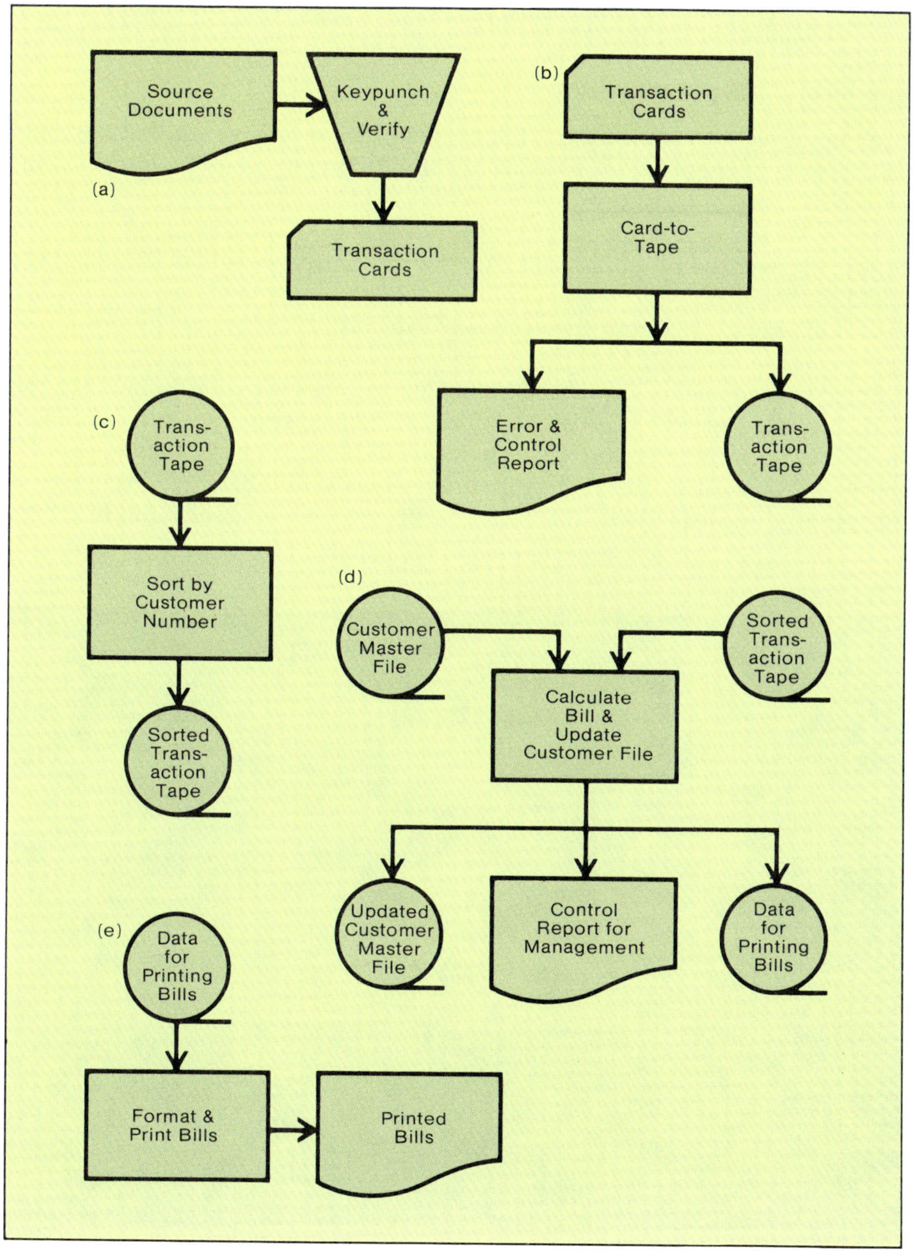

FIGURE 7–9
Billing Operations

Step d: The sorted transactions are used to update the customer master file. The process involves reading the transaction records and master records into main storage (there may be more than one transaction record for a master record). The master record is updated to reflect the final amount owed by the customer. Usually, during an update, a report is also printed for management. For example, during the billing update, a listing of customers who have exceeded their credit limits may be printed (see Figure 7–9d).

Step e: The customers' bills are prepared from the data generated in the previous step (see Figure 7–9e).

Interrogating Sequential Files

How inquiries into a sequential file on magnetic tape are handled depends on the type of inquiry. Let us consider the following inquiries into the employee file shown in Figure 7–7.

1. List the records of employees with social security numbers 234–02–1532 and 372–84–7436.
2. List all employees from the area with zip code 43403.

The employee file is sequenced according to social security number. In the first case the file will be searched for the correct social security numbers from the beginning of the file, but only the key of each record will be checked. As soon as the required social security numbers are located and the required records listed, the search is stopped. Of course, if the numbers

Shown here is a minicomputer system with magnetic tapes stacked in the background.

are in the last two records on the file, then the entire file must be searched. For the second inquiry, the entire file will have to be searched. In this case, the zip code field of each record must be checked to see if it matches 43403. This illustrates one problem with referring to a non-key field on sequential files. If an inquiry is based on a field other than the key, then a great deal of time may be wasted in the search process. To alleviate this problem a second employee file ordered by zip code could be created; however, this approach requires maintaining multiple files that contain duplicate data.

Assessment of Sequential Design

Advantages of sequential processing and file design include the following.

- It is suitable for many types of applications—payroll, billing, preparation of customer statements, and so forth—that require periodic updating of large numbers of records.
- If at least half the records in a master file are updated during a processing run, the large volume of transactions reduces the processing cost per record.
- The design of sequential files is simple.
- Magnetic tape, a low-cost medium, can be used to maximum advantage.
- Input and output speeds are higher than those achieved with direct input of transactions from terminal keyboards.

The disadvantages of this mode of processing include the following.

- The entire master file must be processed and a new master file written even if only a few master records have to be updated.
- Transactions must be sorted in a particular sequence; this takes time and can be expensive.
- The master file is only as up to date as the last processing run. In many instances, the delay in processing the master file results in use of old (and thus incorrect) information.
- The sequential nature of the file organization is a serious handicap when unanticipated inquiries must be made.

DIRECT-ACCESS MEDIA

Magnetic Disk

The conventional **magnetic disk** is a metal platter fourteen inches in diameter coated on both sides with a magnetizable material like iron oxide. In many respects, a magnetic disk resembles a phonograph record. However, it does not have a phonograph record's characteristic grooves; its surfaces are smooth. Nevertheless, a disk unit does store and retrieve data in much the same fashion as a phonograph. The disk is rotated while a read/write head is positioned above its magnetic surface. Instead of spiraling into the center of the disk like the needle of a phonograph, however, the data is

HIGHLIGHT
Jackpot Banking

A modern day Jesse James might have more luck robbing banks with a plastic card than with blazing guns—although the odds for success are slim in either instance. In Phoenix, an insurance clerk "asked" an automatic teller machine to dispense her $40 from her checking account. By the time her transaction was over with, she had walked away with $5,140. It seems that she had hit the "savings" button accidentally. Instead of rejecting her request—as it was programmed to do—the machine spewed out $600 in $20 bills. Intrigued by such largesse, the clerk kept pressing buttons until she had the $5,140 in hand. The machine didn't end the game, she did. Not having Jesse James' outlook, the clerk notified the bank of the botch, but not before she took the money home and played with it for a while. A bank official, predictably, refused to say what the defect in the automatic philanthropist was. Maybe it just wanted to make friends.

stored in a set of concentric circles. Each circle is referred to as a **track.** One track never touches another, as shown in Figure 7–10. A typical disk has two hundred tracks per surface.

In most disk storage devices, several disks are assembled to form a **disk pack** (see Figure 7–11) and mounted on a center shaft. The individual disks are spaced on the shaft to allow room for a mechanism to move between them (see Figure 7–12). The disk pack in Figure 7–12 has eleven disks and provides twenty usable recording surfaces; the top and bottom surfaces are not used for storing data because they are likely to become scratched or nicked. A disk pack may contain anywhere from six to eleven disks.

A disk pack must be positioned in a disk drive when the data on the pack is to be processed. The **disk drive** rotates all disks in unison at a speed ranging from 40 to 3,600 revolutions per second. In some models, the disk packs are removable; in others, the disks are permanently mounted on the disk drive. Removable disk packs allow disk files to be removed when the data they contain is not needed. Users of removable disk packs typically have many more disk packs than disk drives (see Figure 7–13).

FIGURE 7–10
Top View of Disk Surface Showing Concentric Tracks

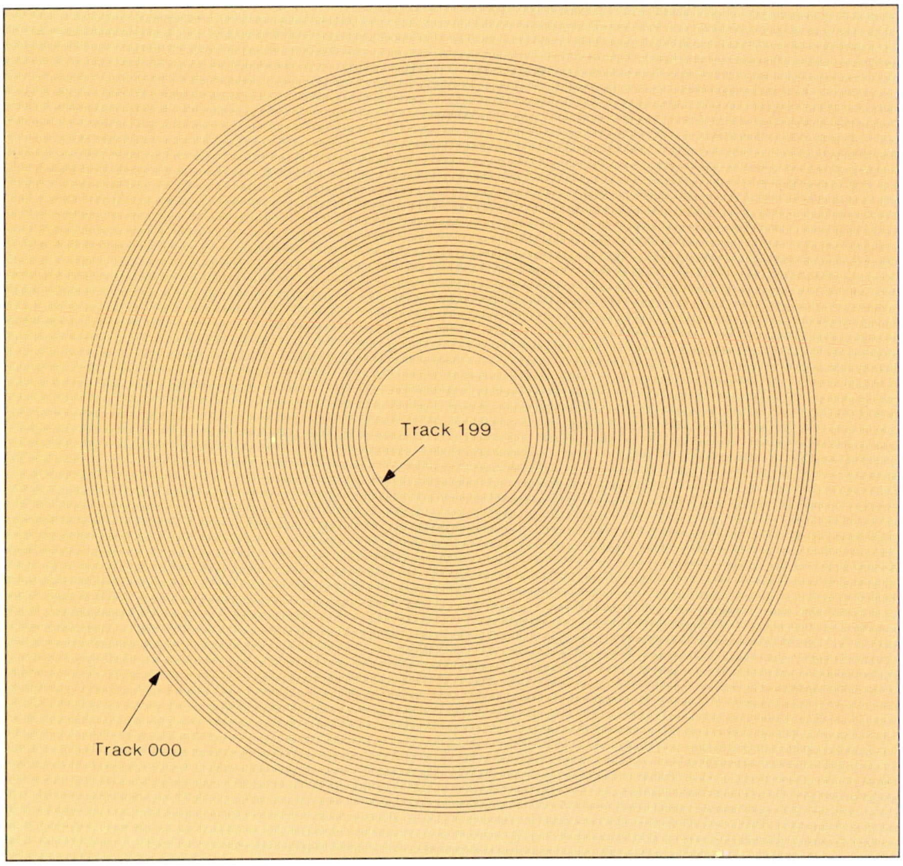

FIGURE 7–11
Disk Pack

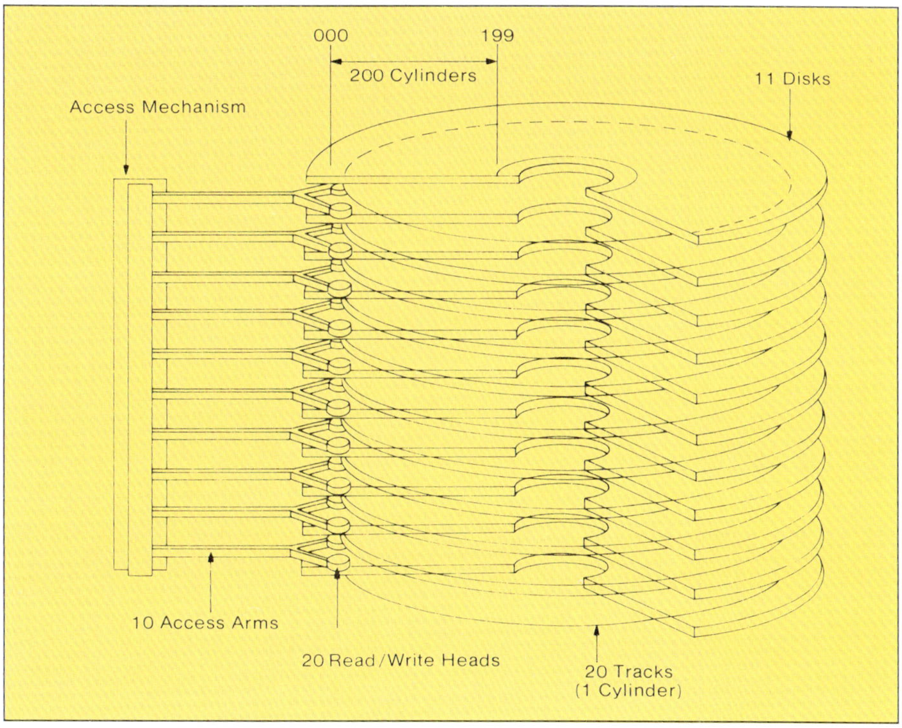

FIGURE 7–12
Disk Pack Showing Read/Write Heads

FIGURE 7–13
Disk Storage Units with Removable Disk Packs

The data on a disk is read or written by the read/write heads between the disks. Most disk units have one read/write head for each disk recording surface. All the heads are permanently connected to an **access mechanism.** When reading or writing occurs, the heads are positioned over the appropriate track by the in-and-out movement of the access mechanism (see Figure 7–12). Some disk units have one read/write head for each track. The access time is much faster with this type of disk unit since the access mechanism does not need to move from track to track, but such units are rarely used because of their high costs.

A technician checks a disk pack for flaws, scratches or dust. Even minute flaws in the disk, such as fingerprints, can cause major damage to the system.

Because disks provide direct access, they are typically used to store data against which frequent inquiries are required. Depending upon the disk drive, transfer rates of up to 850,000 characters per second are possible.

Floppy Disk

The **flexible disk, diskette,** or **floppy disk** was introduced in 1973 (see Figure 7–14) to replace punched cards as a medium for data entry, but it can also store programs and data files. These floppy disks are made of plastic and coated with an oxide substance. They are, in most respects, miniature magnetic disks. The diskettes often sell for as little as $5 and are very popular for use with minicomputer systems and point-of-sale terminals. They are reusable, easy to store, and weigh less than two ounces. They are readily interchangeable and can even be mailed. Because flexible disks are removable, they provide added security for a computer system. A typical disk can store as much as 3,000 punched cards. Advances in technology are greatly expanding the floppy disk's storage capacity.

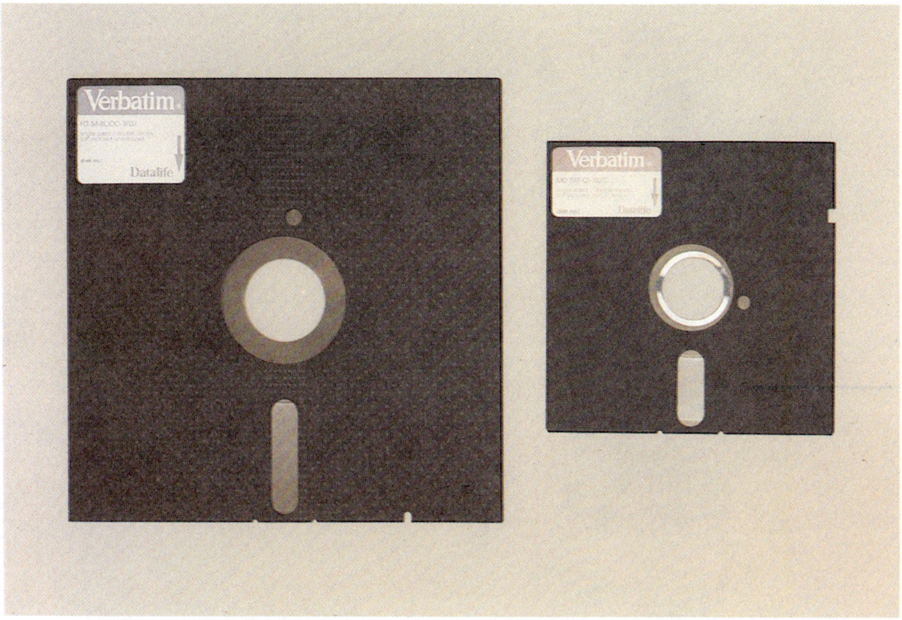

FIGURE 7–14
Eight-Inch and Five-and-A-Quarter-Inch Floppy Disks

DIRECT-ACCESS DESIGN

Direct-access processing is suited to applications involving files with **low activity** and **high volatility.** Activity refers to the proportion of records processed during an updating run, and volatility refers to the frequency of changes to a file during a certain time period.

In contrast to a batch-processing system, a direct-access system does not require that transaction records be grouped or sorted before they are processed. Data is submitted to the computer in the order it occurs. **Direct-access storage devices (DASDs),** such as magnetic-disk drive units, make this type of processing possible. A particular record on a master file can be accessed directly using its assigned keys and updated without all preceding records on the file being read. Only the key to the record need be known. Thus, up-to-the-minute reports can be provided. For example, assume Ralph Smith's address in the employee master file in Figure 7–7 had to be changed. With direct-access processing, the computer can locate the record to be updated without sequentially processing all records that precede it. Figure 7–15 shows how direct-access processing would be used in a business.

A major consideration in the use of direct-access processing is finding the record to be updated. For the record to be located, its address or location on the disk must be known. The address is usually a number from five to seven digits in length that is related to the physical characteristics of the direct-access storage device (see Figure 7–16). The address can be obtained through a transformation process on the record key (also called **randomizing** or **hashing**) or from a **directory.** Directories list reference numbers along with their corresponding addresses in storage (see Figure 7–17). During pro-

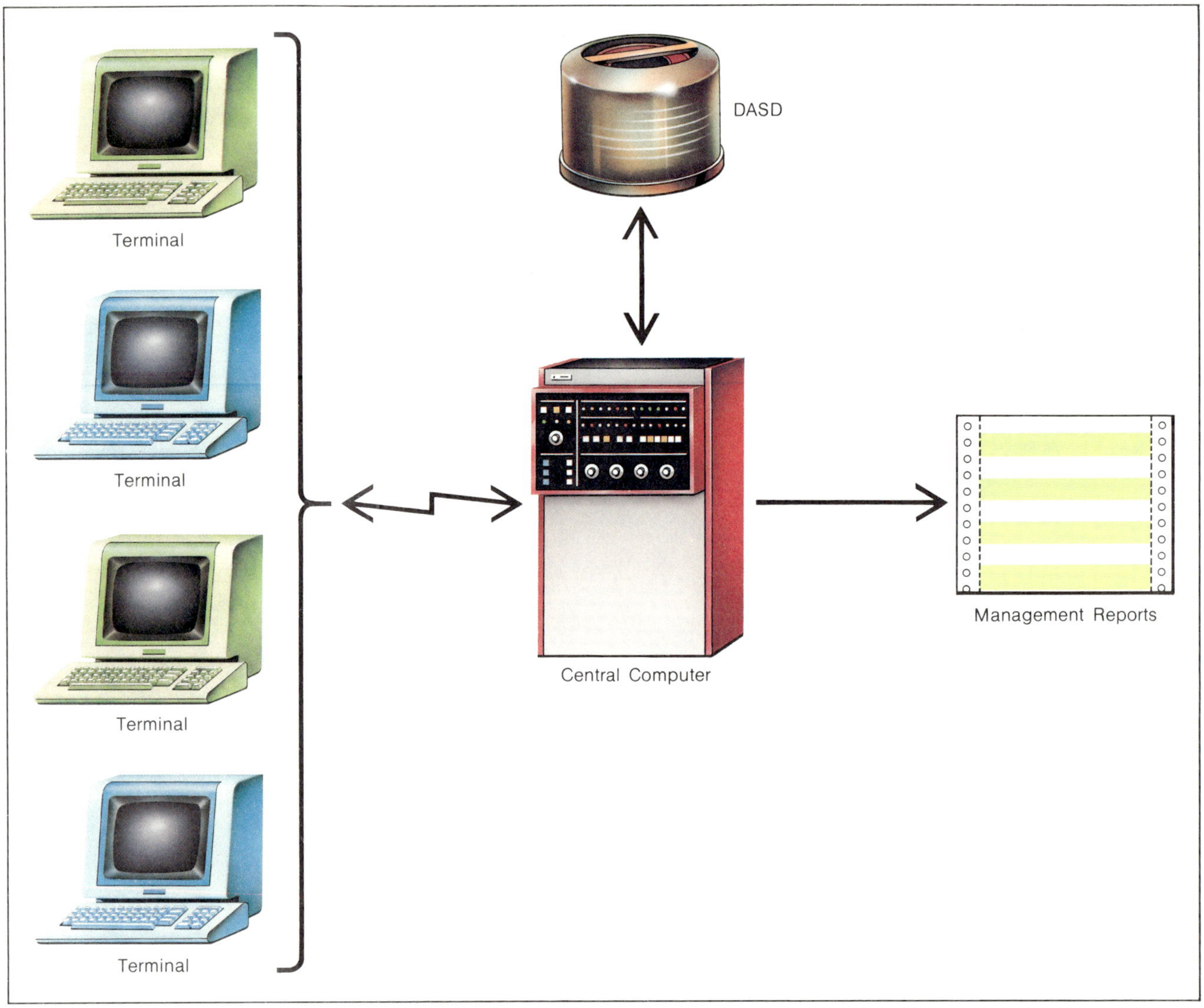

FIGURE 7–15
Direct-Access Processing

cessing, the computer searches the directory to locate the address of a particular record.

Interrogating Direct-Access Files

To see how direct-access files handle inquiries, let us look again at the two inquiries discussed in connection with sequential files:

1. List the records of employees with social security numbers 234–02–1532 and 372–84–7436.
2. List all employees from the area with zip code 43403.

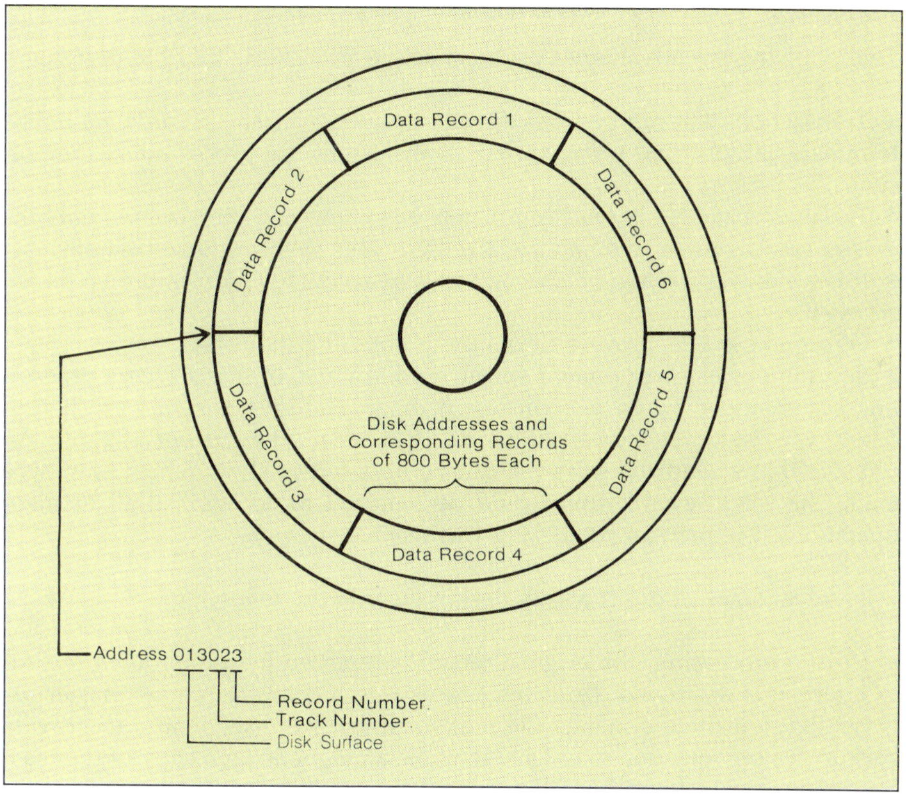

FIGURE 7–16
Disk Address

With regard to the first inquiry, the records of the two employees can be located directly, assuming the social security number is used as the key.

The approach used for the second inquiry will depend on the organization of the file. If much processing is done based on a geographic breakdown of employees, a directory relating zip codes and their record addresses can be created (as in Figure 7–17). However, if ABC is a small company, a directory to locate employee records by zip code may have little value. In this case, we encounter the same situation we did with sequential files: The entire file must be read to obtain the desired information. This could take a great deal of time.

ZIP CODE	ADDRESS
43403	12043
43403	12140
44151	12046
44153	12143
44200	12146
44201	12045

FIGURE 7–17
Directory for Zip Codes

Assessment of Direct-Access Design

The following are advantages of direct-access processing and file design.

- Transaction data can be used directly to update master records via online terminals without first being sorted. Transactions are processed as they occur.
- The master file is not read completely each time updating occurs; only the master records to be updated are accessed. This saves time and money.
- It takes only a fraction of a second to gain access to any record on a direct-access file.
- Direct-access files provide flexibility in handling inquiries.
- Several files can be updated concurrently by use of direct-access processing. For example, when a credit sale is made, the inventory file can be updated, the customer file can be changed to reflect the current accounts receivable figure, and the sales file can be updated to show which employee made the sale. Several runs would be required to accomplish all of these operations if sequential processing was used.

Disadvantages of direct-access design include the following.

- During processing, the original record is replaced by the updated record. In effect, it is destroyed. (In batch processing, a completely new master file is created, but the old master file remains intact.) Consequently, to provide backup, an organization may have to make a magnetic-tape copy of the master file weekly and also keep the current week's transactions so that master records can be reconstructed if necessary.
- Since many users may have access to records stored on direct-access devices in online systems, the chances of accidental destruction of data are greater. Special programs are required to edit input data and to perform other checks to ensure that data is not lost. Also, there exists the possibility of confidential information falling into unauthorized hands; additional security procedures are necessary to reduce this risk.
- Implementation of direct-access systems is often difficult because of their complexity and the high level of programming (software) support that such systems need.

INDEXED-SEQUENTIAL DESIGN

Sequential processing is suitable for applications where the proportion of records processed in an updating run is high. However, sequential files provide slow response times and cannot adequately handle file inquiries. On the other hand, direct-access processing is inappropriate for applications like payroll where most records are processed during a single run. When a single file must be used for both batch processing and online processing, neither direct-access nor sequential file organization is appropriate. The same customer file that is used in a weekly batch run for preparing bills by the accounting department may be used daily by order-entry personnel to record orders and check credit status. To some extent, the limitations of both types of file design can be minimized by using another approach to file organization—**indexed-sequential design.**

In this structure, the records are stored sequentially on a direct-access storage device according to a primary key. A **primary key** is a field that will be unique for each record on the file. In addition, secondary keys can also be established. **Secondary keys** are fields that are to be used to gain access to records on the file, but which may not be unique. For instance, if zip code is chosen as a secondary key, there may be several records with the same value. Records on an indexed-sequential file can be accessed randomly by using either the primary or one of the secondary keys, or the file can be read sequentially—in primary-key sequential order.

The method used to gain access to a record on an indexed-sequential file is a little different than on a direct-access file. Every record on an indexed-sequential file may not have its own unique address. Rather, several records may be grouped together and one address given for the entire group. An index table is created for all fields which are primary or secondary keys. The index table lists the value of the key (such as social security number) and the corresponding address on the direct-access storage device at which the group containing that record can be found. A key given by the user is matched against the index table to get an approximate address for the required record. The computer then goes to that location on the direct-access storage device and checks records sequentially until the desired record is found. In the case of secondary keys, all records with that key may be retrieved.

Figure 7–18 shows the employee file from Figure 7–7 set up as an indexed-sequential file. The primary key is a social security number, while zip code is a secondary key. Notice how the records are in sequence according to the social security number on the file. To locate an employee with a zip code equal to 43403, the computer goes to the index table for zip code (see Figure 7–19). Next to the value 43403 is the address on the direct-access storage device at which the group containing that record can be found, 1015. The computer goes to that address and reads each record in the group until the one with zip code 43403 is found. In this case, it is the first record in the group.

Thus, an indexed-sequential file provides direct-access capability. Since all the records are ordered according to a primary key, it also allows efficient sequential processing.

HIGHLIGHT
Computer Tutor

Programmed instruction is nothing new, nor is it technologically exotic. But by linking the step-by-step teaching system to a computer, the process can be truly individualized and made more interesting to the learner. By combining an instruction videotape, a floppy disk, and a video screen, the student can find himself or herself linked to a system that will type out an individualized greeting at the beginning of the lesson, recall how far the student has progressed in the overall instructional program, ask suitably tailored questions and give the right answers, and even flash words of approval on the screen for signs of improvement.

Examples of Indexed-Sequential Processing

The customer file referred to earlier in this chapter is an example of a file suitable for indexed-sequential processing. The file could be read sequentially for the billing operation. In addition, it could be accessed one record

FIGURE 7–18
Indexed-Sequential Design—Physical Layout of Records on a Disk

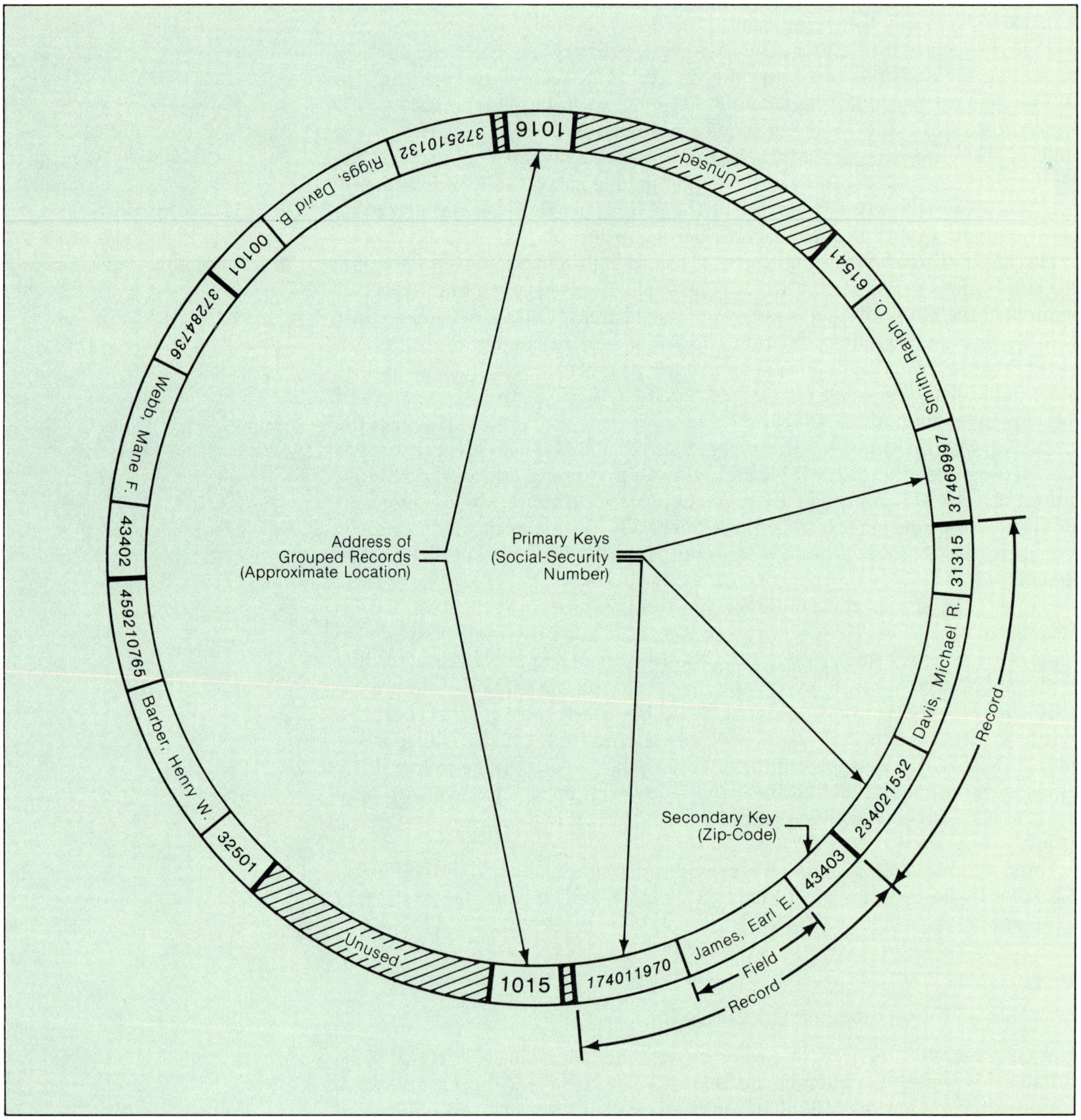

PRIMARY KEY (Social Security Number)		SECONDARY KEY (Zip Code)	
Number	*Address*	*Number*	*Address*
174–01–1970	1015	00101	1016
234–02–1532	1015	31315	1015
371–46–9997	1015	32501	1016
372–51–0132	1016	43402	1016
372–84–7436	1016	43403	1015
459–21–0765	1016	61541	1015

FIGURE 7–19
Index Tables of Primary and Secondary Keys

at a time for order-entry transactions. The following steps outline the procedures involved in preparing a customer order:

Step 1: A customer mails or phones an order to ABC Company for equipment. The clerk receives the order and enters the customer number on a visual display terminal. This number acts as a key to the file.

Step 2: The index to the customer number on the customer file is searched until it is located. The record's approximate address is used to begin the search on the disk file. Once at that location, records are looked at sequentially until a match is found between the number entered and the appropriate record. Once the appropriate record is found, the information appears on the terminal's screen. The clerk verifies shipping and billing addresses.

Step 3: The order is entered on the keyboard, and a sales order is generated by a printer connected to the system.

Step 4: The customer's record is updated to reflect the current order.

Assessment of Indexed-Sequential Design

Advantages of indexed-sequential design include the following.

- Indexed-sequential files are well suited for both inquiries and large processing runs.
- Access time to specific records is apt to be faster than it would be if the file were sequentially organized.

Disadvantages of indexed-sequential design include the following.

- More direct-access storage space is required for an indexed-sequential file than for a sequential file holding the same data because of the storage space required for indexes.
- Processing time for specific record selection is longer than it would be in a direct-access system.

MASS STORAGE

Using primary storage is very fast because access to data is direct and requires no physical movement. The speed of electricity is, in effect, the limiting factor. However, primary storage is also very expensive. Disk storage is less expensive and it provides direct-access capabilities, but even disk storage tends to be too expensive when very large amounts of data must be stored for direct-access processing.

To meet this need, mass storage devices have been developed. They allow rapid access to data, although their access times are much slower than those of primary storage or magnetic disk. Large files, backup files, and infrequently used files can be placed in mass storage at a relatively low cost.

One approach to mass storage uses a cartridge tape as the storage medium. The cartridges are similar to cassette tapes; however, the high-density tape used requires 90 percent less storage space than common magnetic tape. A mass storage system such as this can hold the equivalent of up to 1,000 tape reels. The mounting of the tapes is under the control of the system, rather than of an operator, and tends to be faster than the traditional operator-controlled mounting of magnetic tapes (see Figure 7–20).

Mass storage is not limited to high-density magnetic tape. Recently, a mass storage system for minicomputers using small floppy disks as the storage medium was introduced. However, unlike the cartridge system described above, most mass storage devices require extensive physical movement because the needed files must first be found and then mounted mechanically before data can be read or written. Although direct access is possible, the retrieval time is relatively slow (normally measured in seconds).

FIGURE 7–20
Honeycomb Mass Storage. Because these data cartridges are stored in a fashion resembling a honeycomb, it is often referred to as honeycomb mass storage and is well suited for applications with large volumes of data requiring slower access time.

SUMMARY POINTS

- Auxiliary, or secondary, storage is not part of the CPU. It is used to store data not immediately required for processing, at a lower cost than primary storage. The most common auxiliary storage media are magnetic tapes and magnetic disks.
- Access to data in auxiliary storage can be either direct or sequential. Magnetic disks provide for either indexed-sequential or direct-access storage, while magnetic tapes are used for sequential storage.
- Magnetic tape consists of a plastic base coated with iron oxide. Data is stored by magnetizing small areas on the surface of the tape.
- In sequential design, all data is stored in sequential order on a master file; it may be ordered by some key field. Transactions to be processed against the master file are stored on a transaction file. Transactions are usually collected and processed against the master in one batch. During processing, transactions are matched against the master file and the master file is updated. Updates to the master file are made by rewriting a new master file during processing. The entire master must be read when sequential processing is used.

- Direct access processing is possible with magnetic disks. Any record on the file can be located directly without having to read the records preceding it.
- In direct-access processing, records are accessed according to their key. The computer determines the physical location of the record on the disk by a transformation process on the key or by using a directory. Once the physical address is known, the record can be retrieved.
- Indexed-sequential processing is used when the same file may be required for sequential processing and single-record updates. A primary key is used to identify each unique record, and records are stored in sequence according to the primary key. Secondary keys are set up for those fields used to gain access to the file. The computer uses the key value to determine the approximate physical location of the record (or records), and then reads the records sequentially until the desired one is found.
- Mass storage allows rapid access to data, but at a slower speed than most secondary-storage devices. Its cost is significantly lower for a given volume of storage.

REVIEW QUESTIONS

1. Describe how a computer accesses data in main storage. Compare this to data stored on secondary-storage devices.
2. What are the advantages of blocking records on magnetic tape?
3. Define the term *key*. Explain the use of a key in sequential processing. How does the use of a key in direct-access processing differ from sequential processing?
4. Distinguish between a master file and a transaction file.
5. Give an example, other than the one used in the book, for a sequential-processing application.
6. One of the advantages of batch processing is that a backup file is automatically created during processing. Is this true of direct-access processing? What are the implications of this?
7. What is a disk track? How does this track differ from the track on a phonograph record? How many tracks are typically on one disk surface?
8. An airline company is interested in automating its reservation system. What type of processing is most suitable for this application? What would be an appropriate key? Define the steps involved in the procedure of making a flight reservation.
9. Explain the similarities between indexed-sequential processing and sequential processing. How is direct-access processing similar to indexed-sequential processing?
10. How does the computer use its directory?
11. Give an example of an instance where mass storage might be useful to a firm.

Data Storage

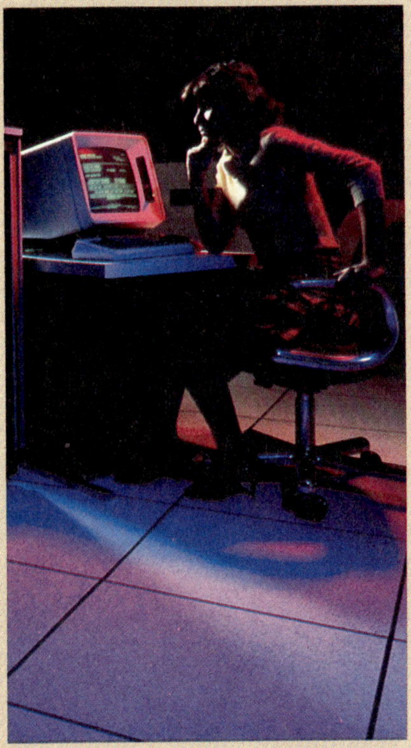

For a computer system to be of much use, the programs to be used and the data to be manipulated must be instantly available. Since the amount of internal memory in a microcomputer is generally not adequate for the storage of all the applications you might have for it, peripheral forms of storage are necessary.

An inexpensive form of storage for microcomputers is magnetic tape in the form of tape cassettes and cartridges. These are similar to the type used in audio recording but use a higher-quality, higher-density digital recording tape.

Magnetic tape cassettes and cartridges are well suited for temporary storage of short programs and data that are suitable to a sequential format. For those who have no greater need or whose budget won't allow more, the relatively low cost of the equipment and medium offers an affordable alternative to the more expensive disk drives. It does, however, become tedious loading cassettes and cartridges into memory for long programs or for large amounts of data manipulation. This is because of their relative slowness compared with other peripheral storage formats and the fact that programs and data must be stored and accessed sequentially.

Floppy disks, the most widely used form of peripheral storage for microcomputers, overcome these drawbacks. A single disk can hold relatively huge chunks of programs and data and can access them randomly at many times the speed of magnetic tape. They are available in two standard sizes—8 inches and 5¼ inches, and a new 3-inch micro disk is being introduced. Their storage capacity presently extends from 100K to 1 megabyte (one million bytes) on 5¼-inch disks and 125K to 1.2 megabytes on 8-inch disks. However, increased storage capacity can be expected in the near future, pushing the upper boundaries even further.

Data is stored as magnetized spots in tracks and is addressed by track number and sector number. A standard 8-inch disk contains 77 tracks and 26 sectors while a mini-floppy disk (5¼-inch) has 35 tracks and 18 sectors.

The format for data storage on a floppy disk can take any of the following combinations: single-sided/single-density, single-sided/double-density, double-sided/single-density, and double-sided/double-density. Double-sided means that the system allows using both sides of a disk. Double-density means that the system permits "doubling" the amount of data, no matter how many sides are used.

As long as disks are used on the drives for which they are designed, there is usually no problem. If your system allows for a variety of disk drives to be used, there is a danger that a disk designed for a specific type of drive will cause problems if you try to use it on a different type of drive. Unless it is stated otherwise, some good rules of thumb are: data on double-sided disks cannot be used by single-sided drives; data on double-density disks cannot be used by single-density drives; however, data on single-sided/single-density disks can be used by double-sided/double-density drives. A recent innovation by Omni is a reversible disk for use on single-sided 5¼-inch disk drives. It works just like the present single-sided disks, except that it can be flipped over, allowing you to record on the reverse side.

Some users, though, may have storage requirements greater than those provided by even the largest-capacity floppy disks. Some personal computing systems allow the use of hard disks that offer, in addition to the storage, greater speed in accessing data. There are two forms, the hard disk pack—a totally sealed unit with no user access—and the removable disk pack. The hard-disk pack has a number of positive features: relatively low price, reliability, security from damage by untrained persons (because of the sealed unit), small size, and large storage capacity. The removable system, however, provides easier and quicker back-up. For example, a "standard" basic hard-disk system consists of a floppy disk for back-up and the enclosed hard-disk unit. If the floppy disk has, say, a storage capacity of 500,000 characters and the hard-disk unit is capable of holding 5 million characters, there will be a marked unbalance when it comes to copying the data from the hard disks to floppy disks. It would require a box of ten disks and at least twenty minutes to complete back-up. This in itself may not seem to be too great a problem; however, one should know that standard software for file copying will only deal with complete files, and any file greater than the size of the floppy cannot be backed up without a special "back-up routine." Therefore, it is advisable to make sure that this is available before purchasing a hard-disk system. The disks in the removable disk pack are physically detachable from the system and, therefore, avoid this problem, since spare disks can be inserted for back-up purposes. At present, however, predominant use is with the sealed hard-disk packs rather than with the removable disk packs because of the latter's high cost.

Recent advances in technology will soon make available new types of storage devices. Two devices that have already made an appearance are optical (laser) disks and RAM chips that act like disk drives.

The optical disks are much faster than hard disks but are still fairly slow when compared to RAM. One big advantage, though, is their capacity. A single optical disk the size of a 12-inch record can hold the text equivalent of 1735 average books per side. Bits of data are stored on an optical disk as the presence or absence of a tiny pit burned into the disk by a pinpoint laser beam. A line one inch long contains about 5000 pits, or bits, of data. Optical disks are limited in that they cannot be erased or rerecorded and as such are now being used mainly for permanent storage of data.

Inputting data from disks is relatively slow when compared with the speed at which a microprocessor can manipulate data. RAM chips are, at the present, the only type of memory device that can approximate the speed of a microprocessor. A new peripheral storage device using RAM chips is now available. It plugs into the same slot that the disk drive would and is indistinguishable from a disk drive to the computer. Since RAM chips require a continuous power supply, some manufacturers are providing battery back-up units for use in case of power failures. A back-up floppy disk could be read into the RAM device that would enable processing to be done more rapidly, and then dumped back on to the floppy disk for permanent storage after processing is completed. RAM Card by Microsoft is an example of this type of device for use with the IBM Personal Computer. It has up to 256K bytes of memory and has a retrieval time that's typically fifty times faster than disk.

As new technologies continue to be developed, we can expect increases in both the amount of data that can be stored on a given medium and the speed at which the data can be retrieved. In the future, floppy disks may become as obsolete an magnetic tape cassettes for microcomputers. These new developments in storage formats greatly increase the efficiency of microcomputers and open up many new areas of possible use.

DISCUSSION QUESTIONS

1. Describe three types of peripheral storage media and the types of applications that each are suited for.
2. Describe two new types of peripheral storage media and their implications.

CHAPTER 8

Software

INTRODUCTION

The benefits of smaller, faster, and more efficient computers brought about by technological achievements cannot be realized unless programs exist that utilize those computers well. Programs are used not only to direct the computer to solve business problems, but are used by the computer itself to direct and oversee its own operations. These programs, called software, go hand in hand with computer hardware.

This chapter discusses the difference between system and application programs. The various functions of a computer's operating system and the programs used by the computer for its own operations are discussed. Various application programming languages are overviewed, along with their advantages and disadvantages. Finally, developments that increase the effectiveness and efficiency of the computer are reviewed.

FACING PAGE
The software developed at Burlington Industries, Inc., tracks work in progress in the production plant and handles the data on customers' orders.

CHAPTER OUTLINE

PROGRAMS

Despite the apparent complexity and power of the computer, it is merely a tool manipulated by an individual. It requires step-by-step instructions to reach the solution to a problem. As stated earlier, this series of instructions is known as a **program,** or **software,** and the individual who creates the program is the **programmer.** There are two basic types of programs: **system programs,** which coordinate the operation of computer circuitry; and **application programs,** which solve particular user problems.

System programs directly affect the operation of the computer. They are designed to facilitate the use of hardware and to help the computer system run quickly and efficiently. For example, a system program allocates storage for data being entered into the system. It has already been shown that computers differ in main storage capacity, in methods used to store and code data, and in the number of instructions they can perform. Consequently, system programs are written specifically for a particular type of computer and cannot be used (without modification) on different machines.

Application programs perform specific data-processing or computational tasks to solve the organization's information needs. They can be developed within the organization or purchased from software firms. Typical examples of application programs are those used in inventory control and accounting, and those used in banks to update checking and savings account balances.

OPERATING SYSTEMS

In early computer systems, human operators monitored computer operations, determined the order in which submitted programs were run (the priority), and readied input and output devices. While early electronic development increased the processing speeds of CPUs, the speed of human operators remained constant. Time delays and errors caused by human operator intervention became a serious problem.

In the 1960s, operating systems were developed to help overcome this problem. An **operating system** is a collection of programs used by the computer to manage its own operations. This approach provides a control system that can operate at computer speeds. Instead of a human operator, the operating system is given the responsibility for all jobs to be run.

Types of Operating Systems

There are two basic types of operating systems: **batch** (or **stacked job**) and **real time.** In a stacked-job processing environment, several user programs (jobs or job steps) are grouped into a batch and processed one after the other in a continuous stream. A real-time operating system can respond to spontaneous requests for system resources, such as management inquiries entered from terminals.

Many operating systems can handle both batch and real-time applications simultaneously. These systems direct processing of a job stream but also respond to interrupts from other devices, such as terminals, in direct communication with the CPU. (An **interrupt** is a condition or event that temporarily suspends normal processing operations—for example, a request to accept data from an input device or a request for transfer of data to an output device.)

Components

An operating system is an integrated collection of subsystems. Each subsystem consists of programs that perform specific duties (see Figure 8–1). Since all operating system programs work as a team, CPU idle time is avoided and utilization of computer facilities is increased. Operating system programs are usually stored on an auxiliary device known as the **system residence device.** They are called into primary storage when needed.

Although operating systems allow the computer to direct its own operations, they do have some disadvantages. Space must be provided in primary storage for operating programs. This is space that otherwise could be used by application programs. Since this space must be reserved, it is called **overhead.** The computer must constantly refer back to operating system programs in order to know what to do next. In doing so, some 50 percent of processing time is taken up by operating system programs.

Two types of programs make up the operating system: control programs and processing programs. **Control programs** oversee system operations and perform tasks such as input/output, scheduling, handling interrupts, and communicating with the computer operator or programmers. **Processing programs** are executed under the supervision of control programs and are used by the programmer to simplify program preparation for the computer system.

Control Programs The **supervisor program** (also called the **monitor** or **executive**), the major component of the operating system, coordinates the activ-

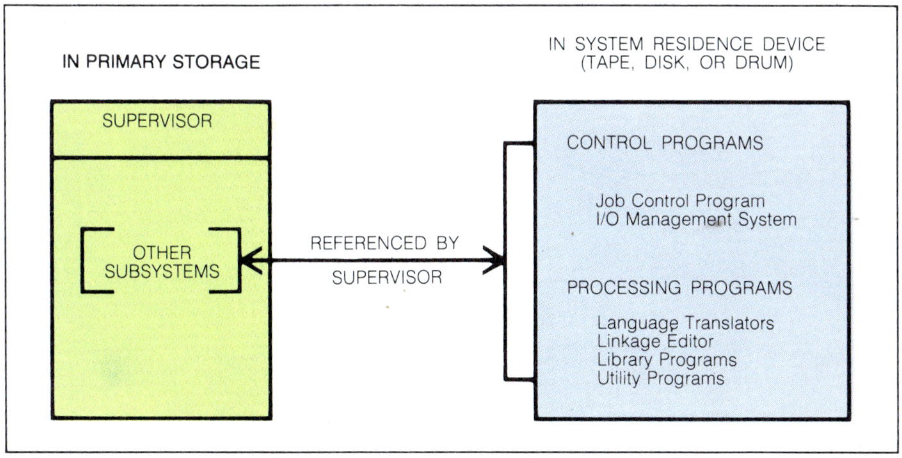

FIGURE 8–1
Operating System in Primary Storage and System Residence Device

ities of all other parts of the operating system. When the computer is first put into use, the supervisor is the first program to be transferred into primary storage from the system residence device. The supervisor schedules input/output operations and allocates resources to various input/output devices. It also sends messages to the computer operator indicating the status of particular jobs, error conditions, and so on.

The operating system requires job-control information in order to perform its mission. (A **job** is a unit of work to be processed by the CPU.) A **job-control language (JCL)** serves as the communication link between the programmer and the operating system. Job-control statements are used to identify the beginning of a job, to identify the specific program to be executed, to describe the work to be done, and to indicate the input/output devices required (see Figure 8–2). The **job-control program** translates the job-control statements written by a programmer into machine-language instructions that can be executed by the computer.

The control programs of the operating system must be able to control and coordinate the CPU while receiving input, executing instructions of programs in storage, and regulating output. Input/output devices must be assigned to specific programs, and data must be moved between them and specific memory locations. The **input/output management system** oversees and coordinates these processes.

Processing Programs The operating system contains several processing programs that facilitate efficient processing operations by simplifying program preparation and execution for users. The major processing programs con-

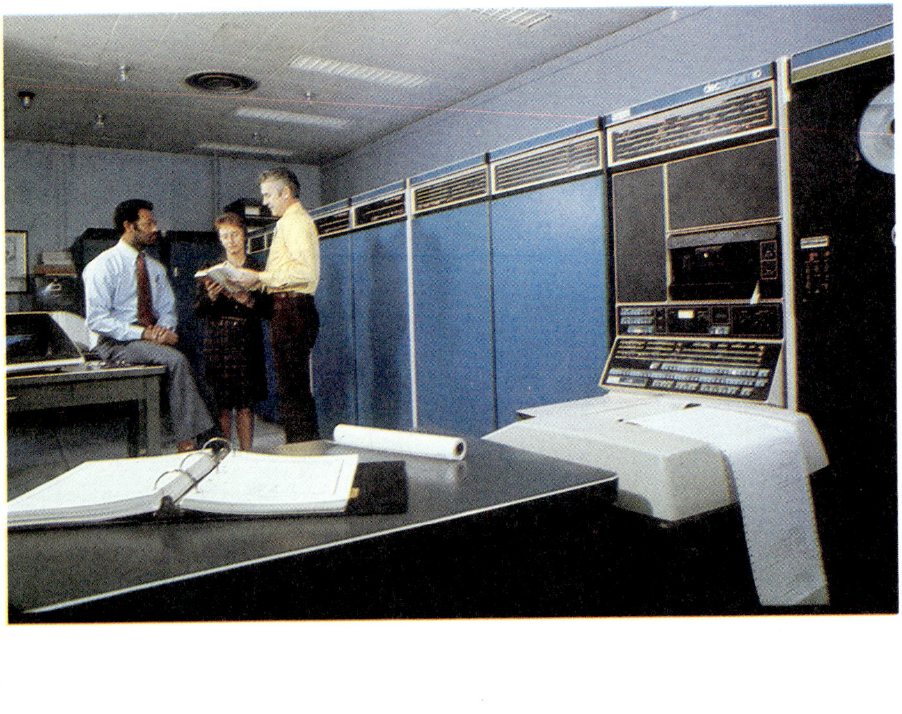

Time-sharing helps employees of Armstrong World Industries research and development organization get maximum utilization from their computers.

tained in the operating system are the language translators, linkage editor, library programs, and utility programs.

A **language-translator program** (also known as a **compiler**) translates English-like programs (such as FORTRAN or COBOL) written by programmers into machine-language instructions. The original, untranslated program is called the **source program.** The translated application program is called the **object program,** and often remains on the system residence device until the supervisor calls for it to be loaded into primary storage for execution. It is the task of the **linkage editor** to "link" the object program from the system residence device to main storage by assigning appropriate main storage addresses to each byte of the object program.

Library programs are user-written or manufacturer-supplied programs and subroutines that are frequently used in other programs. So that these routines will not have to be rewritten every time they are needed, they are stored in a **system library** (usually on magnetic disk or tape) and called into main storage when needed. They are then linked together with other programs to perform specific tasks. A **librarian program** manages the storage and use of library programs by maintaining a directory of programs in the system library; it also contains appropriate procedures for adding and deleting programs.

Operating systems also include a set of **utility programs** that perform specialized functions. For example, a utility program can be used to transfer data from tape to tape, tape to disk, card to tape, or tape to printer. Other utility programs, known as **sort/merge programs,** are used to order (sort)

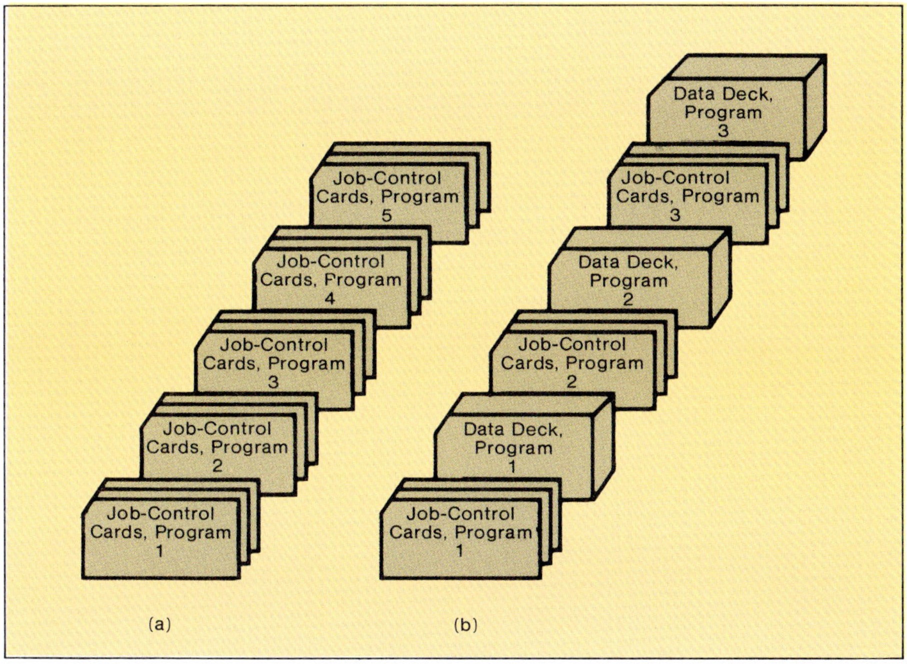

FIGURE 8–2
Continuous Job Streams for Stacked-Job Processing System

records into a particular sequence to facilitate updating of files. Once sorted, several files can be merged to form a single, updated file. Job-control statements are used to specify the sort and merge programs; these programs or routines are then called into main storage when needed.

HIGHLIGHT
Sometimes The Output Is Wet

The computerized bartender installed at a military officers' club in Colorado is said to be super—except in the sympathetic listener category. Designed by American Beverage Control Corporation, the dispenser is controlled by a microprocessor and is capable of mixing with precision 1,200 different drinks.

The human bartender receives the customer's order and enters it on a keyboard, which has more than 200 keys. The entry station also includes pictures of the drinks to show the bartender the kind of serving glass to place at the pouring tower. Three seconds after the bartender's signal, the computer sends an exact mixture of the required liquids from the "rack room" through tubing to the pouring tower. Then the bartender serves the drink and is free to do what he or she does better than the computer—listen.

The computer, meanwhile, has done its other tasks: updating the liquid inventory, printing the customer's receipt, and running the customer's tab. The economic advantages of the computer's skill and efficiency may mean the initial investment can be recovered in as little as six months.

PROGRAMMING LANGUAGES

A number of languages have been developed to allow programmers to communicate with the computer. Each has different objectives. For instance, one language may be designed to utilize the computer's computational abilities for scientific applications. Another may use the tremendous storage capabilities of the computer for business processing. Overall, there are two main categories of programming languages—batch-oriented and interactive. **Batch-oriented** programming languages are used to solve problems for which immediate responses are not required. A batch job is a series of programs submitted to the computer as a single unit. Once the instructions and data have been loaded into the CPU, processing takes place without intervention from programmers or users.

Interactive languages, on the other hand, allow the programmer or program user to communicate directly with the computer in a conversational fashion. Programs and data can be submitted directly to the computer from remote terminals. The programs are translated (compiled) and executed, and the results are returned to the remote terminal in a matter of seconds. (In contrast, programs submitted in a batch environment may spend several hours waiting in line before they are executed and the results returned to the user.)

Batch programming languages can be divided according to the overall goal or by the orientation of the language. **Machine-oriented languages** seek to make the most efficient use of computer resources. **Procedure-oriented languages** focus on the various processing steps required of a particular application and are designed to help the programmer direct the computer to perform these tasks easily. Finally, **problem-oriented languages** attempt to solve processing requirements with minimal programming effort—allowing the user to focus on what results are desired, rather than on the individual steps needed to get those results. The following section discusses examples of batch programming languages according to these three divisions: machine-, procedure-, and problem-oriented.

Machine-Oriented Languages

Machine Language **Machine language** is the language of the computer, the only language it can recognize and act upon. High-level languages must first be translated into machine language before the computer will recognize their instructions. Remember that machine language is represented as 1s and 0s. Coding a program in this binary form is very tedious, so machine language is often coded in hexadecimal codes, which is still considered by some to be quite tedious as the following example illustrates:

```
48   00   23C0
4C   00   23C2
40   00   2310
D2   01   2310   2310
48   00   2310
4E   00   2028
F3   17   3002   2028
96   F0   3003
```

The programmer using machine language must specify *everything* to the computer. Every step the computer must take to execute a program must be coded. This means that the programmer must know exactly how the computer works. Actual numerical addresses of storage locations for instructions and data must be specified. Every switch and register (temporary storage areas for holding data and instructions) must be known.

Assembly Language **Assembly languages** were developed to alleviate many of the disadvantages of machine-language programming. When programming in an assembly language, the programmer uses symbolic names, or **mnemonics,** to specify machine operations; thus, coding in 0s and 1s is no longer required. Mnemonics are English-like abbreviations for the machine-language instructions. For example, Table 8–1 shows some common arithmetic operations coded in an assembly language and in binary.

Many of the operations listed in Table 8–1 involve the use of registers. Further, the mnemonic codes for assembly-language instructions differ depending on the type and model of computer. Thus, assembly-language programs, like machine-language programs, can be written only by persons who know the internal operation of the computers that will execute the statements. Figure 8–3 shows the sample payroll program now written in assembly language.

TABLE 8–1
Examples of Assembly-Language Mnemonic Codes

OPERATION	TYPICAL ASSEMBLY-LANGUAGE MNEMONIC CODE	TYPICAL BINARY OP CODE
Add memory to register	A	01011010
Add register to register	AR	00011010
Compare memory locations	CLC	11010101
Divide register by memory	D	01011101
Load from memory into register	L	01011000
Multiply register by memory	M	01011100
Store register in memory	ST	01010000
Subtract memory from register	S	01011011

FIGURE 8–3
Payroll Problem in Assembly Language (Continued on Facing Page)

```
     SOURCE  STATEMENT
             START
PAYROLL      BALR      12,0            Set Up Registers
             USING     *,12
             XPRNT     HEADING,45      Print Headings
READCRD      XREAD     CARD80          Read Data Card
             CLC       EOF,''C'99'
             BE        DONE
             PACK      WKHR!,HOURS     Convert Data to Decimal
             PACK      WKRATE,RATE     Form and Initialize Variables
             ZAP       GROSS,ZERO
             ZAP       OVRTME,ZERO
             ZAP       REG,ZERO
             CP        WKHRS,FORTY     Compute Regular Pay
             BH        OVERTIME
             AP        GROSS,WKRATE
             MP        GROSS,WKHRS
             B         TAXRATE
OVERTIME     AP        OVRTME, FORTY   Compute Overtime Pay
             MP        OVRTME,WKRATE
             AP        GROSS,WKRATE
             SP        WKHRS,FORTY
             MP        WKHRS,ONEHLF
             MP        GROSS,WKHRS
             MVN       GROSS+5(1),GROSS+6
             ZAP       GROSS(7),GROSS(6)
             AP        GROSS,OVRTME
TAXRATE      CP        GROSS,=P'25000' Determine Tax Rate
             BH        UPPERRTE
             ZAP       RATE,LOW
             B         TAXES
UPPERRTE     ZAP       RATE,HIGH
TAXES        ZAP       TOTAXES,GROSS   Compute Taxes
             MP        TOTAXES,RATE
             AP        TOTAXES,=P'50'
             MVN       TOTAXES+5(1),TOTAXES+6
             ZAP       TOTAXES(7),TOTAXES(6)
             SP        GROSS,TOTAXES   Calculate Net Pay and Edit Print Line
             MVC       PRPAY,MASK
             ED        PRPAY,GROSS
             MVC       PRNAME,NAME     Print Output Line
             XPRNT     LINE,32
     SOURCE  STATEMENT
             B         READCRD
DONE         XPRNT     HEADING,1
             BR        14
*
*
*
```

```
CARD      DS    0CL80  ┐
NAME      DS    CL16   │
HOURS     DS    CL2    │  Input Card File
          DS    CL2    │  Definitions
RATE      DS    CL4    │
          DS    CL54   │
EOF       DS    CL2    ┘
HEADING   DS    0CL45                ┐
          DC    CL1'1'               │
          DC    CL13,EMPLOYEE NAME'  │
          DC    CL10'                │
          DC    CL7'NET PAY'         │  Output Print
          DC    CL14'  '             │  File Definitions
LINE      DS    0CL30                │
          DC    CL1'  '              │
PRNAME    DS    CL16                 │
PRPAY     DS    CL15                 ┘
GROSS     DS    PL7          ┐
WKRATE    DS    PL3          │
OVRTME    DS    PL7          │
REG       DS    PL7          │
WKHRS     DS    PL4          │
FORTY     DC    PL2'40'      │  Variable Definitions
ONEHLF    DC    PL2'150'     │
LOW       DC    PL2'14'      │
HIGH      DC    PL2'20'      │
ZERO      DC    PL4'0000'    │
TOTAXES   DS    PL7          ┘
MASK      DC    X'402020202020202020202021 4B2121' }  Edit Field
          END   PAYROLL
                =C'99'
                =P'50'
                =P'25000'
```

```
EMPLOYEE NAME        NET PAY

LYNN MANGINO         224.00
THOMAS RITTER        212.42
MARIE OLSON          209.00
LORI DUNLEVY         172.00
WILLIAM WILSON       308.00
```

Procedure-Oriented Languages

COBOL **COBOL** (COmmon Business-Oriented Language) is the most frequently used business programming language. Before 1960, no language well suited to solving business problems existed. Recognizing this inadequacy, the Department of Defense called together representatives of computer users, manufacturers, and government installations to examine the feasibility of establishing a common business programming language. That was the beginning of the CODASYL (Conference Of DAta SYstems Languages) Committee. By 1960, the committee had established the specifications for COBOL, and the first commercial versions of the language were offered later that year. The government furthered its cause in the mid–1960s by refusing to buy or lease any computer that could not process a program written in COBOL.

FIGURE 8–4
Payroll Program in COBOL

```
IDENTIFICATION DIVISION.
PROGRAM-ID. PAYROLL.
ENVIRONMENT DIVISION.
INPUT-OUTPUT SECTION.
FILE-CONTROL.
    SELECT CARD-FILE ASSIGN TO UR-2540R-S-SYSIN.
    SELECT PRINT-FILE ASSIGN TO UR-S-SYSPRINT.
DATA DIVISION.
FILE SECTION.
FD  CARD-FILE LABEL RECORDS ARE OMITTED.
01  PAY-CARD.
    02 EMPLOYEE-NAME PICTURE A(16).
    02 HOURS-WORKED PICTURE 99.
    02 WAGE-PER-HOUR PICTURE 99V99.
FD  PRINT-FILE LABEL RECORDS ARE OMITTED.
01  PRINT-LINE.
    02 NAME          PICTURE A(16).
    02 FILLER        PICTURE X(5).
    02 AMOUNT        PICTURE $$$$.99.
WORKING-STORAGE SECTION.
77  GROSS-PAY        PICTURE 999V99.
77  REGULAR-PAY      PICTURE 999V99.
77  OVERTIME-PAY     PICTURE 999V99.
77  NET-PAY          PICTURE 999V99.
77  TAX              PICTURE 999V99.
77  OVERTIME-HOURS   PICTURE 99.
77  OVERTIME-RATE    PICTURE 999V999.
77  BLANK-LINE       PICTURE X(132) VALUE SPACES.
PROCEDURE DIVISION.
    DISPLAY 'EMPLOYEE NAME              ', 'NET PAY'.
    DISPLAY BLANK-LINE.
    OPEN INPUT CARD-FILE, OUTPUT PRINT-FILE.
```

One of the objectives of the CODASYL group was to establish a language that was machine-independent—that could be used on any computer. Thus, when several manufacturers began offering their own modifications and extensions of COBOL, a need for standardization became apparent. Consequently, in 1968 the American National Standards Institute (ANSI) established and published guidelines for a standardized COBOL that became known as ANSI COBOL. In 1974, ANSI published a revised version of the standard in which the language definition was expanded. The CODASYL committee continues to examine the feasibility of modifying or incorporating new features into COBOL.

Another key objective of the designers of COBOL was to make the language look like English. Their intent was that the program written in COBOL should be understandable even to casual readers, and hence self-documenting. Judge how successful they were by looking at Figure 8–4, which shows the payroll application coded in COBOL.

FIGURE 8–4
continued

```
WORK-LOOP.
    READ CARD-FILE AT END GO TO FINISH.
    IF HOURS-WORKED IS GREATER THAN 40 THEN GO TO
        OVERTIME-ROUTINE.
    MULTIPLY HOURS-WORKED BY WAGE-PER-HOUR GIVING GROSS-PAY.
    GO TO TAX-COMPUTATION.
OVERTIME-ROUTINE.
    MULTIPLY WAGE-PER-HOUR BY 40 GIVING REGULAR-PAY.
    SUBTRACT 40 FROM HOURS-WORKED GIVING OVERTIME-HOURS.
    MULTIPLY WAGE-PER-HOUR BY 1.5 GIVING OVERTIME-RATE.
    MULTIPLY OVERTIME-HOURS BY OVERTIME-RATE GIVING
        OVERTIME-PAY.
    ADD REGULAR-PAY, OVERTIME-PAY GIVING GROSS-PAY.
TAX-COMPUTATION.
    IF GROSS-PAY IS GREATER THAN 250 THEN MULTIPLY GROSS-PAY
        BY 0.20 GIVING TAX ELSE MULTIPLY GROSS-PAY BY 0.14
        GIVING TAX.
    SUBTRACT TAX FROM GROSS-PAY GIVING NET-PAY.
    MOVE EMPLOYEE-NAME TO NAME.
    MOVE NET-PAY TO AMOUNT.
    WRITE PRINT-LINE.
    GO TO WORK-LOOP.
FINISH.
    CLOSE CARD-FILE, PRINT-FILE.
    STOP RUN.
```

EMPLOYEE NAME	NET PAY
LYNN MANGINO	224.00
THOMAS RITTER	212.42
MARIE OLSON	209.00
LORI DUNLEVY	172.00
WILLIAM WILSON	308.00

"By Jove . . . this is written in COBOL!"

DATAMATION
April 1, 1981.
Reprinted by permission

COBOL offers many advantages for business. Because of its English-like nature, programs require little additional documentation; well-written COBOL programs tend to be self-explanatory. COBOL also has strong file-handling capabilities; it supports sequential, indexed, and direct-access files. Since COBOL is standardized, a firm may switch computer equipment with little or no rewriting of existing programs.

A disadvantage of COBOL is that it tends to be wordy. Using COBOL may require more statements to solve a problem than using a more compact language such as FORTRAN (discussed next). Similarly, COBOL's computational abilities are limited. It is designed for business applications requiring little mathematics. This makes it undesirable for scientific applications.

FORTRAN **FORTRAN** (FORmula TRANslator) is the oldest high-level programming language. Its origins can be found in the mid–1950s, when most programs were written in either assembly language or machine language. Efforts were made to develop a programming language that resembled English but could be translated into machine language by the computer. This effort, backed by IBM, produced FORTRAN—the first commercially available high-level language.

Early FORTRAN compilers contained many errors and were not always efficient. Moreover, several manufacturers offered variations of FORTRAN that could be used only on their computers. In response to this problem,

In Southern Bell's computer room in Atlanta, a computer operator discusses a problem.

ANSI laid the groundwork for a standardized FORTRAN. In 1966, two standard versions of FORTRAN were recognized—ANSI FORTRAN and Basic FORTRAN. They were very similar to two earlier versions, FORTRAN IV and FORTRAN II. A more recent version of FORTRAN, FORTRAN 77, provides more enhancements to the language and supports structured programming.

A group from the University of Waterloo in Ontario developed a subset of FORTRAN—WATFOR (WATerloo FORTRAN)—specifically for the beginning or student programmer. Improvements were added to WATFOR, and the enhanced version was called WATFIV. In spite of the attempts to standardize FORTRAN, however, most computer manufacturers have continued to offer their own extensions of the language. Therefore, the compatibility of FORTRAN with different computer systems remains a problem today.

In 1957, when FORTRAN was first released, the computer was primarily used by engineers, scientists, and mathematicians. Consequently, FORTRAN was developed to meet their needs, and its purpose has remained unchanged. FORTRAN is a procedure-oriented language with extraordinary mathematical capabilities. It is especially applicable where numerous complex arithmetic calculations are necessary. However, it is not well suited for programs involving file maintenance, editing of data, or production of documents. Figure 8–5 shows the sample payroll program in FORTRAN.

PL/I **PL/I** (Programming Language One) was designed to be an all-purpose, procedure-oriented language for both scientific and business applica-

HIGHLIGHT
Political Speeches by Program

Putting programming skills to a new use, two communications professors in St. Louis have programmed a computer to write the perfect foreign-policy speech. Although they have been approached several times by political office candidates for a speech-writing tip or two, the professors are not selling their speech-writing services.

They hypothesize that, by always saying the things we want to hear, any "idiot" could be elected. In order to prove this notion, the two men had to develop a computer program that would use their market research and spew out the most politically expedient script.

The pair hope that, after these speeches are published, the public will start to wonder why their candidates sound so "canned" and will demand more from the office-seekers. Perhaps the word is already spreading. The candidates who asked the professors for a little help were all turned down, and all lost their races.

FIGURE 8–5
Payroll Program in FORTRAN

```
FORTRAN IV G LEVEL 21        MAIN                    DATE = 81214

      WRITE (6,1)
1     FORMAT('1','EMPLOYEENAME',5X,'NETPAY'/'')
2     READ (5,3) NA,NB,NC,ND,NHOURS, WAGE, IEND
3     FORMAT (4A4, I2, 2X, F4.2, 54X, I2)
      IF (IEND. EQ.99) STOP
      IF (NHOURS.GT.40) GO TO 10
      GROSS = FLOAT(NHOURS)*WAGE
      GO TO 15
10    REG = 40.*WAGE
      OVERTM=FLOAT(NHOURS-40)*(1.5*WAGE)
      GROSS=REG+OVERTM
15    IF (GROSS.GT.250.) GO TO 20
      RATE = .14
      GO TO 25
20    RATE = .20
25    TAX=RATE*GROSS
      PAY = GROSS - TAX
      WRITE (6,50) NA,NB,NC,ND,PAY
50     FORMAT (' ', 4A4, 3X, F6.2)
      GO TO 2
      END
```

```
EMPLOYEE NAME          NET PAY

LYNN MANGINO           224.00
THOMAS RITTER          212.42
MARIE OLSON            209.00
LORI DUNLEVY           172.00
WILLIAM WILSON         308.00
```

tions. With the increased use of management-science techniques such as linear programming and regression analysis, the business programmer needed a language with greater computational capabilities than COBOL. By the same token, a language with greater file-manipulation ability than FORTRAN was desired by the scientific programmer. PL/I combines features of both COBOL and FORTRAN; it is a flexible high-level language. PL/I was introduced during the early 1960s for use with IBM System/360 computers and is still primarily an IBM-sponsored language.

All the languages discussed so far—machine language, assembly language, FORTRAN, and COBOL—impose some rather strict coding rules on the programmer. Column restrictions are prevalent. In contrast, PL/I is a free-form language with very few such restrictions.

PL/I was designed to be used by both novice and expert programmers. The beginning programmer can learn to write programs using basic features

```
PAYROLL: PROCEDURE OPTIONS (MAIN);

PAYROLL: PROCEDURE OPTIONS (MAIN);
DECLARE NAME        CHARACTER (16);
DECLARE HOURS       FIXED DECIMAL (2);
DECLARE WAGE        FIXED DECIMAL (3,2);
DECLARE GROSS_PAY FIXED DECIMAL(5,2);
DECLARE TAXRATE     FIXED DECIMAL (2,2);
DECLARE TAX         FIXED DECIMAL (4,2);
DECLARE NET_PAY    FIXED DECIMAL (5,2);
PUT PAGE LIST ('EMPLOYEE NAME', 'NET PAY');
PUT SKIP;
START: GET LIST (NAME, HOURS, WAGE);
ON ENDFILE GO TO FINISH;
IF HOURS>40 THEN
   GROSS_PAY→40*WAGE + 1.5*WAGE*(HOURS-40);
  ELSE GROSS_PAY=HOURS*WAGE;
IF GROSS_PAY>250 THEN TAXRATE=.20;
   ELSE TAXRATE=.14;
TAX=TAXRATE*GROSS_PAY;
NET_PAY=GROSS_PAY - TAX;
PUT SKIP (1) LIST (NAME, NET_PAY);
GO TO START;
FINISH: END PAYROLL

PAYROLL        14:50     AUGUST 3RD, 1981
```

```
        EMPLOYEE NAME          NET PAY

        LYNN MANGINO           224.00
        THOMAS RITTER          212.42
        MARIE OLSON            209.00
        LORI DUNLEVY           172.00
        WILLIAM WILSON         308.00
```

FIGURE 8–6
Payroll Program in PL/I

of the language. As knowledge of the language increases, the programmer can use more powerful features to write programs to solve complex programs.

Various aspects of PL/I containing only portions of the full language have been developed. These subsets are especially geared toward educational use (just as WATFIV is geared to educational use for FORTRAN). The PL/I program in Figure 8–6 is actually written in PL/C, a subset of PL/I developed at Cornell University.

The greatest strength of PL/I is its power—it is a language with many features, the most attractive of which is its ability to support structured programming through modularity features. It is also less wordy than COBOL

This console for a remote minicomputer site interfaces with the major computer center.

and is well suited for short programming projects. Because it is such a broad, powerful language, however, a large amount of storage is required for its compiler. This precludes its use on smaller computers. As minicomputers and microcomputers become more powerful, however, subsets of PL/I may be applied in those environments as well.

Problem-Oriented Languages

RPG **RPG** (Report Program Generator) is a problem-oriented language originally designed to produce business reports. Basically, the programmer using RPG describes the type of report desired without having to specify much of the logic involved. A generator program is then used to build (generate) a program to produce the report. Therefore, little programming skill is required to use RPG.

Since RPG was initially intended to support the logic of punched-card equipment, it is used primarily with small computer systems. Many firms that formerly used electromechanical punched-card processing equipment have upgraded their data-processing operations to small computer systems. These firms usually have relatively simple, straightforward data-processing needs. In such cases, a small computer system supporting RPG can provide significantly improved data-processing operations. Management reports can be produced in a fraction of the time required by electromechanical methods.

The programmer does not code statements; instead, he or she completes specification forms such as those shown in Figure 8–7. All files to be used by RPG must be defined once using the specification forms. Once the files

FIGURE 8–7 RPG Program Specification Forms

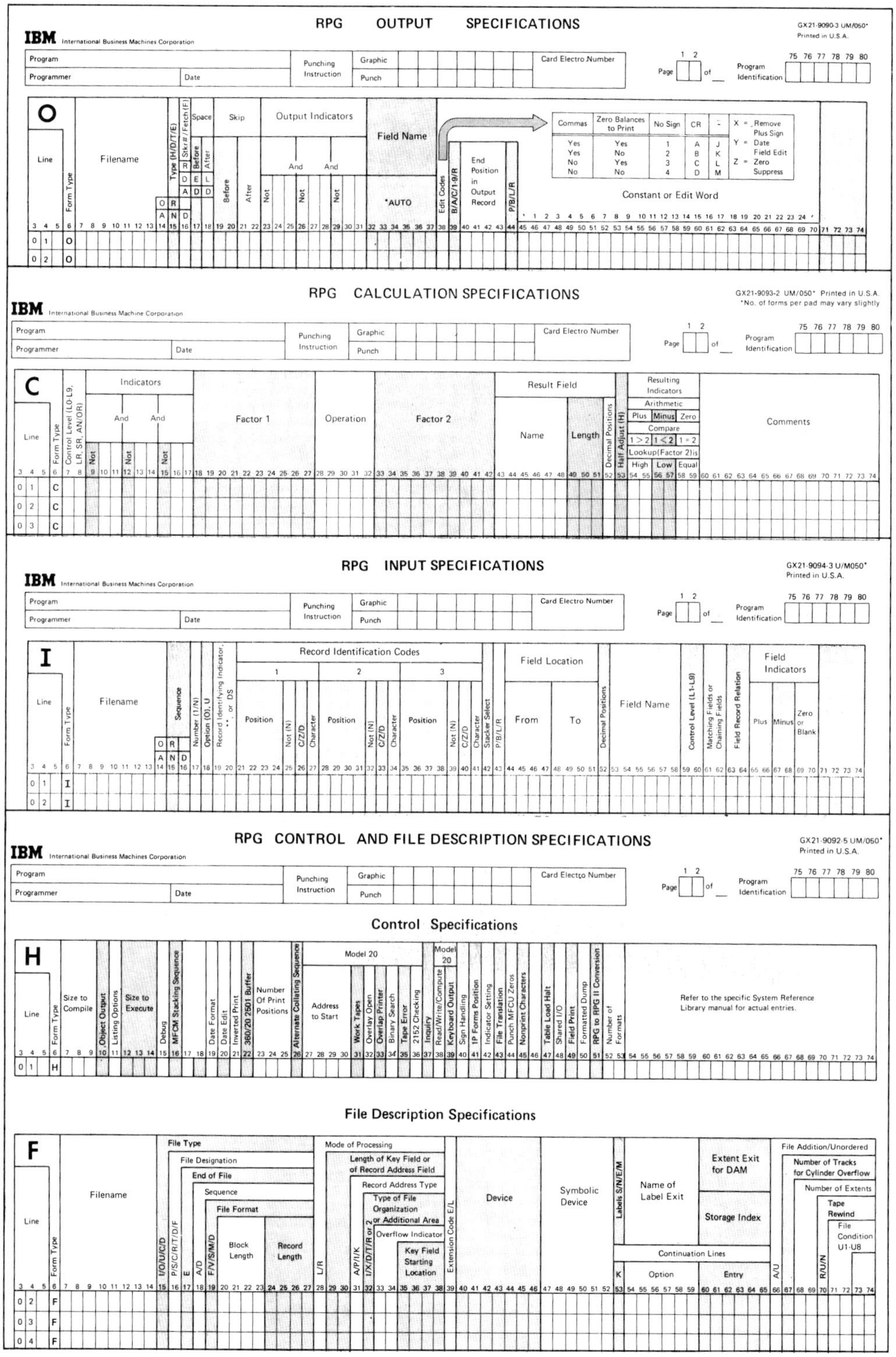

PROFILE
Captain Grace Hopper

Captain Grace Hopper of the United States Navy has led a very active life since officially retiring from the Navy in 1967. In fact, she has worked full time for the Navy during her retirement.

Captain Hopper was one of three original programmers of the first large computer in 1945. Responsible for the development of the first assembler program in the early 1950s, she opened the door for higher-level language programming. Captain Hopper has also played a major role in standardizing COBOL; she headed a team of Navy personnel that wrote a complex computer program to test whether COBOL compilers met the ANSI COBOL standards. This had a major impact on the computer industry, for it allowed the federal government to *require* that *all* computers purchased or leased by the government after the late 1960s had to meet the ANSI COBOL standards. Partly because of this requirement, COBOL is now one of the few standardized languages.

Captain Hopper has received many awards for her contributions to data processing. The Data Processing Management Association (DPMA) awarded her the "Computer Sciences Man of the Year" award in 1969—she was the first person so honored. An original thinker, Captain Hopper continues to search for new ideas to improve data processing.

have been defined to RPG, the programmer need only code the operations to be performed and the content and format of the desired output. The entries on the RPG forms are keypunched, combined with job-control cards, and submitted to the computer. The RPG generator program builds an object program from the source program, and the object program is executed by the computer (see Figure 8–8).

RPG is easy to learn and to use, since the basic pattern of execution is fixed. Since it does not require large amounts of main storage, it is one of the primary languages of small computers and minicomputers. However, the computational capabilities of RPG are limited. Also, RPG is not a standardized language; therefore, RPG programs may require a significant degree of modification in order to be executed on another computer.

Interactive Programming Languages

Interactive programming languages are designed to utilize input from the programmer or user to direct processing. They provide instantaneous response from the computer for queries into computer files or for processing data. More and more applications are utilizing interactive languages in the development of their information systems. Some traditional batch languages (such as COBOL and PL/I) are being modified to accommodate interactive capabilities.

FIGURE 8–8
Payroll Program in RPG

```
00010H       0003         132
00020F*                      PAYROLL EXAMPLE
00030FCDIN    IP  F  80  80           READ01
00040FPRINTR  O   F 132 132      OF   PRINTER
00050I* DEFINES INPUT
00060ICDIN     ZZ  01  80 CD
00070I                                        1    6 DATE
00080I         ZZ  02
00090I                                        1    10DEPT  L1
00100I                                        2    5 EMPNO
00110I                                        6    92HRS
00120I                                       10   133RATE
00130I                                       14   140EXEMP
00510C*TO FIND GROSS PAY, NET PAY
00511C     40              SETOF                      30
00512C    N40 02           SETON                      3040
00520C     02      HRS     COMP   40.00               100909
00530C     02 09   RATE    MULT   HRS      GROSS  52H
00540C     02 10   HRS     SUB    40.00    OTHRS  42
00550C     02 10   RATE    MULT   40.00    REG    52
00560C     02 10   RATE    MULT   1.5      OTRT   43
00570C     02 10   OTHRS   MULT   OTRT     OVER   52
00580C     02 10   REG     ADD    OVER     GROSS  52
00590C     02      EXEMP   MULT   14.40    EXAMT  52H         EXEMPT AMT
00600C     02      GROSS   SUB    EXAMT    BASE   52
00610C     02      BASE    MULT   .12      INCTX  52H         INCOME TAX DED
00620C     02      GROSS   SUB    INCTX    NET    52
00630C     02      GROSS   ADD    DGROSS   DGROSS 62
00640C     02      HRS     ADD    DHRS     DHRS   52
00650C     02      GROSS   ADD    GGROSS   GGROSS 72
00660C     02      HRS.    ADD    GHRS     GHRS   62
001400* DEFINES HEADINGS AND OUTPUT
001500PRINTR    H 0201    01
001600         OR         OF
001700                                  10'DATE'
001800                        DATE      19'  /  /  '
002100                                  67'PAYROLL'
002200                                 120'PAGE'
002300                        PAGE     125'   0'
002400          H 02      L1
002500         OR         OF
002600                                  10'DEPT'
002700                                  24'EMP NO'
002800                                  37'HOURS'
002900                                  49'RATE'
003000                                  63'GROSS'
003100                                  81'EXEMPTIONS'
003200                                 100'INCOME TAX'
003300                                 115'NET PAY'
003400          D 02      02
003500                    L1  DEPT        8
003510                    30  DEPT        8
003600                        EMPNO      23
003700                        HRS        37'  .  '
003800                        RATE       49'  .  '
003900                        GROSS      63'  0.  '
004000                        EXEMP      76
004100                        INCTX      97'  0.  '
004200                        NET       114'  0.  '
004300          T 33      L1
004400                                  27'DEPARTMENT
004500                        DGROSS B   63'  . $0.  '
004600                        DHRS   B   37'  0.  '
004700          T 30      LR
004800                                  29'GRAND TOTALS
004900                        GGROSS B   63'  ., $0.  '
005000                        GHRS   B   39'   0.  '
```

FIGURE 8–8
continued

```
//GO.PRINTR DD SYSOUT=A
//GO.CDIN   DD *
052775
10029400031753
10087410029002
10141420044401
10160400026754
10387445049954
10401510037502
10403400029003
20037400024502
20098400029701
20201400044501
20221440041503
20485478541705
/*EOF
```

PAYROLL

DEPT	EMP NO	HOURS	RATE	GROSS	EXEMPTIONS	INCOME TAX	NET PAY
1	0029	40.00	3.175	127.00	3	10.06	116.94
	0087	41.00	2.900	120.35	2	10.99	109.36
	0141	42.00	4.440	190.92	1	21.18	169.74
	0160	40.00	2.675	107.00	4	5.93	101.07
	0387	44.50	4.995	233.51	4	21.11	212.40
	0401	51.00	3.750	211.87	2	21.97	189.90
	0403	40.00	2.900	116.00	3	8.74	107.26
DEPARTMENT TOTALS		298.50		$1,106.65			

DEPT	EMP NO	HOURS	RATE	GROSS	EXEMPTIONS	INCOME TAX	NET PAY
2	0037	40.00	2.450	98.00	2	8.30	89.70
	0098	40.00	2.970	118.80	1	12.53	106.27
	0201	40.00	4.450	178.00	1	19.63	158.37
	0221	44.00	4.150	190.90	3	17.72	173.18
	0485	47.85	4.170	215.90	5	17.27	198.63
DEPARTMENT TOTALS		211.85		$801.60			
GRAND TOTALS		510.35		$1,908.25			

Some interactive languages on small computer systems utilize an interpreter rather than a compiler to translate source statements to object code. Unlike a compiler, which translates an entire program into object code at one time (for later execution), an **interpreter** evaluates and translates program statements as the program is executed, one instruction at a time. The interpreter takes one source program instruction, translates it into machine code, and then executes it. It then takes the next instruction, translates it, and so on. Using an interpreter can save space since the interpreter program itself can be quite small, and it eliminates the need to store the program's translated object code in the computer. It may also be inefficient—program statements that are used multiple times must be translated each time they are executed.

This system at Santa Fe Railway utilizes software designed by Sperry Univac to monitor and control the movement and inventory of railway cars.

BASIC **BASIC** (Beginners' All-purpose Symbolic Instruction Code) was developed at Dartmouth College for use with time-sharing systems. Because BASIC is easy to learn, it can be used by people with little or no programming experience—novice programmers can write fairly complex programs in BASIC in only a matter of hours.

The growth in the use of time-sharing systems has been accompanied by an increase in the use of BASIC. Most computer manufacturers offer BASIC support on their computers. Although BASIC was originally intended to be used by colleges and universities for instructional purposes, many companies have adopted it for their data-processing needs. In addition, the increasing popularity of microcomputers in homes is furthering the use of BASIC, since it is the language most often supported by these microcomputers.

Among BASIC's most attractive features are its simplicity and flexibility. It is very easy to learn. It can be used for both scientific and business applications. And although BASIC was intended for use as an interactive programming language, it is finding increased use as a batch language.

The simplicity of BASIC has led many manufacturers to offer different versions of the language. A BASIC standard was established in 1978, but it covers only a small subset of the BASIC language. BASIC programs written for one system may need substantial modification before being used on another. Many extensions to BASIC have been developed, but only at the expense of increasing the difficulty of learning and using the language. As

HIGHLIGHT
BASIC Software Packages

Learning a new computer language can be fun and profitable at the same time. BASIC, for example, is relatively easy to learn and is becoming the predominant language available with personal computers. As the microcomputer market matures and hundreds of thousands of these machines come into use, the demand for software increases. Manufacturers of most microcomputers offer a very limited selection of software, and thus the need grows for alternative suppliers. This need is being met largely by individual owners of microcomputers who write programs for their own machines and offer them for sale to others.

Packaged programs can be marketed in several ways: advertise in magazines such as *BYTE* and *Creative Computing;* sell software to one of the computer utilities forming around the country; write a collection of programs and offer the entire selection for sale in book form. One final method, which might be the best, involves marketing through the user newsletters of the various microcomputer manufacturers.

firms continue to expand online, real-time programming applications, however, the use of BASIC will no doubt continue to increase (see Figure 8–9).

Pascal **Pascal** is the only language mentioned in this chapter whose name is not an acronym. Pascal is named after the French philosopher and mathematician, Blaise Pascal. (Remember from Chapter 2 that Pascal invented the

FIGURE 8–9
Payroll Program in BASIC

```
PAYROLL          14:50     AUGUST 3RD, 1981

10   REM THIS PROGRAM CALCULATES A WEEKLY
15   REM PAYROLL FOR FIVE EMPLOYEES
20   PRINT 'EMPLOYEE NAME', 'NET PAY'
30   PRINT
40   READ N$, H, W
50   IF H > 40 THEN 70
60   LET G = H*W
65   GO TO 100
70   LET R = 40*W
80   LET O = (H-40) * (1.5*W)
90   LET G = R+O
100  IF G > 250 THEN 130
110  LET T = .14
120  GO TO 140
130  LET T = .20
140  LET T2 = T*G
150  LET P = G-T2
160  PRINT N$, P
170  GO TO 40
180  DATA 'LYNN MANGINO', 35, 8.00
190  DATA 'THOMAS RITTER', 48, 4.75
200  DATA 'MARIE OLSON', 45, 5.50
210  DATA 'LORI DUNLEVY', 40, 5.00
220  DATA 'WILLIAM WILSON', 50, 7.00
230  END

RUN PAYROLL
```

```
EMPLOYEE NAME        NET PAY

LYNN MANGINO         224.00
THOMAS RITTER        212.42
MARIE OLSON          209.00
LORI DUNLEVY         172.00
WILLIAM WILSON       308.00
```

first mechanical adding machine.) Niklaus Wirth, a computer scientist from Switzerland, developed Pascal between 1968 and 1970. The first Pascal compiler became available in 1971.

Like BASIC, Pascal was first developed to teach programming concepts to students but is rapidly expanding beyond its initial purpose and finding increased acceptance in business and scientific applications. Pascal is well suited for both batch and interactive modes, although most Pascal business applications are batch-oriented.

Pascal receives avid support from its users because, while it is relatively easy to learn (like BASIC,) it is powerful (like PL/I). Unlike PL/I, Pascal is available on microcomputers and seems to be a good alternative to BASIC for use on small computers.

At first, Pascal's availability was limited, but more computer manufacturers now are offering Pascal compilers with their machines. Perhaps the major disadvantage of Pascal is that it is not yet standardized. Many versions and enhancements are available from manufacturers, which may cause programs written in Pascal to differ depending upon the specific compiler used. In addition, some people believe that Pascal has poor input/output capabilities. Figure 8–10 shows the payroll program in Pascal.

A software application development by Informatics called TAPS, seen on the terminal screen, is compatible with main frames, minicomputers, and microcomputers while most software is designed for use on only one type of processor.

FIGURE 8–10
Payroll Program in Pascal

```
PROGRAM PAYROLL (INPUT,OUTPUT);
VAR HOURS,REGULAR,WAGE,OVERTIME,GROSS,TAX,NETPAY : REAL;
NAME : ARRAY(.1..17.) OF CHAR;
I : INTEGER;
BEGIN
WRITELN('1','EMPLOYEE NAME','                    NET PAY');
WRITELN('   ');
WHILE NOT EOF DO
   BEGIN
   FOR I:=1 TO 17 DO
      READ (NAME(.I.));
      READLN (HOURS,WAGE);
      IF HOURS> 40
         THEN BEGIN
            REGULAR:=40*WAGE;
            OVERTIME:=(HOURS-40)*(1.5*WAGE);
            GROSS:=REGULAR + OVERTIME
         END
         ELSE BEGIN
            GROSS:=HOURS*WAGE
         END;
      IF GROSS>250
         THEN BEGIN
            TAX:=0.20*GROSS;
            NETPAY:=GROSS-TAX
         END
         ELSE BEGIN
            TAX:=0.14*GROSS;
            NETPAY:=GROSS-TAX
         END;
   WRITE(' ');
FOR I :=1 TO 17 DO
      WRITE(NAME(.I.));
      WRITELN(NETPAY:12:12);
   END
END.
```

```
EMPLOYEE NAME         NET PAY

LYNN MANGINO          224.00
THOMAS RITTER         212.42
MARIE OLSON           209.00
LORI DUNLEVY          172.00
WILLIAM WILSON        308.00
```

APL CODING	ENGLISH TRANSLATION
A + B	A plus B
A ← 25	A = 25
A⌊B	Finds the smaller of A and B
V1 ← 2 5 11 17	Creates a vector of 4 components and assigns this vector to V1
⌉/V1	Finds the maximum value in the vector V1

FIGURE 8–11
APL Coding

APL **APL** (A Programming Language), conceived in 1962 by Kenneth Iverson in his book of the same name, APL, became available to the public through IBM in 1968 and, over the years, has been expanded and has gained many enthusiastic supporters. Several businesses now use APL as their programming language.

The full power of APL is best realized when it is used for interactive processing via a terminal. A programmer can use APL in two modes. In the **execution mode,** the terminal can be used much as a desk calculator. An instruction is keyed in on one line and the response is returned immediately on the following line. In the **definition mode,** a series of instructions is entered into memory and the entire program is executed on command from the programmer. APL bears little resemblance to any high-level programming language discussed this far.

APL operators can be combined to perform some very complex operations with a minimum of coding (see Figure 8–11). APL's lack of formal restrictions on input and output and its free-form style make it a very powerful language. APL is also available through time-sharing networks for organizations that need only a limited amount of data processing.

APL involves a few disadvantages as well. It is very difficult to read. A special keyboard is required to enter APL statements; fortunately, however, the larger offering of new, low-cost terminals capable of handling several type fonts has greatly reduced this problem (see Figure 8–12). Many people do not believe that APL is suitable for handling large data files. Another limitation of APL is the large amount of primary storage required by its compiler. Finally, APL is not as widely supported as are COBOL and Pascal. Figure 8–13 shows an interactive APL session.

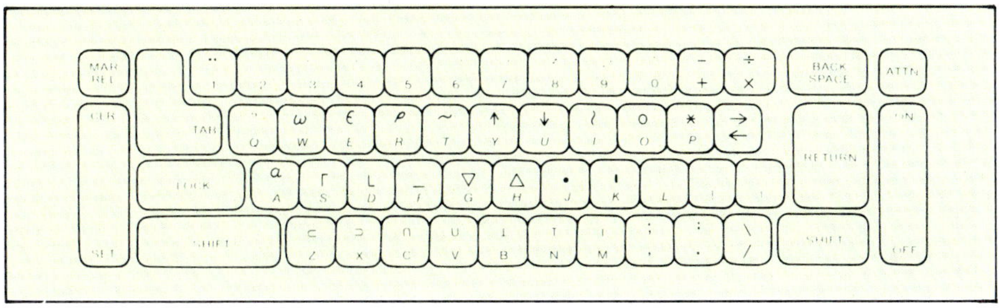

FIGURE 8–12
APL Keyboard

FIGURE 8–13
Interactive APL Session

```
      ∇PALINDROME[⎕]∇

    ∇ PALINDROME PHRASE;ALPHA;COMPRESSED;REVERSE
[1]   ⍝  PROGRAM TO DETERMINE IF A PHRASE IS A PALINDROME
[2]   ⍝  THE PHRASE MUST BE CHARACTER DATA AND HAVE AT LEAST ONE
[3]     ALPHA←'ABCDEFGHIJKLMNOPQRSTUVWXYZ'
[4]     COMPRESSED←(PHRASE∊ALPHA)/PHRASE
[5]     →(0 =⍴COMPRESSED)/NONE
[6]     REVERSE←COMPRESSED[⍒⍳⍴COMPRESSED]
[7]     →( ∧/REVERSE=COMPRESSED)/YES
[8]     PHRASE,'  IS NOT A PALINDROME'
[9]     →0
[10]  YES:PHRASE,'  IS A PALINDROME'
[11]    →0
[12]  NONE:'THERE ARE NO ALPHABETIC CHARACTER IN PHRASE'
    ∇

      PALINDROME 'MOM'
MOM  IS A PALINDROME

      PALINDROME 'THIS'
THIS  IS NOT A PALINDROME

      PALINDROME 'MADAM IN EDEN I''M ADAM'
MADAM IN EDEN I'M ADAM  IS A PALINDROME

      PALINDROME '1 21 '
THERE ARE NO ALPHABETIC CHARACTER IN PHRASE
```

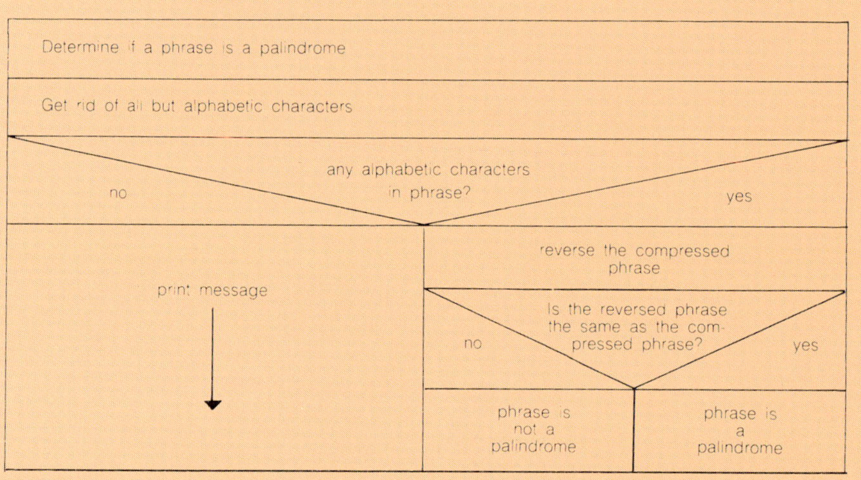

Table 8–2 shows a comparison between all the batch and interactive languages discussed in this chapter.

MULTIPROGRAMMING, VIRTUAL STORAGE, MULTIPROCESSING

Just as application programs have become more sophisticated over the years, so have system programs. Early computer systems were plagued by inefficient use of computer resources, either because human intervention was required or because system programs were not sophisticated enough to allocate resources well. Several developments have come about that greatly increase the overall efficiency of the computer. These are multiprogramming, virtual storage, and multiprocessing. **Multiprogramming** allows the computer to work with more than one program at a time. **Virtual storage** makes main storage appear larger than it is, while **multiprocessing** provides for simultaneous execution of more than one program by several computers. These are all discussed in more detail below.

Multiprogramming

When the CPU is very active, the system as a whole is more efficient. However, the CPU frequently must remain idle because input/output devices are not fast enough. The CPU can operate on only one instruction at a time; furthermore, it cannot operate on data that is not in primary storage. If an

TABLE 8–2
Comparison of Programming Languages

	ASSEMBLY LANGUAGE	FORTRAN	COBOL	PL/I	RPG	BASIC	PASCAL	APL
Strong math capabilities	X	X		X		X	X	X
Good character-manipulation capabilities	X		X	X		X	X	X
English-like			X	X			X	
Available on many computers	X	X	X		X	X	X	
Highly efficient	X							
Standardized		X	X	X		X		
Requires large amount of storage			X	X				X
Good interactive capability						X	X	X
Procedure-oriented		X	X	X		X	X	X
Problem-oriented					X			
Machine-dependent	X							

input device is slow in providing data or instructions, the CPU must wait until input/output operations have been completed before executing a program.

Multiprogramming increases CPU active time by effectively allocating computer resources and offsetting low input/output speeds. Under multiprogramming, several programs reside in the primary storage unit at the same time. Although the CPU can execute only one instruction at a time, it can execute instructions from one program, then another, then another, and back to the first again. Instructions from one program are executed until an interrupt for either input or output is generated. While the input/output operation takes place, the CPU can shift its attention to another program in memory. The computer executes the second program until it, too, requires input or output. This rotation occurs so quickly that the execution of the programs in storage appears to be simultaneous. More precisely, the CPU executes the different programs **concurrently,** which means "over the same period of time."

Virtual Storage

Multiprogramming increases system efficiency because the CPU can concurrently execute programs instead of waiting while input/output operations occur. A limitation of multiprogramming, however, is that all the instructions of a program are kept in primary storage throughout its execution, whether they are needed or not. Yet, a large program may contain many sequences of instructions that are executed infrequently. As processing requirements increase, the physical limitations of memory become a critical constraint, and the productive use of memory becomes increasingly important.

To alleviate the problem, an extension of multiprogramming called **virtual storage** has been developed on the principle that only a portion of a program (that portion needed immediately) has to be in primary storage at any given time. The rest of the program and data can be kept in auxiliary storage. Since only part of a program is in primary storage, more programs can be placed there at one time. More programs can be executed within a given time period. This gives the illusion that main storage is unlimited.

To implement virtual storage (or **virtual memory,** as it is sometimes called), a direct-access storage device such as a magnetic-disk unit is used to augment primary storage. The term **real storage** is usually given to primary storage within the CPU, while virtual storage refers to the direct-access storage (see Figure 8–14). Both real and virtual storage locations are given addresses by the operating system. If data or instructions needed are not in the real (primary) storage area, the portion of the program containing them is transferred from virtual storage into real storage, while another portion currently in real storage may be written back to virtual storage (or merely overlaid in primary storage). This process is known as **swapping.**

One of the major limitations of virtual storage is the requirement for extensive online auxiliary storage. Also, the virtual-storage operating system is highly sophisticated and requires significant amounts of internal storage.

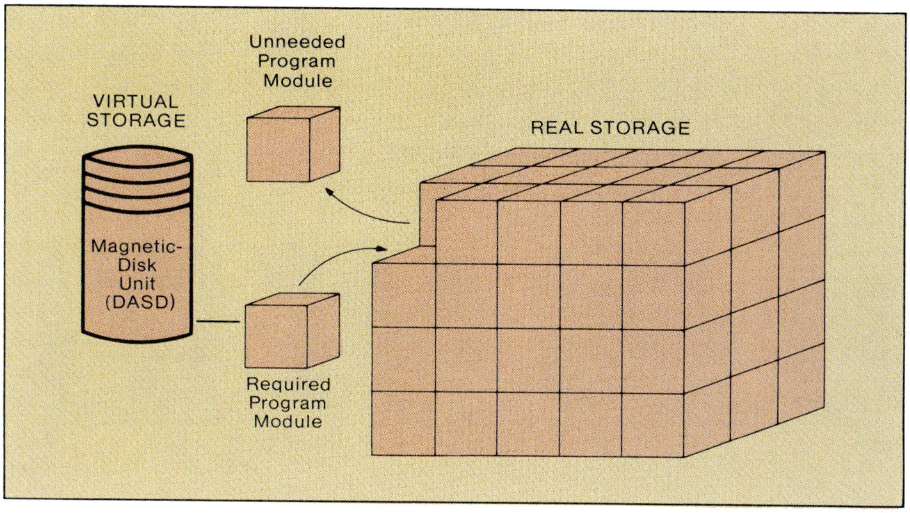

FIGURE 8–14
Schematic Drawing of Virtual Storage and Swapping

If virtual storage is not used wisely, much time can be spent swapping portions of a program in and out of real storage. Very little processing occurs compared with the amount of swapping. This is known as **thrashing.**

Multiprocessing

Multiprocessing involves the use of two or more central processing units linked together for coordinated operation. Stored-program instructions are executed simultaneously, but by different CPUs. The CPUs may execute different instructions from the same program, or they may execute totally different programs. (In contrast, under multiprogramming, the computer appears to be processing different jobs simultaneously, but is actually processing them concurrently.)

Multiprocessing systems are designed to achieve a particular objective. One common objective is to relieve a large CPU of tasks such as scheduling, editing data, and maintaining files so that it can continue high-priority or complex processing without interruption. To do this, a small CPU (often a minicomputer) is linked to the large CPU. All work coming into the system from remote terminals or other peripheral devices is first channeled through the small CPU, which coordinates the activities of the large one. Generally, the small CPU handles all input/output interrupts and so on, while the large CPU handles the "number crunching" (large mathematical calculations). A schematic diagram of this type of multiprocessing system is shown in Figure 8–15. The small CPU in Figure 8–15 is commonly referred to as a **front-end processor.** It is an interface between the large CPU and peripheral devices such as online terminals.

Coordinating the efforts of several CPUs requires highly sophisticated software and careful planning. The scheduling of workloads for the CPUs involves making the most efficient use of computer resources. Implementing such a system is a time-consuming endeavor that may require the services

FIGURE 8–15
Multiprocessing System with Small Front-End Processor and Large Main Frame

of outside consultants as well as those provided by the equipment manufacturers. The payoff from this effort is a system with capabilities extending far beyond those of a single-CPU system.

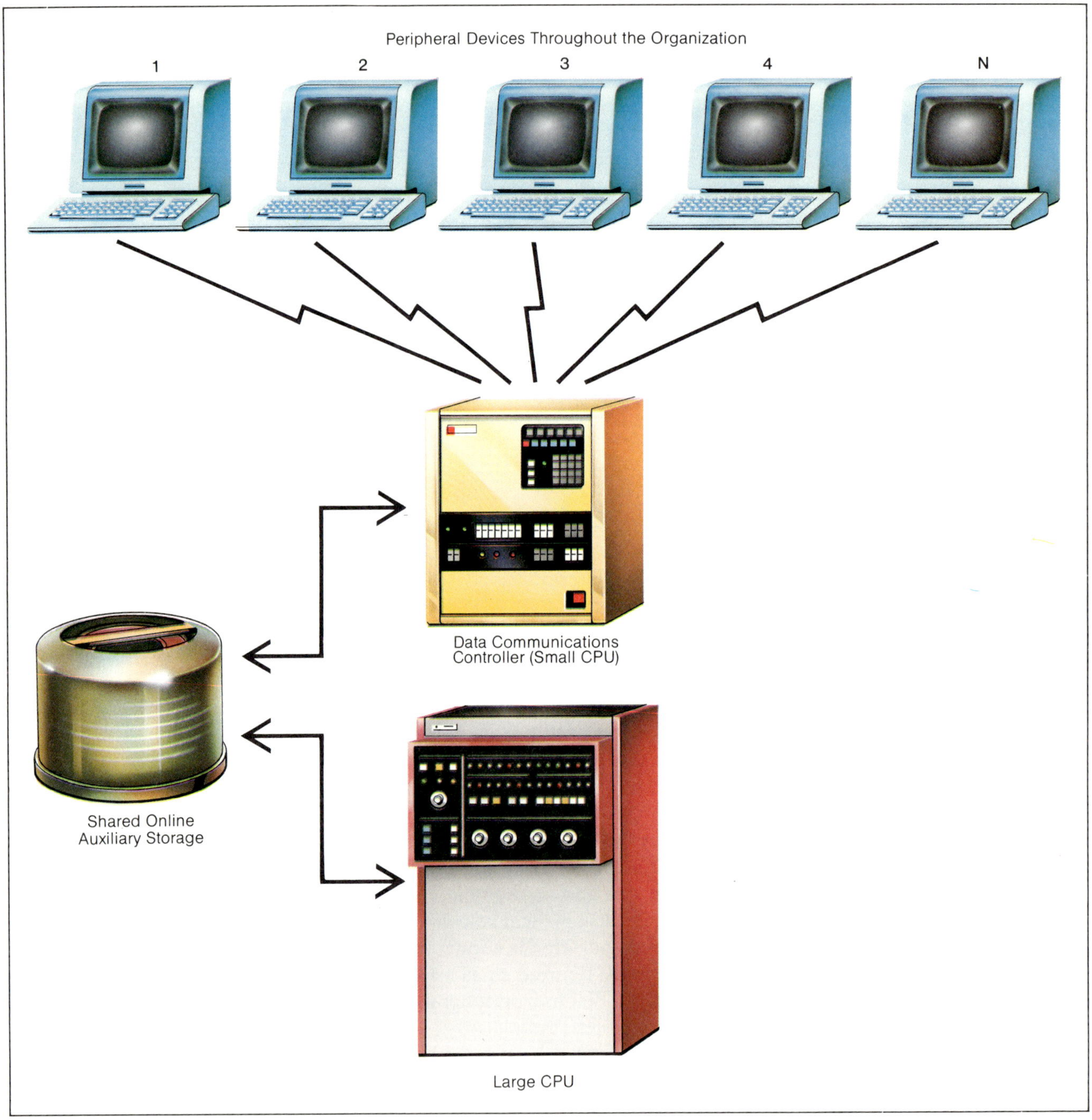

SUMMARY POINTS

- System programs coordinate the operation of computer circuitry while application programs solve particular user problems.
- Operating systems are groups of system programs with specific functions. Batch operating systems direct computer processing without interruption until all jobs are complete. Real-time operating systems respond to spontaneous requests for system resources such as user requests from online terminals.
- Control programs oversee system operations and perform input/output, scheduling, handling interrupts, and communicating with the computer operator.
- Processing programs are executed under the supervision of control programs and are used by the programmer to simplify program preparation.
- Programming languages can be either batch or interactive. Batch-oriented programming languages solve problems for which immediate responses are not required. Interactive programs allow the user to interact with the program in a conversational fashion.
- Machine-oriented languages make the most efficient use of computer resources, but are also the most difficult to program in. Examples of machine-oriented languages are machine language and assembly language.
- Procedure-oriented languages focus on the processing steps required to solve a problem and are designed to aid the programmer in performing those steps.
- COBOL, a procedure-oriented programming language, is the most common business programming language. It is self-documenting and very English-like.
- FORTRAN, also a procedure-oriented programming language, is used extensively in scientific and mathematical applications.
- PL/I combines the best of COBOL and FORTRAN and is a free-form programming language. It can be programmed modularly, making it a good choice for structured programming.
- Problem-oriented languages are designed to allow the programmer to focus on the end result desired of a program, rather than on the individual steps required.
- RPG was first designed to provide business reports quickly and accurately. The programmer or user merely designates the qualities desired of the output on special forms, and RPG generates the program required to provide that output.
- Interactive programming languages provide for interaction with the user or programmer. BASIC, Pascal, and APL are examples of interactive languages.
- Interpreters are often used with interactive languages. They do not translate an entire program at one time (like a compiler), but rather evaluate program statements one at a time.
- Multiprogramming increases computer efficiency by having more than one program in main storage at one time. When an interrupt is issued by

one program, the computer can process another program while the required input/output functions for the first are executed.

- Virtual storage keeps only those portions of a program required for processing in main memory. As other parts of the program are required, they are brought into main memory.
- Multiprocessing provides for simultaneous execution of commands by more than one computer. This is often accomplished by using a smaller computer to manage input/output operations.

REVIEW QUESTIONS

1. Discuss the major differences between application and system programs.
2. How do control programs in operating systems differ from processing programs? Give examples of each one, and how each would be used by the computer during its operation.
3. What is the function of the supervisor program?
4. Distinguish between a source program and an object program. What does a compiler do?
5. Under what types of conditions would you suggest using a machine-oriented language? Procedure-oriented? Problem-oriented? Interactive?
6. List some advantages of COBOL for business use. What is its principal disadvantage?
7. Discuss why former users of FORTRAN might be interested in learning to program in PL/I.
8. What does it mean when a language is said to be "standardized?" Why is this important?
9. What is the difference between multiprocessing and multiprogramming?
10. How are programs written in high-level languages translated into machine-readable form? What is the difference between a compiler and an interpreter?
11. How does virtual storage differ from real storage?

Programming Languages and the Microcomputer

BASIC is by far the most popular language on microcomputers today. Its interactive nature and relative ease of programming for nonprofessional programmers has helped earn this status. It is also more efficient than standard versions of COBOL because BASIC commands and statements require less memory. For this reason, when the first hobby computers with very small RAMs were built, the makers incorporated BASIC. One drawback to this popularity, however, has been a lack of uniformity on the computer manufacturer's implementation of the BASIC language, and as a result, there are differences in the BASIC versions found on various computers. BASIC in ROM, written by Microsoft, is the most common form. It is available on Apple, TRS-80, Commodore PET/CBM, Atari, and Ohio Scientific computers, among others. There are also many disk-based versions of BASIC, with the computer manufacturers adding "quirks" of their own.

Pascal is an interactive language that has been gaining popularity, and there is some speculation that it may soon replace BASIC as the most popular language. It has several advantages over BASIC. It has a modular structure, which forces a programmer to think in a more structured, organized fashion; it allows creation of complex data structures, such as an array, that can define tables including different data types; it uses a compiler that catches common consistency errors; and it includes program statements that replace BASIC's common GOTO statement. One reason Pascal hasn't come to the forefront sooner is because it requires a lot of memory to implement it. Most versions require about 64K bytes of RAM, but with the increasing number of sixteen-bit computers (IBM Personal, Apple III, TRS-80 Model 16) able to support more internal memory, this restriction may soon vanish.

A wide variety of other languages can also be implemented on microcomputers. These include FORTRAN, COBOL, C, Forth, Ada, and a number of new educationally oriented languages such as Logo and Pilot.

The full versions of FORTRAN and COBOL require a large amount of memory and therefore are not normally found on microcomputers. However, with the increasing memory capacity of microcomputers, some of these computers are now supporting these languages. In addition, some manufactures have developed a chip containing the computer language, which can be added without using additional memory.

Ada, a new high-level language developed for use by the Department of Defense, is intended as a common language for all its applications. They envision it as someday replacing COBOL in the business world. Because of its large size, only subsets of Ada are presently available for personal computers.

Among the educational languages, Logo is receiving a good deal of attention. It is presently available for the Apple II and III and the Texas Instruments 99/4 computers with versions for others in the works. It is a high-powered language set up in a "kiddie" format. Its main attraction is that it allows children to communicate with computers, drawing images, animating them, and coloring them by giving very simple instructions. It does this through a triangular object called a "turtle" that leaves a trail in its path that children can easily command to draw straight lines or rotate in the directions in which they want it to draw.

Pilot is another of the current, easy-to-learn educational languages. It features the same unusually powerful set of simple graphics instructions known as "turtle" graphics found in Logo.

Let's take a look at an example of how "turtle" graphics works. When graphics mode is first entered, the turtle is located near the middle of the screen and is pointed straight up (0 degrees) "holding" a yellow pen. The color of the line that the turtle draws can be changed with the proper command. If we want the turtle to draw a square with each side 30 screen units in length, we would enter the following statements:

```
 10 GR:CLEAR
 20 GR:GOTO -15,5
 30 GR:DRAW 30
 40 GR:TURN 90
 50 GR:DRAW 30
 60 GR:TURN 90
 70 GR:DRAW 30
 80 GR:TURN 90
 90 GR:DRAW 30
100 GR:TURN 90
110 E:
```

The GR indicates a graphics command. Line 10 clears the screen of any previous drawings. Line 20 directs the turtle to go to the coordinates -15, 5 on the screen where it is to begin drawing. The turtle is then directed to draw a line 30 units long by line 30 and then turn 90 degrees by line 40. It continues in this fashion through line 100, which completes the square. Line 110 signals the end of the program. "Turtle" graphics also allows shortcuts in the programming steps. For example, the following program accomplishes the same feat as the one above:

```
10 GR:CLEAR
20 GR:GOTO -15,5
30 4(DRAW 30;TURN 90)
40 E:
```

Microcomputers have a lot more functions available now than they used to. Some systems allow you to play music and/or display graphics. Even inexpensive models such as the Atari 400 and the Commodore VIC 20 have these features. We saw above one example for the Atari 400 of how graphics are being used in educational programs. Let's take a look at how we can use the VIC 20 to produce music. Two statements that are allowing microcomputers to do many of the things that they are now doing are PEEK and POKE. The PEEK and POKE statements allow machine language subroutines to be called from BASIC programs.

PEEK allows you to find a particular memory location and *identify* what is stored there. POKE allows you to find a particular memory location and *change* what is stored there. The VIC 20 has four voices that can sound individually or in any combination. They are each indicated by a memory location. Speaker 1 is 36874 (alto), speaker 2 is 36875 (tenor), speaker 3 is 36876 (soprano), and speaker 4 is 36877 (white noise generator). The volume is set through the address 36878 and has fifteen levels. The user can regulate the four voices and volume levels to create the desired music.

As programming languages are becoming more user-friendly, the world of computing is being opened up to more than just the professional programmer. New languages, along with new features for older languages, are now enabling users to accomplish many things that previously could not be done or only the highly skilled could accomplish. These user-friendly languages should help propel the acceptance of the personal computer into our everyday lives.

DISCUSSION QUESTIONS

1. What factors led to BASIC becoming the most widely used language for personal computers?
2. Why have languages such as FORTRAN and COBOL not been widely used with personal computers?

CHAPTER 9

System Analysis and Design

INTRODUCTION

Today's business environment is terribly complex and challenging. Business information systems must be designed to provide the information managers need to make the right decisions. Ineffective systems doom a corporation by providing misleading, incorrect, or tardy information. Too much information yields the same result—managers overlook important facts because of information overload.

This chapter discusses the system approach to information systems and the three stages to system development: system analysis, system design, and system implementation. The concept of management information systems is discussed, along with the various types of information required by managers. Structured design as a methodology for designing systems is reviewed along with various design alternatives. Finally, the concepts of a data base and data-base management systems are presented.

FACING PAGE
A computer system specially designed to handle a variety of trading and reporting services for stock brokers.

JANUARY
Quotron

CHAPTER OUTLINE

INFORMATION SYSTEM THEORY

A business is too complex to be studied directly, just as the forest sometimes cannot be seen for the trees. The analyst needs tools to help remove the complexities of business information systems in order to better understand and evaluate them.

The system approach to system analysis is one such tool. It is a model that aids in the analysis of information systems by attempting to mirror events in the real world while reducing the complexity of the activities involved in those events. The system model highlights important factors, patterns, and flows. Instead of accurately representing each tree in the forest, the model shows the overall pattern of the trees, their outline in the forest, and the countryside bordering its edges.

Definition of a System

The system approach is based upon system theory. System theory defines a **system** as a group of related elements that work together toward a common goal. One example of a system is a single cell in a human body; each molecule in the cell performs important functions and all these molecules work together in order for the cell to survive.

A system is made up of inputs, processes, and outputs. **Inputs** enter the system from the surrounding environment. In the cell, the inputs might be oxygen and nutrients. These inputs are transformed by some **process** into outputs. The cell processes its inputs into energy and wastes. Most of the **outputs** leave the system, going to the environment; but some may stay within the system.

Feedback is another important concept in system theory; it can take the form of either internal or external communication. That is, information can flow within the system's internal environment or between the system and the outside. Its purpose is to inform the system whether or not predetermined standards are being met. Figure 9–1 shows a diagrammatic representation of a system and its components.

FIGURE 9–1
A Simple System with Feedback

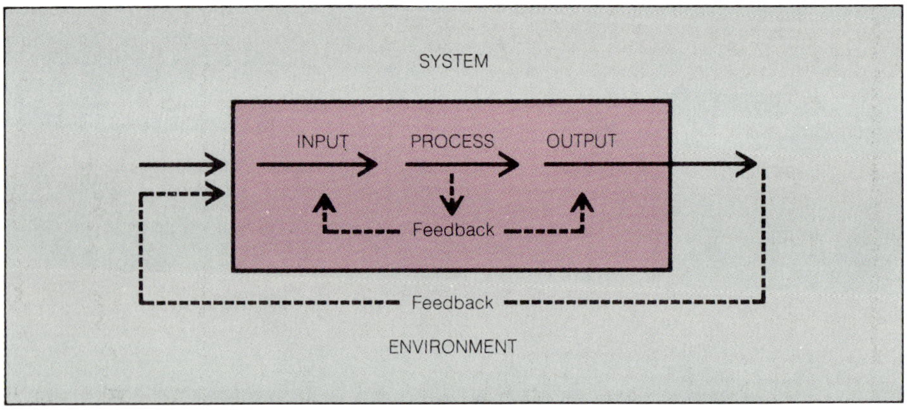

The System's Interaction with Other Systems

System analysis is an inexact science—the boundaries between systems are not always easy to define, and neither are the elements of a system that might stand alone as systems in themselves. The determination depends on the level at which one views the system. A doctor who is a general practitioner views the body as the system; an ophthalmologist views the eye as the system.

The fact that one system may belong to another, larger one is an important concept in system theory because it implies the existence of interaction among systems. All of these concepts are put to good use when system theory is used to view the organization.

The Organization as a System

The concepts of system theory can be used to analyze the information flow within a business firm. A firm has a group of related elements (departments of employees) working together toward a common goal (survival and profit). Figure 9–1 could easily represent the firm using inputs from the surrounding environment to create outputs through a transformation process. Figure 9–2 shows a business firm (Centron) as a system within a larger one—the economic system of today's business world.

FIGURE 9–2
Interacting Systems

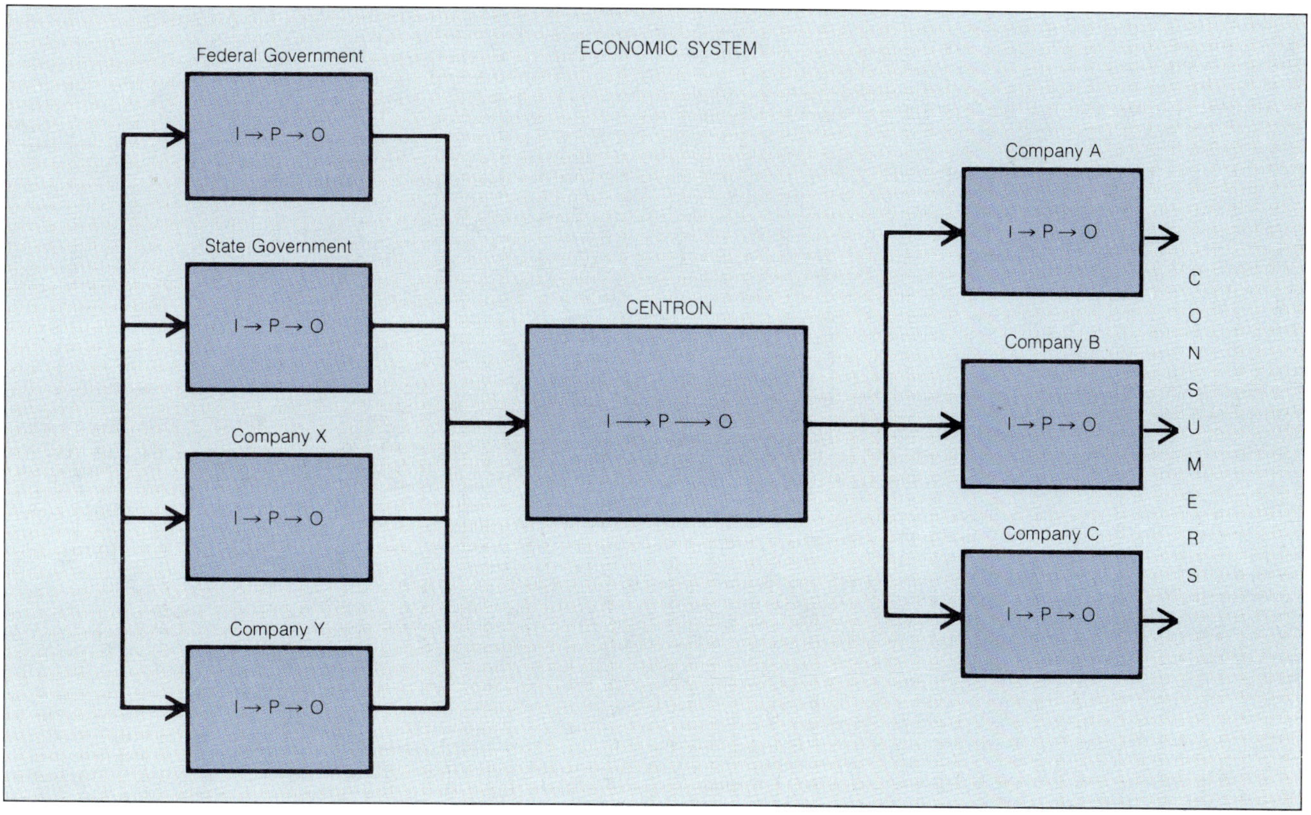

Each department within Centron also can be thought of as a system. The various methods and procedures used by a department to gather data, process it, and distribute the resulting information is called its information system. An **information system** has all of the characteristics of a system as described earlier—the input to an information system is data, the processing is either manual or computer manipulation, and the output is information. Feedback is the other action taken by company employees based on that information. A planner in the production department of Centron (one system) needs information about forecasted sales from the sales department (another system). In making sales forecasts, the sales department probably uses past history and information from its own salespeople (internal environment) as well as stated customer intentions and projected economic conditions (external environment). Information about the availability of raw materials is provided by the purchasing department, which communicates with suppliers. The list of interactions goes on and on (see Figure 9–3).

FIGURE 9–3
The Company as a System

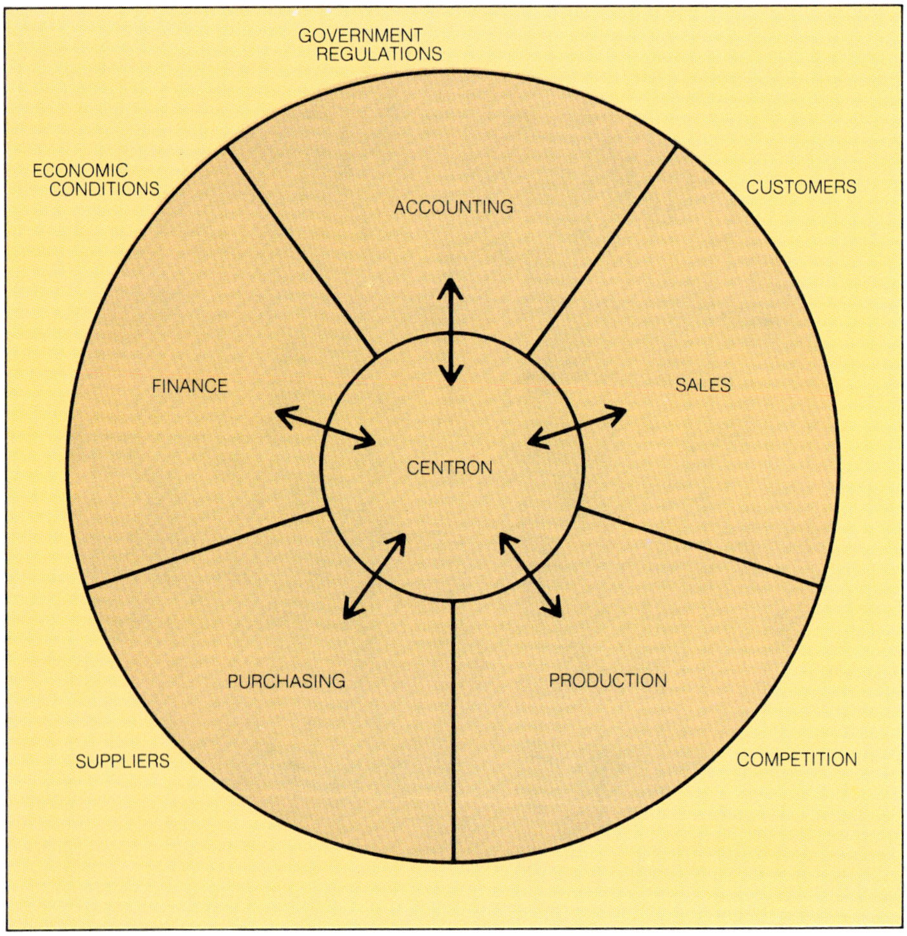

SYSTEM METHODOLOGY

An information system is designed to satisfy the needs of decision makers. Some information systems are computerized; others are manual. The output from both types must provide management with the information it needs. If management believes an information system is not functioning properly, it may need to be analyzed. However, even when there are reasons to review an existing system, it does not necessarily follow that a new system should be developed. Developing an information system may cost hundreds of thousands of dollars, and it is a complex and time-consuming process. This process involves three steps: **analysis, design,** and **implementation** (see Figure 9–4). The goal of the first step, system analysis, is to determine whether or not a need for a new information system exists.

System Analysis

System analysis may be required because of a need to solve a problem, respond to new information requirements, incorporate new technology into a system, or make broad system improvements. The reason for the analysis determines the scope or level at which the investigation takes place. The analyst, in conjunction with those requesting the system study, establishes

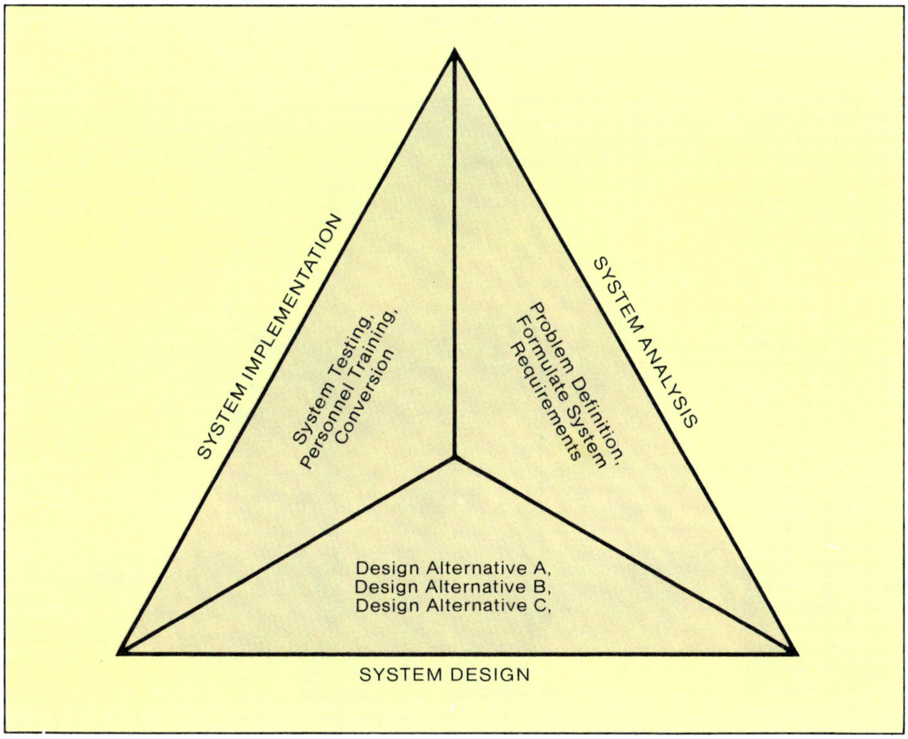

FIGURE 9–4
System Methodology

the proper focus for the two stages of system analysis—data gathering and data analysis.

The type and amount of data gathered depend upon the scope and goal of the system analysis. Data can be supplied by both internal and external sources. Four common sources of internal information are interviews, system flowcharts, questionnaires, and formal reports. Personal interviews provide data about current operations and procedures and the users' perceptions of what the system should do. System flowcharts identify the inputs, processing, and outputs of the system being analyzed. Questionnaires are used to collect information regarding detailed system operations such as frequency of processing, time required for various processing steps, and the personnel and equipment used. Formal reports, the major outputs of the system, give the analyst clues as to the goals of the information system. Potential interfaces with other systems can easily be identified by studying the distribution of these reports.

Sources external to the business could include books, periodicals, brochures, and product specifications from manufacturers. Customers and suppliers are also good sources of information. Analysts also need to identify and contact other companies that may have developed or implemented similar information systems.

After data has been collected, it must be organized and integrated to be seen in proper perspective. Whereas the focus during data collection is on *what* is being done, the focus during data analysis is on *why* certain operations and procedures are being used. The analyst looks for ways to improve these operations. Many tools are available to the analyst to aid in data analysis; one such tool is the system flowchart.

HIGHLIGHT
Computer at the Cinema

At the twenty-one-theater complex at Toronto's giant Eaton Center shopping mall, a specially-designed computer helps sell and monitor tickets to all the viewing rooms, keeps track of how many people are attracted to each movie on any given day, controls advance ticket sales according to space available, and virtually eliminates mistakes and cheating on the daily box office reports. The theaters range in size from 50 to 185 seats and offer all kinds of fare, from special-interest foreign-language movies to current commercial hits.

System analysts at work in the tire development computer center at Goodyear Tire and Rubber Company.

System flowcharts emphasize the flow of data through the entire data-processing system without describing details of internal computer operations. A system flowchart represents the interrelationships among various system elements. Examples of different system flowchart symbols and what they represent are shown in Figure 9–5.

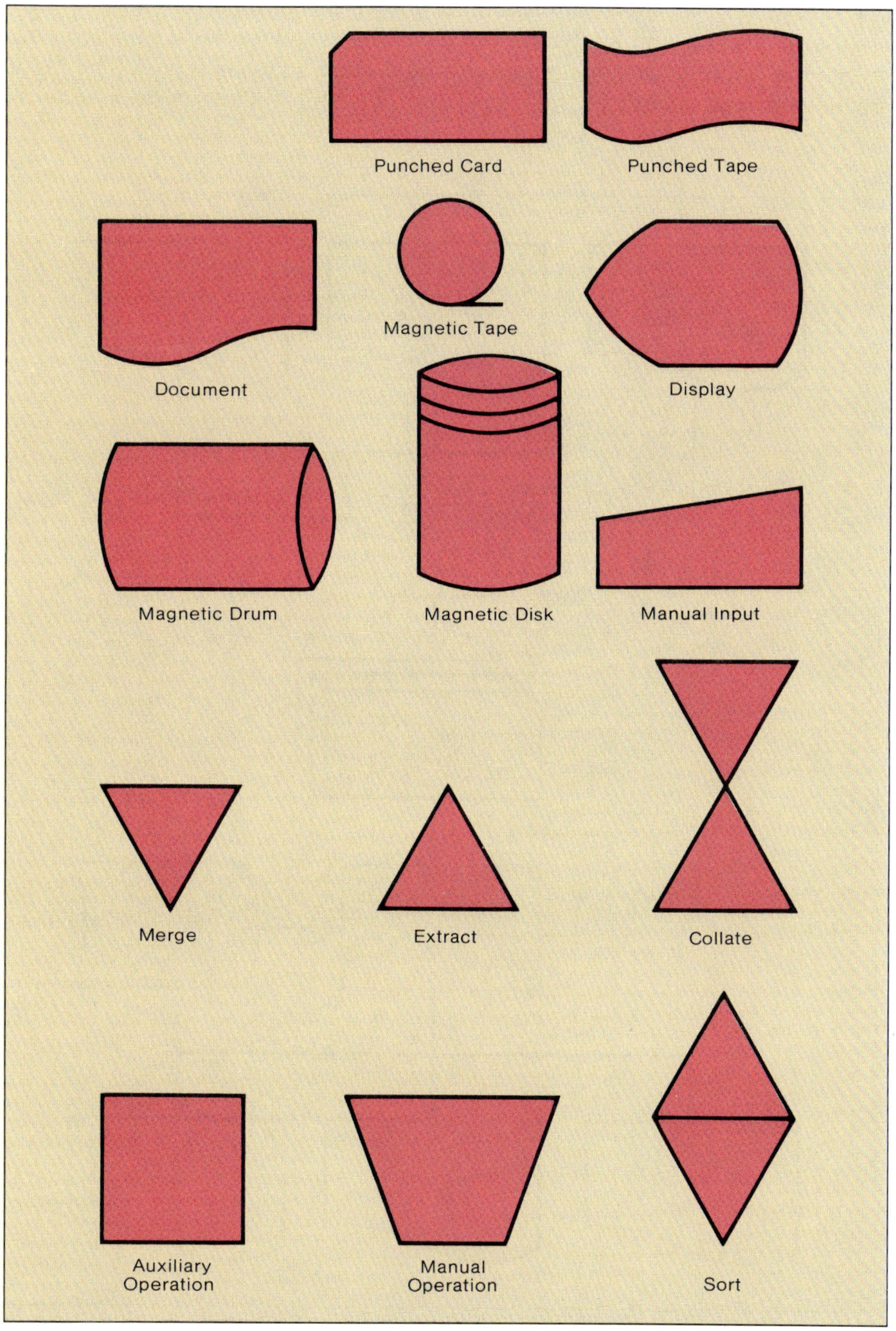

FIGURE 9–5
Specialized Input/Output and Process Symbols for System Flowcharts

The difference between program and system flowcharts is in the purposes they serve. A program flowchart aids the programmer in writing a source program by specifying the details of operations so that the programmer can code the steps more easily. In contrast, system flowcharts are designed to represent the general information flow; they often represent many operations within one process symbol. An example of a system flowchart showing the updating of an inventory master is shown in Figure 9–6.

After collecting and analyzing the data, the system analyst must communicate the findings to management in the **system analysis report.** The report includes a restatement of the scope and objectives of the system analysis,

FIGURE 9–6
Sample System Flowchart

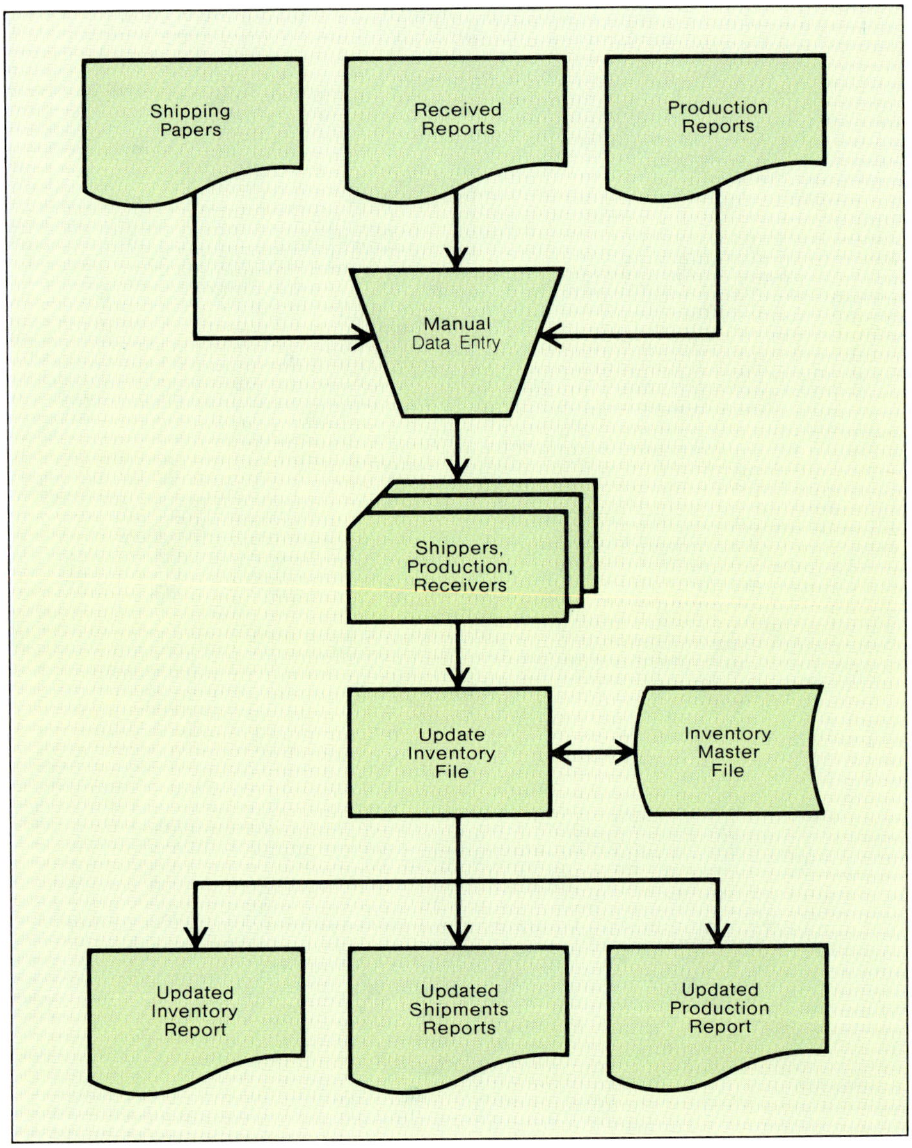

an explanation of the present system, a preliminary report of alternatives that currently seem feasible, and an estimate of the resources and capital required to either modify the present system or design a new one. Only if management approves this report can the system analyst proceed to the detailed system design.

System Design

If management decides to continue the project, the system design stage begins. In **system design** the analyst develops an information system that meets the needs uncovered in the system analysis stage. Designing an information system demands a great deal of creativity and planning. It is also very costly and time-consuming. In the system analysis, the analyst focused on what the current system does and on what it should be doing according to the requirements discovered in the analysis. In the design phase, the analyst changes focus and concentrates on how a system can be developed to meet the information requirements. During the design stage, the analyst

System designers at the Santa Fe Railway always keep user-oriented goals in mind when designing a new system. Currently, their Information System Department is designing a company-wide electronic mail system in which there will eventually be a terminal on every manager's desk.

HIGHLIGHT
Making It Big in System Design

It seems the computer industry still has open arms for the innovator. Paul Rollins was a twenty-one-year veteran of the electronic field—having worked for such giants as General Electric, Honeywell, and Motorola—when big business bureaucracy got the best of him and he decided to strike out on his own. He quit his corporate job in 1978 and took out a Small Business Administration loan to start a consulting firm. At about the same time General Motors of Canada was looking for a company to provide it with a computerized plant-monitoring system. Ultimately, General Motors came to Rollins' new Phoenix Digital company for help. His proposal for a monitoring design was so impressive—and comparatively low-cost—that GM asked Phoenix General to actually manufacture it. By the first quarter of 1982, Rollins' entrepreneurial spirit had resulted in $4 million in sales, and the sky was the limit.

reviews the goals and objectives of the system, develops a system model, evaluates any organizational constraints, develops alternative designs, performs a cost/benefit analysis, and finally prepares a system design report and recommendation. These are all discussed more fully below.

The analyst reviews the goals and objectives of the system in order to maintain a broad approach and flexibility in the system design phase. The analyst should restate users' information requirements so that they reflect the needs of the majority of users. For example, the finance section of an organization may want a report of customers who have been delinquent in payments. This department might be only one of many in a larger accounts-receivable department, so it might be more appropriate to state these requirements more generally as follows: (1) maintain an accurate and timely record of the amounts owed by customers, (2) provide control procedures that ensure detection of abnormal accounts and report them on an exception basis, and (3) provide, on a timely basis, information regarding accounts receivable to different levels of management to help achieve overall company goals.

The analyst next attempts to develop a model, based on system theory, to represent the system's major components. This is to verify his or her understanding of the various components in the system and their interactions. In reviewing the model, the analyst refers to system theory to discover any possible omissions of important subsystems. Are the major interactions among subsystems shown? Are the inputs, processes, and outputs appropriately identified? Does the model provide for appropriate feedback to each of the subsystems? Are too many functions included within one subsystem? Figure 9–7 is an example of a conceptual model of an accounts-receivable system.

No organization has unlimited resources; most have limitations on financial budgets, personnel, and computer facilities as well as time constraints for system development. The system analyst must recognize and evaluate these organizational constraints on system design imposed by a limited availability of resources. The structure of the organization can affect subsequent designs developed by the analyst.

There is more than one way to design a complex information system, and system analysts are generally required to develop alternative designs. This requirement is useful because it forces the analyst to be creative. A complete design of all alternatives is not possible. The analyst instead "roughs out" several possible systems and selects the one that appears most feasible. The alternative systems may be evaluated in ascending order of complexity and cost since management often desires alternatives from which to choose.

Cost/benefit analysis is a technique commonly used in business decision making. The firm has limited financial resources, and they must be allocated to projects that appear to offer the greatest return on the costs of initial development. In order for cost/benefit analysis to be performed, both costs and benefits must be quantified. Many statistical programs are available to use in determining costs and benefits of large system designs. Sampling and modeling enable the analyst to provide cost/benefit figures not readily apparent from available information. Even then, estimating costs or benefits is often not straightforward—they can be extremely difficult to quantify.

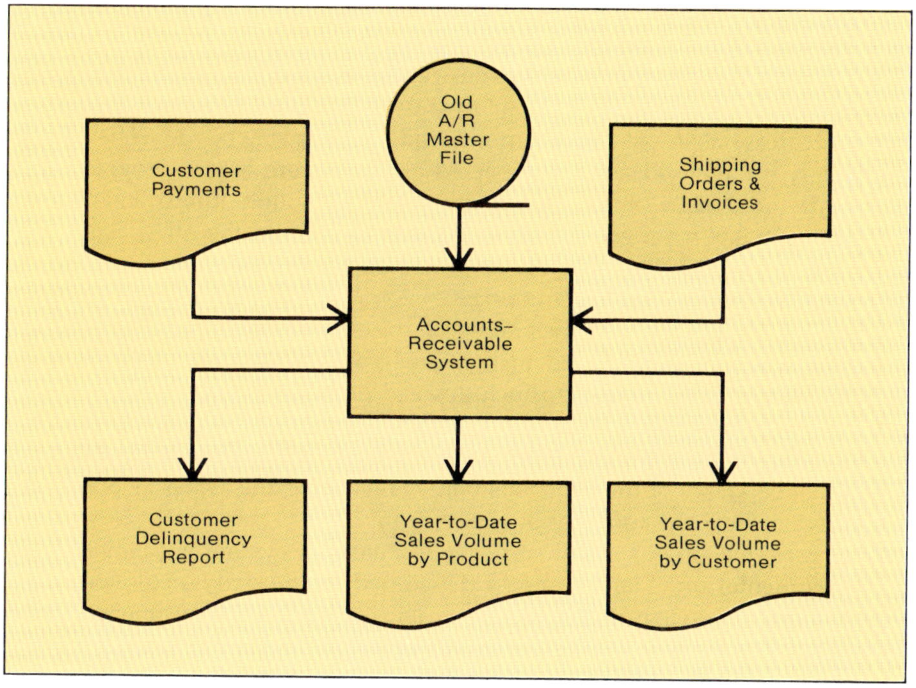

FIGURE 9–7
Model of an Accounts-Receivable System

Once the analyst has completed all of the steps described above, he or she must prepare a report to communicate findings to management. The system design report should explain in general terms how the various designs will satisfy the information requirements determined in the analysis phase. The report should also review the information requirements uncovered in the system analysis, explain in both flowchart and narrative form the proposed designs, detail the corporate resources required to implement each alternative, and make a recommendation. The recommendation should include a more detailed design than the other alternatives and include a set of procedures and forms to be used in the proposed system.

After evaluating the system design report, management can do one of three things: approve the recommendation, approve the recommendation with changes (this includes selecting another alternative), or select none of the alternatives. The "do nothing" alternative is always possible. If the design of the system is approved, the analyst proceeds to implement it.

System Implementation

In the implementation stage of the system methodology, the analyst is able to see the transformation of ideas, flowcharts, and narratives into actual processes, flows, and information. **System implementation** is the adoption of the information system developed in the system design stage. This transition is not performed easily, however. Detailed programming specifications must be coded in a computer language, debugged, and put into production. Personnel must be trained to use the new system procedures, the system must be thoroughly documented and tested, and finally a conversion must be made from the old system to the new one.

A computerized information system requires considerable programming in order to work properly. If the analyst does not program, the system design specifications must be communicated to people who do. They must completely understand what is expected of the system before programming begins. If the design of the system has been thorough, there will be few changes to make in programs during conversion. If, on the other hand, the analyst has not fully considered all processing requirements, considerable time may be spent in reprogramming.

One of the primary responsibilities of the system analyst is to see that personnel training is provided to the two groups of people who interface with a system. The first group includes the people who develop, operate, and maintain the system. The second group includes the people who use the information generated by the system to support their decision making. Both must be aware of their responsibilities regarding the system's operation and of what they can and cannot expect from it.

Until recently, one of the most neglected parts of system implementation was **documentation.** Many systems developed in the early 1970s were implemented with sparse documentation. This presented no problems when the systems were first implemented. Over time, however, changes in the businesses and their information requirements necessitated making system and programming changes. It was at that point that organizations painfully

"After one inning of play, the computer has projected the winner to be the Minnesota Twins."

realized the need to have extensive system documentation. It was often difficult to understand programs written five to ten years earlier. Changes made to them often caused errors in other programs. Thus, most organizations have adopted a system development methodology requiring adequate documentation of both programs and user procedures.

Before a system becomes operational, it must be tested and debugged. Testing occurs at various levels. The lowest level is program testing. Once all program testing is complete, system testing can proceed; this level of testing involves checking all the application programs that support the system. All clerical procedures used in data collection, data processing, and data storage and retrieval are included in system testing.

The switch from an old system to a new one is referred to as **conversion.** Conversion involves not only the changes in the mode of processing data but also the changes in equipment and in clerical procedures. Several approaches can be used to accomplish the conversion process. When **parallel conversion** is used, the new system is operated side-by-side with the old one for some period of time. **Pilot conversion** involves converting only a small piece of the business to the new system. With **phased conversion,** the old system is gradually replaced by the new one over a period of time. Finally, **crash conversion,** sometimes referred to as **direct conversion,** takes place all at once.

In parallel conversion, both the old and the new system must operate at the same time; this may require additional personnel and can be expensive. It does, however, provide for verifying the output of the new system against the proven results of the old one. Pilot conversion is useful in discovering problems in the new system while only a small part of the business is affected. These system "bugs" can be corrected before other areas adopt the system. Phased conversion can be used to replace parts of the old system with modules of the new as they are completed. Old data recording procedures may be updated using terminals instead of input forms; the gathered data may nevertheless be input to the old system's processing programs while new ones are developed. Crash conversion may be required when fast adoption of a new system is required or when new procedures are radically different from the old. This is a risky conversion method; there is no old system to fall back on should the new one fail.

System Audit and Review

After the conversion process is complete, the analyst must obtain feedback on the system's performance. This can be done by conducting an audit to evaluate the system's performance in terms of the initial objectives established for it. The evaluation should ask questions like: Does the system perform as planned and deliver the anticipated benefits? Was the system completed on schedule and with the resources estimated? What controls have been established for input, processing, and output of data? Have users been educated about the new system? Is the system accepted by users? As a result of the audit or of user requests, some modification or improvement of the new system may be required.

HIGHLIGHT
Computers in the Leisure Industry

Computers have invaded the leisure industry in a big way. A system at the Harry S. Truman Sports Complex in Kansas City, Missouri, monitors and regulates virtually every aspect of commercial activity at both Royals Stadium and Arrowhead Stadium, which make up the complex. The system tells management, among other things, which concession stands are selling the most, what the precise state of the inventory is at any time in the supply warehouse the two stadiums share, and where cash shortages are. A particular benefit of the system is its ability to handle the complicated payroll for the facility's unionized concession workers, who are subject to such variables as holiday pay rates, overtime rates, shift differentials, and bonuses. The computer's capacity to tie all the income and expenses together into a financial profile permits management to get an instantaneous summary of each event booked into the complex.

A well-designed information system is flexible and adaptable. Minor changes should be easily accommodated without large amounts of reprogramming. This is one of the reasons why structured programming was emphasized in Chapter 3; if each program module is independent, a minor change in one module will not snowball into other changes.

No matter how flexible or adaptable a system is, however, major changes become necessary over time. When the system has to be redesigned, the entire system cycle—analysis, design, and implementation—must be performed again. Keeping information systems responsive to information needs is a never-ending process.

MANAGEMENT INFORMATION SYSTEMS

Managers have recently recognized that the possibilities for computer use extend beyond normal reporting to generating information to support decision making. This application is known as a **management information system (MIS).** An MIS is a formal information network using computers to provide management with information it needs to make decisions. The goal of an MIS is to get the correct information to the appropriate manager at the right time. This is not as easy as it might first appear.

Levels of Management

Three levels of management generally exist within an organization, and managers at each level make different types of decisions that require different types of information. These levels are depicted in Figure 9–8.

FIGURE 9–8
Levels of Decision Making

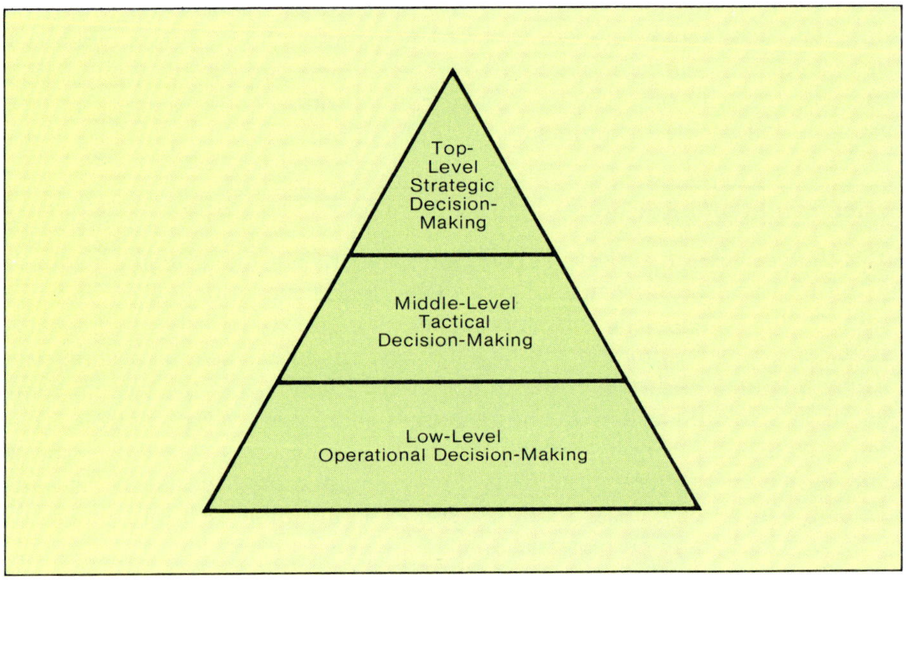

- **Top-level management—strategic decision making.** At the top level, activities are future-oriented and involve a great deal of uncertainty. Examples include establishing goals and determining strategies to achieve the goals. These strategies may involve introducing new product lines, determining new markets, acquiring physical facilities, setting financial policies, generating capital, and so forth.
- **Middle-level management—tactical decision making.** The emphasis in middle levels is on activities required to implement the strategies determined at the top level. Thus, most middle-management decision making is tactical. Activities include planning working capital, scheduling production, formulating budgets, making short-term forecasts, and administering personnel. Much of the decision making at this level pertains to control and short-run planning.
- **Lower-level management—operational decision making.** Members of the lowest level in the management hierarchy (first-line supervisors and foremen) make operating decisions to ensure that specific jobs are done. Activities at this level include maintaining inventory records, preparing sales invoices, determining raw material requirements, shipping orders, and assigning jobs to workers. The major function of lower-level management is controlling company results—keeping them in line with plans and taking corrective actions if necessary.

Managers at all levels must be provided with decision-oriented information. The fact that the nature of decisions differ at the three levels creates a major difficulty for those attempting to develop an MIS: the information

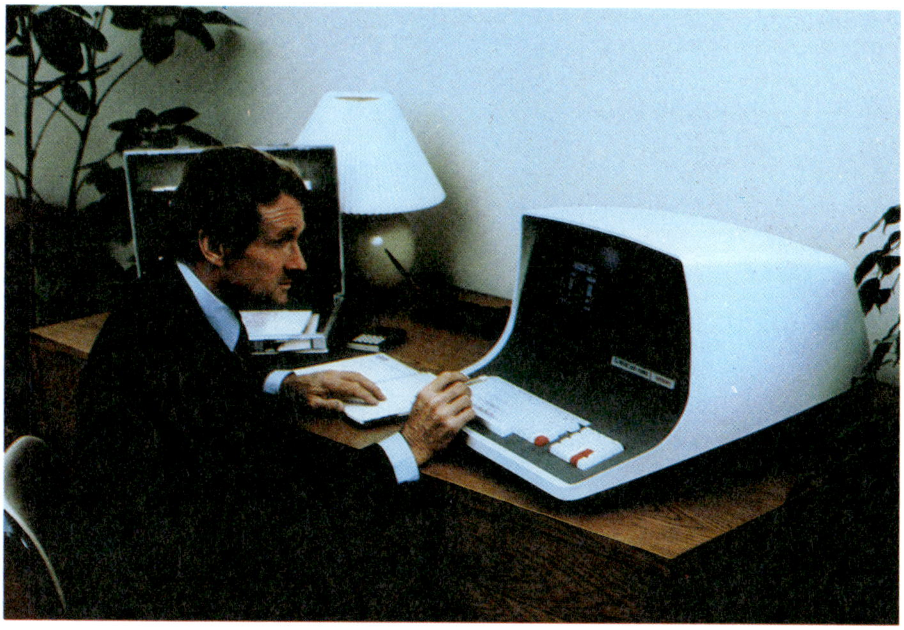

A financial executive utilizes his terminal for creating long-range financial plans.

system must be tailored to provide appropriate information to all levels (See Figure 9–9).

Decisions made at the lower level are generally routine and well defined. The needs of first-level supervisors can be met by normal administrative data-processing activities such as preparation of financial statements and routine record keeping. Although this level of decision making is fairly basic, it provides the data-processing foundation for the entire organization. If the information system is faulty at this level, the organization faces an immediate crisis.

Tactical decision making is characterized by an intermediate time horizon, a high use of internal information, and significant dependence on rapid processing and retrieval of data. Many middle-level decisions are ill-structured. The major focus of tactical decisions is how to make efficient use of organizational resources.

The main problems in MIS design arise when planners attempt to define and meet the information requirements of top-level management. It is extremely difficult, if not impossible, to clearly delineate these information needs. Most problems are nonrepetitive, have great impact on the organization, and involve a great deal of uncertainty. Most information systems serve the needs of the two lower levels but are not adequately designed to cope with the variety of problems encountered by top management. However, well-designed management information systems can help.

Table 9–1 shows the differences among the three levels of decision making.

Decision-Oriented Reporting

No matter what the level of information requirements, management information systems typically generate several types of reports. **Scheduled reports** are produced at regular intervals and provide routine information to a

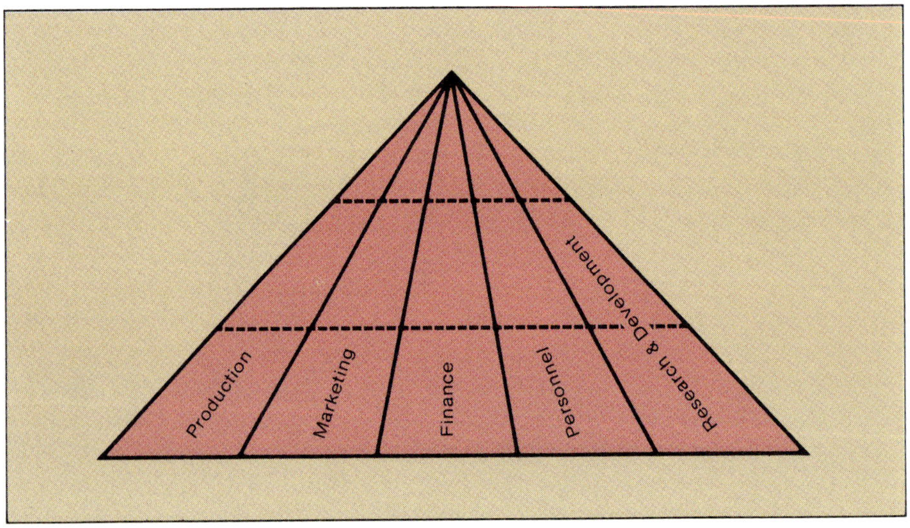

FIGURE 9–9
Functional Information Flow

wide variety of users. **Exception reports** are action-oriented management reports, because they ignore all normal events, reporting only abnormal situations that require special handling. **Predictive reports** are used for tactical and strategic decision making, where management can respond to "what if" kinds of queries. **Demand reports** are produced only on request, usually in response to unanticipated needs.

Management and MIS

Although an MIS can help management make decisions, it cannot guarantee the decisions will be successful. One problem that frequently arises is determining what information is needed by management. To many, decision making is an individual art. Experience, intuition, and chance affect the decision-making process. These inputs are all but impossible to quantify. In designing a system, the analyst relies on the user to determine information requirements. Frequently lacking precise ideas of what they need, managers request everything the computer can provide. The result is an overload of information. Instead of helping the manager, this information overload creates another problem: how to distinguish what is relevant from what is irrelevant.

STRUCTURED DESIGN METHODOLOGY

As the pace of technological innovation accelerates, data-processing departments are hard-pressed to keep up. In fact, most are unable to. Software development is far behind existing technology, because software development is extremely labor-intensive. Thus, data-processing departments today face a productivity problem: they must obtain greater software development for each dollar invested. The basic ways of increasing productivity are: (1) to automate the software development process, (2) to require employees to work harder or longer or both, or (3) to change the way things are done. Structured design attempts to achieve greater productivity by focusing on the third method, changing the way things are done.

TABLE 9–1
Characteristic Differences in Levels of Decision Making

	LEVELS OF DECISION MAKING		
CHARACTERISTICS	Operational	Tactical	Strategic
Time Horizon	Daily	Weekly/Monthly	Yearly
Degree of Structure	High	Moderate	Low
Use of External Information	Low	Moderate	Very high
Use of Internal Information	Very high	High	Moderate/Low
Degree of Judgment	Low	Moderate	Very high
Information Online	Very high	High	Moderate
Level of Complexity	Low	Moderate	Very High
Information in Real Time	High	High	High

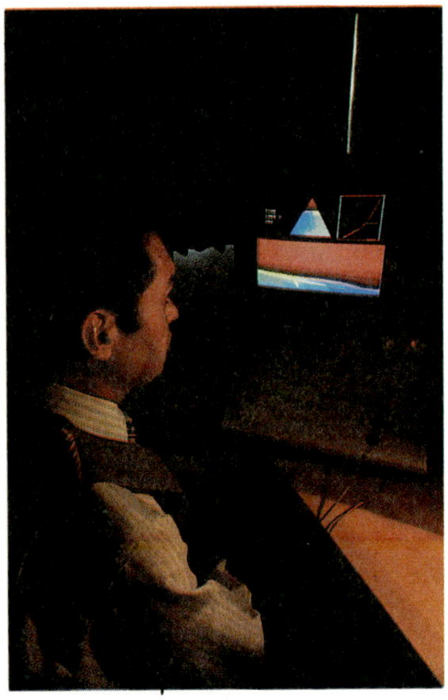

A system has been designed that allows an engineer at Shell Oil Company to analyze information about oil and gas reservoirs using color monitors.

Top-Down Design

Top-down design is a structured approach to system design much like the system approach is to system analysis. It attempts to simplify a problem by breaking it down into logical segments, or modules. These, in turn, are further divided. This is known as a modular approach to problem solving. The solution to a problem is first defined in terms of the functions it must perform. Each of these functions is then translated into a step (or module). The correct solution to a problem may require several of these modules, which together perform the required tasks.

In top-down design, the most general level of organization is the main control logic; this overall view of the problem is the most critical to the success of the solution. Modules at this level contain only broad descriptions of steps in the solution process. These steps are further broken down into several lower-level modules that contain more detail as to the specific steps to be performed. Depending on the complexity of the problem, several levels of modules may be required, with the lowest-level modules containing the greatest amount of detail.

The modules of the problem solution are related to each other in a hierarchical manner. These relationships can be depicted graphically on a **structure chart.** Figure 9–10 shows a portion of such a chart for an inventory processing application.

When top-down design is used, certain rules must be followed. First, each module should be independent of other modules; in other words, each module should be executed only when control is passed to it from the module directly above it. Similarly, once a module has been executed, control should be passed back to the module directly above. The return process continues until the main control module is reached.

DESIGN ALTERNATIVES

The development of an MIS is an integrated approach to organizing a company's activities. The company must be structured in a way that will allow it to fully realize the benefits of integration. When considering alternative organizational structures, the analyst faces virtually unlimited possibilities. This section describes four basic design structures: centralized, hierarchical, distributed, and decentralized. These structures should be viewed as checkpoints along a continuous range of design alternatives rather than as separate, mutually exclusive options.

Centralized design is the most traditional design approach. It involves the centralization of computer power. A separate electronic data-processing (EDP) department is set up to provide data-processing facilities for the organization; this department's personnel, like other staff personnel, support the operating units of the organization. All program development, as well as all equipment acquisition, is controlled by the EDP group. Standard regulations and procedures are employed. Distant units use the centralized equipment through remote access via a communication network. A common

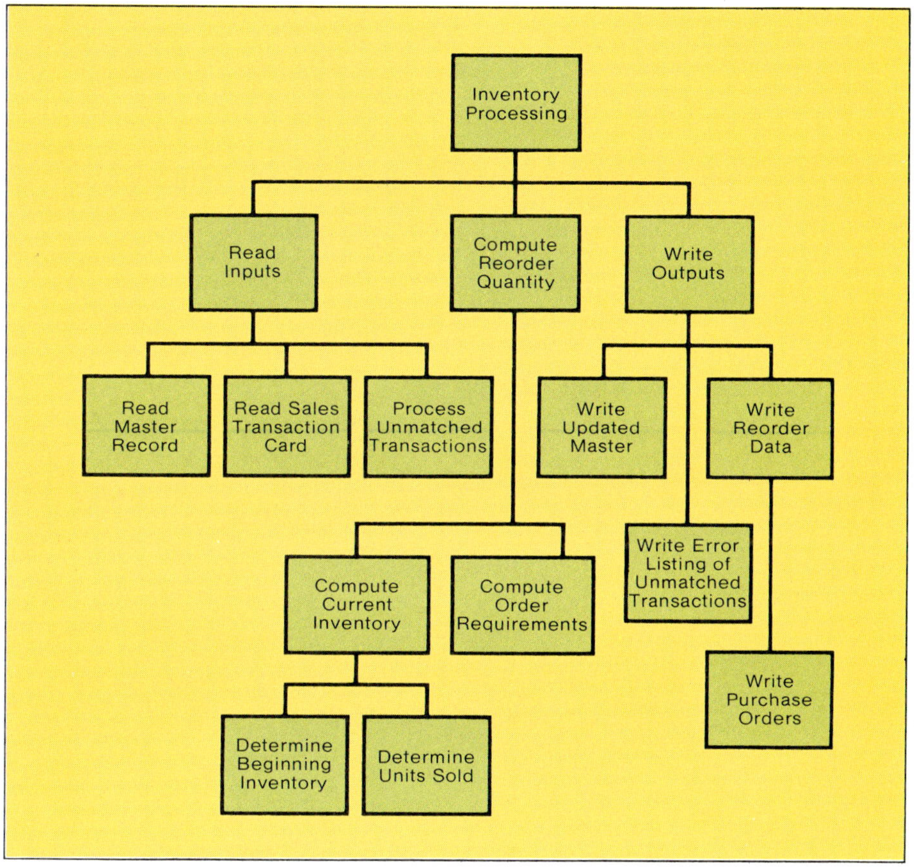

FIGURE 9–10
Structure Chart for Inventory Processing Example with Four Levels of Processing Modules

data base exists, permitting authorized users to access information (See Figure 9–11a).

When **hierarchical design** is used, the organization comprises multiple levels with varying degrees of responsibility and decision-making authority. In hierarchical design, each management level is given the computer power necessary to support its task objectives. At the lowest level, limited support is required, because the work is considered technical in nature. Middle-level support is more extensive, because managerial decisions at this level require more complicated analysis (hence, more information processing). Finally, top-level executives require little detailed information since they deal with general issues that require information available only with greater processing and storage capabilities. An example of this design approach is shown in Figure 9–11b.

The **distributed design** approach identifies the existence of independent operating units but recognizes the benefits of central coordination and control. The organization is broken into the smallest activity centers requiring computer support. These centers may be based on organizational structure, geographical location, functional operations, or a combination of these factors. Hardware (and often people) are placed within these activity centers to

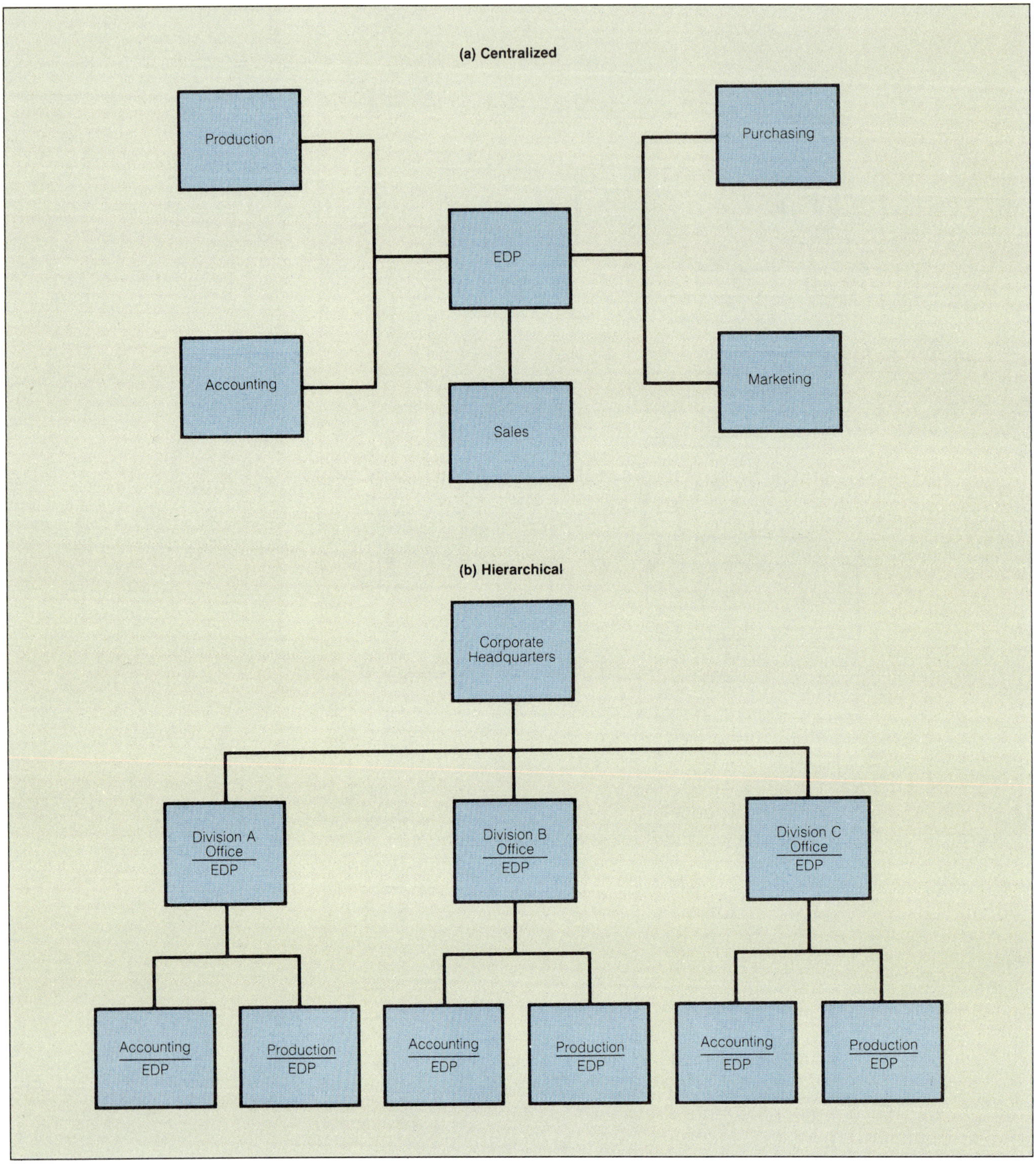

FIGURE 9–11 Sample Design Structures

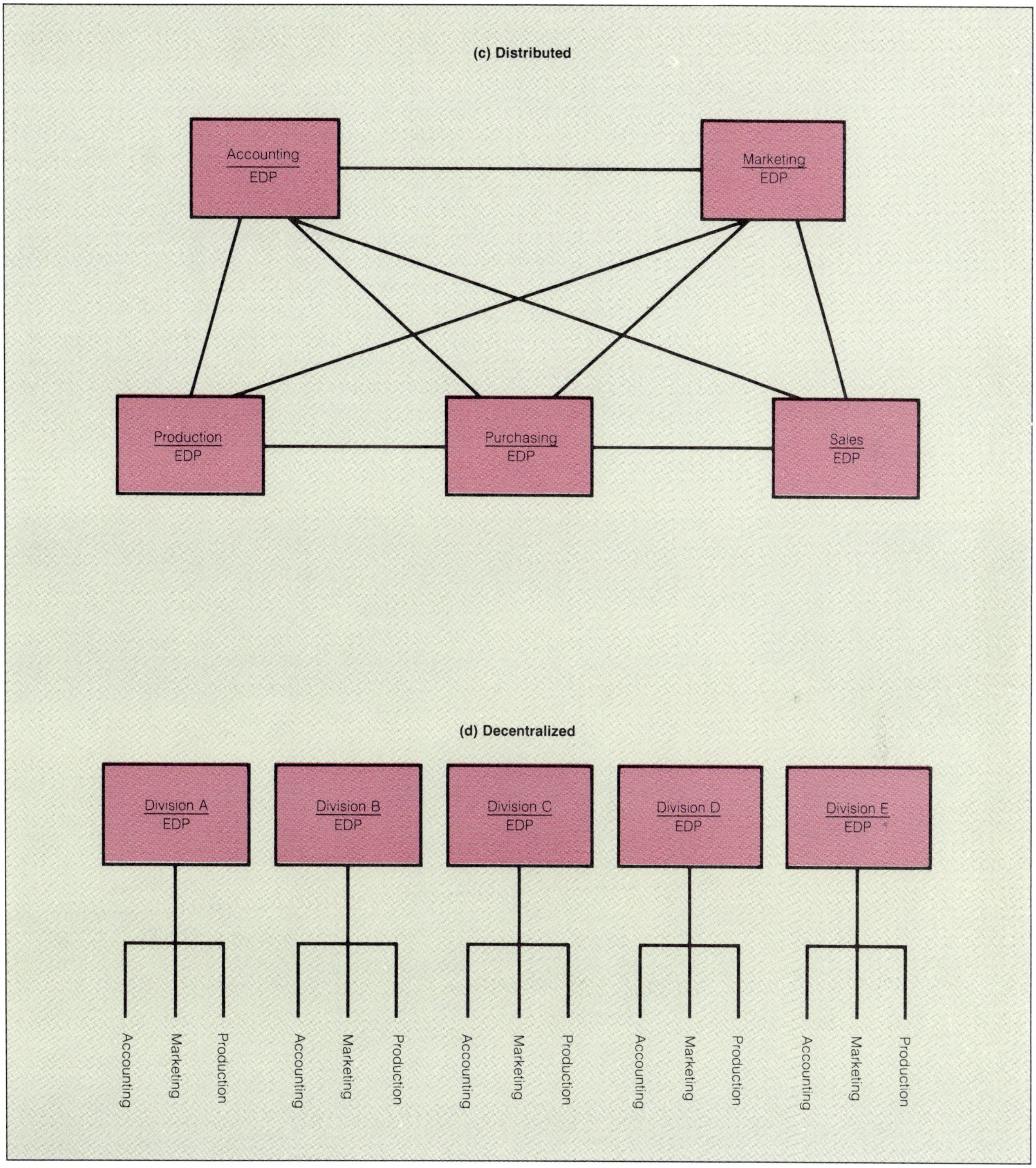

FIGURE 9–11 Continued

support their tasks. Total organization-wide control is often evidenced by the existence of standardized classes of hardware, common data bases, and coordinated system development. The distributed computer sites may or may not share data elements, workloads, and resources, depending on whether or not they are in communication with each other. An example of the distributed design approach is given in Figure 9–11c.

In a **decentralized design,** authority and responsibility for computer support are placed in relatively autonomous organizational operating units. These units usually parallel the management decision-making structure. Normally, no central control point exists; the authority for computer operations goes directly to the managers in charge of the operating units. Since there is no central control, each unit is free to acquire hardware, develop software, and make personnel decisions independently. Responsiveness to user needs is normally high because close working relationships are reinforced by the proximity of the system to its users. Communication among units is limited or nonexistent, thereby ruling out the possibility of common or shared applications. This design approach can only be used where an existing organizational structure supports decentralized management. Fur-

This Hewlett-Packard terminal puts managers in touch with vital information stored in their central computer system.

ther, it is not highly compatible with the management information system concept. An example of the decentralized design approach is shown in Figure 9–11d.

DATA-BASE MANAGEMENT

Before the integrated system approach was introduced, departments had their own separate data files and collected their own input. In contrast, the installation of an MIS requires the use of some form of general data storage. The organization's data must be stored in such a way that the same data can be accessed by multiple users for varied applications. This can be accomplished by use of a **data base,** a grouping of data fields structured to fit the information needs of multiple functions of an organization. Data is independent—it is grouped and organized according to its inherent characteristics and relationships rather than specifically for one application task. Thus, multiple departments can use the data, and duplication of files is avoided.

In addition to reducing redundancy and increasing data independence, the data base increases efficiency. When a particular item is to be updated, the change needs to be made only once. There is no need for multiple updates as is required with separate files. The integration of data also permits the results of updating to be available to the entire organization at the same time. Furthermore, the data base concept provides flexibility because the system can respond to information requests that previously may have bridged several departments' individual data files.

Data Organization

The design of data for a data base is approached from two perspectives. **Physical design** refers to how the data is kept on storage devices and how it is accessed. **Logical design** deals with how data is viewed by application programs or individual users. The logical data design is performed by the system analyst and data analyst. A **data analyst** is a person assigned the task of analyzing the relationships of data in the data base. Together, they attempt to model the real-world relationships that exist among data items. Logical records should be designed independent of physical storage considerations, so the physical design is often performed by the data administration department. The **data administration department** is the area assigned the responsibility for maintaining the data base. Taking into account such problems as data redundancy, access time, and processing constraints, this team tries to implement the logical data design within the physical records and files actually stored on the data base.

A logical unit can extend across more than one physical file. That is to say, what one user views as a logical unit of data may include data from the employee history file and the payroll file. Conversely, one physical file may contain parts of several logical units of data. One user's logical unit may include only an employee's name and address; another may include only the employee's number and job code. In both of these cases, the data is only a part of one physical file—the employee file.

HIGHLIGHT
Ahwatukee—Arizona Dream House

Ahwatukee is a Crow Indian word meaning house of dreams. A computer-controlled dream house in Arizona that goes by that name presents a novel study of systems; it is such a wonder that thousands of visitors monthly pay $2 each for a half-hour tour. (The money goes to charity.) The house is described as the state of the art in technology, ecology, and sociology; but the technology—the computer system—is the real drawing card.

Five linked microcomputers run five systems in the house: (1) The *environmental control system* handles all heating and cooling and all opening and shutting of doors and windows. (2) The *security system* is designed to protect against intruders through use of TV cameras, sensors, and a password-controlled front door. In addition, the sensors provide a fire detection and warning system. (3) The *electrical switching system* also uses the sensors to track paths through the house, adjusting lights (and other) switches wherever people go. (4) The *energy management system* maintains the most cost-efficient use of electricity. (5) Finally, the *information storage and retrieval system* is on hand for personal or home business needs.

HIGHLIGHT
Data Base Corrals Rustlers

Cattle rustling is not an activity found only in history books; rustlers are alive and active in the black market, where a cow can bring $500 and a trailer-truckload $10,000 or so. With this kind of money at stake, Texas and Southwestern Cattle Raisers Association (the nation's largest antirustling organization) has made a computer its defense weapon.

A data base of cattle transactions is stored on an electronic microfilm index. When cattle are reported stolen, the computer checks and lists all sales of cattle with that brand for a specified time period. Then the Texas Ranger assigned to the investigation tracks the sellers. Sometimes the ranger must backtrack through several transactions to get the real crooks. Once the rustlers have been pinpointed, the data base can be searched for their other cattle sales, perhaps identifying multiple crimes.

In just four years, this system has recovered or accounted for stolen merchandise worth over $1.3 million. Since the computer system can also handle more mundane business matters, the organization believes that its decision to automate was a good one.

Data-Base Management System (DBMS)

To facilitate the use of a data base, an organization can use a **data-base management system (DBMS)**—a set of programs that makes data in the data base readily available to its three principal users: the programmer, the operating system, and the manager (or other information user). By installing an available DBMS, an organization greatly reduces the need to develop its own detailed data-handling capabilities.

One of the major purposes of a DBMS is to effect the physical data independence mentioned earlier. This physical data independence permits the

A Tektronix color graphics terminal is used for management reporting.

physical layout of data files to be altered without necessitating changes in application programs. Such insulation between applications and the data with which they interact is extremely desirable. The programmer does not have to pay attention to the physical nature of the file. He or she can simply refer to the specific data that the program needs. Figure 9–12 shows the application, logical, and physical views of a data-base management system.

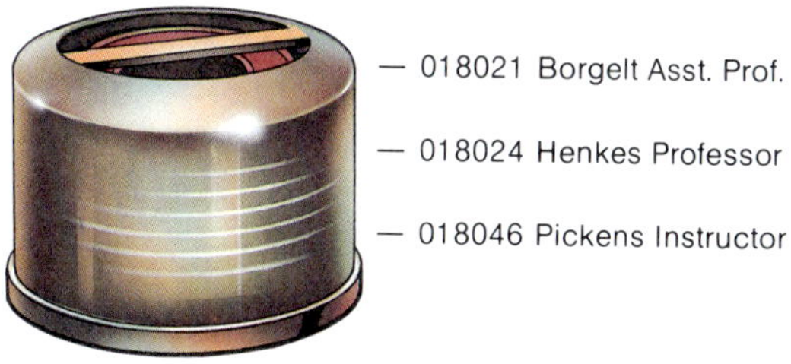

Disk Pack

Physical View of Data-base Organization

NAME		TITLE	
Value	Address	Value	Address
Borgelt	018021	Instructor	018046
Henkes	018024	Asst. Prof.	018021
Pickens	018046	Professor	018024

Logical View of Data-base Organization

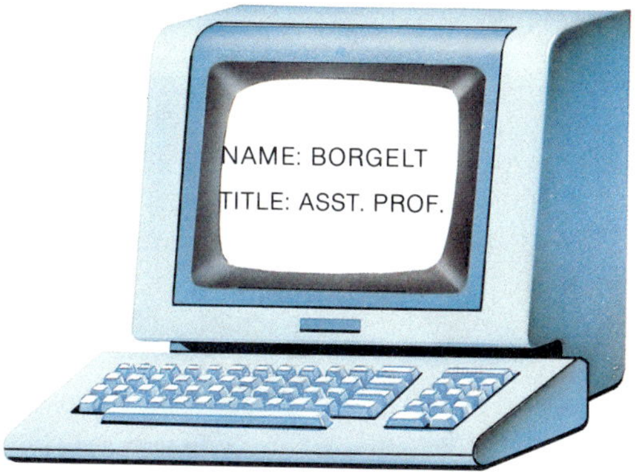

Application of Program Files

FIGURE 9–12
Physical, Logical, and Application Views of Data

SUMMARY POINTS

- A system is a group of related elements working together toward a common goal. The system takes inputs from its environment, processes them into outputs to be used by itself and the surrounding environment, and adjusts its processes through feedback.
- One system may be part of another, larger system, or may in itself be composed of several smaller systems. These systems interact with one another through their environments.
- The organization can be appropriately viewed as a system—it is a group of related elements (departments or employees) working together toward the common goals of profits and survival. It interacts with other systems in its environment, such as the government, the economy, its customers, and its competitors.
- Development of an information system follows three steps: analysis, design, and implementation.
- System analysis defines the scope or magnitude of the study to take place. Once this is agreed upon, the analyst gathers then analyzes data regarding the current system. The result of system analysis is the system analysis report.
- System design focuses on how a system can be developed to better provide the information required by decision makers. The analyst attempts to specify the overall objectives of the new system, designs several alternatives, and selects the most feasible. The design report represents all of these steps in a format easily understood by management.
- System implementation is the putting into production of the proposed design from the system design report. Implementation requires the programming of required procedures, training of personnel, documentation, testing of the programs, and finally, conversion from the old to the new system.
- Once the system is in place, the analyst reviews the results and compares projected to actual benefits. As a result of this audit, some modifications or improvements of the system may be suggested.
- Management information systems seek to provide the correct information to the appropriate manager at the right time. There are three levels of management: top-level management makes strategic and future-oriented decisions, middle-level management makes tactical decisions (implementing the strategies developed by top-level managers), and lower-level management makes the day-to-day decisions that keep the organization operating efficiently.
- Decision-oriented reporting identifies various types of reports required by management. Scheduled reports are produced at regular intervals and provide routine information. Exception reports are action-oriented and monitor performance—they indicate when a particular operation is not behaving as expected. Predictive reports use models to project possible outcomes of different decisions. Demand reports are usually one-time-only requests that cover unanticipated information needs.
- Structured design is a method of breaking down a problem into logical segments, or modules. Each module performs a logical function. These

modules, in turn, may be broken down further. Modules are related to one another in a hierarchical fashion. Each module is independent of another.

- System design may need to focus around organizational structure. Centralized design utilizes a central computer to perform all data-processing functions. Hierarchical design provides each level of an organization with the computing power required to perform its task objectives; information becomes more summarized the higher the point in the hierarchy. Distributed design recognizes the independence of organizational units and each has its own computing power, yet these units must report to a central point. Decentralized design gives each part of the organization its own computing power—there is no central point of control.
- A data base is a grouping of related data fields structured to meet the information needs of a wide variey of users. Data is analyzed logically according to its inherent relationships to other data in the business setting, then designed physically for best processing. Users can relate to the logical view of data without regard to its physical storage.
- A data-base management system is a collection of software that provides users with access to the stored data-base data.

REVIEW QUESTIONS

1. Think of an example of a system. Describe its inputs, processes, and outputs. What do you think its feedback mechanisms are? Using this system, see if you can picture a larger system of which it is a part. What other smaller systems are within your system?
2. Describe what steps you might take in analyzing the checking system at a bank.
3. Name three internal information sources. How is internal information different from external? Are both types needed during the first phase of system analysis?
4. How does the focus of data collection relate to the focus of data analysis.
5. Why is system design a creative stage of the system cycle?
6. What organizational constraints can complicate a system design effort?
7. Why might a system designer initially ignore any constraints and focus instead on an "ideal" system design?
8. Describe four types of conversion. Which is the most preferable? What are your assumptions for this choice?
9. The chapter defines four types of reports. Explain and give examples of each. Which level(s) of management would be interested in each type of report?
10. Why is it beneficial for users and programmers to not have to worry how data is physically stored on a data base?
11. Discuss some of the factors a business may want to consider before implementing a computer network, such as corporate philosophy, control, configurations, and cost.

Using Microcomputers in Business

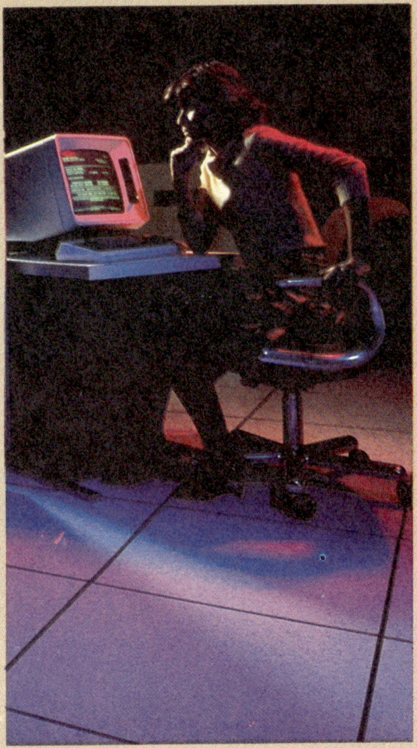

When first introduced, microcomputers were generally envisioned for the home and small-business environments as stand-alone (self-contained) systems. But recently they have begun to make their way into the management information systems of large corporations.

It has been suggested that the entry of major main frame and minicomputer vendors such as IBM, Hewlett-Packard Company, and Xerox Corporation into the personal computer field has caught senior managers' attention and made them curious about the potential of microcomputer technology. For whatever the reason, the number of microcomputers being introduced into the large corporations has been dramatically increasing.

Different companies are taking different approaches to introducing microcomputers. Some, such as Ford Motor Company, are taking a more cautious approach to this new technology. They are using their personal computers in stand-alone mode only. Their strategy is to keep applications in a local mode, allowing no access to remote computer facilities, and thus avoiding the potential problems of on-line use. Even in this restricted mode, Ford has reported an enthusiastic user response and annual average savings greater than the original cost of the microcomputers.

General Electric has taken personal computers one step further. In addition to using microcomputers on a stand-alone basis for applications such as financial analysis and spread-sheets, presentations, and plotting, they are also allowing their microcomputers to have limited access to a remote computer. At present, though, they are employing no formal distributed processing strategy, but instead are waiting to see what the future brings.

North American Philips, one of the Pentagon's largest suppliers, with a company philosophy of distributed data processing, has approached microcomputers with an integrated, decentralized approach. They plan to tie a hierarchy of maxicomputers, minicomputers, and microcomputers together so that they can use the same data base. By linking their IBM 3033s and 4331s and Apple, Radio Shack, and IBM personal computers, managers at various levels could communicate among themselves or pass information up and down the organizational structure. The main frames would continue to manipulate large data files while the microcomputers would enable such applications as inventory analysis to be executed at the manager's desk.

Now that many large organizations have accepted microcomputers, the question of how to maintain control of their use has arisen. Here, again, we see a number of different approaches. One approach is to centralize the purchase of personal computers under the data processing department, which then distributes them to managers throughout the corporation. Another method is for the data processing department to issue a list of approved models from which departments and individuals may choose. Still a third method is for the corporation to set up an in-house computer store to sell company-approved small computers.

Additionally, in an effort to encourage their use, many companies have made mass purchases to secure quantity discount and are allowing their employees to buy microcomputers at cost. And others have negotiated contracts with computer manufacturers to supply discounted systems to their employees.

Regardless of how their distribution is accomplished, the addition of microcomputers into the corporate world still faces many problems that will have to be dealt with before they are completely accepted. Some of these problems are deciding how to allocate information processing resources among microcomputers, minicomputers, and main frames; assessing the effects of the use of microcomputers on organizational communications and stability; and maintaining compatibility among corporate microcomputers and between microcomputers and the larger computers. In addition, because many executives will be using their personal microcomputers to support their decision making, there is the old "garbage in–garbage out" fear that executives might use incorrect data and assumptions in making their decisions.

Even with all these uncertainties, many companies are looking to the future and are seeing substantial benefits in, if not the necessity of, having executives who know how these tools work.

Rockwell International Corporation's Energy Systems Group (ESG), for example, is offering financial incentives to encourage their employees to acquire and learn how to operate their own personal microcomputers. ESG has separately negotiated special purchase agreements with several manufacturers allowing their employees to buy their own personal computers at the same corporate discount that ESG would be entitled to if it were purchasing the equipment in volume. They have also allowed their employees to pay for the computers through a payroll deduction plan, with ESG picking up any monthly finance charges. Most of the microcomputers purchased by Rockwell employees are being used in their own homes strictly as stand-alones; however, a few of these have been equipped with a dial-up communications feature that allows them to gain remote access to some of Rockwell's host main frames. This arrangement allows employees to receive trouble calls from their offices and use their home computers as terminals to communicate with the corporate computing center. They can then analyze and solve business problems at home without having to drive long distances to their offices.

Probably the most limiting factor thus far in the incorporation of microcomputers into a first-rate distributed system has been the slow pace of software development. This, however, is beginning to change as microcomputers become more common. For example, Micro Data Base Systems, Inc., is now offering a genuine managment data-base system called MDBS for use on microcomputers. Its features are comparable to main frame data-base management systems, but beyond these, MDBS also offers several valuable innovations that are not available on any main frame data-base management system. Other available software includes relational data-base management systems from Condor. With just a brief study of the manual, this user-friendly system allows you to start building a data base within fifteen to twenty minutes. Jini Micro-Systems, Inc., has an integrated data manager system called JINSAM, which is being used by NASA, Kennedy Space Center. Despite some initial failures by developers of large-scale, data-base management systems to redesign these systems for utilization by microcomputers, the number of success stories indicate their widespread availability in the future.

DISCUSSION QUESTIONS

1. Describe several approaches being taken by large organizations in the incorporation of personal computers.
2. What are some of the problems facing larger organizations incorporating microcomputers into their systems?

CHAPTER 10

Computer Systems

INTRODUCTION

During the past two decades, all aspects of the computer market have experienced rapid growth. New products and computer systems are constantly being introduced to perform tasks ranging from monitoring fuel mixtures in automobiles to modeling the economies of nations.

This chapter identifies the various categories into which computer systems can be grouped, delineates the characteristics of each category, and describes appropriate applications for the systems in each category.

This chapter discusses important market trends and vendor support within each market sector, and briefly describes the software market and the computer services offered by service bureaus and time-sharing companies. Also discussed are important factors that must be taken into consideration when acquiring a computer system.

FACING PAGE
This sophisticated computer system is capable of providing complex network control and distributed data processing.

CHAPTER OUTLINE

MAIN FRAMES

At the heart of a large-scale computer system is the **main frame,** or CPU (which consists, as you recall from Chapter 4, of control unit, ALU, and primary storage). A main frame can process large amounts of data at very high speeds, hold up to millions of characters in its primary storage, and support many input, output, and auxiliary storage devices.

Vendors

The main-frame sector is the backbone of the computer industry. Major competitors in this market are International Business Machines (IBM), Burroughs, Honeywell, Univac, National Cash Register (NCR), Control Data Corporation (CDC), and Amdahl (see Table 10–1). These vendors appeal to potential users of large, sophisticated computers.

Entry into the market is restricted by the huge capital investment required. However, once in the market, companies can spread the costs of research and development, hardware, and application and system software design over a number of units; this gives them a pricing advantage.

An example of a main-frame computer is any member of IBM's System/370 series. This series includes many models, and an organization can choose the model best suited to its processing needs. Other vendors in the main-frame sector also offer computers in various sizes with various processing speeds and storage capacities. Purchase costs of these computers range from $200,000 to $1 million or more.

Vendor Support

Main-frame vendors do more than sell main frames. A computer is useless to an organization that lacks the knowledge needed to operate it. Most vendors provide support services along with an initial purchase. These services normally include education and training for all levels of users, including top executives and data-entry personnel. Training can involve classes and seminars or self-study, where users pace their own learning through manuals and machine exercises.

Other services may be included in the purchase or lease price of the computer system. Managers must consider any additional costs when purchasing a large computer system.

Market Trends

Though the main-frame sector dominates the computer industry, it has lost part of its market share during the past decade because of the changing nature of the computer business. At one time, as previous chapters have pointed out, the industry was almost purely a hardware business. The price of a computer system was dominated by the cost of the hardware; software costs were included in the total system price (in a selling technique called **bundling** discussed later in the chapter). With recent technological advances, the cost of hardware has been declining at a rate of 15 to 20 percent per year. In contrast, software and service costs have continued to increase significantly.

Another change in the computer industry is the trend toward distributed processing and away from centralized processing. The demand for larger, central-site computer systems has been replaced by a demand for smaller, more flexible systems. Main-frame vendors who have specialized in the production of large CPUs are diversifying into other sectors of the computer industry to remain competitive. For example, IBM has established a General Systems Division to manufacture minicomputers. Honeywell, Burroughs, and Amdahl have diversified into the areas of minicomputers, office products, and telecommunications.

Many companies requiring the processing capabilities of large computers have already had them for some time. Purchases of newer processors are made only when the company needs expanded capacity or when new price/performance ratios make them cost effective. The costs of maintaining large computer systems deter many firms from acquiring them. Some users are

AT&T's computer center in Knightsbridge, New Jersey, is an example of a large, main frame computer system.

TABLE 10–1
Data Processing Top 50

1981 RANK	1980 RANK	COMPANY	1981 DP REVENUE ($MILLIONS)	1981 DP GROWTH RATE	HOW THE DP REVENUES BREAK DOWN ($MILLIONS)							
					Main-Frame	Mini	Micro	Office Systems	Data Commun.	Peripherals/ Terminals	Software/ Services	Other
1	1	International Business Machines	$26,340.0	16.7%	$12,000	$3,000	—	$1,600	$260	$5,000	$4,480	—
2	4	Digital Equipment Corp.	3,586.6	30.7	—	2,223.8	—	—	—	451.9	910.9	—
3	3	Control Data Corp.	3,103.3	12.2	623.4	—	—	—	—	1,116.4	1,153.7	—
4	2	NCR Corp.	3,071.8	4.1	1,027.4	—	—	—	—	1,015	1,029.4	—
5	6	Burroughs Corp.	2,934.0	24.6	1,254.8	575.4	—	50	—	—	837.8	$216
6	5	Sperry Corp.	2,781.0	8.9	917.7	55.6	—	—	—	1,112.4	695.3	—
7	8	Hewlett-Packard Co.	1,875.0	18.4	—	435	$235	—	150	510	545	—
8	7	Honeywell, Inc.	1,773.7	8.5	551	300	—	—	—	88.7	835	—
9	9	Xerox Corp.	1,100.0	15.7	—	—	10	132	—	748	209	—
10	11	Wang Laboratories Inc.	1,008.0	47.9	—	272.3	—	605.1	30.2	—	100.9	—
11	13	Storage Technology	922.0	52.9	—	—	—	—	—	786.4	135.6	—
12	20	TRW, Inc.	855.0	11.1	—	50	—	40	—	40	725	—
13	12	Data General Corporation	764.4	13.6	—	573.2	—	—	—	61.2	130	—
14	17	General Electric Co.	750.0	57.8	—	—	—	—	—	100	570	80
15	14	Texas Instruments, Inc.	666.7	6.7	—	320	13.3	—	—	266.7	66.7	—
16	15	Computer Sciences Corp.	624.7	11.4	—	—	—	—	—	—	624.7	—
17	16	Automatic Data Processing	613.0	20.9	—	—	—	—	—	—	613	—
18	30	ITT Corp.	540.0	33.3	—	—	—	—	56	400	84	—
19	18	Electronic Data Systems	480.6	17.6	—	6.8	—	—	—	—	473.8	—
20	21	Datapoint Corp.	474.1	30.2	—	142.2	—	23.7	47.4	189.6	71.2	—
21	35	Tandy Corp.	460.0	109.0	—	—	293	—	—	84.6	37.7	44.7
22	19	Amdahl Corp.	442.7	12.2	334.6	—	—	—	25.8	—	82.4	—
23	47	Apple Computer, Inc.	401.1	142.7	—	—	401.1	—	—	—	—	—
24	25	McDonnell Douglas Corp.	376.7	23.7	—	—	150	—	—	—	156.2	70.5
25	27	Prime Computer Inc.	365.0	36.1	—	309	—	—	—	—	56	—
26	23	Management Assistance Inc.	349.1	12.4	—	224	—	—	—	—	116	9.1
27	—	Comdisco, Inc.	343.9	25.0	—	—	—	—	—	—	—	343.9
28	91	Rolm Corp.	331.5	32.1	—	—	—	—	331.5	—	—	—
29	32	National Semiconductor	330.0	10.0	175	—	—	—	—	100	55	—
30	26	Mohawk Data Sciences Corp.	320.9	11.6	—	81	—	—	—	198.5	41.4	—
31	28	Harris Corporation	313.0	20.3	—	62.6	—	37.6	—	112.7	50.1	50
32	24	Tektronix, Inc.	308.9	7.8	—	—	—	—	—	308.9	—	—
33	38	Tymshare Inc.	289.7	23.2	—	—	—	—	41	—	248.7	—
34	41	Computervision Corp.	270.7	41.7	—	—	—	—	—	—	—	270.7
35	31	Dataproducts Corp.	270.0	8.7	—	—	—	3.2	35.4	231.4	—	—
36	70	Gould, Inc.	270.0	44.3	—	130	140	—	—	—	—	—
37	34	Raytheon Co.	245.0	8.8	—	25	—	75	—	100	45	—
38	53	Tandem Computers, Inc.	242.5	88.4	212.9	—	—	—	—	—	23.4	6.2
39	37	Racal Corp.	240.0	13.2	—	—	—	—	—	240	—	—
40	40	Four-Phase Systems	233.7	18.5	13.7	—	—	—	—	220	—	—
41	33	Perkin-Elmer	230.0	1.7	—	140.3	—	—	—	66.7	23	—
42	36	Northern Telecom	229.3	5.7	—	—	—	172	—	—	57.3	—
43	63	Lanier Business Products	228.0	18.4	—	—	—	228	—	—	—	—
44	39	3M	225.0	9.7	—	—	—	—	—	—	—	225
45	42	C. Itoh Electronics, Inc.	213.0	12.6	—	34	—	—	—	138	41	—
46	57	Boeing	205.5	46.4	—	—	—	—	—	—	205.5	—
47	44	Motorola Inc.	180.0	42.8	—	—	—	—	180	—	—	—
48	46	Signal Co.	176.0	6.6	—	—	—	—	—	176	—	—
49	49	Sanders Associates Inc.	171.5	45.0	—	—	—	—	—	171.5	—	—
50	48	Allied Corp.	162.0	10.2	—	55	—	—	—	53.5	53.5	—

Source: June 1982 issue of *Datamation*.

finding it more economical to purchase small computer systems. Since few users require the power of a maxicomputer (described below), the potential market for those large computers is limited. The needs of the high-end user are being met, but demands for sophistication and performance continue to challenge the creativity and abilities of manufacturers.

MAXICOMPUTERS

Main-frame vendors sell their products to organizations requiring extensive data-processing capabilities. These organizations may process vast amounts of data or may need to perform millions of calculations per second. In some cases, demand exists for even higher processing speeds and efficiency. To respond to these needs, some vendors offer super-large, sophisticated computers called "maxicomputers."

Maxicomputer systems are very expensive, and their costs are justified in relatively few cases. The CRAY-1 computer, developed by Cray Research, Inc., is an example of a maxicomputer system (see Figure 10–1). The

FIGURE 10–1
The CRAY-1 Computer System

CRAY-1 is offered at a base price of $4.5 million; it is used mainly in the scientific areas of weather forecasting, nuclear weapons development, and energy supply and conservation. Other maxicomputers are used by large corporations and government agencies where the needs for large data bases and complex calculation capabilities justify the costs of obtaining them. Such a configuration is shown in Figure 10–2.

MINICOMPUTERS

Minicomputers have come a long way since their initial development for specific applications such as process control and engineering calculations. Current minicomputers are more flexible, provide greater capabilities, and support a full line of peripherals (see Figure 10–3). The growth in minicomputer applications has led to the concept of distributed processing. Minicomputers are also used in time-sharing applications, numerical control of machine tools, industrial automation, and word processing.

FIGURE 10–2
Maxicomputer Configuration

The distinction between minicomputers and main frames has blurred over the past decade. The minicomputers manufactured today are more powerful than the main frames manufactured ten years ago. Their price ranges from $15,000 to $250,000. Many minicomputer vendors offer support services (education, training, hardware maintenance, and so on).

One reason for the popularity of the minicomputer is its flexibility. Minicomputers can be plugged into standard electrical outlets, they often do not require special facilities such as air conditioning and water cooling, and they can be utilized in an unlimited number of configurations. For example, a minicomputer system for a small firm may consist of a visual display terminal, a disk storage unit, and a printer (see Figure 10–4). A large distributed system may consist of hundreds of minicomputers and peripherals tied together by communication channels to meet the needs of a geographically dispersed organization.

Another important advantage of a minicomputer system is that it can be enlarged to meet the needs of a growing organization since it can be implemented in a modular fashion. For example, a hospital may install one minicomputer in its outpatient section for record keeping and another in the pharmacy section or laboratory. As additional minicomputers are installed, they can be connected to existing ones to share common data.

The minicomputer industry has been growing at a rate of 35 to 40 percent annually. However, recent analysis indicates that the growth rate of this

FIGURE 10–3
A Minicomputer System

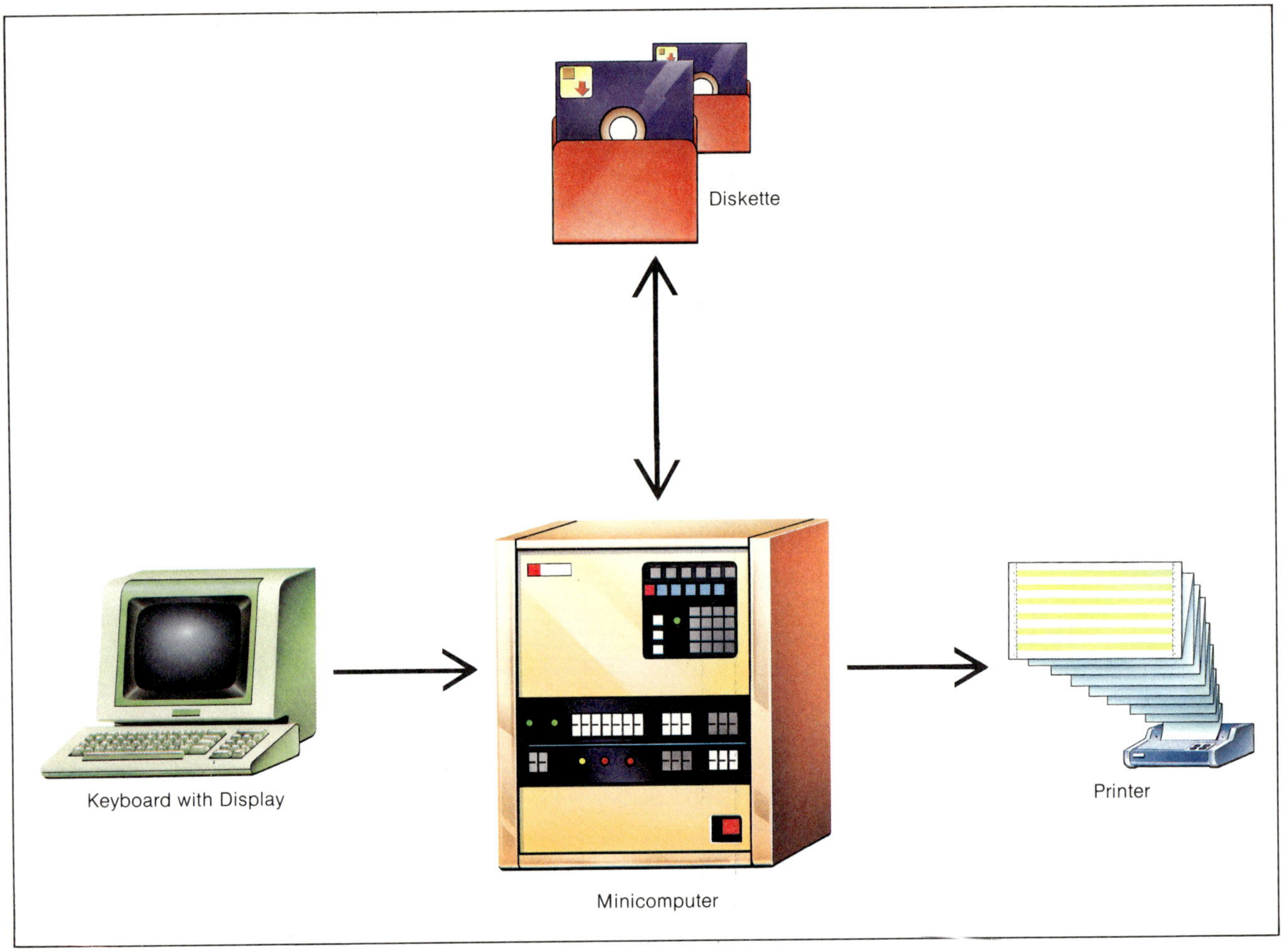

FIGURE 10–4
Diagram of a Small Minicomputer System

sector of the market is declining and may stabilize in the near future. Leading manufacturers include Digital Equipment Corporation (DEC), Hewlett-Packard, Data General, Honeywell, General Automation, and Texas Instruments. Other manufacturers include Wang Laboratories, Systems Engineering Laboratories, Inc. (SEL), and Prime Computer, Inc. IBM and Burroughs have also entered this market.

Distributed Processing

In many cases, minicomputers are used in conjunction with communication facilities to provide remote processing capabilities (see Chapter 6). Most vendors in the minicomputer sector include data-communication equipment to provide powerful, flexible computing capabilities.

Prior to the advent of distributed processing, many organizations depended on large, centrally located computers. As user needs increased, these computers became overloaded. Centralized computer departments were not able to respond quickly to user requirements. Users began to replace or supplement their large computers with a number of minicomputers located where processing was required, reducing the workloads on the large computers. Figure 10–5 diagrams an example of a distributed minicomputer system.

Software Support

At the center of a minicomputer system is the software that directs its operations. For example, a minicomputer and peripherals alone are not enough to implement a distributed system. Hence, many vendors in this market sector sell software packages to accompany their hardware. The vendors realize that low cost and performance will no longer sell their products, and that efficient software may be a primary key to selling hardware. Several firms specialize in software development, although software can also be developed by the user (but such development is time-consuming and costly). Many users choose to buy prewritten packages and tailor them to meet their specific needs. Indeed, when choosing a minicomputer system, managers often base their decisions on the software packages available from vendors, then choose the hardware that supports the software they need.

Many application software packages have been developed for specific industries. Minicomputer users can purchase packages designed for transportation, manufacturing, hospitals, food companies, and so on. Accounting packages containing programs for accounts receivable, payroll, order entry, billing, and general ledger are available for many minicomputer systems.

In addition, system software is now available for minicomputers. High-level language translators are available for FORTRAN, BASIC, COBOL, RPG, and other languages. Software vendors have developed data-base management systems, data dictionaries, and program development aids that allow relatively untrained users to develop their own application programs.

Minicomputer users, then, are finding it increasingly attractive to purchase software packages. The need for in-house staff is decreased, and total systems can be implemented within relatively short time periods. Given the number and variety of software packages available, most users can purchase software that meets their data-processing needs. A later section will further discuss the software market.

HIGHLIGHT
Software Stores

What good is a computer if you don't have plenty of software to feed it? That's the question being happily answered by a new brand of retail operation: the computer software store. Entrepreneurs say that this development is a parallel to the record industry, in which there came to be stores that sold hardware only (phonograph systems) and stores that sold software only (records and tapes). It has been estimated that there are more than 5,000 software packages available in disk and cassette format and that sales rose from $50 million in 1978 to $500 million in 1981. Several software companies have already set up store franchise systems.

MICROCOMPUTERS

The microcomputer market has received a great deal of attention recently. When microcomputers first appeared, they were used by hobby-oriented engineers, programmers, electronics buffs, and other technically competent and inquisitive individuals. These computer hobbyists built their computers from scratch or purchased ready-to-assemble computer kits. The hobbyist could put together a real computer, complete with a keyboard for data entry and a TV-like display tube.

FIGURE 10–5 Distributed Minicomputer System

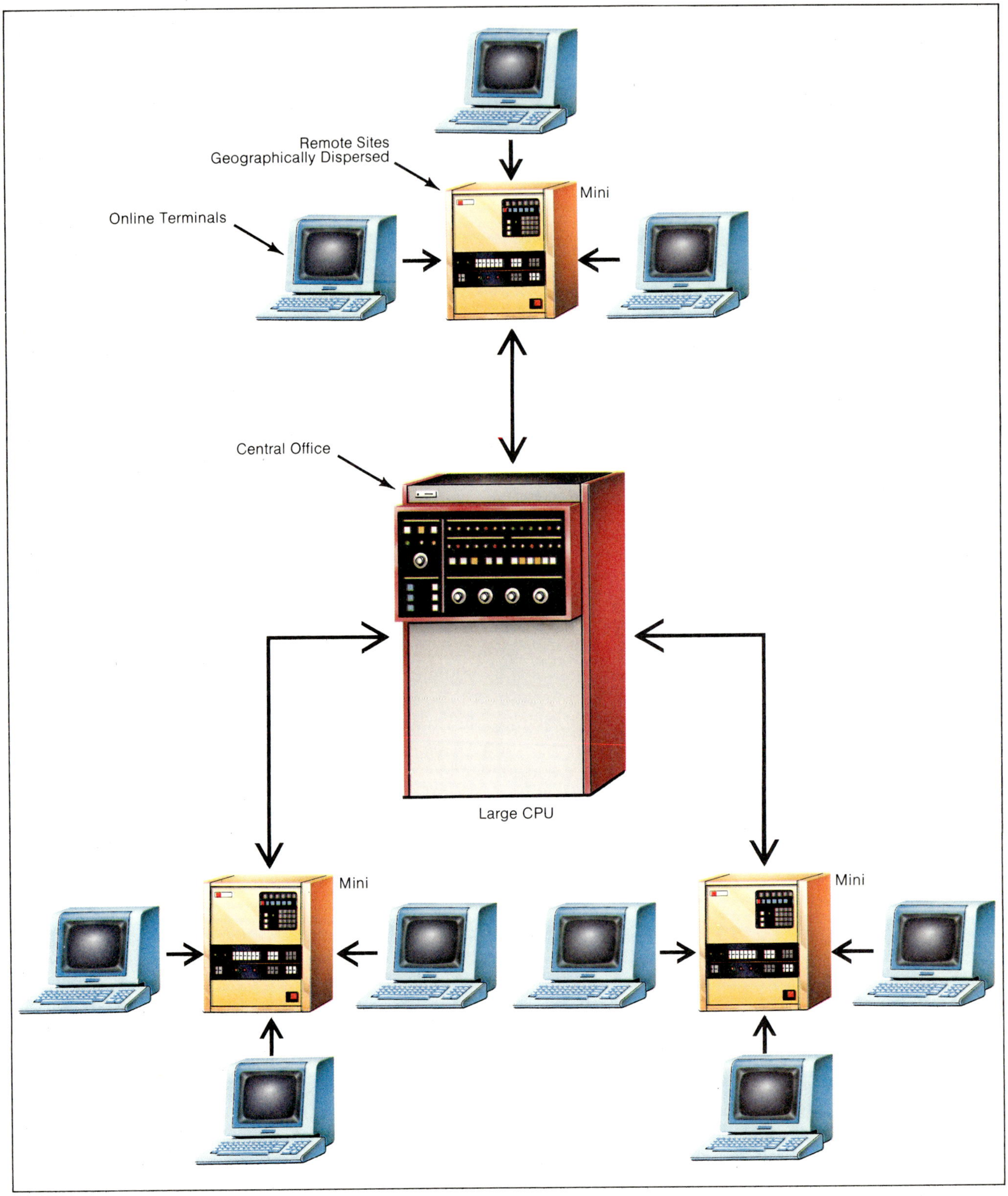

At the heart of a microcomputer is a **microprocessor** that performs arithmetic/logic operations and control functions, much as the CPU of a large computer does. The microprocessor fits on a single silicon chip the size of a nail head (see Figure 10–6). Some cost under $10. Memory and input/output units then are added, as on a large main-frame computer, making microcomputers very powerful for their size.

At the sight of a true consumer market, manufacturers began to offer user-oriented microcomputer systems. These small systems were preassembled and equipped with programs to do simple jobs, such as balancing a checkbook or playing a game of backgammon. The personal computing market started in 1975 when MITS introduced the Altair 8800, a computer kit for under $500. Today a wide range of personal computers offer complete computing capabilities at low costs. A computer for the home can be purchased for about the same price as a good stereo system; those available range in price from $100 to about $5,000.

Vendors and Vendor Support

Two popular personal computer systems are the Apple and the TRS-80 computers. Initially, Radio Shack offered the TRS-80 Model I microcomputer system for about $600. It now offers a larger version, the TRS-80 Model II microcomputer (see Figure 10–7). This system can be expanded by the addition of memory and input/output units. The computer is normally pro-

FIGURE 10–6
Microprocessor on a Chip

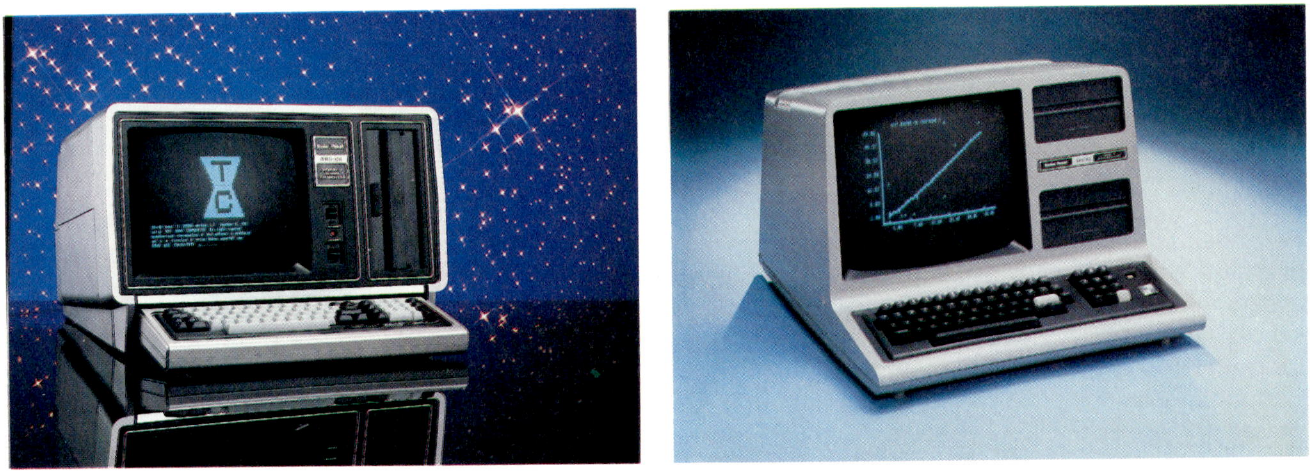

FIGURE 10–7
TRS-80 Microcomputers—Model II and Model III

grammed in BASIC. Radio Shack and a wide variety of other firms and individuals have developed software for use with the TRS-80 Model II, including programs for payroll, finance, home recipes, games, and so on. The replacement for the Model I is the Model III, introduced in 1980. The newest product is a Model 16.

The Apple II computer has standard features including 16K of RAM, five programmed cassettes, a keyboard, and a module for color TV hook-up. The system is designed for growth and has many accessories (disk drives, printers, and so on). A wide range of software for small business owners, engineers and scientists, educators, and home users is available. BASIC, Pascal, or assembly language can be used to write additional programs. The most common Apple II system consists of an Apple II plus, (see Figure 10–8) with 48K of RAM, a monitor, and one 5¼″ floppy disk drive. (The Apple II as opposed to the Apple II plus comes with a version of BASIC that only allows integer numbers; the II plus with floating-point BASIC is much more common. The newest model offered by Apple is the Apple III.

Although the production of microcomputers has been dominated by a host of small firms, large manufacturers such as RCA, Texas Instruments, and Heath have now moved into the field. And IBM has entered the market with a personal computer priced to compete with Apple's and Radio Shack's. The IBM personal computer (Figure 10–9), like the Commodore PET (Figure 10–10), and other personal computers, offers color graphics, word processing, and problem-solving capabilities. Digital Equipment Corporation (DEC) also has a line of personal computers—Rainbow 100 (see Figure 10–11).

Applications

Profitable applications of microcomputers are found in small businesses and in the professions. An estimated one-third of all personal computers are located in private offices, where businesspersons can use them to do word

FIGURE 10–8
Apple II Plus Microcomputer

FIGURE 10–9
IBM Personal Computer

FIGURE 10–10
The Commodore PET Microcomputer

FIGURE 10–11
DEC Rainbow 100 Microcomputer

processing, accounting, inventory control, order processing, customer lists, client records, tax records, mailing labels, and evaluation of bids and contracts. School teachers can use them to devise exams and compute grades; doctors, to keep patients' records; and college football coaches, to figure out potent combinations of players and strategies.

The use of personal computers in small businesses has led to a new phenomenon known as telecommuting. **Telecommuting** is based on computer hookups between offices and homes that allow employees to work at home. This concept enables firms to employ labor resources that might not otherwise be available. For example, handicapped people, women who leave jobs to raise families but still want to work, and commuters who find the rising costs of gasoline prohibitive can be gainfully employed. Work can be done at all hours of the day.

Another area influenced by the low cost of microcomputers is **word processing,** the manipulation of text data to achieve a desired output. Wang Laboratories is the leading manufacturer of word-processing equipment, but many other manufacturers are also developing word processors.

A typical stand-alone word-processing system consists of a keyboard, a visual display screen, a storage unit, and a printer (see Figure 10–12). An operator enters text (in the form of memos, letters, reports, and the like) on the keyboard. The text is stored and can be edited, revised, and reformatted without retyping entire documents. The printer is used to generate hard

FIGURE 10–12
The Xerox 820 is a display word processing system with a daisy wheel, 40-character-per-second printer.

copies when desired. A further advantage is the word processor's ability to store names and addresses that can be used in form letters or for distribution of output.

An Apple II microcomputer in use.

Computer Stores

Personal computing was, until recently, primarily a mail-order business. Products were shipped directly from manufacturers to users. With the emergence of the home-computer concept, however, a new retailing phenomenon has evolved—the **computer store.** These stores are structured to appeal to owners of small businesses and to personal users. Today, thousands of home computer stores exist in the United States. The best ones offer a variety of products and services manufactured by several firms. Demonstration systems are on display so that potential buyers can experiment with the systems, much as they would take test drives before purchasing a car. Microcomputer experts are available to answer questions and to provide technical guidance to the computer novice.

Evaluating Microcomputers

Purchasing a personal computer is like purchasing a stereo component. There are so many models available, with so many different characteristics, and at so many different prices, that a number of key features to consider must be identified. Many people consider the first step in buying a microcomputer to be the selection of software, and then they choose the hardware that it is compatible with. Concerning the computer itself, the buyer might want to look at the type of keyboard and the availability of a programming language (such as BASIC) in read-only memory (ROM). Optional equipment, such as more programming memory, high-level languages, printers, disk drives, and the like, and their costs, should be evaluated. If the computer will be used for business purposes or for writing and editing, it should have the growth capability needed for word processing. For financial or engineering analysis, full memory, a disk drive, a printer, and graphics capability are useful. Both hardware support and software support are important. The buyer should check to determine whether service as well as expansion hardware will be available a few years in the future.

A businessperson anticipating a microcomputer purchase should evaluate several stores' offerings. Many stores specialize in a certain brand of machines, while a few are "computer supermarkets" carrying five or six brands. Businesspersons can learn of current developments by reading about the various microcomputers in publications such as *Byte Magazine*, *Microcomputing*, *Creative Computing*, and *S-100 Microsystems*, which are available at computer stores or book stores. *Interface Age* carries articles for the legal and medical professions as well as inventors and math-oriented types. Finally, the businessperson should meet with computer owners' groups (owners of Apples and TRS-80s, among others, have formed groups around the country) to discuss the pros and cons of the various systems. Local stores know of owners' groups associated with the brands of machines they sell. In this fashion, the potential computer-owner will have the best chance of selecting a microcomputer best fitting his or her requirements.

SOFTWARE

Software and consulting firms specialize in developing information systems for businesses. Usually, firms specialize in either system software or application software. Both are often sold as packages—collections of programs that work together to accomplish specific processing objectives. Such software packages are debugged and well documented. Some suppliers even provide ongoing maintenance.

Vendors

Manufacturers in all market sectors provide software packages to accompany their equipment. However, the overwhelming demand for software in the past decade has made it profitable for firms to specialize in software offerings. The leading suppliers of computer software include Computer Sciences, Automatic Data Processing (ADP), General Electric, Electronic Data Systems (EDS), McDonnell Douglas, and Tymshare. There are a number of smaller firms offering software for use on minicomputers and microcomputers; such offerings include word processing and business packages.

The most popular type of software packages are data management packages. Others include communication packages, in which complete programs are offered to tie together large networks of computers; for example, ADR offers DATACOM, IBM offers CICS (Customer Information Control System), and Cincom offers ENVIRON/1. Operating system software and utilities packages are available from several vendors; common examples are librarian programs and high-level language translators. In addition, application software is available in a multitude of forms, ranging from inventory management to payroll and general ledger.

HIGHLIGHT
Program Piracy

The unlicensed and unauthorized copying of computer programs is costing the minicomputer software industry from $12 to $36 million a year, according to some estimates. Because it's a new and developing field, the copyright protections afforded programs are not clear. Nor are the applications of trade secret safeguards and patents. While laws that are stricter and more stringently applied may be one answer to the piracy problem, another is the basic education that unauthorized copying is wrong, illegal, and ultimately injurious to the whole industry.

Market Trends

The increased purchases of hardware that resulted from declining costs have escalated software demand. Users want sophisticated software such as a data-base management system (DBMS). Many users who once developed their own software are now buying standardized application programs and system programs. Although these standardized programs may need to be tailored for the organization, the benefits of purchasing packages are quickly realized, since the cost of buying a package is a fraction of the cost of developing the software in-house.

Small business users and first-time users are hardest hit by the "software crunch." These users do not have the staff needed to support software development. Software firms are attempting to reach these potential customers through avenues such as retail stores. Some stores offer one-stop shopping: programs ranging from computer games to small business applications are

"We used to have a real problem with other corporations raiding our software people."

provided. The current offerings of any one software company are in a constant state of flux. Many firms offer new releases of their software packages containing the latest developments requested by users. Other firms develop specialized software packages under contractual arrangements. Table 10–2 shows a listing of some of the software packages available to customers.

SERVICE BUREAUS AND TIME-SHARING COMPANIES

Computer systems are a major expense. Many companies cannot afford systems of their own. **Service bureaus** provide data-processing services such as system development and computer operations. **Time-sharing** companies maintain computer facilities rented by a wide variety of users who want the sophistication of a large computer system without incurring all of its costs. Time-sharing companies also provide computer power to companies who do not need twenty-four-hour-a-day processing.

Growth in the time-sharing industry is primarily due to the advances in data-communication equipment. Time-sharing customers usually purchase input/output devices and use them to access the facilities of the time-sharing company. Storage space on magnetic tapes and disks can be rented; the customer pays for CPU resources at a monthly rate. Some time-sharing com-

TABLE 10–2
Consumers' Guide to Software Shopping

TYPE OF SOFTWARE	WHAT IT DOES	WHERE TO BUY IT	SOFTWARE PRICE
DATA BASE MANAGEMENT SYSTEM	Organizes data in line with the informational needs and organizational structure of a business. Makes it easier to access and update files.	Computer vendors Systems software companies	Starts at $7,000 (for use with a minicomputer) and runs to more than $100,000 (for use with a mainframe computer or for custom programming)
NETWORKING	Enables computers in one building or across the country to communicate.	Primarily computer vendors	$5,000 to $15,000 per machine in a minicomputer network and $30,000 to $75,000 for each mainframe computer in a network
TRANSACTION PROCESSING	Permits users to carry on a dialogue with the computer—typing information and getting an immediate response. For use with such commercial applications as check processing and order entry.	Computer vendors Systems software companies	$15,000 and up
PROGRAMMING TOOLS	Helps programmers write applications programs by automatically testing software code and identifying errors. Also known as "debuggers."	Computer vendors Systems software companies	$1,000 to $5,000 (for a minicomputer) and $5,000 to $75,000 (for a large mainframe computer)
QUERIES AND REPORT GENERATORS	Aids the novice user in extracting information from a computer memory and formating it into a report.	Computer vendors Systems software companies	$1,000 to $37,000 for standard software

panies have networks of computers spread throughout the nation. They have the ability to distribute the costs of such a system over many users, thus reducing overall costs.

A disadvantage of using time-sharing is that it becomes very expensive as data-processing needs increase. The more computer time required, the greater the monthly costs. However, time-sharing may be an economical alternative for companies that are first-time EDP users.

TABLE 10–2
Continued

TYPE OF SOFTWARE	WHAT IT DOES	WHERE TO BUY IT	SOFTWARE PRICE
APPLICATIONS GENERATORS	Generates applications software programs without the need for an experienced programmer.	Major computer vendors	$5,000 and up
GENERAL FINANCIAL	Automates the accounting functions of a business, including billing, inventory control, accounts payable, accounts receivable, general ledger, and payroll.	Computer vendors Applications software companies	Packages range from $1,000 to $2,000 (for minicomputer systems) and from $20,000 to $70,000 (for large mainframe computers)
MANUFACTURING RESOURCE PLANNING	Helps the user gain better control over the entire manufacturing process from production planning and inventory control to materials monitoring.	Large computer vendors Applications software companies	$50,000 and up for standard packages, $100,000 and up for custom software.
FINANCIAL PLANNING	Simulates profit-and-loss scenarios for a company based on revenues, sales force location, commissions, and other controllable variables.	Primarily applications software companies	$5,000 to $45,000 for packages; custom work begins at $250,000
CASH-FLOW MANAGEMENT	Assists financial managers in getting the best use of funds within a business.	Primarily applications software companies	$25,000 to $75,000 for packages; custom software begins at $150,000
MANAGEMENT SUPPORT SYSTEMS	Combines software packages such as color graphics and business modeling that aid the manager in making decisions.	Primarily applications software companies	Depends on the packages selected

Data: International Computer Programs Inc., BW

Service bureaus provide a number of data-processing services. Some bureaus perform all data-processing activities for small firms. Others specialize in providing temporary personnel to perform data-entry or programming activities. Many specialize in a particular industry, such as oil companies or savings and loan associations.

An example of a service bureau is McDonnell Douglas Automation Company (MCAUTO). MCAUTO, the largest computer center in the world, services approximately 3,000 customers and processes over 30,000 time-sharing jobs in an average week. The computer center contains thirteen large-scale computers linked to 16,000 terminals (see Figure 10–13). McDonnell Douglas also sells software to various industries (insurance, manufacturing, and construction) and offers computer-related consulting services to computer users.

Thus, managers have countless alternatives from which to choose when acquiring an EDP system, and they will be faced with an even greater number of decisions as computer vendors continually develop new and better ways to gain a share of the market and to reach the consumer with information about their products. The following section discusses some ideas facing management in the future regarding computer systems.

MANAGEMENT PERSPECTIVES IN COMPUTER SYSTEMS

Management is faced with several alternative methods of meeting data-processing requirements. Some firms choose to lease or buy computer resources and do in-house processing; other firms use outside service bureaus. Other alternatives include time-sharing and traditional methods of manual processing. Selecting the best alternative for an organization is an exceedingly complex task.

FIGURE 10–13
MCAUTO Computer Center

HIGHLIGHT
A User's Dream

The development of a truly "user friendly" microcomputer has been the dream of most users and the goal of most microcomputer manufacturers. Now, a new microcomputer called "Lisa" by Apple Computer, Inc., represents a quantum link in this direction. The relatively expensive Lisa represents a new generation of small computers far more sophisticated and easier to use than those now on the market. In direct competition is Visi-on (by Visicorp), a software product that will give the IBM personal computer and other machines many of the same capabilities that Lisa has.

Either of these products will allow all applications to share common data and instruction. This will greatly increase the ease with which the user can manipulate the data and switch from one task to another, which can often be an awkward process. For example, it will be possible to switch immediately from a numerical analysis to a graph, plot the results, and then, if desired, to insert the graph into the middle of a letter being written with a word processing program. An additional feature is that users can point to words or symbols on the screen to request information instead of typing commands or code words.

The selection is further complicated by the myriad equipment configurations available. Given the numerous peripheral devices discussed in Chapter 5, a seemingly infinite number of configurations are possible. The following paragraphs discuss some of the major points organizations should consider when choosing from among available alternatives.

The purchase prices of CPUs and peripheral devices prohibit all but the largest firms from buying and owning large computer systems. Traditionally, therefore, large and medium-sized computer systems have been rented or leased. Normally, it takes several years of lease payments to reach the purchase price of the equipment. On the other hand, minicomputers and microcomputers are much lower in cost and are usually purchased.

The costs and quality of service must not be overlooked. When a system is purchased, maintenance is a separate contractual matter and its cost can be significant (often several thousand dollars a month for large systems). Maintenance services can be performed by the computer manufacturer or by a specialized maintenance firm. The quality of service is vital, because a computer breakdown can totally disrupt work flow.

Vendor support and training are especially important when an organization first installs a computer system or radically changes an existing one. The expertise of the vendor can be invaluable during design and implementation. Most vendors offer training classes to educate users of the systems they sell or lease, but the quality and amount of training offered vary greatly. The cost for these services may be included in the price of the equipment; if so, the support is said to be **bundled.** In contrast, if such items are priced separately, they are said to be **unbundled.** In 1969, IBM set a precedent by unbundling its software. It is becoming evident that the industry is evolving into a business dominated by software and service costs.

Large computer systems are often justified on the basis of the *volume* or the *complexity* or *diversity* of work they can be used to accomplish. Their capabilities stem not only from the equipment within the system but also from the sophisticated software available for use with it. For large firms, multiprogramming and virtual-storage capabilities (discussed in Chapter 8) may be necessities. These capabilities can be exploited fully only with large and medium-size computers.

The speed and storage capacity of the CPU are also of great interest to computer users. The volume and type of processing to be done determine the speed and storage capacity required, and thus the size of computer needed. Large businesses that process data in great volume frequently need large computer systems. Firms that use computers for scientific applications need very fast computers but may not need large storage capacities. Small organizations may find that minicomputers meet all their requirements. Large businesses may use small computers for applications where response times and storage capacities are not critical. For example, a minicomputer costing only $50,000 may do much the same type of work as a computer costing $2,000,000. In other words, a minicomputer that costs one-fortieth as much as a large computer can often do more than one-fortieth the work.

Besides paying for hardware and software, an organization must pay the salaries of its computer staff—managers, system analysts, programmers,

HIGHLIGHT
Looking Ahead

Where is money to be made in the computer industry during the rest of this decade? Forecasters say it will be in software design and sales. As software becomes more recognized for its applied value to a company, it will be an asset on the company's balance sheet and thus a subject of great interest to taxing authorities. This leads to another prediction: that the data-processing industry will need to lobby for laws that will protect software from overtaxation and other dangers to valuable property.

data-entry personnel, computer operators, and computer technicians. Most computer-related jobs require a high degree of skill and training. These specialized services do not come cheaply; the salaries of computer staff may constitute a significant portion of an organization's monthly payroll.

The computer main frame in the background is made by National Semiconductor.

The **flexibility** of a system is the degree to which it can be adapted or tailored to meet changing requirements. Many manufacturers design their systems using a modular approach that permits the addition of components to a system configuration, thereby allowing for growth and adaptation as an organization's needs change. An organization can start with a relatively slow, limited system and then change to a large CPU or add more peripherals when needed. Systems designed with emphasis on modularity are usually flexible.

Software compatibility also affects a system's flexibility. Compatibility refers to the ability to use programs written for one system on another system with little or no change. From a user's point of view, the number of required program changes should be minimal since reprogramming is both costly and time consuming. Fortunately, many manufacturers offer systems that can be expanded with few program changes.

While this list of considerations is by no means complete, it demonstrates the complexities involved in choosing a computer system. Other key considerations include the size of the organization and its structure. For example, a large, highly centralized organization may have little choice but to acquire a large computer system. In contrast, small businesses and decentralized organizations often find that all their data-processing needs can be met with minicomputer systems.

The computer industry is a large and growing sector of the United States economy. Although the largest user of computers is the federal government, the business world is rapidly closing the gap. A computer explosion has occurred, and there is little indication that the industry's rapid growth has slowed or is about to. With the rapidly expanding capabilities of minicomputers and small computer systems and new technological developments in secondary storage and communication systems, the task of evaluating system alternatives will become increasingly complex.

SUMMARY POINTS

- The main-frame sector of the computer industry is limited to a few large companies. This sector dominates the computer industry; however, entry into this market is limited by the huge capital investment needed. Main-frame vendors provide software support and maintenance in various ways. These costs may or may not be included in the initial purchase or lease price.
- Maxicomputer systems are capable of processing large amounts of data and performing millions of calculations per second. These systems are very expensive and are used by large corporations and government agencies that need to support large data bases and complex calculations.
- The declining costs of hardware along with the trends toward distributed processing have resulted in a changing computer industry. Main-frame vendors have found it profitable to diversify into other market sectors.

- Minicomputer systems have led to the concept of distributed processing. Minicomputers are flexible and can support many peripherals. When combined with data-communication equipment, they can be very powerful data-processing tools. Vendors in this market include software and services in their product offerings. In addition, software companies supply various types of software packages. Organizations can purchase prewritten packages or develop programs in-house.
- Microcomputers have rapidly gained popularity in homes, small businesses, and large corporations. Personal computers offer homeowners and hobbyists a wide variety of electronic games and also perform household duties. Small businesses and professionals use microcomputers to perform clerical tasks such as payroll, accounts receivable, appointment scheduling, and billing. Telecommuting allows employees to work at home on computer terminals tied to offices. Large corporations use computers to provide desktop conveniences for managers.
- Word-processing systems ease the typing duties of secretaries in all sizes of organizations. Word processing can be provided by a stand-alone microcomputer, by a distributed minicomputer system, or by a large system.
- A multitude of software and peripheral devices can be used with microcomputers. The microcomputer sector has evolved to serve a mass-merchandise, retail market. Both hardware and software are available at local computer stores. Prospective microcomputer users must consider the importance of software support when buying computer systems.
- The demand for software is growing at an unprecedented rate. Many users find it less expensive to buy software from a software vendor than to create programs in-house. Prewritten packages are documented and debugged. However, an organization must tailor such programs to meet its particular needs.
- Service bureaus provide data-processing activities to firms that are unable to support the costs of a computer system. Time-sharing companies provide the use of computer facilities to customers for a monthly fee. Both of these allow users to realize the benefits of a large computer system without the associated costs.
- Selecting a computer configuration for an organization or for personal use is a complex task. Important factors to be considered include: purchase versus rental prices of hardware, maintenance costs, vendor support, software costs and capabilities, hardware capabilities, staff requirements, and system flexibility and compatibility.

REVIEW QUESTIONS

1. What types of support may be received from the computer vendor?
2. Discuss the importance of software in a computer system. How should a potential buyer choose a software package?
3. Describe the factors a manager must consider before acquiring a computer system.

4. Must selection of hardware be the first decision faced by managers who are implementing a new computer system?
5. How have recent trends in the computer industry affected computer vendors? What has been the effect of these trends on small businesses?
6. What is telecommuting?
7. How have the costs of hardware and software changed over the past decade?
8. Explain the term *compatibility*. How has this factor affected the computer industry?
9. What are some uses of maxicomputer systems? of minicomputers? of microcomputers?
10. How might a firm justify buying a large computer system when the smaller computers are so convenient and inexpensive?
11. Why might a firm contract with a service bureau? What are some advantages and disadvantages of using service bureaus and time-sharing companies?

Selecting Your Microcomputer

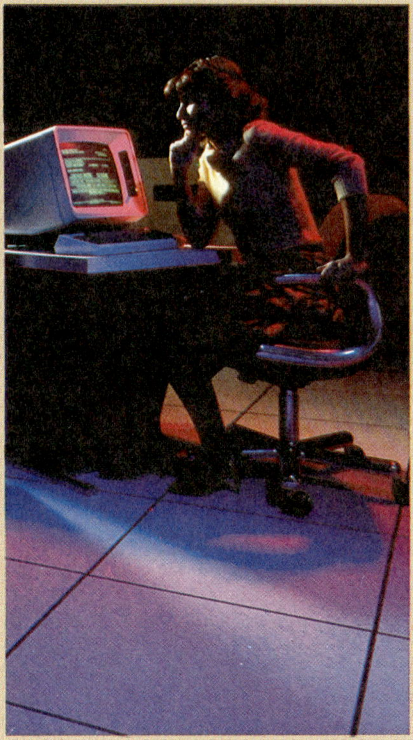

The first step in buying a personal computer is to analyze your situation and determine your software requirements. After you have done this, then select a model that is compatible with your software needs. You will find that life will be much easier with this approach than if you tried matching your situation to a computer that may not have adequate software.

Once you have analyzed your needs and determined the appropriate software, where do you go to buy your computer? Actually, a number of different types of stores sell computers today. One type that is becoming more and more popular is the computer-specialty store. These stores, such as Computerland, deal strictly in microcomputers and their associated hardware and software. Buying through dealer outlets, such as Radio Shack, which sells its TRS-80s, is another option. And many computer manufacturers are marketing their products through department stores and other retail stores. For example, the IBM Personal Computer can now be bought at Sears, while many lower-priced models by Commodore, Atari, Texas Instruments, and Timex can be found at retail outlets such as K-Mart. You can also order your personal computer through a mail-order house.

Now that you have some idea of where to find your personal computer, here are a few tips to help you evaluate the various vendors.

When choosing a vendor, you will probably be better off with a firm whose primary line of business is computers. They generally will have experienced salespeople who are very knowledgeable about computers and can offer you sound advice. A good indication that you're in the right place is if the dealer is more concerned with helping you understand your options rather than just trying to make a sale. You'll also want to make sure that the vendor you buy from is stable and will be around when you need service. Large companies as well as small local dealers should be investigated to make sure they are legitimate and will stand behind the product they sell.

Buying through mail-order houses is not recommended because of the lack of support. Before you buy from a mail-order house, know exactly what to expect in the way of associated services. For example, will the vendor provide prompt and efficient service/maintenance for your computer, or will you have to ship it off to the manufacturer and be without it for an untold number of weeks?

If you're a typical buyer, one of the first considerations to cross your mind is price. Don't be too price conscious, however. A low price could mean lack of support or service, which could cost you more in the long run in both time and money.

With the variety of personal computers available, how do you decide which machine is suitable for your needs? The first thing to do is match your present software needs to the capabilities of the various models, allowing room for future expansion. You'll want to know what languages can be supported. For example, if you want your computer to support one of the educational languages such as Logo, you wouldn't want to buy the Commodore VIC 20, which supports only BASIC.

The type of operating system is also very important. It is the operating system that dictates the amount and type of software that can be used on your computer. CP/M is the operating system that is becoming an industry standard. There is more software available for it than for any other operating system. Once you've determined the computers that will support your software needs, the next step is to look at the hardware that is available. If you're planning to do any kind of substantial work with your computer, the amount of internal memory is important. The IBM Personal Computer and the Apple II offer up to 256K bytes of RAM memory, while some like Radio Shack's TRS-80 Model III come equipped with a maximum of only 64K bytes of RAM memory.

Other features to consider, which can enhance the readability and/or analysis of your output, are the color of the terminal display and the graphics capabilities. Radio Shack's TRS-80 Model III, for example, has no color display capabilities, while the Atari 800 has 256 different colors.

There are also a wide variety of keyboard styles to choose from. Some offer special function keys, editing keys, and/or numeric pads. Most offer the standard touch-sensitive keys, but some like Atari offer a pressure-sensitive, mylar-covered keyboard, which provides excellent keyboard protection of the keys from spills or food crumbs that might be common if the computer is to be used by younger children.

Most, if not all, personal computers now offer a 5¼-inch disk drive for external storage. Some, like the Apple III and the Heath H-89, are even offering hard-disk drives as standard equipment. Cassettes are not used very much anymore because of the problems inherent with loading data from them.

When purchasing a computer, be extremely careful in what you sign. If the salespeople present a contract that in any way disclaims your implied warranty rights, recognize that you are losing a valuable legal remedy in the event of defective goods. In addition, it may prove useful to put in writing that you are not a computer expert and are relying on their expertise to recommend a computer that will solve your specific problems.

To protect your investment in both hardware and software from damage due to "spikes" or "glitches" from electrical circuits, there are AC surge protectors available to eliminate these and provide a constant power source.

For those of you who still feel the need for more protection, there is now insurance such as SAFEWARE from Columbia National General Agency designed to protect your investments in your microcomputer hardware and software if your homeowner's insurance doesn't.

You now know some of the things to look for and look out for. The best advice is to find a trusted dealer with experienced, knowledgeable salespeople.

DISCUSSION QUESTIONS

1. Describe the steps you should take in purchasing a personal computer.
2. What are some of the problems associated with buying a personal computer through a mail-order firm?

CHAPTER 11

Computers in our Future

INTRODUCTION

Computers are evident in all segments of society today and will play a major role in shaping its future. This chapter focuses on some of the new, and often controversial, uses of computers. What are the implications of the automated workplace? Will we be able to stay home and work? What will be the impact of automation and robotics? Will computers ever be able to think? Will they "control" society? What will you be able to do with a personal computer in your home?

FACING PAGE
This futuristic looking "landscape" is actually a wire matrix printer head. It has an expected life of more than 300 million characters—that's equivalent to more than two years' work in normal use.

CHAPTER OUTLINE

OFFICE ELECTRONICS

Automation refers to machine-directed processes. Just as the Industrial Revolution brought automation to the factory, the computer revolution is bringing it to the one place where automation has not had tremendous impact in the past—the office. Recent developments in communications, information storage and retrieval, data analysis, and decision making have made computer applications feasible in office environments.

In communications, for instance, computerized facilities have been designed to handle messages, text and graphics, and conferences. Word-processing systems, electronic mail, reprographics, and computer conferencing systems are simplifying secretarial and managerial work and increasing office productivity. With the rising cost of labor, using such office automation offers great cost savings. One further incentive for office electronics is the increasing amount of reporting required by governmental agencies.

Word Processing

Word processing simply means writing with a computer. It provides a mechanism to prepare material that otherwise would be written by hand or typed. The text is entered on a typewriter-like keyboard. Words appear on a visual-display screen rather than on paper. A word-processing program can edit, rearrange, insert, and delete material until the document is exactly as desired. Then the computer prints the text on paper; it produces a letter-perfect document with much less effort than it takes to produce the same document on a typewriter. Further, the computer can print as many perfectly typed copies as desired. The text can be stored on cassette tape or disk and can be changed at any time.

Word processing is available on computer systems ranging in size from personal computers to huge commercial installations. All word-processing systems involve computers. A CRT display, a printer that can print letter-quality type, and a keyboard from which the user enters text are also parts of all word-processing systems. In addition, an auxiliary storage device (normally using cassettes, floppy disks, or hard disks) is needed to store documents for revision or reuse. (See Figure 11–1.) A stand-alone system includes all of these components with a microcomputer; the user thus has his or her own system (see Figure 11–2). In a larger system (often called a shared-logic word-processing system), the computer may be a large, centrally located machine that does many other data-processing chores. It supports the terminal as a microcomputer does, but on a time-sharing basis. Such a system may include several CRTs and keyboards and several auxiliary storage devices and printers, all controlled by one CPU. Users work at terminals that are functionally their own personal word-processing systems.

The cost of a basic word-processing system is between $5,000 and $20,000. The leading manufacturer of word-processing systems is Wang Laboratories. Others include CPT Corporation, Datapoint Corporation, Lanier, Digital Equipment Corporation, IBM, and Vector Graphics.

Word-processing systems are not restricted to the tasks described above.

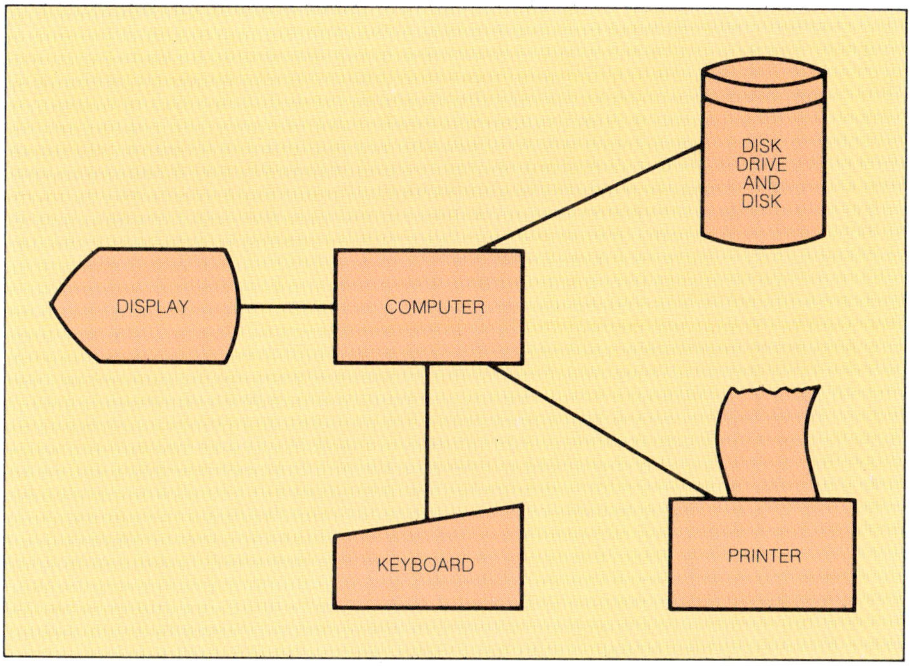

FIGURE 11–1
Hardware Components of a Word-Processing System

In addition to providing sophisticated word-processing functions, they can merge data with text, process files, perform mathematical functions, generate the output of photocomposition devices, facilitate paperwork management (electronic filing), and accept input from optical character recognition devices (typewriter-created text may be put into word-processing systems for subsequent editing). Some systems can communicate with other word-processing systems and can distribute text after it has been created, allowing documents prepared in one location to be printed in others.

FIGURE 11–2
The Wangwriter, Wang's stand-alone word processor, can also perform a variety of personal computing applications.

Electronic Mail

Early word processors could not communicate with each other; text transfers had to be handled manually. Now, however, text transmissions are possible, and any type of message can be sent electronically. Since managers and professionals spend approximately 25 percent of their time reading, and since roughly one trillion pages of paper are exchanged between U.S. businesses and government agencies each year, this capability to transmit text electronically can be put to good use in the office.

Electronic mail is the transmission of messages at high speeds over telecommunication facilities. The main idea behind these computer-based mail systems is that one user of the service sends a message to another by placing it in a special storage area from which the second receives the message by retrieving it and printing it. People using such systems can be in remote locations and need not use the system at the same time in order to send and receive messages.

Electronic mail terminals are often located in centralized communication centers staffed by trained operators. Sometimes, however, the terminals are placed on the desks of managers, professionals, and secretaries. Receivers can view incoming mail items on a CRT screen or can receive paper documents printed with the same typewriter quality as the originals. The mail can be revised, incorporated into other documents, passed along to new recipients, or filed like any other documents in the system.

In some systems, application programs actually send and receive mail items. For example, an application producing sales reports can automatically address, duplicate, and mail the reports to branch offices quickly and easily. Branch office personnel can read their reports the same day—not days later.

There are two basic forms of electronic mail: teletypewriter systems and facsimile systems. **Teletypewriter systems** transmit messages as strings of characters. **Facsimile systems,** sometimes called **telecopier systems,** produce a picture of a page by scanning it, as a television camera scans a scene or a copier scans a printed page. The image is then transmitted to a receiver, where it is printed.

Another type of electronic message system on which much work is currently being done is the **voice message system (VMS).** In VMS, the sender presses a special "message" key on the telephone, dials the receiver's number, and speaks the message. A button lights on the receiver's phone. When he or she presses the "listen" key, the message is played back.

Electronic mail is already a $2 billion industry. Many major computer equipment vendors offer such a service as part of automated office systems now being designed and introduced. Costs of electronic mail are already low and are likely to fall 15 to 25 percent each year. Some problems exist with

This office information system is an integrated system capable of both word and data processing.

electronic mail systems, however. In a system that serves thousands of users, it may be difficult to find a recipient's address (especially if the recipient's name is, say, Robert Smith). Another problem is the possibility of missed or incomplete delivery of messages. With telephone calls, it is easy to tell if you have reached your party; but when you send a message on an electronic message system, there often is no way to know that it has been received.

Reprographics

Another application of electronics in the office, as well as in the publishing industry, is **reprographics,** or computer typesetting. The computer is connected to a typesetting machine and the output is film "repro" paper, or tape to be used ultimately to prepare total page layouts for books, magazines, newspapers, and the like. The type is set automatically from the text stored in computer memory. The text contains special codes to indicate where various typefaces (such as italics and boldface) are to be used. The codes can also specify formatting for insertion of photos and so on.

Word processing, electronic mail, and reprographics are all applications of the computer to assist in communications in the office. The other office functions previously mentioned (information storage and retrieval, data analysis, and decision making) are also being automated.

Office Automation

The **automated office** combines office electronics with data processing. **Office information systems** contain a variety of word processors, data-entry terminals, graphics terminals, information distributors, printers of all kinds, OCR devices, photocomposition devices, and computer-based text editors. For example, a word processor linked to an intelligent copier (a copier that can accept both printed source documents and electronic input) can send instructions and text directly to the copier, with no need for an original paper document.

Chicago's Continental Bank, a leader in office automation, has instituted a sophisticated electronic communication system that includes home data terminals, electronic mail, and remote-location dictation. Ultimately, text, data, voice, and image will be integrated into an information system that can be used as a corporate resource.

Hardware and software systems are being introduced for the automated office. For example, Wang Laboratories has introduced the OIS/BASIC Integrated Office System, which combines word processing and data processing. Users can simultaneously perform word processing, data processing, printing, and communication activities. With this system, users can accomplish a wide variety of tasks, such as general accounting, insurance calculations, cash flow analysis, and project scheduling. For example, sales office personnel can answer customer's letters, write memos, communicate with the home office, enter orders, and do their monthly sales reports on one system.

HIGHLIGHT
Briefcase Offices

The private office, ever the dream of would-be and ambitious executives, may be on its way out—in a briefcase. Those whose job it is to look into the "office of the future" see lots of changes: terminals where there were typewriters, machines that make and answer routine phone calls, conferences conducted by video rather than around a table, electronic and audio mail instead of the printed kind, software files instead of filing cabinets, and on and on. Says one office furniture futurist, "I want to move to deskless offices, take away all the old props. Best of all is a terminal in an attache case—you have the entire office with you all the time."

Office automation can provide many benefits to companies. Staffing costs are reduced because fewer office personnel are needed to perform a given amount of work. Space, for both people and paper, is conserved. Most importantly though, the timeliness of work is increased; this leads to better results and better information, and these in turn lead to better decisions.

Automating the office may be worthwhile, but it can also cause problems. Job displacement and the declining quality of jobs are two main issues. Critics argue that clerical workers' skills are deemphasized and that they are made to feel like extensions of their machines. Jobs are made routine, paced by the computer, and possibly measured by dehumanizing factors such as the number of keystrokes per hour. The implications of such arguments must be considered. What will be their impact on labor relations, management, and job satisfaction?

JOB AUTOMATION

Ever since the Industrial Revolution, automation has been of great concern to people. As technology has advanced, more and more processes have been automated, leading to greater efficiency and lower costs but also to machines replacing people in many jobs. With the advent of computers, fears about automation leading to unemployment and depersonalization have taken on even greater significance. Whether these fears are justified is yet to be seen.

The evidence of the past three decades does not indicate that increased automation leads to increased unemployment. To be sure, workers have

A computer terminal on the finishing line at Burlington Industries, Inc., gives workers information on various manufacturing procedures as well as updates on work in process.

been displaced, but each new technology has created new employment opportunities that more than compensate for the jobs eliminated. For example, the invention of the automatic weaving machine eliminated many jobs in the garment industry, but this effect was offset by the creation of a whole new industry involving the manufacturing and marketing of the new equipment.

Nevertheless, many people argue the impact of computers is going to be much more significant because computer technology provides for much more versatile and complex automation. Computers, instead of humans, can be used to control automatic machines and entire assembly lines. Grocery stores can be automated—a person can call in an order and a computer can record it, find the required items, and even arrange for delivery. Other computers can control entire processes in oil refineries, turning crude oil into tar, heating oil, diesel oil, gasoline, and so forth.

Several studies have been conducted to determine the effects of computer automation on jobs. The results have not been conclusive but have in general indicated that a certain amount of job displacement can be expected,

The entire steel rolling operation of this Bethlehem mill is supervised and monitored from this computerized control center.

At this Shell Oil manufacturing complex, computer technology is used to monitor octane levels in gasoline.

because the computer can take over many routine clerical jobs. However, the extent to which such displacement occurs also depends on other factors, including the following:

- The goals that are sought from the use of the computer. Is the objective to be able to handle an increasing workload with the same personnel, or is it to reduce costs by eliminating jobs?
- The growth rate of the organization. If the organization is expanding, it can more easily absorb workers whose jobs are being eliminated, since many new jobs must be created to cope with the increasing business.
- The planning that has gone into the acquisiton and use of the computer. With careful preparation, an organization can anticipate the personnel changes a computer system will bring about. It can make plans either to reassign the affected people or to help them to find new jobs with other organizations. First-time use of a computer-based system will definitely create new jobs in the areas of computer operations, data-entry, programming, and system analysis and design. Usually, however, the skills and education required for these jobs differ from those required for the eliminated jobs. However, displaced employees can be trained to handle such jobs as operating computer equipment (loading and unloading tapes and the like) and keypunching; they can also be sent to schools for more formal training.

Applications

Perhaps the impact of automation on job displacement is felt more keenly in production-oriented environments, because the nature of mass production is conducive to automation. Robot-like equipment is already common in manufacturing. **Industrial robots,** as these machines are called, are a far cry from the endearing C-3PO pictured in *Star Wars*. Typically, an industrial robot is just a mobile arm ending in some sort of vise-like grip or claw. The arm is attached to a box that houses the control unit. The computer is plugged into an electric outlet, and cables that run from the computer along the arm transmit instructions in the form of electric impulses to the claw (see Figure 11–3). For heavy work, hydraulic pressure is used.

At present, most industrial robots are used to perform very simple, repetitive tasks. They paint cars, assemble appliances, and mine coal. Chrysler is using robots to weld auto bodies; 50 such robots can do the work of 200 human workers. General Motors currently uses 1600 robots in its auto assembly processes. Robots are also found in industrial environments potentially dangerous to humans. For example, robots can be used in high-radiation environments to handle parts too hot or too cold for humans or to clean up the radiation of a damaged nuclear reactor. At a Department of Energy plant, a robot is used to transport reprocessed plutonium, one of the most toxic substances known, in and out of a furnace. The military plans to use robots in place of soldiers to patrol restricted areas and battle zones. Robots can also be used to operate machines such as stamping mills and electric saws that can maim careless operators.

FIGURE 11–3
Industrial Robot

Robots can work faster and more efficiently than humans. They can work around the clock without becoming tired or bored. They don't get hungry or sick or join a union. Robots range in price from $7,500 to $150,000 and have an average life span of about eight years. They can be operated and paid for at a cost of about $5 per hour, while a human worker might cost $20 per hour.

Many efforts in robot development are sponsored by military and space programs. The Voyager I robot traveled 1.3 billion miles to Saturn. In 1986, the Mars Rover, which is currently being built, will travel to Mars and be able to motor around on the planet, looking at rocks with its TV eyes and digging up samples with a shovel. Other robots currently being developed will be able to take off from the space shuttle and repair a satellite in orbit or be sent out aboard an unmanned submarine to find and repair vessels undersea.

The potential ability of robots reaches into fields other than science and manufacturing. One robot manufacturer has been asked to develop a robot that can pluck chickens. In Australia, a robot that shears sheep is being

HIGHLIGHT
A Rampage of Robots

Once the stuff of science fiction, robots are becoming as common as department store Santa Clauses—and like these dittoed Kris Kringles they inspire wonder only among the young and naive. Estimates are that there may be as many as 6,000 robots working in American factories, welding, spray painting, handling material, packaging objects, and the like. Others are in offices, acting as automatic receptionists, mail carriers, and even as guides. (But are they smart enough to unionize?)

tested. Robots are being designed to care for the afflicted, aid nurses and doctors during surgery, and fight crime. Texas Instruments employs robots in the manufacture of pocket calculators. Some day, robot servants may be commonplace in the home.

Future Impact

Today, more than 6,000 robots work throughout the United States, while Japan operates over 10,000. A recent forecast by the American Society of Manufacturing Engineers and the University of Michigan predicts that by 1987, 15 percent of all U.S. assembly systems will use robot technology and that by 1988, 50 percent of the labor in small-component assembly will be replaced by automation. Japan's advanced technology will force the United States to be competitive in employing robots. If this forecast is correct, and if robots continue to become cheaper and more efficient, what will human workers do? So far, robots have been used mainly for boring or dangerous tasks. This has helped workers view robots as more of a help than a threat. But if robots also begin to replace humans in more pleasant and exciting jobs, their use may cause alarm.

The use of robots may cause some difficulties and bring about many changes in our society. The "Robot Revolution" may lead to a shorter work week and more leisure time. This new technology may increase personal freedom in terms of options of occupational choice and leisure-time activities. It may also encourage a shift from manufacturing to service occupations.

Furthermore, the robot industry itself may be a huge new employer, creating many more jobs than robots displace. The North American robot systems market alone is widely expected to have constant dollar growth from $65 million in 1980 to more than $500 million by 1985 and to $1.5 billion by 1990.

ARTIFICIAL INTELLIGENCE

So far, this text has used well structured problems to illustrate using the computer as a problem-solving tool. Each problem could be solved with a carefully defined procedure. For example, to solve the payroll problem, we developed a structure that did not need to be changed each time the payroll was calculated. However, many problems must be solved by processes quite different from the conscious, deliberate methods used to solve problems in mathematics or logic. People do not always think according to a set of strictly defined rules. Many problem solutions involve not only logic but also intuition, creativity, and intelligence. Examples of such problems include deciphering someone's scribbled messages, playing a game that requires strategy or deception, and distinguishing literally intended meanings from sarcasm. Such problems are not difficult for humans to solve; they are natural tasks we do every day. But the question of whether techniques can be developed to enable computers to solve problems that seem to require imagination or intelligence is one that continues to challenge researchers.

Research efforts are currently aimed at preparing programs that can perform tasks never before done automatically and usually assumed to require human intelligence—programs that perform tasks such as thinking, reasoning, making logical deductions, remembering past experiences, or solving present problems by recognizing analogous situations. This field of research is called **artificial intelligence.** Research efforts and technical developments in the field of artificial intelligence are advancing rapidly. Researchers are developing computers that can understand human speech, read and summarize news stories, and compile data about a sick person and diagnose the illness.

Robots at Motorola place electronic engine controls in heating ovens, prior to a computer-controlled environmental test.

The practical applications of artificial intelligence seem endless. Intelligent computers could, for example, read books, newspapers, journals, and magazines, and prepare summaries. They could search libraries for facts pertinent to a decision that must be made and perhaps suggest possible courses of action and their probable consequences. In areas such as law and medicine, computers could understand specialized knowledge and know-how to put it to work.

Research in artificial intelligence has been directed mainly toward such fields as heuristics, speech understanding, print and script reading, and natural-language processing.

Heuristics

The word **heuristic** means "helping to learn or discover." A heuristic problem-solving process suggests a certain course of action to be taken in a certain situation. The action is not guaranteed to be the correct or the only solution for a problem, but one that has worked well in similar situations in the past and is worth trying. Generally, heuristics are used to solve problems too complex or time-consuming to yield to conventional mathematical analysis. An advantage of heuristics is that they can reduce the number of alternatives that have to be explored.

To decide which heuristics to apply in a particular situation, a problem solver can look for patterns. For example, a chess player is guided by patterns formed by the pieces on the board. Heuristic processes are therefore programmed into computers that play chess. The computer can recognize the pattern of pieces on the board and know moves that have worked in the same situation in the past. Thus, the total number of choices of moves has been narrowed.

Speech Interpretation

Researchers are also attempting to program computers to understand speech—a very difficult task because of variations in intonation and pitch, pauses, errors, hesitations, incomplete words, and different pronunciations of words. Consequently, most research in this area has been restricted to programming machines to perform specified tasks in response to spoken commands, using a very limited vocabulary and simple sentence structure. One such system, for example, accepts spoken commands to move chess pieces. There are only thirty-one words and a small number of action statements like "move" and "check" in the computer's vocabulary. The computer can test whether a statement makes sense, because it has a record of where all the pieces are on the board and, through its program "knows" the legal moves.

One of the most practical applications in this area of research is in aiding handicapped people. In one such application, a wheelchair controlled by a computer can understand spoken English commands. A user can instruct the computer to move the wheelchair in certain directions. A mechanical arm attached to the wheelchair and controlled by the computer can be instructed, for example, to manipulate eating utensils. Systems such as this one can greatly increase the self-sufficiency of handicapped persons.

Print and Script Reading

Researchers are now trying to program computers to read handwritten script. Even this limited capability to read handwritten print can be very useful for such applications as sorting mail. In fact, the USSR and Japan use such readers to process 20,000 pieces of mail an hour with 93 percent accuracy. (Address codes must be written in preprinted boxes on envelopes.)

Natural-Language Processing

Considerable research has been devoted to developing techniques whereby computers can process natural languages, for example, to summarize text or

Planning Research Corporation has assisted police and fire departments throughout the United States in designing and installing local and statewide information system networks for dispatching vehicles, message switching, and operations control.

to translate text from one language to another. As suggested in the discussion of speech interpretation, this is very difficult, because many of the statements people speak, hear, and read are highly ambiguous and assume a thorough understanding of words, grammar, and their context. However, approximate translations of technical text (which is more straightforward than general writing) from Russian to English are now possible.

In order for computer programs to understand the written word, they must be able to link words with ideas and make logical conclusions. A program written at Yale University called FRUMP reads short news stories and writes one-sentence summaries in English, Spanish, and Chinese. In one instance, FRUMP was presented with a 600-word story about the death of Margaret Mead, the anthropologist. The computer wrote the following summary: "Anthropologist Margaret Mead, 76, has died from cancer." FRUMP has made some mistakes, however. One story of the shooting of the mayor of San Francisco in 1978 contained the phrase "shooting shook San Francisco." FRUMP concluded there had been an earthquake in California!

HIGHLIGHT
Talking Computers

If the notions of computers talking to you is a trifle unsettling, then you'd better head for the hills. Computers are chattering all around us. They announce the time—on demand and on their own. They tell us we have dialed the wrong number and scold us to check the directory (or, presumably, they'll give us a real talking-to the next time). They are imbedded in some arcade games to talk us out of our quarters. A relatively benign talking device can scan printed matter and turn it into talk for the blind to listen to. Another one can scan the bar coding on assembly line parts and tell the workers on the line how the parts are to be put together. Well, just as long as it doesn't insist on joining the bowling team. . . .

Concerns for the Future

One of the major hindrances in the advancement of research into artificial intelligence is the difficulty of developing programs that work the same way the mind does. So far, biologists have not been able to explain how the brain thinks well enough for it to be mimicked by programs; researchers have not been able to duplicate its functions in the laboratory. In fact, the most difficult problems arise in the attempt to mimic the simplest elements of human behavior, such as simple eye-to-hand coordination and recognition of spoken words. On the other hand, the successes in artificial intelligence have been in modeling some extremely complex skills that often require years of effort for humans to accomplish, such as playing chess well, diagnosing diseases, and solving problems in college physics.

Artificial intelligence researchers are studying human behavior, what happens to information when the brain processes it, and how human memory is organized so that one particular piece of information can be retrieved from the vast amounts of information stored in the brain. As new clues are discovered, researchers try to mimic them with a computer. The consequences of using computers to understand the human mind may be extremely beneficial. As we get a deeper understanding of how the mind works, we may be able to make the process of education more effective and may become more effective at solving problems and making decisions.

On the dark side of this forecast, the misuse of such powerful computers could endanger personal freedom. For example, what if computers that understood speech were programmed to listen in on every human conversation? Would there be any individual privacy? Humans are perhaps most troubled by the idea that computers can learn to think, maybe even at a range and scope approaching that of human thinking; it presents a strange encroachment on people's feeling of uniqueness. What if society became too dependent on such computers? What if they became so complex people lost the ability to understand why they reached the decisions and took the actions they did? And then there is the ultimate fear that computers would conspire to take over.

Like any new technology, computers must be used properly. If computing knowledge and resources are sufficiently available to people on both sides of the issues, the risks of misuse will decrease. Society must be aware of the consequences of new technology and take responsibility for them.

> **HIGHLIGHT**
> ***Video Game Designers***
>
> Video game designers are being treated like superstars by their companies, and with good reason. Their creativity is leading to superprofits. The materials that actually go into a video game are simple and fairly inexpensive, amounting to about $4 a unit. Yet the game may sell for $25 or more. It's what the games can do—the fantasies they can conjure up—that is really valuable, and this is where the designers come in. Their mastery of the technical and the imaginative are essential to the low-cost, high-profit and very hot industry. David Crane, a designer for Activision, estimates that there are fewer than 100 designers in the industry now and that only a dozen or so of these are "top flight." To honor the genius of its designers, Activision puts their pictures on the instruction sheets for the games they create.

PERSONAL COMPUTING

A concept which for years was discussed only as a science fiction novelty is now a trend—acquiring computers for personal use. Because microcomputers are inexpensive and widely available, computing power is available to almost anyone. In the past five years, the personal computer industry has grown from nothing to nearly $1 billion in annual sales to the hobbyist, the consumer at home, and the small business. Today there are more than 750,000 general-purpose microcomputers in U.S. homes and small businesses, and the number is increasing by over 40 percent per year.

The most promising market for the microcomputer is in the home; it may soon be as common in homes as color television. The most popular use of home computers thus far has been for entertainment. Computer games that simulate sports such as golf, hockey, baseball, and tennis are available (see Figure 11–4). Conventional games such as chess and backgammon, in which the computer is a formidable opponent, are also popular. The graphical and audio capabilities and fast operation of microcomputers allow them to display action in spectacular detail in games such as Space Invaders and Star Raiders.

The microcomputer is natural as an aid in financial matters. It can keep track of your checkbook, savings account, and loans, and can maintain the family budget and tell you the best time to buy a new car. It can keep personal records, inventory, mailing lists, and property lists.

The homemaker can make extensive use of a microcomputer. It can be used to maintain a Christmas-card list, monitor biorhythms, file recipes, work out a dinner menu with what food is in the refrigerator, monitor calorie intake, or start the roast when triggered by a phone call from the office. As an educational aid, it can enhance children's basic math, reading, and spelling abilities; tutor high school and college subjects; and teach the fundamentals of computers and computer programming. Software is available to teach both typing and Chinese!

Adding sensors, motors, and switches to a microcomputer enables it to run a wide range of gadgets around the home. A microprocessor-controlled microwave oven allows the user to specify how long food should be defrosted or cooked as well as what time cooking should begin. A microcomputer can manage energy use by keeping various rooms of the house at desired temperatures. It can monitor for fire and enhance security by locking doors and controlling burglar alarms. The microcomputers can water the lawn according to ground moisture, send a signal if water begins seeping into the basement, open and shut drapes, and control lights. Also, minute

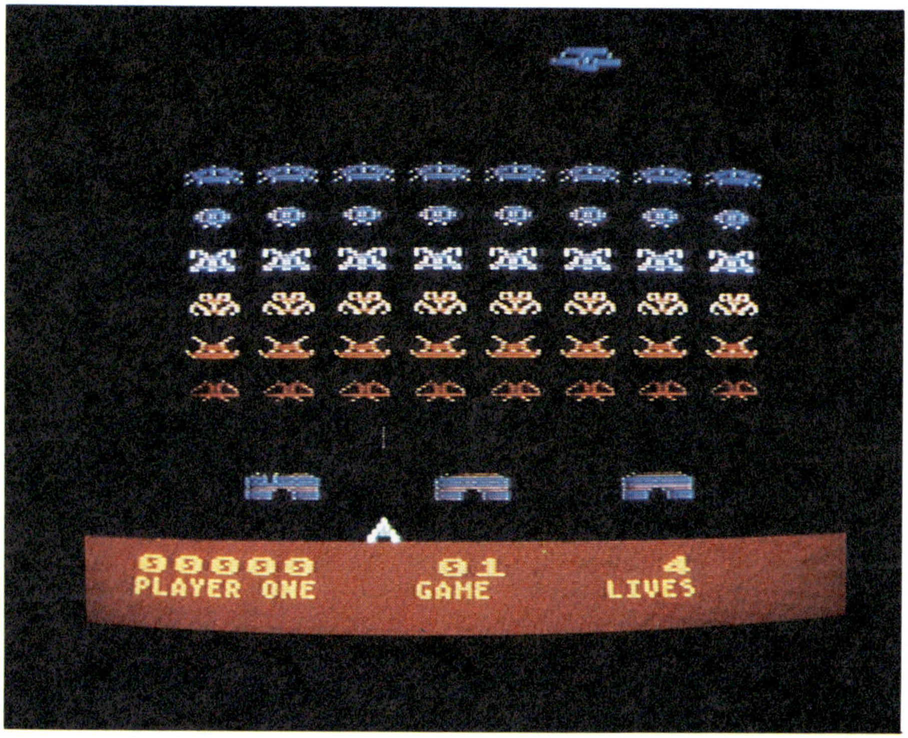

FIGURE 11–4
Computer Games in the Home

wires placed underneath a baby's crib mattress can allow the computer to signal the baby's movements in the crib or even detect irregularity in the baby's breathing and sound an alarm.

This may seem like a lot of uses for personal computers, but it only includes applications limited to computers isolated from one another. A whole new range of usefulness opens up when we consider networks that allow home computers to communicate with one another and with commercial installations. There are available, for example, a number of personal computer information services (see Figure 11–5). Some provide a link to a library or to a nationwide want-ad service. The Dow Jones News/Retrieval service allows users access to current quotations for stocks, bonds, mutual funds, and treasury notes for more than 6,000 companies and enables them to look up articles in *The Wall Street Journal.*

Communication networks linking home computers to banks will provide computer-based home banking services. At least one such service is being tested. The customers can pay bills using their home computers by authorizing the bank to pay specified amounts to certain merchants from their accounts. The service also includes a news and information network that customers can use to obtain national, international, and financial news, as well as information about the bank's services. Customers have access to a statement that shows all their banking activities since the last formal statement. They can see which items have cleared and which direct deposit checks have

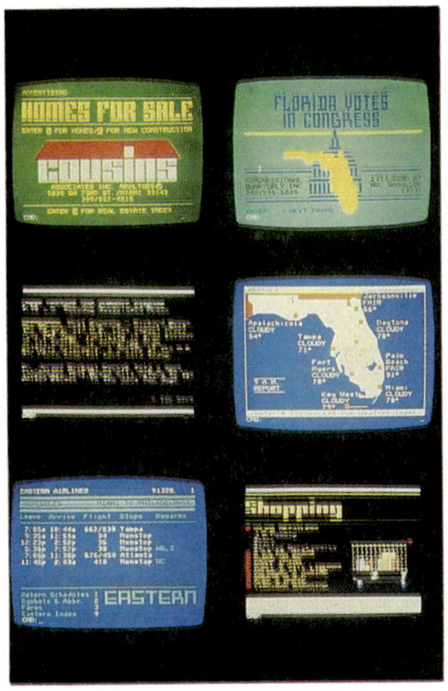

FIGURE 11–5
Home Information System

reached their accounts. Deposits and withdrawals still must be handled at branches or by mail. The fee for such a system is only $5 per month.

In the future, the home-computer owner will also be able to shop from home. In a computerized shopping system, the user dials a store, identifies items of interest to be displayed on the screen, and then selects the items to be purchased and delivered. The user can purchase not only groceries but also clothes and furniture without leaving home.

The personal computer may be the answer to many problems ranging from energy regulation to food consumption. The time has come for the machine that has changed people's lives to become a part of their lives.

PERSPECTIVE

Computer technology has had a more significant impact on society than any other factor since the Industrial Revolution. The extent of the impact has led many to classify the present era as the **Information Revolution** (or **Computer Revolution**). In an extremely short time, computers have moved out of the laboratory and into an indispensable position in modern life. This rapid progress has generated many problems as well as spectacular benefits.

Some people born and educated before widespread implementation of computers refuse to recognize their existence. Psychological barriers are raised, and no attempt is made to understand the logical base of computer operations. The technological obsolescence associated with computer advances often requires job restructuring or retraining; this tends to increase resistance to computer applications. Computer professionals must commit themselves to continuing education if they want to remain current in this dynamic field. These problems are people-oriented rather than dependent upon scientific advancements. As such, they are more difficult to solve.

The world would be very different today if all the advances attributed to computers were removed. For example, airlines could not continue to function without computerized airline reservations systems, space travel would be impossible without simulation and control programs, and many economic systems would grind to a halt without the tremendous speed of the computer upon which the banking industry relies so heavily for processing cash flow.

One point must be understood: not all computer applications are beneficial or even effective. The computer is only a tool used by analysts and programmers to help people solve problems. If instructions are inappropriate or incorrect, then the computer system has the same deficiencies. Computer power is a fact of technological achievement; harnessing this power is a function of the individuals who control computer use. The principal limitation on computer applications is the imagination and ingenuity of the humans who use them.

SUMMARY POINTS

- Office electronics is a rapidly growing application of computerization. Word-processing systems, electronic mail, reprographics, and office automation simplify secretarial and managerial work, decrease costs, and increase productivity and the flow of information in the office. The "office of the future" is fast becoming the "office of the present."
- Job automation refers to machine-directed processes. Automation through the use of computers has created new jobs while eliminating some jobs and modifying others. The amount of job displacement that results from computer use depends on the goals sought from its use, the growth rate of the organization, and the amount of planning that went into the acquisition and use of the computer.
- Computer-controlled machines, including robots, are now used for simple, repetitive tasks and for tasks deemed too dangerous for humans. Though often used in industrial environments, these machines are far from displacing the working class.
- Personal computing is a trend gaining widespread popularity, both in small businesses and in the home. Applications of microcomputers in the home range from entertainment to more practical tasks such as monitoring energy and security devices.

HIGHLIGHT
Computer Animation

If you've given up hope that animated cartoons can still be as realistic and artful as they were in Walt Disney's heyday, you can start hoping again. Computers at the New York Institute of Technology are now able to do the frame-by-frame animation drawings that simulate movement and action when shown at a rapid speed. Done the old way by hand, the animation process was painfully slow and extremely expensive. That's why more recent cartoons—such as those of the Saturday morning variety—have been so jerky and mechanical looking. With computer assistance, an animator makes the initial drawing (A), the final drawing (B), and the determination of how many frames there are to be between A and B. Then the computer creates appropriate drawings on that number of frames. The effect is the same as if the frames were hand drawn. Computers at the institute have also been programmed to simulate three-dimensional movement and to do quick and subtle coloring and shading effects.

REVIEW QUESTIONS

1. Give several examples of office electronics. What changes do you think the automated office will bring to the working day as people now know it?
2. What benefits does office automation extend to the firm?
3. Why would clerical work at a computer terminal be considered dehumanizing?
4. Do you feel that the Computer Revolution will lead to greater levels of unemployment?
5. Robots and other computer gadgets are used extensively in science-fiction movies and television shows. What are possible practical applications for such robots?
6. To what use would you, or do you, put a personal computer?
7. What is meant by artificial intelligence? What are the limitations to research in this area?
8. How are heuristics used to solve problems?
9. What difficulties does the computer face when trying to recognize and interpret human speech?
10. In the 1982 movie, *TRON*, a computer aims to abandon the users' needs and gain more "personal" power. If scientists continue to strive to model computers after human brains, do you feel that the computer can become a threat to humankind? Why or why not?
11. How do you think future computer applications will affect society? Discuss the consequences of displacement and privacy.

A Glimpse into the Future

From tabulating machines to microcomputers. The progression has occurred at an astounding pace! There is an industry saying that goes like this: "If the auto industry had done what the computer industry has done in the last thirty years, a Rolls Royce would cost $2.50 and get two million miles per gallon. . . . It would also be only three inches long." Such an increase in potential at such a small cost cannot help but change the way we live. And we see evidence of this change daily.

Amid concern that the computer is going to master our minds, misdirect our children, and invade our privacy, the personal microcomputer is gain ing ground. Not only are the microcomputers very adaptable, but they are also becoming much more user-friendly. Menu options (where you can select various functions or programs listed on your screen) and touch panels (where you merely touch the screen to give a command or response) make it easy to interact with the machine, but the future holds even more. Some scientists anticipate the development of a computer that will talk to the users to help build files, design new programs, and work through problems verbally.

The expected advances in the medicine and health field alone will affect us greatly. Small computers are being attached to bedpans to analyze urine and report the results. Other microcomputers are helping doctors examine symptoms and diagnose the disease. Genetic study is so enhanced by computers that in the not-so-distant future, we may be able to have a blood sample analyzed at the local clinic and receive a printout of the diseases to which we are susceptible. Our personal computers at home could then be programmed to help monitor our health in light of these susceptibilities.

At work, microcomputers already are aiding productivity improvement by monitoring tasks and progress toward goal achievement. And we can make factory work more pleasant by using noise-level projection techniques, based on the building or room structure, and then adapting the physical design for minimum noise. Robots will become more common; General Motors hopes to be using, by 1990, ten times the 1600 robots it has today.

Home after work, we reach for the newspaper. Already the electronic newspaper is appearing on personal computers. Over a dozen dailies, including the *Washington Post,* publish an electronic edition that allows a reader to select the articles of interest and omit the rest.

Need to make a phone call? An experiment by the French will soon replace 300,000 phone directories with video consoles in homes. To locate the telephone number desired, the user will type in the person's name—you can even misspell it—and the computer will search phonetically and display on the screen several names and phone numbers that are spelled like or similar to the one asked for. Searching the yellow pages may be simplified; the computer has up-to-date information and is user-friendly.

For instance, finding a nearby mechanic may be as easy as typing in the make of auto and the owner's address; the computer will then respond with all the Renault repair services in the user's geographic area. Or a teenager who wants to go dancing Friday night can type in the commands that will display the names of all discos open Friday night in that geographic area, their phone numbers, and their hours open for business. Banking, too, will become revolutionized. In some cities, banking via personal computer hookups to the bank computer is becoming more common. Banking-at-home is convenient to both bank and customer: The bank saves paperwork and employee costs and the customer doesn't have to waste time in long bank lines.

Giant strides will be made in the field of education. Today's children are being hailed as the first computer generation. While many adults are still suspicious and fearful of computers, computers are a way of life for children—at home, at school, at play. Computer firms like Tandy and Apple are donating computers to schools. Chips are steadily getting smaller so that children will soon have supercomputer power readily available. Their minds will explore many intriguing concepts such as chemical structures or space with their computers and three-dimensional graphic display. They will be able to simulate what it's like to fly into space or be jostled by atoms bouncing around in a fluid.

Some educators fear that this computer power may cause a great split between those who can control the computer and those who cannot. Fortunately, all types of young people seem attracted to—and are usually successful with—computers. Smart kids are challenged; slower ones are met on their own level. Even prereaders can learn to work with a computer with the help of touch panels (where the child can simply touch the screen to answer a question or give a command) or special languages like Logo.

One report claims that children working at a computer spend 88% of the time with their attention directed at their task. In normal classrooms, attention wanders about half of the time. And computers can answer more questions for a single student than a teacher can in the normal classroom.

An interesting sidelight is that a computer language, now usually BASIC, frequently is the first "foreign" language a student learns. This alone may change our future, since computer languages have both verbal and mathematical aspects. In the past, students have been found to be "good with numbers" or "skilled in verbal expression." Familiarity with computers will, hopefully, integrate these skills for most students and help us bring together the worlds of science and literature.

Computers seem to force children—and older people, too—to notice *how* people think when they solve a problem. Computers can only answer yes or no to a problem, whereas humans can answer yes, no, or maybe. A major aim of the computer industry is to get the computer to function more and more like a human brain. Already a program called AURA (automated reasoning assistant) has the ability to reason and narrow alternatives to those most likely for success in that particular application. While AURA now runs on an IBM 370, a large-scale computer system, its designers are considering a program for home computers to help people through the logic inherent in making decisions that affect their daily lives.

Scientists in Japan have announced their intentions to carry the "human brain" analogy to its limit. They plan to build an electronic brain, as efficient as its human model, by 1985. It will be the size of a human brain, with storage capacity equal to that of human memory complete with reasoning capabilities, and it will run on even less electrical power!

With intentions like those stated by the Japanese, with computer access like that available to U.S. school children, and with the widespread desire to advance our human situation, anything can happen. We can be certain that the computer will continue to revolutionize our world.

DISCUSSION QUESTIONS

1. In what ways will learning to program a computer "improve" a student's mind? Do you think such knowledge may be harmful?
2. What home task do you now encounter that you wish were computerized?

APPENDIX A

Career Opportunities

PEOPLE AND THEIR ROLES

Men and women with technical or managerial skills in data processing are employed in almost every industry. The need for data-processing personnel exists not only in business firms but also in hospitals, schools, government agencies, banks, and libraries. However, the major emphasis of this section will be on computer-related career opportunities in a business environment.

A typical computer installation in a business organization is expected to perform at least three basic functions: system analysis and design, programming, and computer operation. Personnel with the education and experience required to work in these areas are needed; in addition, data-base technology has created the need for specialists in data-base analysis and administration. Further, an information system manager is needed to coordinate activities, set goals for the data-processing department, and establish procedures to control and evaluate both personnel and projects in progress.

Information System Managers

Historically, data-processing managers have been programmers or system analysts who worked their way up to management positions with little formal management training. But the increasing emphasis on information systems and information management has brought a change; professional managers with demonstrable leadership qualities and communication skills are being hired to manage information system departments.

The *management information system (MIS) manager* is responsible for planning and tying together all the information resources of the firm. The manager must organize the physical and human resources of the department to achieve company goals and must devise effective control mechanisms to monitor progress. This means that the MIS manager must possess the following knowledge and skills:

- A thorough understanding of the organization, its goals, and its business activities.
- Leadership qualities to motivate and control highly skilled people.
- Knowledge of data-processing methods and familiarity with available hardware and software.

A man or woman seeking a career in information system management should have a college degree. For managing business data-processing centers, a degree in business administration with a concentration in the area of management information systems is desirable. Some employers prefer to hire someone with an MBA degree. Furthermore, to handle high-level management responsibilities such as those outlined above, a candidate for a position as MIS director should have at least two years of extensive management experience, as well as advanced knowledge of the industry and competence in all technical, professional, and business skills.

This office computer system, Wang Alliance 250, integrates data, word, audio, and image processing. The proliferation of office information systems such as these, and the impact they're making in the business world, opens a wide-range of career possibilities for people with business and data processing skills.

System Development Personnel

Programmers Generally, three types of programming are done in an organization: *application programming, maintenance programming,* and *system programming*. Persons working in any of these areas should possess the following basic skills:

- Good command of the programming language or languages in which programs are written.
- A knowledge of general programming methodology and of the relationships between programs and hardware.
- Analytical reasoning ability and attention to detail.
- Creativity and discipline to develop new problem-solving methods.
- Patience and persistence.

Application programs perform data-processing or computational tasks to solve specific problems facing an organization. This type of programming constitutes the bulk of all programming tasks. It involves taking a broad system design prepared by an analyst and converting it into instructions for the computer. The responsibilities of application programmers also include testing, debugging, documenting, and implementing programs.

An application programmer in business data processing must apply the capabilities of the computer to problems such as customer billing and inventory control. In addition to the basic skills outlined earlier, a business-oriented application programmer should know the objectives of the organization and have a basic understanding of accounting and management science.

Besides business-oriented application programmers, there are scientific application programmers who work on scientific or engineering problems, which usually require complex mathematical solutions. Thus, a scientific application programmer needs a basic knowledge of science or engineering.

Program maintenance is a very important but often neglected activity. Many large programs are never completely debugged, and there is a continuing need for changes to and improvement of major programs. It is the responsibility of maintenance programmers to change and improve existing programs. In some organizations, maintenance programming is done by application programmers. To be effective, a maintenance programmer needs considerable programming experience and a high level of analytical ability.

A different type of specialist, the system programmer, is responsible for creating and maintaining system software. System programmers are not

A programmer at work in a computer center at Hilheim, West Germany. The opportunities available to skilled programmers are truly international.

concerned with writing programs to solve day-to-day organizational problems. Instead, they are expected to develop utility programs; maintain operating systems, data-base packages, compilers, and assemblers; and be involved in decisions concerning additions and deletions of hardware and software. Because of their knowledge of operating systems, system programmers typically offer technical help to application programmers. To be able to perform these duties effectively, a system programmer should have: (1) a background in the theory of computer language structure and syntax and (2) extensive and detailed knowledge of the hardware being used and the software that controls it.

This on-the-job computer training program at TRW, Inc. in Cleveland, Ohio, is one of many such programs throughout the country.

In hiring any of these types of programmers, employers may also look for specialized skills. For example, the increasing impact of minicomputers and microcomputers is creating a demand for programmers with experience in real-time or interactive systems using mini and micro hardware. Also, the advanced technology of today's communication networks provides excellent opportunities for programmers skilled in designing, coding, testing, debugging, documenting, and implementing data communication software.

Educational requirements for programmers vary, because employers' needs vary. For a business-oriented application programming job, a college degree, though desirable, is usually not required. However, most employers prefer applicants who have had college courses in data processing, accounting, and business administration. Sometimes, workers experienced in computer operation or specific functional areas of business are promoted to programming jobs and, with additional data-processing courses, become fully qualified programmers.

Scientific application programming usually requires a degree in computer or information science, mathematics, engineering, or a physical science. Some jobs require graduate degrees. Few scientific organizations are interested in applicants with no college training.

Persons seeking to enter the system programming field should have at least one year of assembly language programming experience or a college degree in computer science. In addition to a degree, work experience, although not essential for a job as a programmer, is extremely beneficial.

Computer programming is taught in technical and vocational schools, community and junior colleges, and universities. Many high schools offer computer programming courses.

Application and system programmers will continue to be in exceptionally high demand. Application programmers with some exposure to data-base management and direct-access techniques, remote processing, conversational programming, structured design, and distributed processing will be in greatest demand. As the use of minicomputers and microcomputers increases knowledge of BASIC, RPGII, and Pascal will be valuable. System programmers knowledgeable in data communications, network planning and analysis, data-base concepts, and terminal-oriented systems will be in great demand. With these trends in mind, data processing, computer science, and business administration students may choose to direct their education toward some degree of specialization.

Computers are an integral part of Shell Oil Company's business. The following are only some of the functional areas within the company that present computer-related opportunities: information systems; financial planning; operations research; engineering; technical services; telecommunications; research and development.

Within an organization, a programmer's chances for advancement are usually good. A programmer who has demonstrated his or her technical competence and ability to handle responsibility may be promoted to lead programmer and given supervisory responsibilities. Some application programmers become system programmers, and vice versa.

System Analysts The *system analyst* is the key person in the analysis, design, and implementation of a formal information system. The analyst has the following responsibilities:

- Helping the user determine information needs.
- Gathering facts about existing systems and analyzing them to determine the effectiveness of current processing methods and procedures.
- Designing new systems, recommending changes to existing systems, and being involved in implementing these changes.

The analyst's role is critical to the success of any management information system. He or she acts as an interface between users of the MIS and tech-

At sea . . . a crewman of the Guided Missile Frigate USS Richard K. Turner operates Navy tactical data system equipment in the ship's combat information center.

nical personnel such as programmers, machine operators, and data-base specialists. This role becomes more important as the cost of designing, implementing, and maintaining information systems rises.

To be effective, the system analyst should possess the following characteristics:

- A general knowledge of the firm, its goals and objectives, and the products and services it provides.
- Familiarity with the organizational structure of the company and management's rationale for selecting that structure.
- Comprehensive knowledge of data-processing methods and current hardware and familiarity with available programming languages.
- The ability to plan and organize work and to cooperate and interact effectively with both technical and nontechnical personnel.
- A high level of creativity.
- The ability to communicate clearly and persuasively with technical personnel as well as with persons who have little or no computer background.

The minimum requirements for a job as a system analyst generally include work experience in system design and programming and some specialized industry experience. System analysts seeking jobs in a business environment should be college graduates with backgrounds in business management, accounting, economics, computer science, information systems, or data processing. An MBA or some graduate study is often desired. For work in a scientifically oriented organization, a college background in the physical sciences, mathematics, or engineering is preferred. Many universities offer majors in management information systems; their curricula are designed to train people to be system analysts.

Some organizations, particularly small ones, do not employ system analysts. Instead, *programmer/analysts* are responsible for system analysis and programming. In other companies, system analysts begin as programmers and are promoted to analyst positions after gaining experience. However, the qualities that make for a good analyst are significantly different from those that characterize a good programmer. Hence, there is no clear career path *from* programming *to* analysis, though such movement is possible.

System analysis is a growing field. According to data from the United States Department of Labor, computer system analysts can look forward throughout the 1980s to employment prospects brighter than those for workers in almost any other occupation. There is a continuing growth of management consulting firms and computer services organizations, as well as a high demand for system professionals by computer manufacturers. The growth rate in jobs is estimated to be 37 percent by 1990. Also, the increas-

Designing and implementing management information systems such as the one pictured here is the work of system analysts. The need for system analysts is growing steadily—it is estimated that by the year 1990, the number of jobs for system analysts will have grown by 37 percent.

ing use of minicomputers and microcomputers will cause an increase in the small user's needs for analysts to design systems for small computers.

Data-Base Specialists

Data-base specialists are responsible for designing and controlling the use of the organization's data resources. A *data-base analyst*—the key person in the analysis, design, and implementation of data structures—must plan and coordinate data use within the system. The analyst has the following responsibilities:

- Helping the user or system analyst to analyze the interrelationships of data.
- Defining physical data structures and logical views of data.
- Designing new data-base systems, recommending changes to existing ones, and being involved in the implementation of these changes.
- Eliminating data redundance.

In some organizations, the function of data analysis and coordination is incorporated in the system analysis function.

A data-base analyst needs technical knowledge of programming and system methodologies. A background in system software is valuable for persons planning physical data-base structures. The job requires a college education with concentration in the areas of computer science, business data processing, and data-base management system design. Many colleges offer courses in data-base management to train people to be data analysts.

The career path within the data-base specialty often leads to the position of corporate *data-base administrator (DBA)*. Data-base administrator is a management-level position responsible for control of all the data resources of the organization. The primary responsibilities of this position include:

- Developing a dictionary of standard data definitions so that all records are consistent.
- Designing data bases.
- Maintaining the accuracy, completeness, and timeliness of data bases.
- Designing procedures to ensure data security and data-base backup and recovery.
- Facilitating communications between analysts and users.
- Advising analysts, programmers, and system users as to the best ways to use data bases.

To handle these responsibilities, a data-base administrator must have a high level of technical expertise as well as an ability to communicate effectively with diverse groups of people. This person must exhibit supervisory and leadership skills developed through experience.

Demand is strong for data-base specialists. With the increasing trend toward data-base management, the need for persons with the technical knowledge to design data-base-oriented application systems is increasing.

Data-Processing Operations Personnel

Data-processing operations personnel are responsible for entering data and instructions into the computer, operating the computer and attached devices, retrieving output, and ensuring the smooth operation of the computing center and associated libraries. An efficient operations staff is crucial to the effective use of an organization's computer resources.

The *librarian* is responsible for classifying, cataloging, and maintaining files and programs stored on cards, tapes, disks, diskettes, and all other storage media and kept in a computer library for subsequent processing or historical purposes. The librarian's tasks include transferring backup files to alternate storage sites, purging old files, and supervising the periodic cleaning of magnetic tapes and disks.

The librarian's job is important because he or she controls access to stored master files and programs. Computer operators and programmers do not have access to the tapes or disks without the approval of the librarian. This prevents unauthorized changes or processing runs.

This office information system combines word and data processing along with a company-wide communications network. The time is rapidly approaching where virtually everyone in a business environment will have some exposure to computers.

The educational background required for this particular job is not extensive; a high-school diploma is adequate. In addition, the individual must have some knowledge of basic data-processing concepts and should possess clerical record-keeping skills.

A *computer operator's* duties include setting up equipment for particular jobs; mounting and removing tapes, disks, and diskettes as needed; and monitoring the operation of the computer. This person should be able to identify operational problems and take appropriate corrective actions. Most computers run under sophisticated operating systems that direct the operator through messages generated during processing. However, the operator is responsible for reviewing errors that occur during operation, determining their causes, and maintaining operating records.

Direct data-entry on a computer terminal. As the use of computers continues to expand, so too does the demand for terminal operators.

People seeking jobs as computer operators should enjoy working with machines and be able to read and understand technical literature. A computer operator has to act quickly and properly; a good operator can prevent the loss of a great deal of valuable computer time, as well as the loss or destruction of files and input data. An operator must also possess communication skills so that he or she can explain to users why programs worked or did not work.

Most operators receive training as apprentice operators. Few have college degrees. However, formal operator training is available through technical schools and junior colleges. To be effective, training must include several weeks of on-the-job experience with equipment similar to that the operator will be using.

A *data-entry operator's* job involves transcribing data into a form suitable for computer processing. A *keypunch operator* uses a keypunch machine to transfer data from source documents to punched cards. Operators of other key-entry devices transfer data to magnetic tape or magnetic disk for subsequent processing.

A *remote terminal operator* is also involved with the preparation of input data. The operator is located at a remote site, probably some distance from the computer itself. The data is entered into the computer directly, from the location at which it is generated.

Data-entry jobs usually require manual dexterity, typing or keying skills, and alertness. No extensive formal education is required; a high-school diploma is sufficient. However, all personnel in this category should be trained carefully to minimize the incidence of errors. Usually several weeks of on-the-job training is provided for new operators to familiarize them with the documents they will be reading and the data-entry devices they will be using.

Occupations in computer operations are being affected by changes in data-processing technology. The demand for keypunch operators will continue to decline as new methods of data preparation are developed and as the use of computer terminals and direct data-entry techniques continues to flourish. However, as the use of computers continues to expand, especially in small businesses, demand for computer operating personnel should remain strong.

MANAGING INFORMATION SYSTEMS

Organization of Data Processing

Traditionally, data-processing activities have been performed within the functional departments of organizations. However, because of increased record-keeping requirements, the ever-present need for current information, and the necessity to adapt to a complex, changing environment, many organizations have consolidated their data-processing operations. The computer has been used increasingly as a tool to manage the paper explosion that threatens to engulf many organizations.

The rapid growth of computer-based data processing has affected the location of the EDP department in an organization's structure. In most organizations, data processing originated in the accounting area, since most record keeping was done there. However, management has recognized that information is a scarce and valuable resource of the entire organization and has increasingly emphasized the data-processing activity and elevated it in the organizational structure.

Figure A–1 shows two versions of an organizational chart for a typical manufacturing firm, each with a different general location for the EDP department. Figure A–1a shows the traditional location: the EDP manager reports to the vice-president of finance and accounting. This location is satisfactory only if the other functional areas do not demand extensive use of computer capabilities. Unless the processing requirements of the accounting and finance department are extensive, the computer is not used to its full potential under such an arrangement. Further, this location has the following drawbacks:

- It is biased toward accounting and financial applications in the setting of job priorities. Since the data-processing manager reports to the controller he or she will obviously give high priority to financial applications.
- It discourages involvement of data-processing personnel with the other functional divisions and inhibits overall integration of the data-processing function.

Figure A–1b shows an alternative location that overcomes these limitations. Elevating the data-processing activity to the same status as the traditional line functions (production, marketing, finance) reflects its corporate-wide scope. When it occupies this position, the EDP department's name is often changed to management information system (MIS) department, to stress the importance of its function. The independent status of the MIS department helps to ensure that each functional area gets impartial service and that their particular information requirements are integrated to meet organizational goals.

The internal organizational structure of the MIS department can take various forms. Perhaps the most common breakdown is by data-processing function—system analysis and design, programming, and computer operations—as illustrated in Figure A–2.

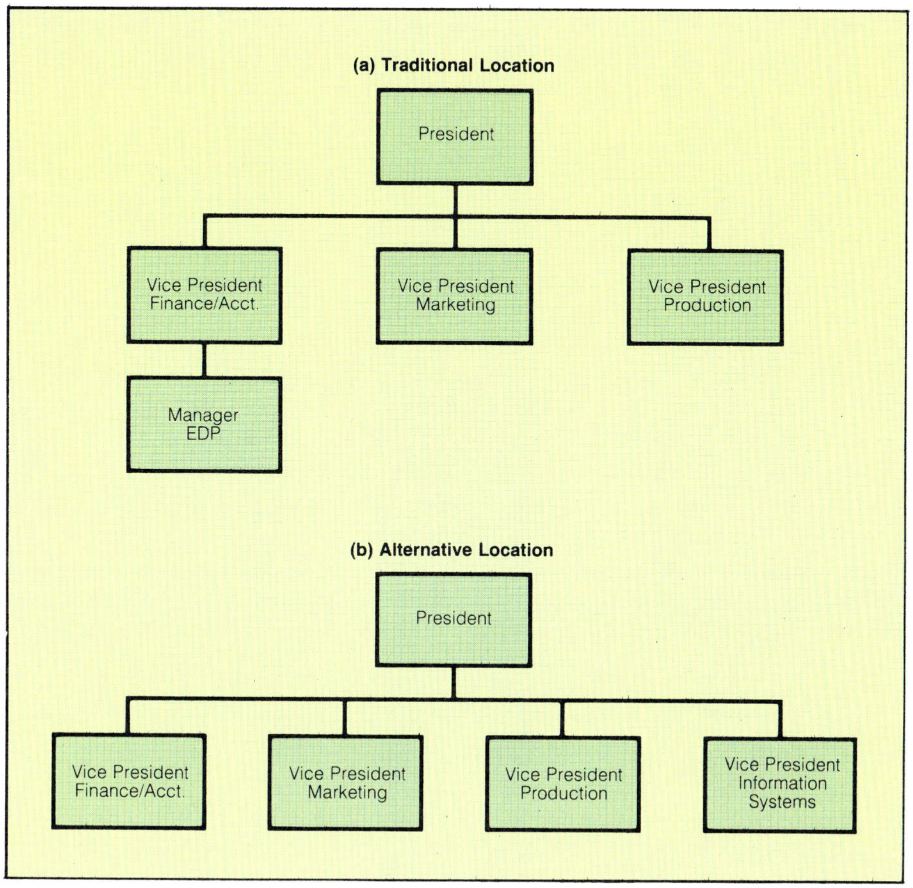

FIGURE A–1
Possible Locations for EDP Department in Organizational Structure

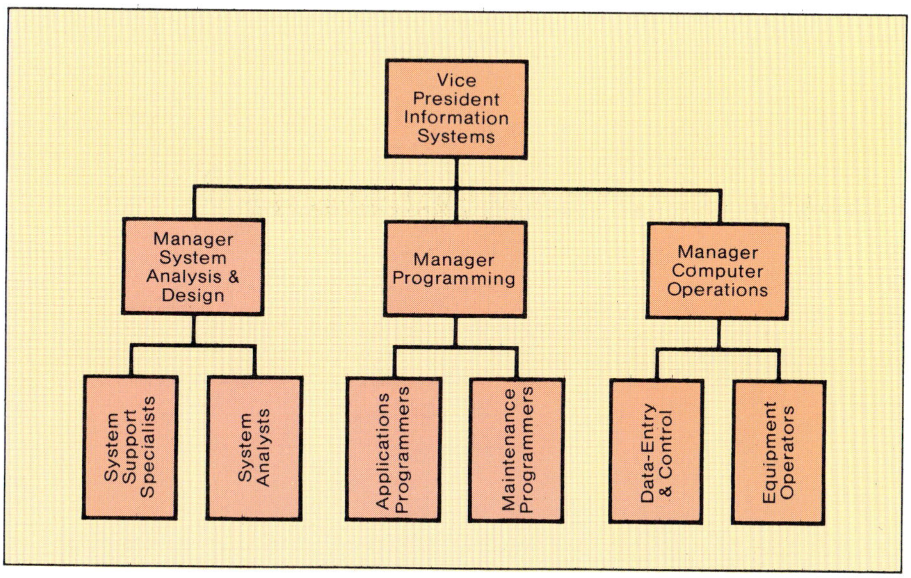

FIGURE A–2
Functional Organization of MIS Department

An alternative structure emphasizes project assignments. Analysts and programmers work on specific projects in teams that include personnel from user departments. As projects are completed, teams are restructured and team members are assigned to new projects. Such an approach is illustrated in Figure A–3.

Managing System Development

System analysis, design, and implementation were discussed in detail in Chapter 9. It is the responsibility of the MIS (data-processing) manager to monitor the total system development cycle to ensure that projects are completed within reasonable time schedules. Various formal network techniques like *PERT* (Program Evaluation and Review Technique) and *CPM* (Critical Path Method) are available for project planning and control. To use such techniques, the manager must break the project into distinct activities, determine the sequence in which the activities are to be performed, and establish a time estimate for each activity. Then, a scheduling chart can be designed. The responsible manager monitors the progress of the project by comparing estimated completion times with actual times. If delays occur, the reasons behind them must be identified and corrective actions taken.

Managing Computer Operations

Most modern computer systems cost millions of dollars; thus, there is increasing concern that the systems' CPUs and peripheral devices be used efficiently. Management can collect data and analyze it to determine the degree of utilization of the hardware and encourage higher efficiency and increased throughput by proper job scheduling and balancing of hardware capabilities.

FIGURE A–3
Project Organization of MIS Department

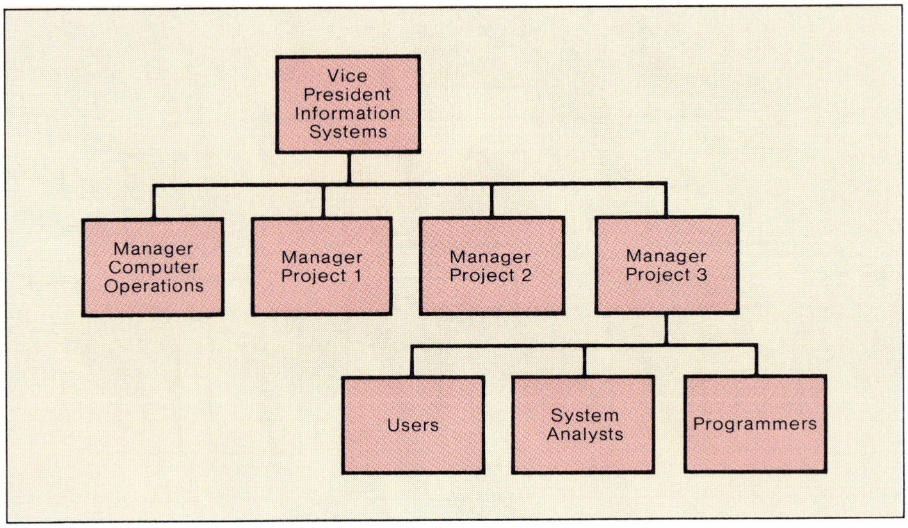

In addition to improving hardware utilization, the data-processing manager must strive for a high degree of maintainability and reliability; preventive maintenance schemes must be developed for both hardware and software. Better systems can be achieved through use of the following practices:

- Establishing standard procedures to control actions that initiate and implement change.
- Using a modular approach for both hardware and software so that systems can be expanded; a complete switch to new equipment and new programs is a costly undertaking and should be avoided if possible.
- Strictly adhering to documentation standards. Software maintenance is impossible without extensive documentation to clarify how specific programs work.
- Implementing standard control and audit procedures to ascertain that the administrative policies and procedures established by management are followed.
- Planning for all contingencies so that data-processing interruptions are not catastrophic.

Managing an MIS is a difficult but important task. Managers must keep in mind that an MIS is an integrated set of people and machines. No matter how sophisticated the MIS, success in using it can be achieved only through its acceptance by users at all levels of the organization.

PROFESSIONAL ASSOCIATIONS

Professional societies have been formed to increase communication among professional people in computer fields, to continue the professional education of members, and to distribute current knowledge through publications of professional journals.

AFIPS

The American Federation of Information Processing Societies (AFIPS), organized in 1961, is a national federation of professional societies established to represent member societies on an international basis and to advance and disseminate knowledge of these societies. There are two categories of AFIPS participation: (1) member societies that have a principal interest in computers and information processing and (2) affiliated societies that, although not primarily concerned with computers and information processing, have a major interest in this area. Some of the prominent constituent societies of AFIPS are the Association for Computing Machinery (ACM), the Data Processing Management Association (DPMA), the Institute of Electrical and Electronic Engineers (IEEE), and the American Society for Information Science (ASIS). Affiliated societies of AFIPS include the American Institute of Certified Public Accountants (AICPA) and the American Statistical Association (ASA).

ACM

The Association for Computing Machinery (ACM) is the largest scientific, educational, and technical society of the computing community. Founded in 1947, this association is dedicated to the development of information processing as a discipline and to the responsible use of computers in increasingly complex and diverse applications. The objectives of the association are:

- To advance the science and art of information processing, including the study, design, development, construction, and application of modern machinery, computing techniques, and programming software.
- To promote the free exchange of ideas in the field of information processing in a professional manner between specialists and the public.
- To develop and maintain the integrity and competence of individuals engaged in the field of information processing

The ACM has established special interest groups (known as SIGs) to address the wide range of interests in the computing field. For example, SIGSMALL was established for ACM members interested in small computers; SIGPLAN, for those interested in programming languages; and SIGCSE, for those interested in computer science education.

DPMA

Founded in Chicago as the National Machine Accountants Association, the Data Processing Management Association (DPMA) was chartered in December 1951. At that time the first electronic computer had yet to come into commercial use. The name "machine accountants" was chosen to identify persons associated with the operation and supervision of punched-card equipment. The society took its present name in 1962.

DPMA is one of the largest world-wide organizations serving the information-processing and management communities. It comprises all levels of management personnel. Through its educational and publishing activities, DPMA seeks to encourage high standards in the field of data processing and to promote a professional attitude among its members.

One of DPMA's specific purposes is to promote and develop educational and scientific inquiry in the field of data processing and data-processing management. As such, it sponsors college student organizations interested in data processing and encourages members to serve as counselors for the Scout computer merit badge. The organization also presents the "Computer Sciences Man of the Year" award for outstanding contributions to the profession.

ASM

The Association for Systems Management (ASM), founded in 1947, is headquartered in Cleveland, Ohio. The ASM is an international organization en-

A scientist uses a handheld calculator to control and interpret tests performed by a new battery-operated instrument. Communication among the devices is via a new, two-wire cable called the Hewlett-Packard Interface Loop.

gaged in keeping its members abreast of the rapid growth and change occurring in the field of systems management and information processing. It provides for the professional growth and development of its members and of the systems profession through:

- Extended programs in local and regional areas in the fields of education and research.
- Annual conferences and committee functions in research, education, and public relations.
- Promotion of high standards of work performance by members of the ASM and members of the systems profession.
- Publication of the *Journal of Systems Management,* technical reports, and other works on subjects of current interest to systems practitioners.

The ASM has five technical departments: Data Communications, Data Processing, Management Information Systems, Organization Planning, and

Written Communications. An ASM member can belong to one or more of these departments.

ICCP

The Institute for Certification of Computer Professionals (ICCP) is a non-profit organization established in 1973 for the purpose of testing and certifying knowledge and skills of computing personnel. A primary objective of the ICCP is to pool the resources of constituent societies so that the full attention of the information-processing industry can be focused on the vital tasks of development and recognition of qualified personnel.

The establishment of the ICCP was an outgrowth of studies made by committees of the DPMA and the ASM, which developed the concept of a "computer foundation" to foster testing and certification programs. In 1974, the ICCP acquired the testing and certification programs of DPMA, including the *Certificate in Data Processing (CDP)* examination, which DPMA had begun in 1962. All candidates for the CDP examination must have at least five years of work experience in a computer-based information system environment. The examination consists of five sections: data-processing equipment, computer programming and software, principles of management, quantitative methods, and system analysis and design. Any qualified person may take the examination; he or she must successfully complete all five sections to receive the certificate. Another certification, the *Certificate in Computer Programming (CCP),* recognizes experience and professional competence at the senior programmer level. Candidates for this certification must also pass a basic five-part examination.

The ICCP is involved in improving existing programs and establishing new examinations for various specialties. A framework for a broad spectrum of tests and the relationship of these tests to job functions and curricula is under development.

SMIS

The Society for Management Information Systems (SMIS) was founded in 1968 to serve persons concerned with all aspects of management information systems in the electronic data-processing industry, including business system designers, managers, and educators. The organization aims to be an exchange or marketplace for technical information about management information systems and to enhance communications between MIS directors and executives responsible for the management of the business enterprise. SMIS also offers educational and research programs, sponsors competitions, bestows awards, and maintains placement programs.

APPENDIX B

Common Program Logic Flowcharts

There are several common program logic problems that are encountered in business applications. Six basic problems are described in this appendix. Each of these utilizes one or more of the four basic logic patterns discussed in Chapter 3. To understand the problems better, an example is provided for each including a flowchart and pseudocode.

INPUT/OUTPUT USING COUNTERS

When processing several input records, one method for detecting the end of the file is a counter. Each time an additional record is processed, the counter is incremented. When the counter equals the number of records in the file, execution stops. To effectively utilize a counter, the program can provide for input of the number of records to be processed. This allows the number of records to change each time the program is executed. To ensure that the counter reflects the proper number of executions, the counter should be initialized to zero prior to the first execution. This replaces any previously stored value.

The processing of customer statements is one example when the number of records may change. The number of current customers is input at the start of execution. Customer data will be read and statements will be printed the specified number of times. Figure B–1 illustrates the basic logic for this process.

MULTIPLE DECISIONS

Managers make decisions daily. Often, these decisions are based on several criteria. Just as often, these multiple criteria or decisions are answered through a computer program. Various answers are generated depending on how many of the required criteria are met.

As an example, a used car dealer who operates several lots may wish to provide fast responses to customer inquiries concerning cars in stock. A master inventory listing is maintained for the cars on all lots. Inquiries can be made via a CRT for the required make, model, and year. The customer will obtain almost instantaneous results concerning the in-stock status and location of the car. This logic is shown in Figure B–2.

ACCUMULATING SUBTOTALS AND TOTALS

Various subtotals and totals are needed in decision making. These are indicators of business activity. The subtotals may be categorized by department, item, account classification, or otherwise. The subtotals and totals are accumulated as records are read or as values are calculated.

Figure B–3 illustrates the logic for subtotaling various types of checking accounts in a bank's files. These may include minimum balance accounts,

FIGURE B–1
Input/Output Using Counters

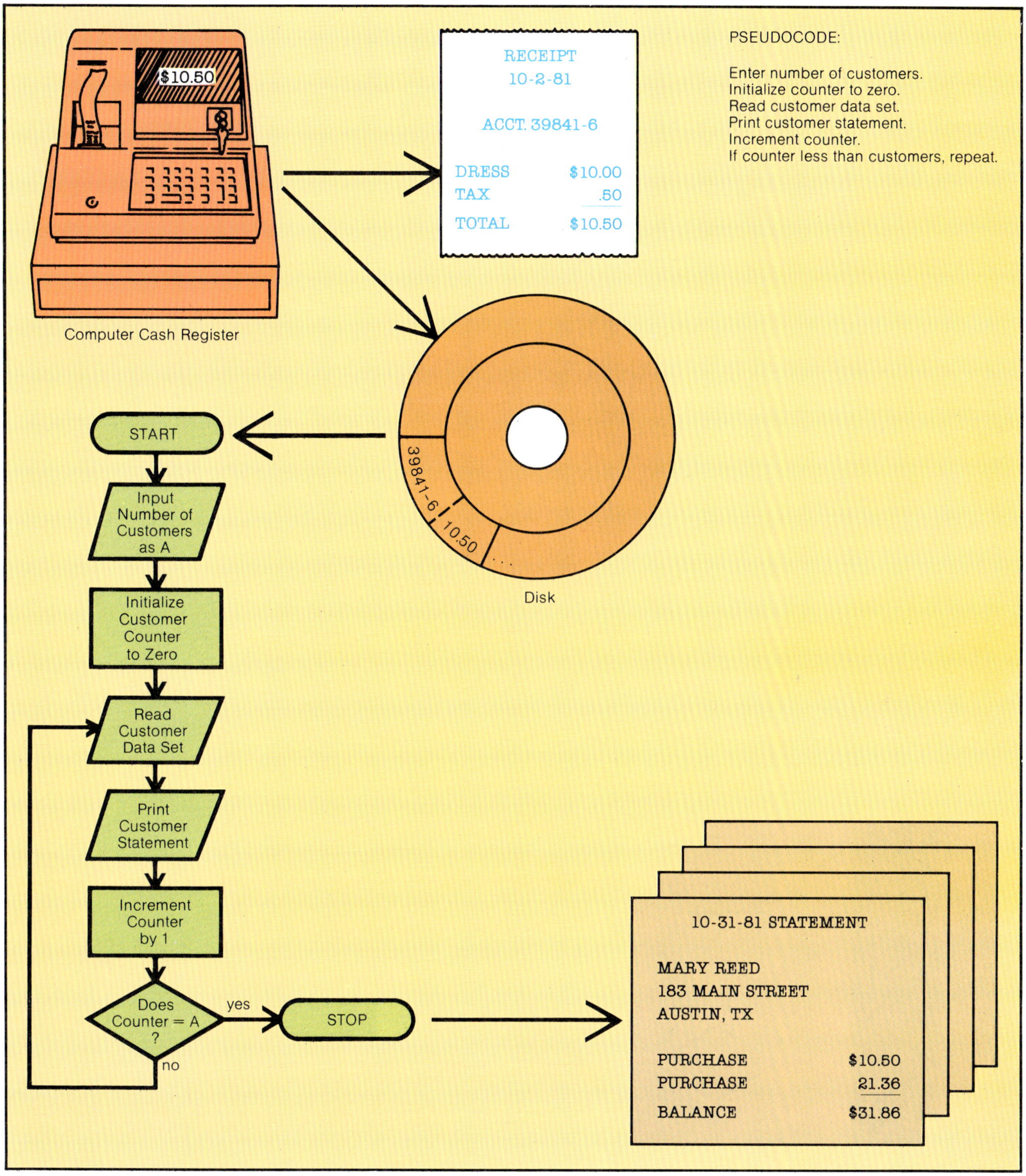

FIGURE B–2
Multiple Decisions

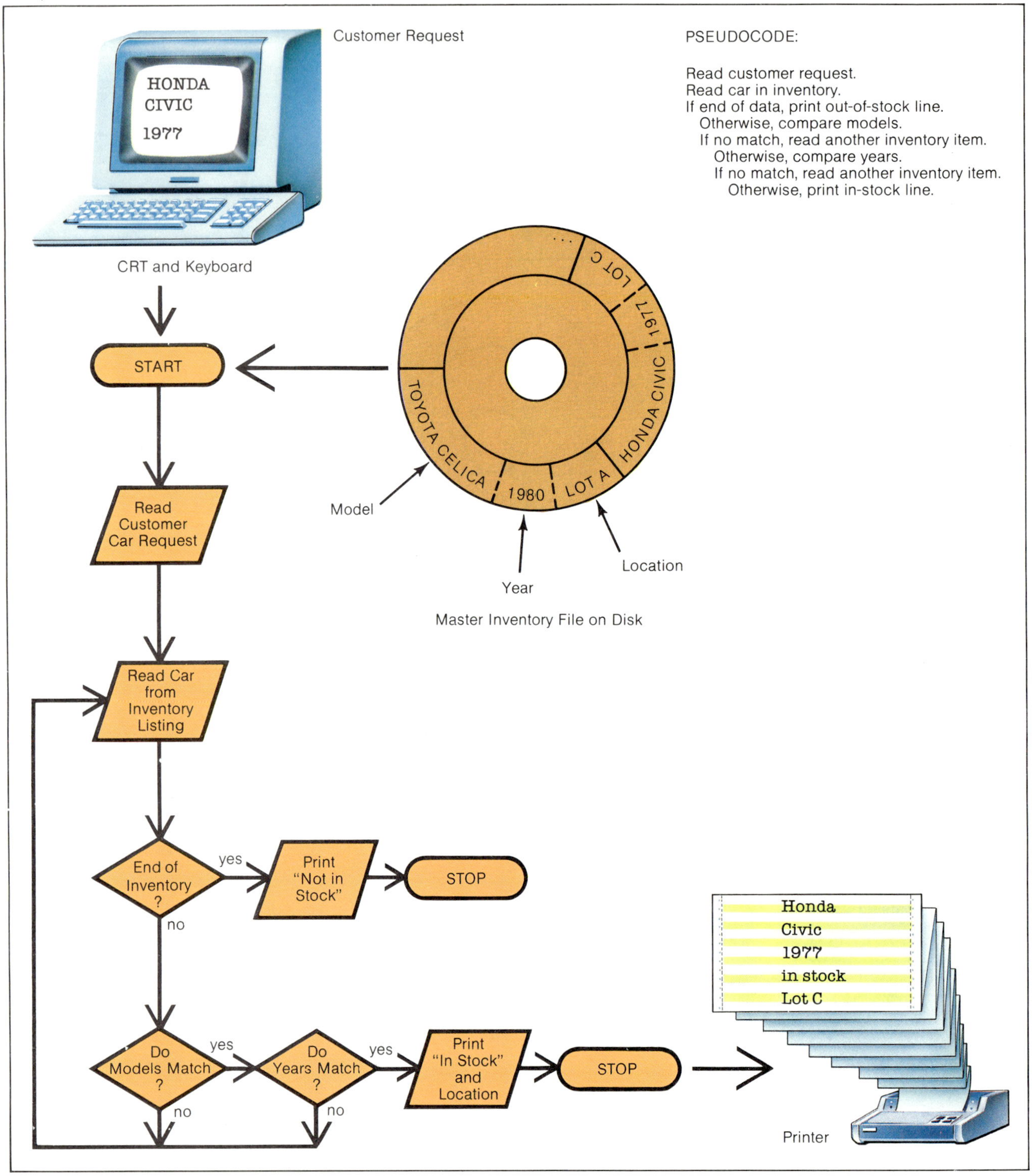

PSEUDOCODE:

```
Read customer request.
Read car in inventory.
If end of data, print out-of-stock line.
  Otherwise, compare models.
  If no match, read another inventory item.
    Otherwise, compare years.
    If no match, read another inventory item.
      Otherwise, print in-stock line.
```

FIGURE B–3
Accumulating Subtotals and Totals

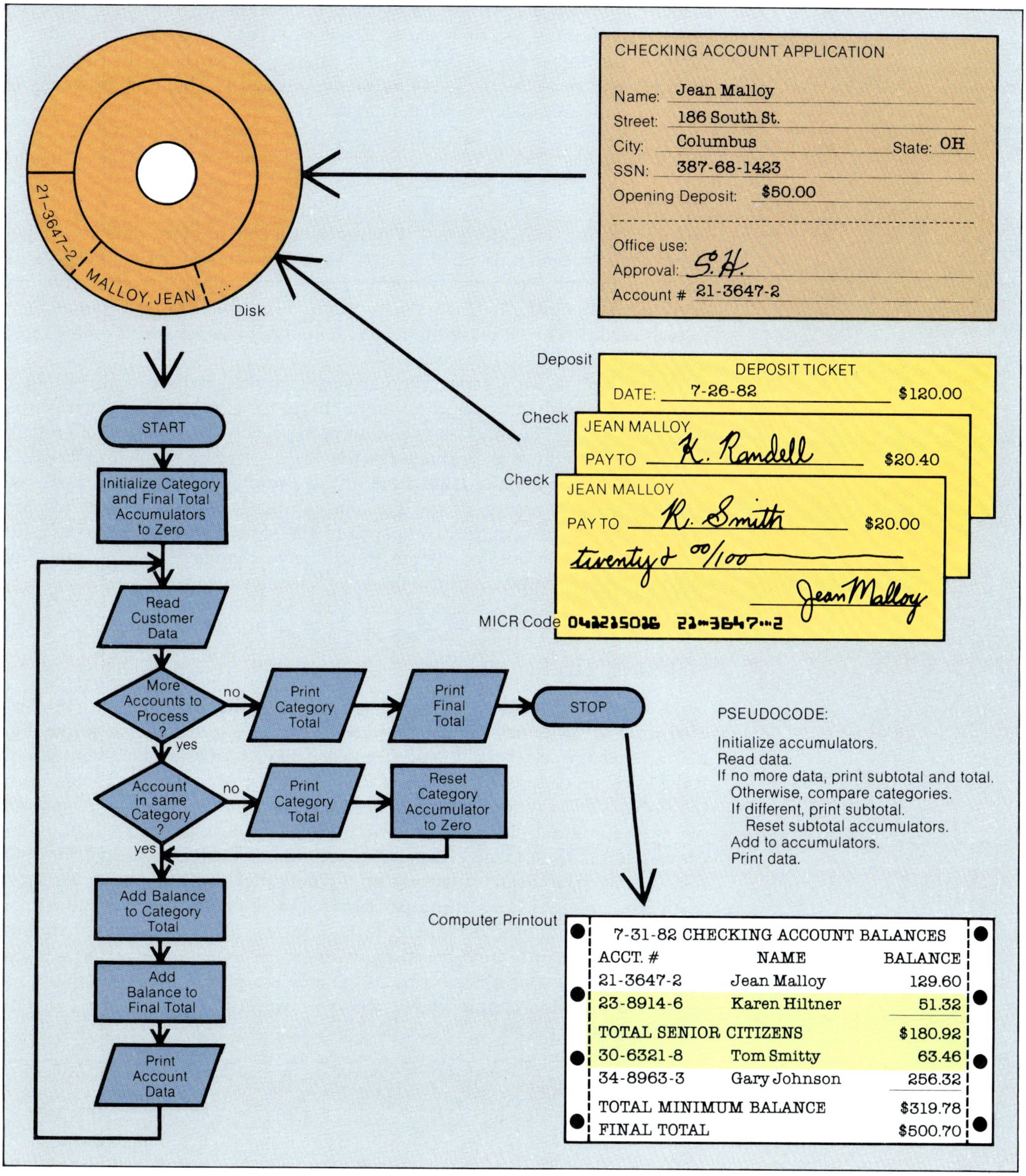

senior citizen accounts, corporate accounts plus others. Each type of account is identified with a different leading digit. Checking accounts are typically ordered by number. As each account balance is read, it is added to both the subtotal and total. When the end of a category is reached, the subtotal is recorded and reset to zero to begin the next category. The total, however, is retained until all categories are completed.

TABLES

In some business applications, it is more efficient to store data in a table rather than on each individual record. A code written on the record permits access to the table as needed during processing. When the stored values need to be changed, the changes are made directly to the table rather than to each record. The code on the record remains the same and the new table value is accessed with that code.

For example, a wholesaler in Indiana may service retailers in all 50 states. A table is utilized that lists the freight charges for shipping to each of the states. These are identified on each shipping record by the two-letter state abbreviations. Figure B–4 illustrates the logic for generating freight statements using this table. At the start of the program, all the data from the table is read into arrays so that the data is read only once. The state code from the shipping record is compared to the state codes in the array until the correct code is located. If the freight rates change at a later date, the table is changed rather than the numerous retailer records.

MERGING FILES

Some applications may routinely or periodically require the merging of files. This process combines two or more files into one larger file. If sequential files are used, one record is read from each file and the keys are compared. If the keys are ordered from lowest to highest, for example, the record with the lowest key is written to the new file. An additional record is read from one of the original files to replace the record that was transferred. Another comparison is then made. This process continues until all records from the original files have been transferred to the new file.

An automobile insurance company may merge a new customer file with a master file as often as daily. Figure B–5 shows the logic for this process assuming the records are ordered sequentially by policy number. Depending on the circumstances, a hard copy of the new master file may or may not be generated. In this example, a new file is in computer readable form for future processing.

FIGURE 8–4
Tables

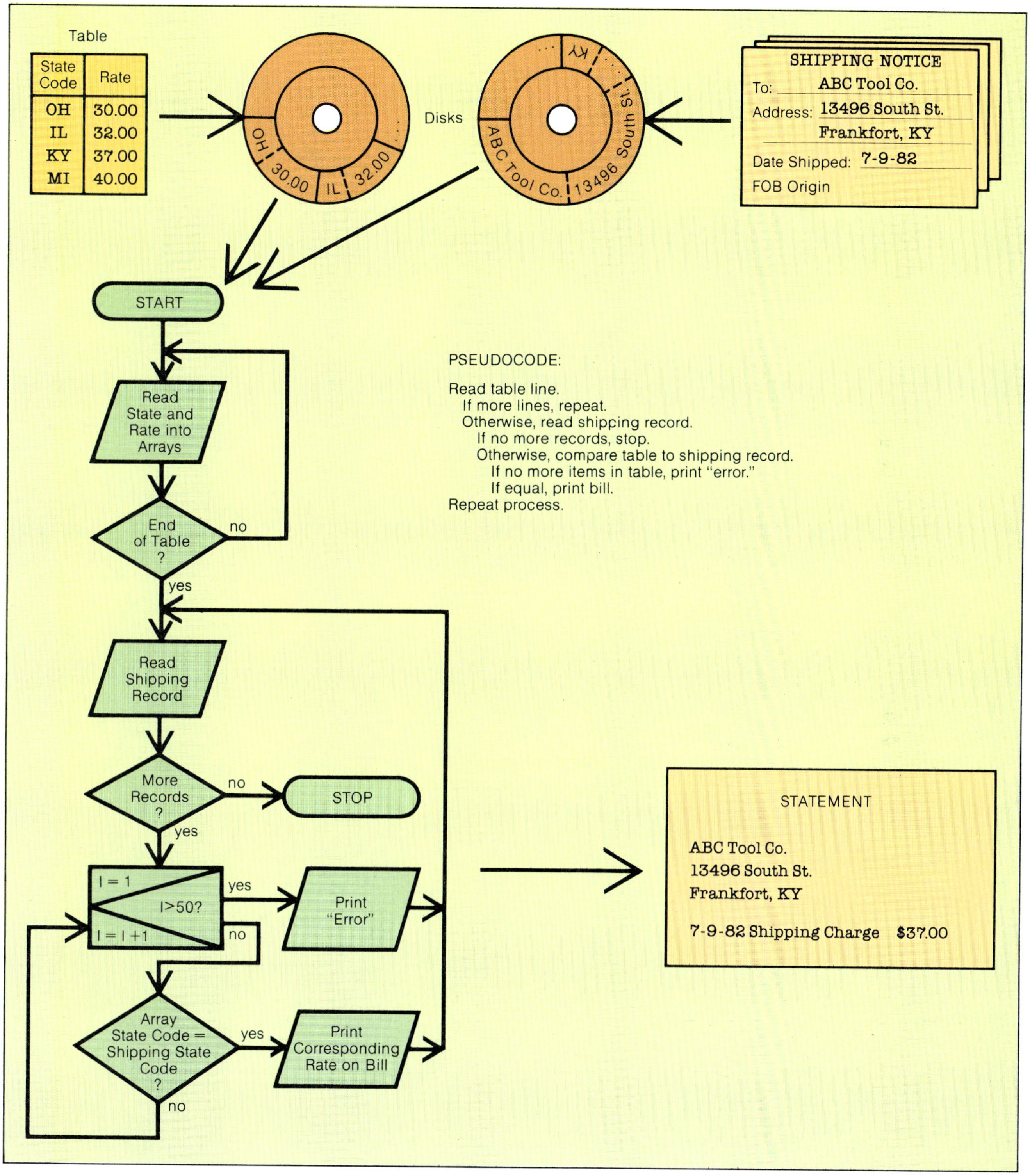

FIGURE B–5
Merging Files

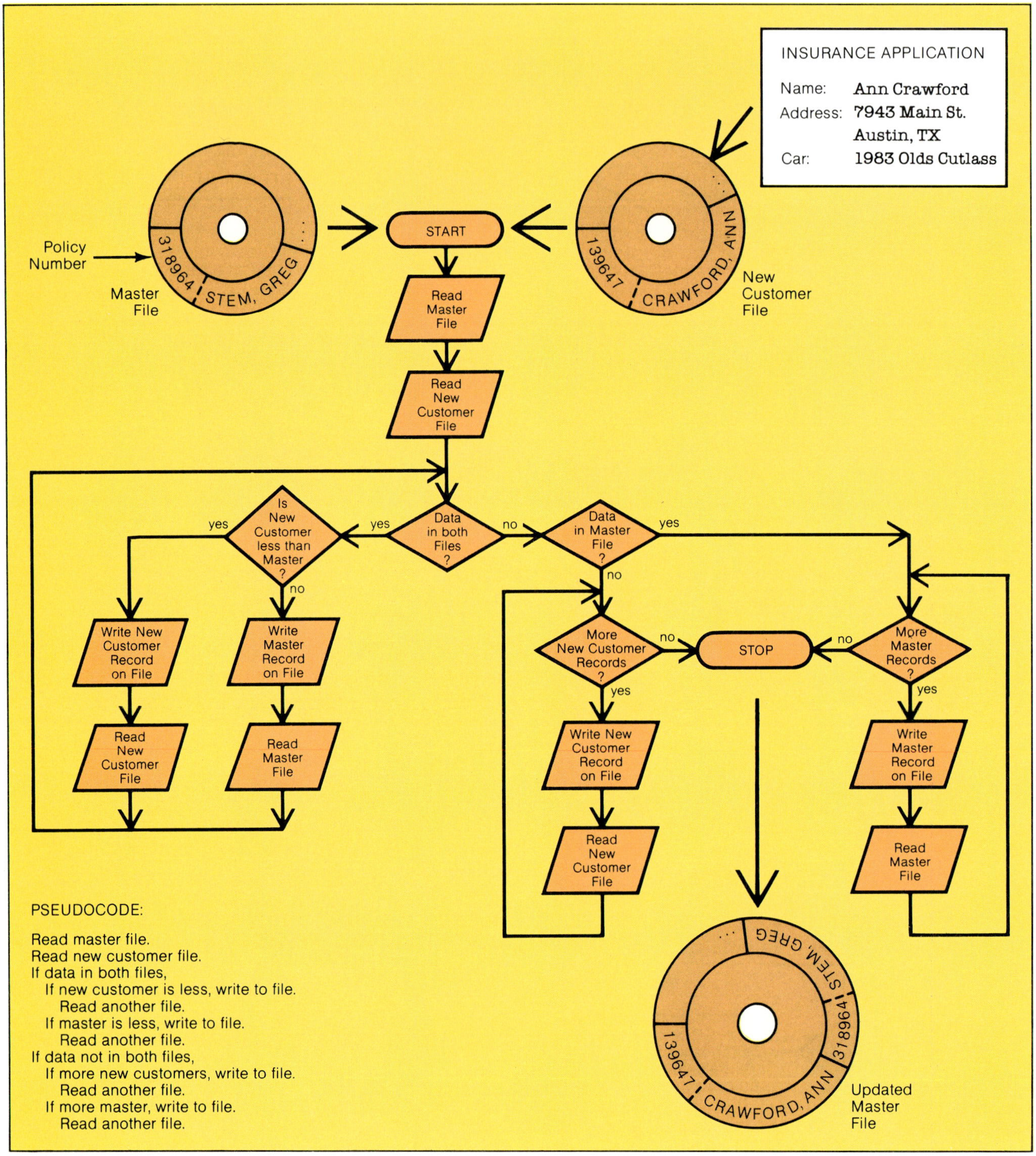

PSEUDOCODE:

Read master file.
Read new customer file.
If data in both files,
  If new customer is less, write to file.
    Read another file.
  If master is less, write to file.
    Read another file.
If data not in both files,
  If more new customers, write to file.
    Read another file.
  If more master, write to file.
    Read another file.

SORTING

In many business applications, it is necessary to sort, or order, data sets alphabetically or numerically. This can occur when data is collected or stored in an order different from that required for sequential file processing or printing reports. Arrays are utilized to sort the data with comparisons made between the array locations to determine which items need to be switched within a given list. This is referred to as a bubble sort.

Figure B–6 illustrates the logic for sorting ten new employees by ascending employee number so that the new employee file may be merged with the master employee file. The new employee data was originally input as the applications were submitted and, therefore, is not in order.

There are several points to note when sorting. First, a flag is used to indicate whether any positions within the array are switched as the loop is executed. If the flag equals one, at least one switch was made. The loop is repeatedly executed until the flag remains zero throughout the execution, indicating the data is in order. Second, the loop terminal value is one less than the number of positions in the array. This prevents an error message when I equals the terminal value and the I position is compared to the I+1 position. Finally, when ordering a set of data that includes more than one field, such as name and number, each field must be switched. Otherwise, the numbers would be in order but they would not correspond to the correct name.

FIGURE B–6
Sorting

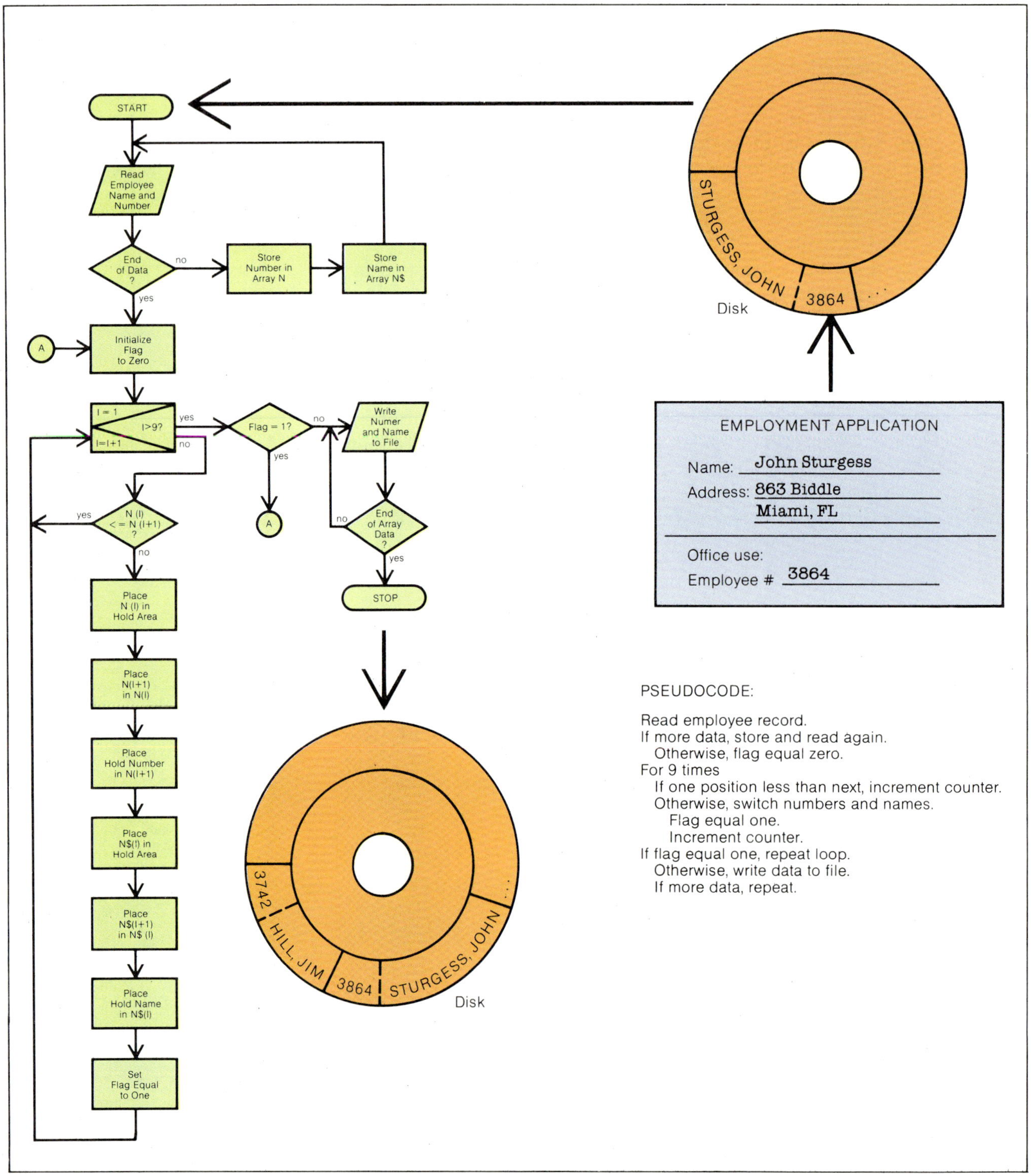

GLOSSARY

A

Access mechanism The physical device that positions the read/write head of a direct-access storage device over a particular track.

Accounting machines Forerunner of the computer; could mechanically read data from punched cards, perform calculations, rearrange data, and print results in varied formats.

Accumulator A register that accumulates results of computations.

Activity The proportion of records processed during an updating run.

Address register A register that holds the address of a location containing a data item called for by an instruction.

American Standard Code for Information Interchange (ASCII) A seven-bit standard code used for information interchange among data-processing systems, communication systems, and associated equipment.

Analog computer A computer that measures continuous electrical or physical magnitudes rather than operating on digits; contrast with digital computer.

Analog transmission Transmission of data over communication channels in a continuous wave form.

APL *A Programming Language*; a terminal-oriented, symbolic programming language especially suitable for interactive problem-solving.

Application program A sequence of instructions written to solve a specific problem.

Arithmetic/logic unit (ALU) The section of the CPU that handles arithmetic computations and logical operations.

Artificial intelligence A field of inquiry, developing techniques whereby computers can be used to solve problems that appear to require imagination, intuition, or intelligence.

Assembler program The translator program for an assembly language; produces a machine-language program.

Assembly language A symbolic programming language that uses convenient abbreviations rather than groupings of 0s and 1s; intermediate-level language in terms of user orientation.

Audio input See Voice recognition system.

Audio output See Voice response unit.

Automated office The combination of office electronics and data processing.

Automatic data processing (ADP) The collection, manipulation, and dissemination of data by electromechanical machines to attain specified objectives.

Automation Machine-directed processes.

Auxiliary storage Also known as external storage or secondary storage; supplements primary storage but operates at slower speeds.

B

Bandwidth The range, or width, of the frequencies available for transmission on a given channel.

Bar-code reader A device used to read a bar code by means of reflected light, such as a scanner that reads the Universal Product Code on supermarket products.

BASIC *B*eginners' *A*ll-Purpose *S*ymbolic *I*nstruction *C*ode; a programming language commonly used for interactive problem solving by users who may not be professional programmers.

Batch (stacked) job The grouping of several user programs (jobs or job steps) into a batch and processed one after the other in a continuous stream.

Batch oriented Refers to programming languages that are used to solve problems for which immediate responses are not required.

Batch/sequential processing A method of processing data in which data items are collected and forwarded to the computer in a group; normally uses punched cards or magnetic tape for generating periodic output, e.g., payroll.

Binary digit The smallest unit of information that can be represented by binary notation.

Binary number system The numeric system, used in computer operations, that uses the digits 0 and 1 and has a base of 2.

Binary representation The use of the binary system to represent data.

Binary system A form of data representation in the computer in which two possible states exist in the machine's circuitry—"on" and "off."

Bit (short for *Bi*nary digi*t*) See Binary digit.

Bit cells Locations where data is stored in semiconductors.

Block diagram See Flowchart.

Blocked records (blocks) Records grouped on magnetic tape or magnetic disk to reduce the number of interrecord gaps and more fully utilize the storage medium.

Branch A statement used to bypass or alter the normal flow of execution.

Broad-band channels Communication channels that can transmit data at rates of up to 120,000 bits per second; e.g., laser beams and microwaves.

Bubble memory A recently developed memory device in which data is represented by magnetized spots (or bubbles) that rest on a thin film of semiconductor material.

Bundled When the price of the computer sold by the vendor includes training, maintenance costs, software and other computer products and services.

Business applications Tasks that traditionally require simple calculations such as addition and subtraction (for accounting records).

Byte Some number of bits; a unit of storage.

C

CAD/CAM (computer-assisted design/computer-assisted manufacturing) Processes where engineers or technicians input certain requirements into the computer for a product or design and receive a computer-generated picture of the product. From here, computerized tasks use those calculations to manufacture the finished product.

Calculations Data that has been arithmetically or logically manipulated.

Cathode-ray tube (CRT) A visual display device that receives electrical impulses and translates them into a picture on a television-like screen.

Central processing unit (CPU) The heart of the computer; composed of three sections—primary storage unit, arithmetic/logic unit (ALU), and control unit.

Centralized design An information structure in which a separate data-processing department is utilized to provide data-processing facilities for the organization.

Chain printer An output device that has the character set engraved in type and assembled in a chain that revolves horizontally past all print positions; prints when a print hammer (one for each column on the paper) presses against an inked ribbon that presses against the characters on the print chain.

Check bit See Parity bit.

Classify To categorize data according to certain characteristics so that it is meaningful to the user.

COBOL *CO*mmon *B*usiness-*O*riented *L*anguage; a high-level programming language generally used for accounting and business data processing.

Coding The process of expressing a problem solution in a programming language; a set of rules for data conversion and representation.

Collection The process of gathering data from various sources and assembling it at one location.

Communication The process of transferring information in intelligible form to a user.

Communication channel A medium for carrying data from one location to another.

Compiler program The translator program for a high-level language, such as FORTRAN or COBOL; translates source-program statements into machine-executable code.

Computer A general-purpose machine with applications limited only by the creativity of the humans who use it; its power is derived from its speed, accuracy, and memory.

Computer output microfilm (COM) Miniature photographic images of output. Computer output is placed on magnetic tape which serves as the input to a microfilm processor.

Computer store Retail store that sells computers and is structured to appeal to the small business person or personal user.

Computer-assisted instruction (CAI) Direct interaction between a computer and a student in which the computer serves as an instructor.

Concentrator A device that systematically allocates communication channels among several terminals.

Concurrently Over the same period of time; in multiprogramming, processing of operations rotates between different programs, giving the illusion of simultaneous processing.

Control program A routine, usually part of an operating system, that aids in controlling the operations and management of a computer system.

Control unit (of CPU) The section of the CPU that directs the sequence of operations by electrical signals and governs the actions of the various units that make up the computer.

Conversion The process of switching from an old to a new information system.

Converting The process of translating information stored in a computer into a humanly readable form.

Crash (Direct) conversion A method of system implementation in which the old information system is abandoned and the new one implemented at once.

D

Daisy-wheel printer An output device resembling an office typewriter; it employs a flat disk with petal-like projections with characters on the surfaces; printing occurs one character at a time.

Data Facts; the raw material of information.

Data administration department The area of a firm assigned the responsibility for maintaining the data base.

Data analyst A person who analyzes the relationships of data in the data base.

Data base The cornerstone of a management information system; basic data is commonly defined and consistently organized to fit the information needs of a wide variety of users within an organization.

Data-base management system (DBMS) A set of programs that serves as an interface between the data base and three principal users—the programmer, the operating system, and the manager (or other information user); provides a method of arranging data to limit duplication, an ability to make changes easily, and a capability to handle direct inquiries.

Data communication The electronic transmission of data from one site to another, usually over communication channels such as telephone/telegraph lines or microwaves.

Data processing A systematic set of techniques for collecting, manipulating, and disseminating data to achieve specified objectives.

Data set A grouping of related records; also called a file.

Debugging Checking and correcting errors found in the program.

Decentralized design. An information structure in which the authority and responsibility for computer support are placed in relatively autonomous organizational operating units.

Decimal number system A number system based on powers of 10.

Definition mode When APL is used in this mode, a series of instructions is entered into memory, and the entire program is executed on command from the programmer.

Demand reports Reports produced only upon request.

Demodulation The process of retrieving data from a modulated carrier wave; the conversion of data back to digital (''on''/''off'') form from analog (wave) form after it has been transmitted.

Desk-checking A method used in both system and program debugging in which the sequence of operations is mentally traced to verify the correctness of the processing logic.

Desk-debugging See Desk-checking.

Difference engine A machine developed by Charles Babbage in 1822; used to compute mathematical tables with results up to five significant digits in length.

Digital computer The type of computer commonly used in business applications; operates on distinct data (e.g., digits) by performing arithmetic and logic processes on specific data units.

Digital transmission The transmission of data as distinct "on"/"off" pulses.

Direct-access storage A method of storing data whereby it can be retrieved in any order, at random.

Direct-access storage devices (DASDs) Auxiliary storage devices that allow data to be stored and accessed either randomly or sequentially.

Directory Consists of two columns, the first containing the key of the record and the second containing the address of the record with that key.

Disk drive The mechanical device used to rotate a disk pack during data transmission; common speeds range between 40 and 3,600 revolutions per second.

Disk pack A stack of magnetic disks.

Distributed data processing system A system in which several CPUs are linked together by communication channels to form a network. This allows faster response to inquiries and provides the power to perform complex calculations.

Distributed design An information structure that identifies the existence of independent operating units but recognizes the benefits of central coordination and control.

Documentation Written descriptions of a system; include flowcharts, major processing flows, input/output forms, file designs, and a narrative.

Dot-matrix printer Also wire-matrix printer; a type of impact printer that creates characters through the use of dot-matrix patterns.

Downtime The time the system is not working because of equipment problems.

Drum printer An output device consisting of a metal cylinder that contains rows of characters engraved across its surface; one line of print is produced with each rotation of the drum.

Dumb terminal A terminal that cannot be programmed.

Dump Hard-copy printout of the contents of computer memory; valuable in debugging programs.

E

EDSAC *E*lectronic *D*elay *S*torage *A*utomatic *C*omputer; the first "stored-program computer."

EDVAC *E*lectronic *D*iscrete *V*ariable *A*utomatic *C*omputer; performed arithmetic and logic operations without human intervention.

Electronic data processing (EDP) Data processing performed largely by electronic equipment such as computers rather than by manual or mechanical methods.

Electronic funds transfer (EFT) A cashless method of paying for services or goods; the accounts of the two parties involved in the transaction are adjusted by electronic communication between computers.

Electronic mail The transmission of messages at high speeds over telecommunication facilities.

Electrostatic printer A nonimpact printer that forms an image of a character on special paper using a dot matrix of charged wires or pins. When the paper is moved through a solution containing ink particles of an opposite charge from the pattern, the particles adhere to each charged pattern on the paper.

Electrothermal printer A nonimpact printer that uses heat in the print element to create characters on heat-sensitive paper.

ENIAC *E*lectronic *N*umerical *I*ntegrator *A*nd *C*alculator; the first "electronic digital calculator."

Erasable programmable read-only memory (EPROM) This memory unit can be erased and reprogrammed but only by being submitted to a special process.

Exception reports Action-oriented management reports which report abnormal situations that require special handling.

Execution mode When APL is used in this mode, the terminal can be used much like a desk calculator.

Executive See Supervisor program.

Extended Binary Coded Decimal Interchange Code (EBCDIC) An 8-bit code for character representation.

Facsimile system Produces a picture of a page by scanning it.

Feedback Information used to evaluate the performance of a processing system; a concept in system theory, a check on the system to see whether or not predetermined standards are being met.

Field A meaningful item of data, such as social security number.

File A grouping of related records; sometimes referred to as a data set.

First-generation computers Used vacuum tubes; developed in the 1950s; much faster than earlier mechanical devices, but very slow in comparison to today's computer.

Fixed scanner A device used to scan and read source data in bar code form or in human readable characters.

Flexibility The degree to which a computer system can be adapted or tailored to the changing requirements of the user.

Flexible disk Also called a flexible diskette or floppy disk; a low-cost, random-access form of data storage made of plastic and having a storage capacity equivalent to that of 3,000 punched cards.

Flowchart A graphic representation of the processing that is performed in a program.

FORTRAN *FOR*mula *TRAN*slator; a programming language used primarily in performing mathematical or scientific operations.

Four-bit-binary coded decimal (BCD) A four binary digit computer code that uses unique combinations of 0s and 1s to represent specific characters.

Front-end processor A small CPU, which provides message-switching, as well as more sophisticated operations such as validating transmitted data and pre-processing data before it is transmitted to the central computer; serves as an interface between a large CPU and peripheral devices.

Full-duplex A type of communication channel capable of the most versatile mode of data transmission; can transmit data in both directions simultaneously.

G

Garbage in-garbage out A phrase used to exemplify the fact that the meaningfulness of data-processing results relies on the accuracy or relevancy of the data fed to the processor.

General-purpose registers Registers that can be used for both arithmetic and addressing functions.

Grade The range, or width, of the frequencies available for transmission on a given channel.

Graphic display device A visual display device that projects output in the form of graphs and line drawings and accepts input from a keyboard or light pen.

H

Half-duplex A type of communication channel through which communication can occur in only one direction at a time, but that direction can change.

Hard copy Printed output.

Hard-wired Memory instructions that cannot be changed or deleted by other stored-program instructions.

Hashing See Randomize.

Heuristics Rules of operation that may or may not work every time; they have to be tested to see if they have value; used to solve complex problems and in situations that do not yield to conventional mathematics.

Hexadecimal number system A base-16 number system commonly used when printing the contents of main memory to aid programmers in detecting errors.

Hierarchical design An information structure in which each level within an organization is provided with necessary computer power; responsibility for control and coordination goes to the top level.

Hierarchical network A design approach used to implement the multiple CPU concept in which an organization's needs are divided into multiple levels that receive different levels of support.

High-level languages English-like coding schemes that are procedure-, problem-, and user-oriented.

Hollerith code A method of data representation named for the man who invented it; represents numbers, letters, and special characters by the placement of holes in 80-column punched cards.

I

Impact printer A printer that forms characters by physically striking a ribbon against paper.

Indexed-sequential A file organization technique in which records are placed on a file in sequence and a multiple-level index is maintained, thus allowing both sequential and direct-access processing.

Industrial robots Industrial machines that are controlled by computers, usually to do simple, repetitive tasks.

Information Data that has been organized and processed so that it is meaningful.

Information Revolution The name given to the present era because of the impact of computer technology on society; also called the Computer Revolution.

Information system A system designed to process input data for output as information. Feedback is provided by the information users, as to the quality and how adequate the information is.

Ink-jet printer A nonimpact printer that uses a stream of charged ink to form dot-matrix characters.

Input Data that is submitted to the computer for processing.

Input/output management system A subsystem of the operating system that controls and coordinates the CPU while receiving input from channels, executing instructions of programs in storage, and regulating output.

Instruction register A register where each instruction is decoded by the control unit.

Integrated circuit Electronic circuits etched on a small silicon chip less than ⅛-inch square; permits much faster processing than with transistors and at a greatly reduced price.

Intelligent terminal A terminal with an internal processor that can be programmed to perform specified functions, such as data editing, data conversion, and control of other terminals.

Interactive languages Computer languages that allow the programmer or program user to communicate directly with the computer in a conversational fashion.

Interblock gap A space on magnetic tape that facilitates processing; records are grouped and separated by interblock gaps.

Internal storage See Primary storage.

Interpreter A device used by small computer systems to evaluate and translate program statements as the program is executed, one instruction at a time.

Interrecord gap A space that separates records stored on magnetic tape; allows the tape drive to regain speed during processing.

Interrupt A control signal from a sensor-band input or output unit that requests the attention of the control unit of the CPU from the current operation.

J

Job A unit of work to be processed by the CPU.

Job-control language (JCL) A language that serves as the communication link between the programmer and the operating system.

Job-control program A control program that translates the job-control statements written by a programmer into machine-language instructions that can be executed by the computer.

K

K A symbol used to represent 1024 storage units (1024 bytes) when referring to a computer's main memory.

Key A unique indentifier for a record; used to sort records for processing or to locate a particular record within a file.

Keypunch A keyboard device that punches holes in a card to represent data.

Key-to-disk Hardware designed to transfer data entered via a keyboard to magnetic disk or diskette.

Key-to-diskette A floppy disk is used instead of the conventional (hard) disk.

Key-to-tape Hardware designed to transfer data entered via a keyboard to magnetic tape.

L

Language-translator program The sequence of instructions (software) that translate the English-like programs written by programmers into machine-executable code.

Large-scale integrated (LSI) circuits Circuits containing thousands of transistors densely packed in a single silicon chip.

Laser printer A type of nonimpact printer that combines laser beams and electrophotographic technology to form images on paper.

Librarian program Software that manages the storage and use of library programs by maintaining a directory of programs in the system library and appropriate procedures for additions or deletions.

Library programs User-written or manufacturer-supplied programs and subroutines that are frequently used in other programs; they are written and stored on secondary media and called into main storage when needed.

Light pen A pen-shaped object with a photoelectric cell at its end; used to draw lines on a visual display screen.

Linkage editor A subprogram of the operating system that links the object program from the system residence device to main storage.

Local system Peripherals connected directly to the CPU.

Logic diagram See Flowchart.

Logical design Deals with how data is viewed by application programs or individual users.

Loop A series of instructions in a program that is executed repeatedly as long as specified conditions remain constant.

Lower-level management First-line supervisors and foremen who make the operating decisions to ensure that specific jobs are done.

M

Machine language The only set of instructions that a computer can execute directly; a code that designates the proper electrical states in the computer as combinations of 0s and 1s.

Machine-oriented language Examples are machine language and assembly languages.

Magnetic core An iron-alloy doughnut-shaped ring about the size of a pinhead. This is strung on thin wires through which an electrical current passes thus magnetizing it to represent either an "on" or "off" state.

Magnetic disk A storage medium consisting of a metal platter coated on both sides with a magnetic recording material upon which data is stored in the form of magnetized spots.

Magnetic drum A cylinder with a magnetic outer surface on which data can be stored by magnetizing specific positions of the surface.

Magnetic tape A storage medium consisting of a narrow strip of material upon which spots are magnetized to represent data; a sequential storage medium.

Magnetic-ink character reader A device that reads characters composed of magnetized particles; often used to sort checks for subsequent processing.

Magnetic-ink character recognition (MICR) The process that allows magnetized characters to be read by a magnetic-ink character reader.

Main frame The central processing unit (CPU) of a full-scale computer.

Main storage See Primary storage.

Management information system (MIS) A formal network that extends computer use beyond routine reporting and into the area of management decision-making; its goal is to get the correct information to the appropriate manager at the right time.

Mark I The first automatic calculator.

Master file A file that contains relatively permanent data; updated by records in a transaction file.

Materials requirement planning (MRP) An inventory control system that allows the manufacturer to enter future demands into a computer, and receive a report that lists the scheduling dates and raw materials needed to manipulate the product to meet those demands.

Memory The part of a computer that provides the ability to recall information; storage.

Message-switching A communications processor with the principal task of receiving messages and routing them to appropriate destinations.

Microcomputer A very small computer; often a special-purpose or single-function computer on a single chip.

Microprocessor The CPU of a microcomputer; fits on a small silicon chip.

Microprogram A sequence of instructions wired in read-only memory; used to tailor a system to meet the user's processing requirements.

Microprogramming The process of building a sequence of instructions into read-only memory to carry out functions that would otherwise be directed by stored-program instructions at a much slower speed.

Middle-level management Those managers who make tactical decisions, and implement the strategies determined at the top level.

Minicomputer A computer with the components of a full-size system but having a smaller memory.

Mnenomics A symbolic name (memory aid); used in symbolic languages (e.g., assembly language) and high-level programming languages.

Modem Also called data set; a device that modulates and demodulates signals transmitted over communcation facilities.

Modulation A process used in modems (data sets) to make business-machine signals compatible with communication facilities; the conversion of data from digital ("on"/"off") form to analog (wave) form before transmitting it.

Monitor See Supervisor program.

Multiplexer A device that permits more than one terminal to transmit data over the same communication channel.

Multiprocessing A multiple CPU configuration in which jobs are processed simultaneously.

Multiprogramming A technique whereby several programs are placed in primary storage at the same time, giving the illusion that they are being executed simultaneously; results in increased CPU activity time.

Narrow bandwidth channels Communication channels that can only transmit data at a rate of forty-five to ninety bits per second; e.g., telegraph channels.

Network The linking together of several CPUs.

Next-sequential-instruction feature The ability of a computer to execute program steps in the order in which they are stored in memory unless branching takes place.

Nondestructive read/destructive write The feature of computer memory that permits data to be read and retained in its original state allowing it to be referenced repeatedly during processing.

Nonimpact printer The use of heat, laser technology, or photographic techniques to print output.

Object program A sequence of machine-executable instructions derived from source-program statements by a language-translator program.

Office information system Can include a variety of word processors, data-entry terminals, graphics terminals, information distributors, and printers.

Online In direct communication with the computer.

Operand The part of an instruction that tells where to find the data or equipment to be operated on.

Operating system A collection of programs designed to permit a computer system to manage itself and to avoid idle CPU time while increasing utilization of computer facilities.

Operation code The part of an instruction that tells what operation is to be performed; also op code.

Optical characters Special types of characters that can be read by optical-character readers.

Optical recognition device A device that can read marks or symbols coded on paper documents and can convert them into electrical pulses.

Optical-character recognition (OCR) A capability of devices with electronic scanners that read numbers, letters, and other characters and convert the optical images into appropriate electrical signals.

Optical-mark page reader A device that senses marks on an OMR document as the document passes under a light source.

Optical-mark recognition (OMR) Also mark sensing; a capability of devices with electronic scanners that read marks on a page and convert the optical images into appropriate electrical signals.

Output Information that comes from the computer as a result of processing.

Overhead The space reserved in primary storage for operating programs.

P

Parallel conversion A system-implementation approach in which the new information system is operated side-by-side with the old one until all differences are reconciled.

Parity (check) bit A means of detecting erroneous transmission of data; internal self-checking to determine if the number of 1 bits in a bit pattern is either odd or even.

Pascal Named after French mathematician Blaise Pascal, a programming language developed for educational purposes, to teach programming concepts to students.

Peripherals Also referred to as peripheral devices; includes input/output devices, secondary storage devices, and other auxiliary computer equipment.

Phased conversion A method of system implementation in which the old information system is gradually replaced by the new one; the new system is segmented and gradually applied.

Physical design Refers to how the data is kept on storage devices and how it is accessed.

Pilot conversion The implementation of a new information system into the organization whereby only a small part of the business uses the new system until it has proved to be successful.

PL/I *P*rogramming *L*anguage *O*ne; a general-purpose programming language used for both business and scientific functions.

Plotter An output device that converts data emitted from the CPU into graphic form; produces hard-copy output.

Point-of-sale (POS) terminal A terminal that serves the same purpose as a cash register but is also capable of relaying sales and inventory data to a central computer for immediate updating of records.

Predictive reports Reports used for tactical and strategic decision making.

Primary key A unique field for a record; used to sort records for processing or to locate a particular record within a file.

Primary storage Also known as internal storage, memory, or main storage; primary storage unit is the section of the CPU that holds instructions, data, and intermediate and final results during processing.

Print-wheel printer An output device consisting of 120 print wheels, each containing 48 characters. The print wheels rotate until an entire line is in the appropriate print position, then a hammer presses the paper against the print wheels.

Printer A device to produce permanent (hard-copy) computer output; impact printers are designed to work mechanically; nonimpact printers use electronic technology.

Printer-keyboard An impact printer similar to an office typewriter; instructions for printing come from the CPU; a keyboard allows an operator to communicate with the system.

Privacy An individual's rights regarding the collection, processing, storage, dissemination, and use of data about his or her personal attributes and activities.

Problem-oriented language A programming language designed to solve specific kinds of problems allowing the user to focus on desired results rather than the individual steps needed to get those results; RPG is an example of this type of language.

Procedure-oriented language A programming language designed to define processing steps required of a particular application; examples consist of COBOL, FORTRAN, and PL/I.

Process To transform raw data into useful information.

Processing The various steps taken by a computer to manipulate data in order to provide information for management.

Processing program A routine, usually part of the operating system, that is used to simplify program preparation and execution.

Program A series of step-by-step instructions that provides a problem solution and tells the computer exactly what to do; of two types—application and system.

Programmable communications processor A device that relieves the CPU of the task of monitoring data transmissions.

Programmable read-only memory (PROM) Read-only memory that can be programmed by the manufacturer or can be programmed by the user for special functions to meet the unique needs of the user.

Programmer The person who writes step-by-step instructions for the computer to execute.

Propagation delay A time delay in a satellite communication system.

Proper program A program using the structured approach and top-down design and having only one entrance and one exit.

Pseudocode An informal design language used to represent the control structures of structured programming.

Punched cards A commonly used storage medium in which data is represented by the presence or absence of holes in them according to a coding scheme much like Hollerith's cards. Each particular set of holes has a distinct meaning which is translated into machine language for the computer.

R

RAM (Random-access memory) Storage in which programs and data can be written into and read from speedily.

Randomize To compute relative record numbers from actual keys through any of a number of mathematical techniques.

Read-only memory (ROM) The part of computer hardware containing items that cannot be deleted or changed by stored-program instructions because they are wired into the computer.

Read/write head An electromagnet used as a component of a tape or disk drive; in reading, it detects magnetized areas and translates them into electrical pulses; in writing, it magnetizes appropriate areas, thereby erasing data stored previously.

Real storage Also known as main storage or primary storage within the CPU.

Real time Refers to the capability of a system or device to receive data, process it, and provide output fast enough to control an activity being performed.

Record A collection of data items, or fields, that relate to a single unit.

Register An internal computer component used for temporary storage of an instruction or data; capable of accepting, holding, and transferring that instruction or data very rapidly.

Remote terminal A terminal that is placed at a location distant from the central computer.

Remote system A system where terminals are connected to the central computer by a communication channel.

Reprographics A technique of producing output whereby the computer is connected to a typesetting machine and the output is film "repro" paper.

Retrieving The process of accessing previously stored information by the computer so it can be referenced by the user.

Ring configuration A type of distributed system in which a number of computers are connected by a single transmission line in a ring arrangement.

RPG *R*eport *P*rogram *G*enerator; an example of a problem-oriented language originally designed to produce business reports.

S

Scheduled reports Those reports produced at regular intervals to provide routine information to users.

Scientific applications Tasks that are traditionally numerically oriented and require advanced mathematical capabilities.

Second-generation computers Used transistors; smaller, faster, and had larger storage capacity than first-generation computers.

Secondary key Fields that are to be used to gain access to records on a file, but which may not be unique.

Secondary storage See Auxiliary storage.

Selection Program logic that includes a test; depending on the results of the test, one of two paths is taken.

Semiconductor memory Circuitry on silicon chips that are smaller than magnetic cores and allow for faster processing; more expensive than core memory and requires a constant source of power.

Sequential file Data (records) stored in a specific order, one right after the other.

Sequential processing See Batch/sequential processing.

Sequential-access storage Auxiliary storage from which records must be read, one after another, in a fixed sequence, until the needed data is located; e.g., magnetic tape.

Service bureau A business that provides data-processing services such as system development and computer operations.

Silicon chip Solid-logic circuitry on a small piece of silicon used to form the primary storage of third-generation computers.

Simple sequence Program logic where one statement, or instruction, after another is executed in order, as stored.

Simplex A type of communication channel that provides for unidirectional, or one-way, transmission of data.

Soft copy Data displayed on a CRT screen; not a permanent record; contrast with hard copy.

Software Programs used to direct the computer for problem solving and overseeing operations.

Software compatibility Refers to the ability to use programs written for one system on another system with little or no change.

Sort To arrange data elements into a predetermined sequence to facilitate processing.

Sort/merge programs A part of the operating-system utility program; used to sort records to facilitate updating and subsequent combining of files to form a single, updated file.

Source program A sequence of instructions written in either assembly language or high-level language by the programmer.

Source-data automation The use of special equipment to collect data at its source.

Star configuration A structure used to implement the multiple CPU concept, in which all transactions must go through a central computer before being routed to the appropriate network computer.

Storage register A register that holds information being sent to or taken from the primary storage unit.

Store To retain data for future reference or processing.

Stored program Instructions stored in the computer's memory in electronic form; can be executed repeatedly during processing.

Stored-program computer A computer that stores instructions for operations to be performed in electronic form, in main memory.

Stored-program concept The concept of storing instructions in the computer's memory in electronic form. This allows the computer to process at its own speed without human intervention.

Structure chart A graphic representation of top-down programming; displaying modules of the problem solution and relationships between modules; of two types—system and process.

Structured programming A top-down modular approach to programming that emphasizes dividing a program into logical sections in order to reduce testing time, increase programmer productivity, and bring clarity to programming.

Summarize To reduce large amounts of data to a more concise and usable form.

Supervisor program Also called a monitor or an executive; the major component of the operating system; coordinates the activities of all other parts of the operating system.

Swapping In a virtual-storage environment, the process of transferring a program section from virtual storage to real storage, and vice versa.

Symbolic language Also called assembly language; uses mnemonic symbols to represent instructions; must be translated into machine language before it can be executed by the computer.

Syntax Refers to the way rules must be followed while coding instructions, just as grammatical rules must be followed in English.

System A group of related elements that work together toward a common goal.

System analysis A detailed, step-by-step investigation of an organization for the purpose of determining what must be done and the best way to do it.

System analysis report A report given to top management after the system analysis phase has been completed to report the findings of the system study; includes a statement of objectives, constraints, and possible alternatives.

System design Alternative solutions to problems uncovered in the system analysis phase are designed, the cost effectiveness of the alternatives is determined, and final recommendations are made.

System flowchart The group of symbols to represent the general information flow; focuses on inputs and outputs rather than on internal computer operations.

System implementation The final phase in the development of a new or revised system; during implementation, the analyst makes sure that the system is completely debugged and operational and is accepted by the users.

System library A collection of data sets in which various parts of an operating system are stored.

System program A sequence of instructions written to coordinate the operation of all computer circuitry and to help the computer run quickly and efficiently.

System residence device An auxiliary storage device (disk, tape, or drum) on which operating-system programs are stored and from which they are loaded into main storage.

T

Tape cassette A sequential-access storage medium (similar to cassettes used in audio recording) used in small computer systems for high-density digital recording.

Tape drive A device that moves tape past a read/write head.

Telecommunications See Teleprocessing.

Telecommuting Computer hookups between offices and homes, which allow employees to work at home.

Telecopier system See Facsimile system.

Teleprocessing The combined use of communication facilities, such as the telephone system, and data-processing equipment.

Teletypewriter system Transmits messages as strings of characters.

Third-generation computers Characterized by the use of integrated circuits, reduced size, lower costs, and increased speed and reliability.

Thrashing Programs in which little actual processing occurs in comparison to the amount of swapping.

Time-sharing An arrangement in which two or more users can access the same central computer resources and receive what seems to be simultaneous results.

Top-down design A method of defining a solution in terms of major functions to be performed and further breaking down the major functions into subfunctions; the further the breakdown, the greater the detail.

Top-level management Management at the top of the organization who make strategic decision.

Touch-tone device A type of terminal used with ordinary telephone lines to transmit data.

Track A horizontal row stretching the length of a magnetic tape on which data can be recorded; one of a series of concentric circles on the surface of a disk; one of a series of circular bands on a drum.

Transaction file A file that contains relatively permanent data; updated by records in a transaction file.

Transistor A type of circuitry characteristic of second-generation computers; smaller, faster, and more reliable than vacuum tubes but inferior to third-generation, large-scale integration.

Transponders Small amplifiers located on satellites that receive the signals from the earth station and reflect them to the receiving station.

U

Unbundled The practice of establishing a separate price for each segment of a computer system.

UNIVAC I *UNIV*ersal *A*utomatic *C*omputer; the first commercial electronic computer; became available in 1951.

Universal Product Code (UPC) A code consisting of ten pairs of vertical bars that represent the manufacturer's identity and the identity code of the item; commonly used on most grocery items.

Utility program A subsystem of the operating system that is capable of performing specialized, repeatedly used functions such as sorting, merging, and transferring data from one input/output device to another.

V

Variables Meaningful names assigned by the programmer to storage locations.

Verification The process of checking the accuracy and completeness of data.

Virtual storage Also called virtual memory; an extension of multiprogramming in which portions of programs not being used are kept in secondary storage until needed, giving the impression that primary storage is unlimited; contrast with real storage.

Visual display terminal A terminal capable of receiving output on a cathode-ray tube (CRT) and, with special provisions, of transmitting data through a keyboard.

Voice message system (VMS) The sender activates a special "message" key on the telephone, dials the receiver's number, and speaks the message. A button lights on the receiver's phone; and, when it is convenient, the receiver can activate the phone and listen to the message.

Voice recognition system A system that allows the user to "train" the computer to understand his or her voice and vocabulary. The user must follow only the patterns the computer is programmed to recognize.

Voice response unit The computer can "speak" through this device by arranging half-second records of voice sounds or pre-recorded words.

Voice-grade channels Communication channels that have a wider frequency range and can transmit data at a rate of forty-five to ninety bits per second, e.g., telegraph channels.

Volatility The frequency of changes to a file during a specific time period.

W

Wand reader A hand-held device used to scan and read source data represented in optical bar-code form or in human-readable characters.

Word processing The manipulation of text data to achieve a desired output.

X

Xerographic printer A type of nonimpact printer that uses printing methods similar to those used in common xerographic copying machines.

INDEX

Credits (Continued)

Morris. **114** courtesy of Inforex, Inc. **120** courtesy NCR Corp. **121** courtesy of Anderson Jacobson Inc. **122** (top) courtesy of Interstate Electronics Corp. **123** photo courtesy of DATAPRODUCTS CORP. **124** Photo courtesy of DATAPRODUCTS CORP. **126** photo courtesy of DATAPRODUCTS CORP. **127** courtesy of Datagraphix, Inc. **128** courtesy of IBM. **129** (top) photo courtesy of Hewlett-Packard Company. **129** (bottom) courtesy of Bell Laboratories. **130** (top) Armstrong World Industries, Inc. **130** (bottom) courtesy of Lockheed Corporation. **131** (top) photo courtesy of Hewlett-Packard Company. **131** (bottom) courtesy of Bell Laboratories. **134** courtesy of Paradyne Corporation. **137** courtesy of Paradyne Corporation. **139** (top) courtesy of Bell Laboratories. **139** (bottom) courtesy of Universal Data Systems. **141** courtesy of Informatics General Corporation. **142** courtesy of Paradyne Corporation. **144** courtesy of Timeplex Inc. **146** courtesy of Inforex, Inc. **148** (top) courtesy of Western Union Corporation. **148** (bottom) courtesy of Quotron Systems, Inc. **149** courtesy of IBM. **151** courtesy of the Atchison, Topeka and the Santa Fe Railway Company. **152** all three photos by Norma Morris. **154** courtesy of Atlantic Richfield Company. **155** photograph courtesy TRW Inc. **158** courtesy of Paradyne Corporation. **161** reproduced with permission of AT&T. **164** courtesy of Dialog Information Services, Inc. **166** courtesy Verbatim Corporation. **170** courtesy of Federal Bureau of Investigation. **172** courtesy of Comshare Incorporated. **175** courtesy of BASF Systems Corporation. **176** (top) courtesy of Control Data Corporation. **176** (bottom) courtesy of Comshare Incorporated. **177** courtesy of Verbatim Corporation. **184** courtesy of IBM. **186** courtesy of Paradyne Corporation. **189** photo courtesy of Burlington Industries, Inc. **192** courtesy of Amstrong World Industries, Inc. **201** reproduced with permission of AT&T. **204** courtesy of Agway, Inc. **209** courtesy of the Atchinson, Topeka and the Santa Fe Railway Company. **211** courtesy of Informatics General Corporation. **222** courtesy of Paradyne Corporation. **225** courtesy of Quotron Systems, Inc. **230** courtesy of Goodyear Tire & Rubber Company. **233** courtesy of the Atchison, Topeka and the Santa Fe Railway Company. **239** courtesy of Corvus Systems. **242** courtesy of Shell Oil Company. **246** photo courtesy of Hewlett-Packard Company. **248** courtesy of Tektronix, Inc. **252** courtesy of Paradyne Corporation. **255** courtesy of Paradyne Corporation. **257** reproduced with permission of AT&T. **259** courtesy of Cray Research, Inc. **260** courtesy of IBM. **261** courtesy of Sperry Univac. **265** courtesy Intel Corporation. **266** courtesy of Radio Shack, a division of Tandy Corporation. **267** (top left) courtesy of Apple Computer Inc. **267** (top right) courtesy of IBM. **267** (bottom left) courtesy of Commodore Business Machines, Inc. **267** (bottom right) courtesy of Digital Equipment Corporation. **268** courtesy of Xerox Corporation. **269** courtesy of Apple Computer Inc. **274** courtesy of McDonnell Douglas Automation Company. **276** courtesy of National Semiconductor. **280** courtesy of Paradyne Corporation. **283** photo courtesy of DATAPRODUCTS CORP. **285** courtesy of Wang Laboratories, Inc. **286** courtesy of Wang Laboratories, Inc. **288** photo courtesy of Burlington Industries, Inc. **289** courtesy of Bethlehem Steel Corporation. **290** courtesy of Shell Oil Company. **291** courtesy of Cincinnati Milacron, Inc. **293** courtesy of Motorola, Inc. **295** courtesy of Planning Research Corporation. **297** (left and upper right) courtesy of Atari Incorporated. **297** (lower right) courtesy of Tomy Corporation. **298** both photos reproduced with permission of AT&T. **302** courtesy of Paradyne Corporation. **307** courtesy of Wang Laboratories, Inc. **308** photograph courtesy TRW, Inc. **309** photograph courtesy TRW, Inc. **310** courtesy of Shell Oil Company. **311** courtesy Department of the Navy. **312** courtesy of Trivex, Inc., a Mohawk Datu Sciences Company. **314** courtesy of Paradyne Corporation. **315** courtesy of Wang Laboratories, Inc. **321** photo courtesy of Hewlett-Packard Company.

Cartoon Credits

49 Reproduced from *Computerworld* with permission from Jack Schmidt. **70** Reproduced from *Computerword* with permission from Lorett Treese. **92** Reproduced from *Computerworld* with permission from Tom Niemann. **119** Reproduced from *Output* with permission from Stuart Leeds. **155** Reproduced from *Computerworld* with permission from John Demchuck. **168** Reprinted courtesy OMNI Magazine © 1983. **200** Reproduced from *Datamation* with permission from Dale Jennings. **236** Reprinted by permission of Bo Brown. **271** Reprinted with permission from *Personal Computing*, December, 1981, p. 76, Copyright 1981, Hayden Publishing Company.

†